GUSTAV MAHLER

Gustav Mahler, Vienna, 1898. Inscription to Arnold Rosé.

GUSTAV MAHLER

A Life in Crisis

Stuart Feder

Yale University Press
New Haven & London

Published with assistance from the foundation established in memory of Philip Hamilton McMillan of the Class of 1894, Yale College.

Set in Galliard type by Achorn Graphic Services. Printed in the United States of America by Vail Ballou Press, Binghamton, New York.

Library of Congress Cataloging-in-Publication Data
Feder, Stuart.
Gustav Mahler: a life in crisis / Stuart Feder.
    p.   cm.
Includes bibliographical references and index.
ISBN 0-300-10340-9 (cloth : alk. paper)
Mahler, Gustav, 1860–1911—Psychology.
ML410.M23 F43 2004
780.92 B 22
2004042219

A catalogue record for this book is available from the British Library.

The paper in this book meets the guidelines for permanence and durability of the Committee on Production Guidelines for Book Longevity of the Council on Library Resources.

10 9 8 7 6 5 4 3 2 1

TO CHARLOTTE

CONTENTS

1 The Summer of 1910   1

2 The Family Mahler   9

3 Family Crisis, 1889   30

4 The Music of Fratricide   47

5 Mahler at Midnight   60

6 Family Romances   75

7 Mahler in Love   92

8 The "Splendid" Years   108

9 A Child's Death   137

10 Old World, New World   152

11 Alma at Tobelbad   173

12 Marital Crisis   188

13 The Walking Cure   206

14 The Precious Word   227

15 Triumph and Despair   243

16 Mahler Dying   265

17 Forever Alma   284

18 Epilogue   302

Acknowledgments   317

Illustration Credits   319

List of Abbreviations   321

Notes   323

Index   345

1

THE SUMMER OF 1910

Vienna, 1925—
Sigmund Freud reminiscing about Gustav Mahler and the summer of
1910:

> I once analyzed Mahler for four hours. He had strong obses-
> sions, I can tell you. I was vacationing in Holland, at Noord-
> wijk by the sea, near Leiden. There I received a telegram from
> Mahler, who was then in the Austrian Tirol. "May I come to
> see you?" I answer, "Yes." Then I received another telegram
> from him saying that he is not able to come. I say, "All right."
> Then a new telegram from him saying that he will come; then
> another that he won't come. Then a third time that he is com-
> ing. So I say "yes," but he must come at a certain time, other-
> wise I would be leaving with a friend on a trip to Sicily. (At that
> time such trips were nothing for me.) I made an exception in
> receiving someone during my vacation, but for a man like
> Mahler . . .
>
> So then he comes to Leiden to meet me at a hotel. I go and
> we walk all over the village for four hours, he telling me his life.
> It begins to be late and I tell him I have to take the steam trol-
> ley now, or else I won't be able to get back. "And you," I ask
> Mahler, "What are you going to do?" "Me?" he answered, "I'm
> going right back to the Tirol."[1]

Altschluderbach, near Toblach, the Austrian Tirol, 1910—

The path to Altschluderbach turns sharply uphill from the road to Toblach. Ascending, one can view the lush Pusteral Valley opposite, in which the road is situated. Visible, too, are the brightly colored blue-and-green onion-shaped spires of the churches of the nearby town. In the far distance, the Alps imperceptibly join the Dolomites, the low-lying clouds elaborating a sense of space, a spiritual space Mahler had already captured forever in the music of *Das Lied von der Erde* (The Song of the Earth).

Climbing the path, Mahler approached the house he and his wife now occupied for the third summer. The Tirolian white-stucco and brown-beamed structure served them well, Mahler regularly spending summers composing while devoting the rest of the year to conducting and revising. But more than this, Toblach was a refuge from an earlier summer locale tainted with tragedy: in Maiernigg, on the Wörthersee of the Austrian Alps, a nearly five-year-old daughter had died of scarlet fever three years earlier. The elder of two, she was called Putzi and was said to be her father's favorite. The couple could not bear the thought of returning there, and the following spring, Alma Mahler, still in mourning, was dispatched along with her mother, Anna Moll, to Toblach to seek a suitable place for the summer's work. Trudging through the snow of a lingering winter, they inspected every available house in the area, finally settling on an eleven-room farmhouse at the outskirts of the village, owned by the Trenkers. The farmer and his family occupied the ground floor, and the Mahlers rented the upper story.

Near the house, Mahler had built a small wooden structure, scarcely twelve-feet square, which served as his workplace. It was furnished simply, with a table, chair, and a small piano. Two large windows in front looked out over the Pusteral Valley. On the steep slope opposite, a serpentine path led to a tiny baroque church in the middle distance. Mahler, still composing mentally, would frequently climb the trail, contrary to doctors' orders to avoid vigorous exercise. Beyond were the mountains. Alone in the silence of the hut, Mahler would feel his creative universe extend toward him from the vastness of this space, through his *Waldhäuschen*, as he called his work space, along its final course into his composer's mind. It was here that Mahler had completed his Ninth

Symphony in a single summer in 1909; and, only the summer previous, *Das Lied von der Erde*, whose spiritual landscape he had entered through the physical world surrounding Toblach and Altschluderbach.

The summer of 1910 was crucial in Mahler's life. It was charged with a crisis—a marital crisis—and marked by the resulting inner turmoil that Mahler sought to heal in a meeting with Freud. The entire episode played itself out over the course of the summer, its pivotal point the four-hour walk mentioned by Freud, in Leiden, Holland, on 26 August. Although Mahler emerged strengthened from his visit with Freud, with his considerable resources mobilized for strenuous undertakings ahead, he never recovered fully and remained vulnerable to physical illness. Within a year he was dead.

From the onset, the summer of 1910 was different from earlier summers. The family—now consisting of three—had returned to Europe in April from New York, where Mahler had conducted his third season. Mahler had resigned his ten-year post as director of the Vienna Court Opera during the tragic year of 1907 that witnessed his daughter's death. Although the American seasons were supposed to relieve Mahler from his strenuous duties and allow for a more leisurely composition period, he already had conducting commitments in May in Paris and Rome. Nevertheless—and despite his characteristic anxiety about starting new work—Mahler was optimistic about the composing summer before him. He would be working on his Tenth Symphony, the seeds of which were germinating in mind only; there were as yet no sketches.

In addition to this, a massive undertaking would permeate the summer's plans, preoccupying Mahler creatively and drawing heavily on his energy: the premiere of his Eighth Symphony, scheduled in Munich on 12 September 1910. It was heralded by the Munich impresario as the "Symphony of a Thousand," Mahler's largest work to date. Although Mahler had not been consulted about the subtitle (and hardly approved of it), he would experience the challenges and rigors of rehearsing its multiple-component performing groups in Munich, Vienna, and Leipzig. Traversing the geographic triangle was an anticipated task of the summer.

Mahler was chiefly in Vienna until well into June, rehearsing the Eighth Symphony. At the beginning of that month, however, Alma had

entered a sanatorium in Tobelbad, near Graz. She brought their surviving daughter, Anna, called Gucki, and a governess with her; later, Alma's
mother would visit. It was not the first year that Alma spent a portion of
the summer at a sanatorium; indeed, for many individuals it was customary to do so. But this time Alma's stay was on medical advice. Treatment
in a sanatorium was frequently recommended for depression, psychosomatic disorders, neurasthenia, and "women's illnesses." Alma suffered
from chronic depression and probable alcohol abuse.

The marriage was not a happy one from her point of view. Mahler, on
tour conducting, often left her alone. He was capable of being an ardent
lover and particularly expressive in letters, but remained insensitive to
her feelings and baffled by her moods. He tended to respond with philosophy, admonitions, and advice for self-improvement, whereas Alma
longed for empathy, intimacy, and appreciation for gifts other than beauty
and childbearing. When he was a younger man of thirty-four, Mahler had
confided his criteria for a wife to his friend the Czech composer Josef
Förster (1859–1951):

> You must understand that I could not bear the sight of an untidy
> woman with messy hair and neglected appearance. I must also
> admit that solitude is essential to me when I am composing; as a
> creative artist I require it without condition. My wife would have
> to agree to my living apart from her, possibly several rooms away,
> and to my having a separate entrance. She would have to consent
> to sharing my company only at certain times decided in advance,
> and then I would expect her to be perfectly groomed and well
> dressed . . . in a word she would need qualities that even the best
> and most devoted women do not possess.[2]

How little had he understood himself! Mahler could never have been as
passionately attracted to the bourgeois model of a woman he described
as he had been to Alma. Nor, with such requirements, could he ever have
found his perfect woman.

Gustav and Alma were more alike in some respects than either might
have acknowledged. They had been in love, each seeking gratification
from the other as well as a family. But now love struggled with narcissism
within each of them. He had married a woman said to be the most

beautiful in Vienna;[3] she, a famous man who occupied the premiere musical post of the Austro-Hungarian Empire. Fifteen years after Mahler shared his marriage requirements with Förster, life had chastised him severely, but his earlier image of the perfect wife persisted and he often found himself puzzled by Alma's needs. Alma, too, sought the ideal mate from what appeared to be her unlimited choice in Vienna. As she saw it in their ninth year of marriage, she had sacrificed much in gaining Gustav as a husband. She was twenty years his junior, a well-known beauty who had come from a family of artistic note and had herself been a serious student of composition. In the early weeks of summer Mahler knew that Alma was becoming depressed. He perceived it in the letters she sent him while he was rehearsing in Vienna and, after she entered the sanatorium, in Leipzig. Although concerned, Mahler was unable to come to terms with its proximal cause, which lay in good measure within his own character and in his behavior toward Alma.

Alma would later describe her condition as "a complete breakdown." Her mention of "melancholy" is consistent with Mahler's own observations at the time and there can be little doubt that she had fallen into a depression.[4] However, Mahler was unable to respond to the "submerged self-confidence" of which she would later write; perhaps by that point in the depression, there was little a spouse could do in any event. Neither could appreciate in the slightest any responsibility for the flaws in their marriage, nor could Mahler acknowledge any role in bringing Alma to this pass. Mahler was dumbfounded, although he did all he could to help Alma recover. After all, much of their current life plan, which already left both exhausted, had been a compromise between Gustav's needs for time to compose along with his family responsibilities, and Alma's for the physical comforts to which she was accustomed. For her part she attributed her state fully to "the wear and tear of being driven on without respite by a spirit so intense as his."[5]

Both still carried the scars of losing their daughter Putzi. But Gustav had been able to submerge himself in the fervor of his two careers and the stimulation—sometimes overstimulation—of multiple locales. Above all, he was capable of transforming loss into creative issue. For Mahler conducting in America and continued success in Europe had replaced the glory of the Vienna opera without its harsh politics and

resident anti-Semitism. His heart disease, diagnosed that same summer of 1907, was quiescent. The unremitting valvular heart disease
that stemmed from childhood rheumatic fever was slowly setting the
stage for the fatal cardiac infection only months distant. Nevertheless
Mahler was symptom-free at the moment and leading an uncommonly
active life.

But restitution was not so easy for Alma. Her own considerable
musical gift as a composer, long since renounced, had been stifled and
eclipsed by her husband's. Her life as Frau Direktor was circumscribed,
constricted and complicated by maternal responsibilities. Now she found
herself a bereaved mother, the wife of a famous but aging man and no
longer quite so young herself: she had turned thirty the previous
summer.

As the month of June elapsed Mahler had looked forward to his return
to Toblach. The last rehearsals in Munich had been somewhat discourag-
ing and despite his own constant correspondence with Alma, detailing the
progress of the rehearsals, he had heard little from her. "Thank God," he
had written to Alma, "tomorrow I will breathe the pure air of Toblach
and truly find some rest."[6] He was eager to devote himself finally to the
creative work of the summer and gradually enter the tone-world of the
Tenth Symphony. Meanwhile, he enjoyed the respite, the good meals prepared by the Trenker family who looked after him, and the sense of
Gemütlichkeit he felt in their midst. With restored energy he walked in the
balmy summer mountain air, once again taking the strenuous path up the
mountainside opposite the villa and his *häuschen*. Shortly after that first
week back in Toblach, on 7 July 1910, Mahler would reach his fiftieth
birthday. He looked for a letter from Alma but none was forthcoming.

Two days before his birthday Mahler wrote to Alma of his disappointment: "Not a single line from you! Almschi, is it that you don't have five
minutes to write a card?"[7] In writing to Alma, Mahler imagined her as he
had left her in Tobelbad, only days before. But Alma had already met
Walter Gropius during her first days at the sanatorium and was by now
deeply involved in an affair that would continue in the months ahead.
When Mahler learned of it, he was devastated.

Thus began Mahler's terminal crisis—the marital turmoil of the summer of 1910. The long-latent themes in Mahler's ordeal—those of Alma's

alienation and her frightening withdrawal of love—now flared to critical proportions. Mahler was enveloped in a breakdown that threatened to stifle the creative efforts of his last summer. Desperate, he finally sought consultation with Sigmund Freud.

There had been three earlier crises in Mahler's life. Unlike the marital crisis of 1910, he had survived these and prevailed. Gustav Mahler is one of the few composers whose works address the question, Can music be in some sense autobiographical? Mahler himself provided a partial answer—as well as a challenge—when, following the completion of his Second Symphony, he wrote,

> My whole life is contained in my two symphonies. In them I have set down my experience and suffering, truth and poetry in words. To anyone who knows how to listen my whole life will become clear.[8]

Mahler affirmed that a composer might consciously choose to reveal autobiographical material in his or her music. Yet in music, no less than in other spheres of life, there will also be a latent component of personal meaning of which the composer is unaware. The attuned listener may successfully hear and interpret both.

Since Mahler endeavored to compose continuously throughout his creative lifetime, and through each of the personal crises he experienced, particular works are associated with such critical periods in what follows. Thus certain pieces of music are privileged in analysis—analysis both musical and psychological. In this sense, a single song may be as important as a massive symphony, depending on its autobiographical role in the composer's life history.

The first crisis in Mahler's life occurred between 1889 and 1894, in the course of which he turned thirty. This crisis was associated with a creative block in the completion of his Second Symphony. A single song ("St. Anthony's Sermon to the Fish") eventually heralded the solution. Elaborated, it became the central movement in the work.

A second crisis erupted a decade later, soon after Mahler's fortieth birthday, when the composer believed himself to be close to death. The event powerfully affected Mahler's musical style, as he subsequently wrote the last of his early *Wunderhorn* songs, and the first of his mature Friedrich Rückert lieder. The concurrent Fifth Symphony was a creative watershed. Mahler's personal life, too, took a turn, his whirlwind courtship of Alma taking place soon after.

Each of these early crises took its toll emotionally but grudgingly yielded a return in creative life. The third crisis was that of 1907, involving the multiple losses of child, physical health, and position in Vienna. The death of Mahler's daughter, in particular, spawned the massive work of mourning, melancholia, and redemptive spirituality that was *Das Lied von der Erde*.

This triple crisis had scarcely been mastered when the marital crisis of 1910 supervened. The Tenth Symphony comprises the music of autobiography par excellence as, under the pressure of anxiety, the boundaries of music and diaristic communication blur in the marginalia of the manuscript score.

Mahler was not destined to overcome the crisis of 1910. Although the session with Freud stabilized him emotionally for a time, Mahler failed to emerge on a new plateau as he had earlier. Nor would there be any further masterpieces as evidence of his prodigious mastery of the ordeals of his life; the Tenth Symphony would remain incomplete. This time he found his footing only temporarily as the faults in his emotional life were tested and its strains revealed. The consultation did enable Mahler as conductor to achieve a new pinnacle in performance: the celebratory and spectacular premiere of his Eighth Symphony. But during the course of Mahler's last year, emotional strains invaded the physical domain. He contracted an acute illness that superimposed on the chronic heart ailment with which he had lived for many years. The promise of the voyage homeward from New York in April 1910 ushered in a year of triumph and despair. And in the course of this final year he not only had to face Alma's infidelity in the summer of 1910—tantamount in Mahler's psyche to abandonment and annihilation—but later, the ultimate trial of life, terminal illness and death.

This then is the story of the crises in Gustav Mahler's life, his struggles to overcome them, and the music of which they were a part. It is a story of the human spirit, its achievements, and its inevitable limitations.

2

THE FAMILY MAHLER

Most characteristic of Bernhard Mahler, Gustav's father, was the alacrity with which he responded to every economic opportunity that arose in the waning years of the Habsburg monarchy. His family history tracks the restrictions on Jewish life during this period, the fitful and eventual emancipation, and a paradoxical amicable tolerance in village life despite endemic and virulent anti-Semitism.

Born in 1827, Bernhard was the eldest son of Simon Mahler (1793–1865) of Chelmna, a typical village in the Czech-Moravian hills, where the paternal ancestor, Abraham Mahler, had settled in the mid–eighteenth century.[1] There, in a tiny Jewish enclave inhabited by a few families, were the three essential buildings for communal Jewish life: synagogue, *cheder* or study house, and *mikvah*, the ritual bath. Close by huddled the stone and wood houses. There was modest domestic farming, and the orthodox Abraham performed the functions of *mischgiach*, the ritual slaughterer. Only five thousand Jewish families lived legally in Moravia at the time, and this great-grandfather of Gustav Mahler could recall the yellow badge that Jews were required to wear before the *Judentenreform* of 1781, a relic of the attempted expulsion of the Jews by the regent Maria Theresa. Still in effect was the ancient *Judenzoll*, or body tax, a fee levied on Jews for a sojourn from one region to another for any purpose.[2]

The *Toleranzpatent* that Maria Theresa's son, Joseph II, enacted the following year was perhaps not quite so liberating in Abraham's own life, as it prohibited the use of Yiddish and Hebrew in commercial affairs, thus

Bernhard Mahler.

ATELIER STAEGER JOH HAUPT JGLAU.

restricting enterprise beyond the small village. Indeed, many traditional Jews considered the edict calamitous. But its thrust, to end the isolation of the Jews in the historic Czech lands and to enrich the social fabric of the state, would certainly benefit Abraham's son Simon and, in the succeeding generation, Bernhard. Simon took advantage of freedom of movement at the time of Bernhard's birth, relocating to the small village of Kaliste, where he purchased a house and leased a small distillery attached to it. The business choice was one of the few areas of commerce traditionally open to Jews; some friends and family had already settled in the area, and some were in the same business. It was an indication of the progression of the time as well as a requirement of reform laws of 1787 that Simon gave a Germanic name to his firstborn, Bernhard. The name was probably taken from an official list published at the time.

The effects of banning the Yiddish language, which was at the heart of a rich culture, would be seen in subsequent generations and the trend toward assimilation. By Gustav Mahler's time, there was little affection or nostalgia in the Czech lands for the language or the life of *Yiddishkeit*. Mahler himself would be appalled when, in his travels, he encountered Polish Jews who had maintained the tradition. "My God, are these my relations?" he exclaimed.[3]

Kaliste, Gustav Mahler's birthplace, was near Iglau, a commercial center and one of the six historic royal Moravian cities, formally severely restricted to Jewish commerce. *Familiant* laws had limited the numbers of Jewish families that could legally occupy these major cities. Only seventeen Jewish families lived in Iglau legally prior to the revolutionary years 1848–1849 and any business Simon Mahler conducted entailed registration with authorities and payment of the body tax. Joseph II's *Toleranzpatent* of 1848 permitted freer commercial movement for Jews and encouraged them to set up businesses and factories. At the same time it still restricted the numbers of Jewish families in larger towns and although Jews could now learn trades, they could not become master craftsmen. Later many such restrictions were repealed and conditions changed rapidly in Iglau. As a result there was a rapid growth of the Jewish community, which soon numbered more than one thousand.[4] Despite expanding opportunities for Jews and their incorporation into the larger community, anti-Semitism was palpable in the region. Only a few miles from Kaliste, in the tiny village of Polna, a Jewish vagrant was found guilty without evidence of killing a Christian girl at Passover. He was sentenced to death.[5]

At midcentury Bernhard was a vigorous and ambitious young man and would take full advantage of the commercial opportunities available. Records show Bernhard made several overnight journeys to Iglau in the 1850s carting liquor and other goods. One such trip took him to Ledec, where he met the Hermann family through either business contacts or the Jewish congregation then forming there.

Abraham Hermann was a wealthy tradesman who also operated a soap factory. The Hermanns' five children were all daughters, ranging from age ten to twenty, and Abraham was eager for a match for his eldest, Marie. He was in a position to offer this appealing and hard-working young man of similar background a substantial dowry. The traditional wedding, no doubt including the services of local *klezmer* musicians, took place in 1857 among the Jewish community of Ledec. The 3,500-gulden dowry permitted Bernhard to purchase a home that had a small distillery, a shop, and a pub attached. He returned to Kaliste with his young wife, independent.[6]

All character sketches collated retrospectively contain contradictions. Properly viewed, these reflect not only the views and vantage point of the observer but the complexity of lives led over the course of time, and the vicissitudes of memory as well. Further, the requirements of narrative warmly welcome the stuff of general gossip, isolated anecdote, and wherever possible, even legend. Thus a case can be made for a "quiet, affectionate and retiring" Marie Hermann, "a lame and probably insignificant-looking girl . . . forced by her parents to marry the ten year older Bernhard though they scarcely knew each other." The story neatly interlocks with the anxious Hermann parents' belief that their oldest daughter "could not hope to make a better match";[7] and with the character of the "match" as received, namely, the domineering, even brutal Bernhard. Gustav Mahler himself seemed to endorse this story, relating to his friend Natalie Bauer-Lechner that his parents "belonged together like fire and water. He was all stubbornness, she gentleness itself."[8] Sigmund Freud lent further gravitas to the story in citing a single anecdote related to him by Mahler. Thus developed a picture that has been relayed handily from biography to biography.

However, this biographical portrait of Marie has been tempered by hints of character and tradition. The apparent marriage of convenience was doubtless rather a marriage of custom and was probably negotiated by a Ledec matchmaker. Marie's father hardly abandoned a damaged daughter to an irascible stranger. Whatever Bernhard's later emergent character traits, Abraham could see in him kindred qualities that promised success against the background of a changing social order. The generous dowry reflected more than the Hermanns' need to unload a family burden. It helped the young couple settle with a degree of stability and comfort in preparation for the expected raising of a family. The bride's trousseau would have included linens, home furnishings, and other domestic objects such as the heavy brass candlesticks for the Sabbath blessing. The hand-scribed and decorated marriage certificate, the *ketubah*, in which the husband's financial responsibilities in the event of death or divorce were detailed, also belonged to Marie. All were loaded onto Bernhard's horse cart for the winding journey across the Czech-Moravian hills of the Vyoscina to Kaliste. As the newlyweds bid the Hermanns goodbye, there was the full expectation that the occasion for the next trip home, in a year or so, would be the birth of a child.

Perhaps it was the dowry and fine furnishings that led Kaliste neighbors to call Marie Mahler *die Herzogin*, the Duchess.[9] Ironic nicknames were built into provincial language custom and often revealed resentment, envy, and at times frank cruelty with regard to physical characteristics. (With her lame leg, Marie Hermann might have earned a worse nickname.) But beyond this Marie was hardly a cipher. According to custom, she would have received her education at home. She was literate in both German and the vernacular of the region and, from sitting in the rear of the synagogue, could probably read Hebrew by rote, without understanding it. Letters written later in family life reveal a capable and attentive mother and a thrifty homemaker.

Marie Hermann Mahler.

Marie and Bernhard's shared values included the importance of education and the opportunities it was creating for families such as theirs. New reforms funded local German-speaking schools and opened the only university in the empire, in Vienna, to Jews. Although schooling would have been impractical for Bernhard, and impossible for Marie, it was timely for their progeny. Bernhard had a passion for knowledge and always had a supply of books in his wagon, which he would peruse while carting goods. This earned him the nickname *Kutschbockgelehrter* (literally, "cart-seat scholar"), reflecting difference as well as a degree of respect among uneducated neighbors. The French grammar in his possession hinted at some unrealized aspiration or fantasy of faraway places.[10]

Bernhard was further assimilated than Marie, and as head of the household steered her and the family in that direction. The grand scheme of the *Toleranzpatent* and the midcentury reforms were reflected in the Jewish enlightenment, the *haskalah* movement. Liberal thinking had trickled down from the heights of Moses Mendelssohn a century earlier to the likes of Bernhard Mahler. Linguistic assimilation came first, followed by loosened but unbroken ties with the traditional Jewish community and synagogue. At the time, there were only three Jewish families among Kaliste's five hundred inhabitants.[11] Bernhard's *Wirtshaus* and father Simon's distillery served the community's social habits but so small a hamlet could hardly contain Bernhard's ambitions. He had his eye on opportunities in nearby Iglau, where he had already conducted some business. Only an immediate stimulus was lacking; it soon came from an unexpected quarter.

In 1858, the year after their marriage, Marie and Bernhard had a child, named Isador. They returned to Ledec for traditional festivities. A ceremony for the opening of the womb, the *pidyon haben*, would have been joyously celebrated, followed by the circumcision of this first child. But Isador did not survive, succumbing not to the prevalent childhood diseases of the time but to an unspecified accident when the child was one year old. The next child, probably already conceived, would be the more precious. Gustav was born 7 July 1860.

Thus Gustav Mahler, like his ideal, Beethoven, was born in the shadow of death; each was preceded by a brother who died in infancy. (Unlike

Beethoven's parents, who called both their children by the same name, Marie and Bernhard had the good sense to give Gustav his own. Although Jews customarily name children after the recently deceased, the fact that Isador had been a child—as well as a fear that their secondborn would share his fate—would have deterred the Mahlers.) Nonetheless, as a replacement child, Gustav was regarded with high hopes. But the death of this first sibling would cast a long shadow in Mahler's life.

A second journey from Kaliste to Ledec was undertaken for Gustav's circumcision eight days after his birth. A precocious child, he would require close attention throughout his youth. According to a family anecdote, Gustav—passionate for reading, like his father—climbed out of an attic window onto the roof, where, "suspended between heaven and earth on the steep slope, I presumed myself safe . . . there I read away blissful hours, until someone spied me. . . . Terrified, they informed my father, who ran up to the attic. For perhaps an hour he stood at the garret window in mortal fear, not daring to call, lest I should fall."[12] To Gustav's dismay, he was beaten and the window soon walled up.

The year 1860 was significant historically as the emperor, Francis Joseph I, issued a decree permitting Jews to own property within the empire. As a result, a Jewish school, as well as a religious association that would later create a synagogue, was founded that very year.[13] Iglau, the second largest town in Moravia, with a population of seventeen thousand, seemed at that point a land of promise. The time was propitious and the Mahlers joined the stream of Jews who had begun to move from the rural towns and villages surrounding Iglau. The relocation also enabled the family to start anew, after the death of their first child. Prophetically, their new home was on the road to Vienna.

The theme of death that marked Gustav's birth would be a recurrent one. There would be multiple births and deaths of siblings, each leaving its impression according to the comprehension brought to these events by the mind of the growing child. Death in its myriad forms would eventually be represented in tone repeatedly by the composer, from his earliest cantata, *Das klagende Lied* (The Lamenting Song), a saga of fratricide; to the late songs of *Kindertotenlieder* (Songs on the Death of Children), in which the musical understanding of death extended to the bereaved parents, as Mahler's so often were in his early years of life.

In Iglau, Gustav's reading skills flourished as other considerable talents emerged. The boy's affinity for music was apparent from the time when only singing could soothe him on the bumpy road to Ledec. During the course of a visit to his maternal grandparents, Gustav was said to have come upon an "enormous box" while playing in the attic—the piano, of course. The stuff of legend resides in the story of the child's banging out recognizable tunes. Truth or narrative, the account highlights Gustav's already dominant auditory mode. At an extremely early age he learned the folk music of Iglau peasants and townspeople, and the dark, imaginative lore associated with "the Gay rounds . . . and the sad cradle songs that were to make such an impression on him and later so deeply mark his music."[14] These experiences were hardly transitory. Gustav's dreamy, reflective nature processed songs as meaningful objects in themselves—found objects, as it were, which could be variously performed, contemplated, played with as if they were mental toys. For his third birthday, Gustav received a tiny accordion and so could make audible to others what was already alive in his creative inner ear.

The boy's ear was nurtured by an extraordinary auditory environment—that of military music—which would imprint the mind of the composer-to-be from his earliest improvisations to his final works. The local geography of Iglau served as catalyst. Iglau took pride in a town square that was massive in proportion to the town itself. When Bernhard brought his family to Iglau, they rented space in a house at its southern border on Pernitzergasse, diagonally across the large square from the barracks on the northern corner. This was an active site with the military in full operation. Music was an essential part of military life in the barracks and on the field. Bugle calls marked the stations of day and night. Sprightly marches accompanied the men's movement; dirges marked military rites of passage; the regimental band performed concerts. By 1866 the Austrian army would be engaged in the Austro-Prussian War and in Iglau ballads about the shaky bravado of men about to die and the separations and deaths of war could be heard. Mahler would later be drawn to these themes in his selection of texts from the folk anthology *Des knaben Wunderhorn* (The Youth's Magic Horn). This music would become as much a part of the environment as Mahler's physical surroundings, furnishing musical ideas and stimulating his developing mind.[15]

Other music filled gaps in the pastiche of Mahler's aural life. Iglau had a village band consisting of three or four instruments, likely a Jewish *klezmer* group that randomly incorporated other instruments as the occasion provided. In fact the double bass player may have been Mahler's first music teacher.[16] Musical figures reminiscent of synagogue songs with "glitches," or glottal breaks in the voice, were imitated in the treble instruments against the background of the persistent broken rhythm of the bass.

Jewish music in varied forms was another important feature of the composer's childhood auditory environment. The indigenous Moravian folk song had long since incorporated both Jewish lore and the tunes themselves.[17] The Jewish religious community of Iglau was established around the time of Gustav's birth. Later, a fine synagogue was built in quasi-oriental style with two imposing towers. It was a sign of Bernhard's social progress that he was appointed a member of the synagogue committee in 1873. Accordingly, despite the tendency to assimilation, it is likely that the family was observant to a degree, if only for the postsummer High Holidays and rites of passage. Significantly, the date of Bernhard's appointment coincided with Gustav's thirteenth birthday. The bar mitzvah ceremony of that time and place, although of religious import, was a socially modest event, occasionally observed on a weekday. Under the circumstances the Mahlers probably observed Gustav's passage to Jewish manhood. In gymnasium, the study of religion was obligatory and Gustav received a grade of "excellent" in "Mosaic" studies.[18]

There is no question but that the child Mahler experienced the synagogue and its chantings.

> Around the age of three, Mahler was taken to the synagogue by his parents. Suddenly he interrupted the singing of the community with shouts and screams: "Be quiet, be quiet, that's horrible!" And when from his mother's arms, he succeeded in stopping everything, when the whole congregation was in consternation and had all stopped singing, he demanded—singing a verse for them—that they should all sing "Eits a binkel Kasi," one of his favorite songs from earliest childhood.[19]

The song has since been identified as an old street song, a catchy polka-like melody, sung in march step. The text is about "A little wanderer [who] traveled from Hungary to Moravia and right in the first inn, he danced as if he were on water." The title refers to his bundle, which "swung back and forth."[20] The knapsack was "an accessory of artisans," who frequented wayside inns such as Bernhard Mahler's, and young Gustav had plenty of opportunities to witness the drunken, dancing journeymen. The song lent itself to many off-color versions with rough sexual innuendo. Later, the journeyman would reappear in Mahler's *Lieder eines fahrenden Gesellen* (Songs of a Wayfarer).[21]

The synagogue anecdote manifests two early-appearing features of Mahler's sensory endowment: first, a sensitivity to sound itself, in particular its volume, and second, attunement to its meaning. The ardent religious chanting with its associated mournful affects clearly overwhelmed the child. It had to be masked and displaced by the banal, even sacrilegious song, rendered loud to drown out imagined meanings. Herein lies the prelude to Mahler's characteristic ironic style.

Gustav's precociousness was quickly recognized; with the start of music lessons at five and his rapid musical development, he became the star of the family. Life as the only child had been short: Ernst, born in 1861, had been conceived by the time of the move to Iglau. Ernst was probably sickly as a child and had the congenital heart disease that would ultimately claim the lives of both Marie and Gustav. The Mahlers' first daughter, Leopoldine, called Poldi, was born in 1863, a few months before Gustav's third birthday. Thus Gustav enjoyed the exclusive love and attention of his mother and the unrivaled familial pride of Bernhard Mahler for only a matter of months. Paradoxically, the sibling to whom Mahler was most attached as a youth was the one who had displaced him. Gustav's love and caring for brother Ernst masked the premature loss of singular love. Here, the child's emulation of mother love served to defend against the feelings attending perceived desertion: anxiety and rage. This early experience would color all of Mahler's adult relationships with women, rendering him acutely sensitive to any behavior relating to abandonment.

Although interspersed with occasions of apprehensive joy, loss continued to plague the Mahlers' family life. Two boys born in successive years,

1864 and 1865, died within their first year of life. A third boy, Alois, born in 1867, survived as did another sister, Justine, born in 1868. Over the next several years, the family lost three more boys. In 1873, Otto was born. An aspiring musician, he would figure prominently in Mahler's coming to terms with family responsibilities after their parents' deaths. Marie and Bernhard's last child to survive to adulthood was a girl, Emma, born in 1875 and practically a generation younger than the oldest siblings. Marie Mahler's final pregnancy, at forty-two, produced a boy who died of diphtheria before his second birthday.

As the family grew, Gustav enjoyed a unique position by dint of his considerable gifts. Mahler later described his childhood to his friend Natalie Bauer-Lechner: "Draconian measures were introduced into the Mahler household, with Gustav and his art at the focal point of the entire family. Everyone wished to have some small share in his art."[22] It was said that the family considered it a privilege to listen to him when he played music although Gustav, sometimes irritably, preferred to practice alone. Thus the child would dominate the family space—at least the auditory space—establishing an expectation of priority that would continue into adulthood. In this, he would become the natural rival of his dominating father, Bernhard.

Gustav was a dreamer and his music a retreat. Many anecdotes detail his capacity to become lost within his own imagination. Yet he was not unaware of profound family events such as the births and deaths of children. Indeed, he sought mastery in imagination, and the traumatic motivated expression in the child's first compositions. It was following the deaths of two infant siblings, Karl and Rudolf, that the five-year-old Gustav wrote—or at least conceptualized—"A Funeral March with an Introductory Polka." The manuscript is lost—if in fact it ever existed as such—but the ironic turn of mind noted in Gustav's synagogue experience at age three is germinally present here. It is the product of the child who cannot yet mourn and whose anxiety of death is expressed in fervent denial.

Marie Mahler carried fourteen children over the course of twenty-one years, eight of whom—all boys—died of diphtheria, scarlet fever, or other infectious childhood diseases. She would live another decade and by then bore the "careworn" appearance that Mahler described to Freud, who responded that Mahler sought this look in the women he loved. Gustav remained deeply attached to his mother. He would recall her face with its "St. Ursula's smile," the St. Ursula of his Fourth Symphony associated with the text of the *Wunderhorn's Das himmlische Leben* (Heavenly Life): "There is no music, no music on earth, that can be compared with ours; eleven thousand virgins go happily dancing; Saint Ursula laughs to see that."[23] Mahler said that "in it, his mother's face, recalled from childhood, had hovered before his mind's eye: sad and laughing, as if through tears. For she, too, had suffered endlessly, but had always resolved everything in love and forgiveness."[24]

Besides enduring multiple births and deaths, Marie had to contend with raising her surviving children. The two eldest girls, Leopoldine and Justine, would have helped their mother as they assumed the traditional roles expected of young women in the family. But times were rapidly changing and proper education of the girls, as well as their marriage potential, would have to be addressed. Both aging parents would develop health problems, and some of the children would need to be looked after when the parents were gone.

Throughout, Marie remained devoted to family, and despite quarrels with her husband, she was a reliable domestic partner to Bernhard. What little correspondence remains intact reveals an essentially cohesive family with traditional values of caring and mutual responsibility despite internal conflicts. Guilt, too, was a shared family trait.[25] Rooted, in part, in traditional Jewish values, this was strongly reinforced by two realities particular to the Mahler family: communal, posthumous guilt for Isador's accidental death, and Bernhard's angry, confrontational manner. Most prone to the guilt-induced turn of mind, which included self-punishment, was Marie Mahler. This tendency was shared by the two siblings most identified with Marie—Gustav and Justine. Others in the family were polar opposites, most notably Alois, who turned out to be a ne'er-do-well sponge on the family resources and would eventually emigrate to America.[26] Brother Otto was caught between guilt-induced responsibility and flagrant irresponsible behavior.

But Bernhard, too, left his imprint on Mahler's character. Bernhard was ambitious, demanding, autocratic, and shrewd. He held no illusions as to the ways of the world and made a point of remaining alert to changes that might be to his advantage in Iglau and the empire. He was a thoroughly competent and aggressive businessman and he possessed some vision as to how far he might go. But he was constrained by his being a Jew, a circumstance that his son would challenge, although Gustav, too, would have to contend with his origins throughout his professional life. For Bernhard, rules and laws were to be cautiously tested and, if possible, contested. Beyond this were fantasies of the unobtainable, revealed in his love of books and learning. Above all, however, Bernhard alone knew what was best for himself and his family.

In contrast to his warm feelings toward his mother, Mahler rarely spoke of his father with affection. Yet if Gustav carried the smiling image of his mother within him, his father was an unseen presence. After Bernhard's death, Mahler kept a single object as a talisman: his father's chair. But the *Kutschbockgelehrter* endured in his son's passion for books and learning. To his lifelong friend Fritz Löhr, Gustav wrote, "I am 'devouring' an increasing number of books! They are, after all, the only friends I keep by me! And what friends! Heavens, if I had no books! . . . They become ever more familiar and more of a consolation to me, my real brothers, and fathers, and lovers."[27]

When the family first moved to Iglau, Bernhard's first application to the town authorities for a pub license was rejected—probably because there were too many such establishments and the business had been dominated by Jews. Undaunted, Bernhard rented a licensed pub, the first of several he acquired that way, and for good measure he sold spirits there as well. The following year he was granted permission to produce spirits and he eventually built a distillery for manufacturing vinegar and sweetened alcoholic beverages. Bernhard was determined to get rich while establishing himself as a respectable town burgher and respected elder in the growing Jewish community.

Yet on more than one occasion he ran aground of the authorities and was fined. He repeatedly challenged the trade laws by illegally selling foodstuffs at his establishments and failing to observe closing hours. He attempted on two occasions to set up a lottery. No slouch at canny advertisement, he named these ventures Fortune and *Gottes Segen*—God's Blessing.[28] Insulting a district administrator, Bernhard incurred a large penalty that was reduced only after an appeal to the governor of Moravia.

Bernhard's perseverance was rewarded. By 1872 he not only was able to purchase a large house near the apartment the family had rented for a dozen years, but undertook major renovation of the structure. By the time the work was completed the commercial area occupied the entire ground floor. The Mahlers' living quarters were on the first floor; employees and servants resided in the rear. There was also a stable and a separate area for the distillery and storage. With the purchase of the home, Bernhard was eligible to apply for the *Bürgerecht*, or town citizenship. With the approval of the authorities and the payment of a substantial fee, Bernhard became a "burgher of the King's Mining City of Iglau." It was at this point that Bernhard bolstered his new social position by becoming a member of the committee of the Jewish congregation of Iglau. Having built both establishment and home, he became involved in planning for the community synagogue.

By then Gustav was twelve and away from home for the first time. Although his musical ability grew apace and he had given a well-received piano recital in Iglau at the age of ten, he was an average student in the Iglau German Gymnasium. Bernhard, who gave no less attention to his son's accomplishments than to his own, had arranged for his son to attend the Neustadte Gymnasium in Prague. There, Gustav's grades proved to be even more dismal (he was sixty-fourth in a class of sixty-four) and no doubt reflected a troubled state, the result of the forced separation from family and an unfortunate choice of boarding arrangement. Bernhard had in good faith sent Gustav to board with the family of a wealthy merchant who was a music lover and the father of eleven. However, Bernhard was appalled when he learned of his son's poor treatment there—lack of food, inadequate shelter, misappropriation of clothes and shoes—and brought Gustav home immediately. Returning to Iglau in time to celebrate the anniversary of the birth of the poet Friedrich von Schiller (1759–1805), Gustav became something of a celebrity after receiving "an interminable and wildly enthusiastic ovation" at a festival performance.[29]

The rescue by Bernhard, and the return to the motherly ministrations of Marie Mahler, especially in the context of a comfortable new home, invoked a fresh sense of security in Gustav. He seemed to have accepted the punishing conditions in Prague passively, as being "quite normal"—

indicating a degree of masochism and his identification with Marie Mahler. Yet the bewildering experience of banishment had left its mark and vulnerability. Like death and bereavement, exile would become a theme in his life and his music. Years later, looking back, Mahler would say, "I am three times without a country: a Bohemian among Austrians, an Austrian among Germans, and a Jew among all the peoples of the world."[30]

Among the comforts of return for Gustav was a resumed relationship with his younger brother Ernst. The exact date of Ernst's birth is unknown but a census gives it as sometime in 1861. If this is correct, Gustav would have been a mere toddler when his brother was born. It would have seemed to him that there was always another child present. Thus Ernst was something of a twin in the dawning consciousness of Mahler's earliest life. Gustav and Ernst became intensely close, sharing the kind of relationship that may develop when, in the absence of parental harmony, children turn to one another to form a family within a family. Gustav displayed "an almost maternal affection" toward Ernst and was said to lecture him in a "friendly way . . . when he was disobedient." According to Mahler's later accounts, "a charming habit was formed, thanks to which Ernst was 'at his service' all day, fetching things for him, and cleaning his shoes and clothes without a murmur, in return for which Gustav played the piano for him." This was an unusual and distinct privilege in the Mahler household.[31]

Soon after Gustav returned from Prague, Ernst, already an invalid owing to his heart condition, became increasingly disabled. Years later Mahler reminisced: "I once nursed a boy with scarlet fever and to pass the time I invented all sorts of gruesome fairy tales . . . [to] satisfy the feverishly wandering imagination of my charge."[32] By 1874 Ernst was terminally ill with pericarditis. "Gustav followed the phases of its progress with terror, and for many months scarcely left the dying boy's bedside. He was always inventing new stories to cheer him up and take his mind off his suffering. Later he was to say that no other death affected him so deeply." As de La Grange rightly puts it, Ernst's death brought Gustav's "first sorrow."[33] More than this, it marked the end of Mahler's childhood. With Ernst gone, he was ready to leave his family—this time on his own initiative and on his own terms.

To do so as he approached his fifteenth year, Gustav would have to contend with Bernhard once again. Gustav's relationship with his father was buttressed by the burgeoning power of his art that made him universally admired and adored. Bernhard no doubt shared a rivalry with his son as well—the only member of the family who was any competition for the love and admiration he sought. Bernhard's ambivalence toward Gustav is evident in an anecdote from Mahler's childhood. Bernhard had taken the child for a walk in the woods when he suddenly remembered something he had forgotten at home. There, he promptly forgot about his son until evening. Returning to the woods hours later, he found the boy sitting quietly on the log where he had left him. That Gustav was his mother's favorite there can be no doubt, and charming as he was as a youth, he may well have perceived that she favored him over his father.

However, Mahler's love and empathy for his mother blinded him to the kinds of nurturance his father provided. Ambivalent as he may have been, Bernhard, too, was enchanted and impressed by his young son. A businessman to the core and an opportunist in every other respect, Bernhard remarkably showed no tendency whatsoever to exploit the child's talents for any need of his own, financial or other. He was no Leopold Mozart or Johann Beethoven—and not just because he lacked musical knowledge. Bernhard made his son's studies a priority, found the best music teachers Iglau could provide, and insisted that Gustav complete gymnasium education as well. He may have wondered about the source of his son's talents; certainly, there was no one in the Mahler clan he could point to.

Bernhard had worked for his own father and inherited the modest start of his own successful business from him. It would have been natural for him to take Gustav into his business or to encourage the next generational step—to steer him toward a career in law or one of the other professions. Two lifelong Iglau friends of Gustav had pursued this upwardly mobile path: Emil Freund, a lawyer, and Guido Adler, a professor. In encouraging Gustav's musical promise, particularly when there were signs that it might lead to a permanent career, Bernhard was making a personal sacrifice.

Gustav's strongest desire was to enter a conservatory. There were two in the Austro-Hungarian Empire, in Vienna and in Prague. His recent experience in Prague did not warm Gustav to that possibility; besides, Vienna was the capital, and for the child who grew up on the road to that city, a magical place. Indeed, Vienna would always be a wonderland for Mahler. Gustav found his opportunity through his musical ability. But he seized it with his father's perseverance and skill.

Near Iglau there was an estate called Morawan, endowed for the benefit of impecunious royal widows. Its manager, Gustav Schwartz, had some musical manuscripts he needed deciphered. Josef Steiner, a young friend of Mahler's from Iglau, knew Schwartz and had recommended Gustav for the task. Schwartz was astounded by the boy's musical ability and urged him to pursue musical studies professionally. Mahler responded that although nothing would please him more, his father wanted him to pursue college studies rather than attend the Vienna Conservatory. Gustav's relationship with Schwartz was a warm one and the boy visited Morawan on several occasions, finally spending the summer of 1874 or 1875 on the estate with the Schwartz family. He found a benign father in Schwartz and a champion as well. Together, the two Gustavs campaigned to win Bernhard's approval.

Mahler's mourning for Ernst was interwoven in this endeavor. Among the pieces Mahler played that most impressed Schwartz were fragments from an opera that he had started to compose following Ernst's death. He called it *Ernst von Schwaben* and its theme was the inseparable bond between Ernst and his friend Werner. In this effort, Josef Steiner, three years younger than Gustav, served as librettist, artistic confidante, and surrogate for Ernst himself. Several years later, in 1879, a lonely and depressed adolescent Mahler, working as a tutor in Hungary, would write a remarkable letter to Steiner in which he related a dream whose central image was Ernst; superimposed were the hero of their unfinished opera and the dead brother whom Steiner knew from Iglau.

> Now the pale figures of my life pass before me like shadows of a long-lost happiness, and the song of longing sounds again in my ears. And once more we are wandering together in that familiar countryside, and there we see the organ grinder standing, his hat proffered with his fleshless hands. In the discordant sound of his instrument I hear *Ernst von Schwaben*'s greetings. He himself

seems to appear, trying to embrace me and when I look at him closely, I see it is my poor brother.

Mourning and Morawan were also associated with first love. In the same letter Mahler hinted at an intimacy to which his young friend had been privy:

> And I see gardens filled with friendly people and a tree on which is engraved the name Pauline. A blue-eyed maiden curtsies and smiles and brings me a cluster of grapes. My cheeks redden again at the recollection. I see those eyes which once made me a thief—and again everything disappears.[34]

Indeed, to this day there is a gnarled tree in the courtyard of the main house of Morawan in which the initial *P* appears to have been carved many years ago.

Gustav put Bernhard and Schwartz in touch and letters were exchanged. A meeting in Iglau was eventually arranged. Gustav had high hopes, although he did not underestimate their adversary. He wrote to Schwartz: "We still have to fight a few battles to get my father to agree to our project." By now Schwartz, too, had been incorporated into *Ernst von Schwaben*, in what may be the only remnant of the lost libretto: "Dazu musst du, O Werner, mir verhelfen" (And it is you, O Werner, who must help me toward that goal). Feeling helpless, Gustav added to his letter: "I am all alone in this struggle against the superior strength of reasonable and sober folk."[35]

As a result of Schwartz's visit to Mahler's father, it was agreed that Gustav would audition for the famous Viennese teacher Julius Epstein, whom Schwartz knew personally. Epstein alone would decide if the young man's talent merited further training at the conservatory. This was an agreeable outcome for Bernhard, given his respect for learning and penchant for advancement. As a businessman he would have had to consider that the cost of the conservatory was not insignificant, and he would have been unlikely to invest in an unpromising venture of any kind. But what doubtless swayed Bernhard in the end was best put in the words of Mahler's contemporary Stefan Zweig, who wrote of the Jewish community that "Riches are . . . merely a steppingstone, a means to the true end, and in no sense the real goal. The real determination of the Jew is to rise to a higher cultural lane in the intellectual world." In this sense Bernhard's compromise was also self-serving. "It is counted as a title of honor for the entire family," Zweig continued, "to have someone in their midst, a professor, a scientist or a musician, who plays a role in the intellectual world, as if through his achievements he ennobled them all."[36]

Epstein, the professor of piano at the Vienna Conservatory, met Bernhard and Gustav in Baden, not far from Vienna. The audition was not long. After a few minutes Epstein interrupted the youth and turned to Bernhard: "Herr Mahler, your son is a born musician." Bernhard hesitated. The canny Epstein, a Jew who was well familiar with such families as the Mahlers, quipped, "In this case I cannot possibly be wrong. This young man has *spirit*, but not to take over his father's spirit business." During Mahler's time at the Vienna Conservatory, Epstein remained "a powerful friend."[37]

A powerful friend indeed, Epstein, the successor to Schwartz's ministrations, essentially replaced him in Gustav's regard. For once in Vienna, Mahler proved to be a poor correspondent and a disappointment to his earlier proponent. In a letter two years later Gustav showed some remorse that Schwartz would "have reason to complain" of his conduct. "How, you will ask, have I been able to forget for one instant my duty toward you and forgotten to keep you informed of my successes and progress? I cannot understand it myself."[38]

With this, Gustav Schwartz, catalyst, mentor, and friend at this critical juncture, disappeared from the Mahler correspondence and from Gustav's life. The older man had served as a placenta in fostering a new life for Mahler. Severing ties with Schwartz was a sign of the fifteen-year-old's readiness to separate himself from Iglau, from his parents, and from childhood itself. Detachment from Schwartz signaled a move beyond the painful mourning of Ernst as well—just as Josef Steiner, similarly associated with Ernst, would also pass from Mahler's life within a few years. *Ernst von Schwaben*, the music with which the three men had been associated and which had bound them together, remained unfinished as it faded into the past.

From this point on, Gustav would still spend portions of vacations in Iglau, correspond regularly and respectfully with parents and siblings, and maintain lifelong relationships with several close Iglau friends. But his unique musical gift engendered a sense of competence-in-the-world that favored psychological emancipation. Already, a powerful attachment to and involvement with the materials of music counterbalanced sentimental affiliations with the human objects of Gustav's past.

As he passed through adolescence, Mahler's personality developed, including those traits that may seem unattractive. Opportunism would reappear repeatedly as he moved forward in his career. Over time, colleagues would complain that Mahler used people. Even those who did not complain—such as his companion of the *Wunderhorn* years, Natalie Bauer-Lechner—were to a degree exploited.

With the physical leaving of home, and the attenuation of relationships such as those with Schwartz and Steiner that amounted to desertion of friends, Mahler sought to sever a portion of his past. Nevertheless, although he may not have been interested in his past, he would soon experience that the past was interested in him, as the themes of banishment, death, and mourning emerged in his creative life along with brotherly love and its dark underside, fratricide. The adolescent crisis that led up to the fifteen-year-old Mahler's separation was normative, stabilizing, and even creative. Shortly, we will turn to the crises that challenged both stability and creative life.

Years later, Mahler summarized the first portion of his life in telegraph fashion. The occasion was a request by a painter-turned-journalist, Annie Somerfeld-Mincieux (1857–1937), for biographical information. A resident of Berlin, she had become interested in Mahler after hearing one of his compositions—probably the first performance of the Second Symphony in Berlin in 1895. For Mahler the performance represented a personal triumph, the end of a creative block that had impeded earlier completion of the work. Nevertheless, in spite of his growing reputation as a conductor, Mahler was still struggling for appreciation and recognition as a composer. Accordingly, he responded to Somerfeld-Mincieux's request warmly, although he emphasized that "the only way to learn about my life is to have my works in chronological order before you."

Born in Bohemia July 1860. Moved when 15 to Vienna—*conservatoire* and *university*! The need to be active in the world and earn my living led me to the theatre, where I have worked unremittingly since my 20th year. At the start of the whole petty misery of the provinces, and later in the *gross* misery of the "hallowed" places of art. The first work, in which I showed myself to the public, was an arrangement of Weber's *Pinto* sketches[39] and the completing of the whole work. 1888. And this is all I have achieved for the theatre. My whole nature points me in the direction of the symphony. My D major Symphony, which I'm performing on 16 March in Berlin, was written before the C minor, as early as 1888.[40] And I have in my desk a Third, as well as a number of larger or smaller works—Lieder, Ballads etc. I have been engaged in Cassel, Prague, Leipzig, Pest and other towns, and have now been 5 years in Hamburg. I am 35 years old (single, in case that interests you), scarcely known and scarcely *performed*! But I shall not let that get me down! I have patience and shall wait![41]

3

FAMILY CRISIS, 1889

Crisis had a way of coinciding precisely with some exceptional achievement in Mahler's life. His appointment as director of the newly built Budapest Opera in the summer of 1888 was just such an event. It was remarkable for several reasons: having resigned an earlier post in Leipzig, Mahler had no other immediate prospects. Then, a ten-year contract was awarded to him, a relatively unknown twenty-eight-year-old conductor—and a Jew at that, in a city that was notably anti-Semitic even for its time and place. This was indeed something to write home about:

> I would be Director of the royal Opera with absolutely unlimited powers! All-powerful master of an institution as large as the Vienna Opera, and at the same time first conductor. . . . It is all simply incredible! At the same time the responsibilities are immense.[1]

To emphasize the point for complete family appreciation and no doubt Bernhard's approval, Gustav provided full financial details: he would receive an annual salary of 10,000 florins (a considerable sum at the time) and have "at my disposition, with a single stroke of the pen, a treasury of one million florins!" (By contrast in the family, sister Leopoldine—Poldi—had married a merchant whose annual salary was 2,160 florins.) But above all, for Mahler the *composer*, there was the marvel of "four months of vacation! It is all simply incredible!"

Whatever pride the news was greeted with in Iglau, Mahler started out the quintessential outsider in Budapest: a German-speaking foreigner, no less a Jew, who in an opening gambit had the gall to promise the truly Hungarian national opera that had never been achieved—one in which the language would be exclusively Hungarian! The press was hostile, representing "a country governed by blind patriotism."[2] In the early months, journalists were won over less by Mahler's actual conducting than by his administrative abilities, his work ethic for himself and performers, and his sense of mission. He had dedicated himself to rigorous preparation while delegating most of the actual performances. "Neither a diplomat nor a society man," one critic noted, "but a man sure of his purpose, lucid, and gifted with a strong will."[3]

Cannily, Mahler was saving his own conducting debut for performances of Wagner scheduled for the beginning of 1889. Budapest had not yet witnessed the *Ring* and would now hear it in Hungarian! Preparation involved not only individual coaching of the singers but stage direction and acting as well. Mahler's motto was "Discipline, work. Work, discipline." The orchestra pit was lowered and a bridge built over it so that he could dash to the stage to demonstrate some detail or retreat from the podium to the concert hall to listen to some effect.

It was in the midst of these preparations for the *Ring* that troubling news came from Iglau. Both parents had been ailing at least since Mahler's three preceding "Leipzig" years. Bernhard Mahler had begun to consult "professors" in Prague and Vienna during this period for an array of symptoms, diagnosed variously as diabetes and inflammation of the liver. He was sent to Karlsbad to take the waters. Later, from his painfully swollen feet, it was suggested that he was most likely suffering congestive heart failure. As Bernhard attempted to keep the business going but grew increasingly irritable, his condition took its toll on all, particularly twenty-year-old Justine. She was nurse to both her father and her mother, who had developed symptoms of her own, initially diagnosed as "nerves." The waters of Marienbad, where Marie was sent, could of course not alleviate what turned out to be heart disease as well. As Bernhard's condition worsened, Mahler frantically tried to keep family matters under control through letters, not daring to make a surprise visit for fear of alarming his parents, and reluctant to diminish the momentum he had created in Budapest. He saw to it that his father consulted a specialist in Vienna, engaging his longtime friend from

Gustav and sister Justine.

university days, the archaeologist Friedrich Löhr, now married and living in the capital, to supervise in his absence.

The first performances of the operas of the *Ring* in early 1889 rewarded Mahler for his ability to keep family distractions at bay and justified his strategy and careful preparation. His triumph was complete and established him in Budapest, at least for the moment. Only after this did he return briefly to Iglau for a visit, which he knew would be the last with his father. The day after his second performance of *Die Walküre*, he received a telegram with the news of his father's death. Mahler was in Iglau for the funeral the following day and remained there several more days, attempting to regroup the family of which, like it or not, he was now the male head.

Marie Mahler was by now quite ill herself and Mahler worried not only about her but about the toll further nursing might take on Justine. Leopoldine had married and moved to Vienna. (Naturally, Bernhard had not approved of her choice of the merchant Ludwig Quittner, although he had become reconciled to it shortly before his death.) Sixteen-year-old Otto was sent to live with Leopoldine. Otto had shown some gift for music and would attend the conservatory. Alois had been called up for the military and would be serving in Brünn. Thus at home in Iglau remained only Marie, twenty-year-old Justine, and thirteen-year-old Emma.

Mahler himself was suffering physically, from a chronic and severe hemorrhoidal problem, delicately referred to as his "subterranean troubles."[4] He was also debilitated from the year's work and worries. Surgery was scheduled for the summer. Sent home from the hospital, he wrote to Fritz of persistent pain and complained of being "run down." He anticipated a three-week recuperation in Marienbad but family problems were relentless.[5] A visit to Iglau in August to see his mother was disheartening and Mahler feared she was terminal. To his father, Mahler had been respectful and dutiful. Indeed, it was his sense of familial duty that motivated Mahler to assume responsibility following his father's death. But Marie Mahler he loved, and the loss he anticipated was as painful as it was disorienting—the final dissolution of his childhood family. Gustav would soon transfer much of the feeling he had toward Marie to Justine, who would be his counterpart in the restoration of family.

Mahler also visited Vienna, where the temporary stability of the satellite family was rapidly declining. As summer approached, Poldi became ill herself, suffering from neuralgic symptoms initially presumed to be benign. Mahler relieved her of the burden of caring for Otto by renting a room for him with Fritz Löhr and his wife, Uda.

Returning to Budapest to begin the new opera season in September, Mahler was depressed and, still suffering postoperatively from his own physical problems, taking morphine for pain. Matters only worsened as troubling news from both Iglau and Vienna continued. His mother's condition deteriorated daily, and Leopoldine was diagnosed with a brain tumor. In the midst of his conducting a performance of *La Juive*, a telegram arrived summoning Mahler to Iglau. He left the following day only to find the exhausted Justine in frightening shape as well. During what seemed to be a brief remission in Marie's condition, Mahler took Justine to Vienna to have her seen by a doctor there. On his return to

Budapest, Mahler learned that Leopoldine had died on 27 September, while he was tending to Marie in Iglau and Justi in Vienna. In sending remittance for Otto's board he wrote to Uda Löhr of his mother's condition: "Very bad news from home—the catastrophe is awaited hourly." Anguished that he was not free to leave Budapest with the start of the season, he begged Fritz, "If the worst should happen before I can get there[,] go to Iglau for one or two days to support my sister."[6]

Scarcely two weeks later, in early October, another telegram arrived as Mahler was about to go onstage to conduct *Lohengrin*: Marie was dying. According to what Mahler later related to his friend Natalie Bauer-Lechner, "His conscience would not let him abandon the performance, which he was to conduct; he concealed his sorrow deep within his heart, letting no one guess the blow that he had just received."[7] Marie died the following day, 11 October 1889. Justine was at her mother's bedside and signed the death certificate. With Mahler's help, she arranged for the funeral, which he did not attend. Anticipating his mother's death during a prolonged illness had fostered anticipatory mourning. But no loss had touched him as deeply since the death of his brother Ernst fifteen years earlier. Mourning had by now become a fixture in Mahler's inner life and would find expression and representation repeatedly in his music from this point onward.

With both parents dead, the family left the Czech lands forever. Mahler's separation from family fifteen years earlier had inaugurated his independent life. Now the break was complete; Iglau remained alive only in nostalgic imagination as home came to be represented by family friends such as Fritz Löhr. Fritz, who attended Marie's funeral as his friend's surrogate, was called on again. Emma as well as Otto would live with him and his family as Mahler planned to take an apartment for himself and Justine in Budapest. Fritz brought both young women from Iglau to Vienna and put Justine on the train to be met by Mahler in Budapest.

In writing to Fritz about financial arrangements "for the two children" (Otto and Emma) during this chaotic period, Mahler confided, "I must admit I cannot quite suppress a slight groan. Alois, in Brünn, also has to be constantly supplied with money, and here expenses seem to be turning out considerably higher than I had originally hoped, and these owing to Justi's singularly sensitive and debilitated constitution. Well—with God's help!"⁸ As the year drew to an end Mahler seemed increasingly concerned about Otto's health, writing to Fritz to be sure that he had a winter coat.

Characteristically, while still in the throes of recent losses and frantic arrangements, Mahler was preparing a singular artistic event: not simply the premiere of his First Symphony (called at this point *Symphonic Poem*) but the first public performance of any of his orchestral works. Occurring just five weeks after Marie's death, it was a critical disaster. Mahler had had high hopes for the First Symphony, considering it "the most sponta-neous and daringly composed of my works." He dreamed that it would fulfill a lifelong wish, namely, that it "would have such immediate appeal that I should be able to live on the profits and go on composing." The reviews were so negative that friends "avoided me afterwards; no one dared to mention the performance or the work for me, and I went about like a leper or an outlaw."⁹

Mahler was deeply wounded by the critical and public response after the tremendous effort expended in Budapest under trying personal cir-cumstances. He had strived to please and to be a part of this community, attempting to create a truly national opera. But once again he experi-enced himself as the outsider—the pariah, the Wandering Jew. By this point Mahler himself was becoming disillusioned with Hungarian opera and was longing to hear German sung again. As always, he was plotting his next move, although he would continue conducting in Budapest until the end of the 1891 season.

With the family pressures of 1889, Mahler's impetus to compose shriv-eled. He had begun a second symphony the previous year, provisionally titling it *Todtenfeier* (Funeral Service or Rite), with an eye to performing this massive first movement before completing the symphony. He had hastened to finish the movement in the summer of 1888, before the move to Budapest. Only recently had Mahler established his custom of devot-ing summers to composition. During the conducting year, he would revise and refine orchestration. This second symphony was still awaiting completion after the summer of 1889 left Mahler preoccupied with family affairs. Mahler had played some of his musical ideas for the symphony for Fritz over an Easter visit, although he was not in the habit of performing unfinished works even informally for friends. This may have been his way to sustain creative focus in the face of adversity. But by summer Mahler had no new ideas nor the energy to realize them. Indeed, the summer of 1889 was one of the most dismal in Mahler's life. Composition was at a standstill and would remain so until the family crisis reached some resolution.

Just before Christmas Mahler and Justine traveled to Iglau for the last time to sell their father's business and settle his estate. Returning to Vienna, the entire newly constituted Mahler family spent Christmas with the Löhrs. Yet their troubles did not subside. With the start of the new year, the "slight groan" Mahler could not quite suppress in his earlier letter to Löhr would rise to a full-scale lament. Fragments of letters to Löhr reveal the ensuing months in Budapest as difficult: "There's always one of us ill in bed . . . have to bottle up so much vexation that I am incapable of writing! . . . —How is Otto turning out? . . . Write soon to your careworn, Gustav."[10] Mahler remained incapable of writing the following summer as well, although there were finally signs of healing as he reunited the younger Mahlers to spend several months sharing a villa with the Löhrs in Hinter Brühl in the Wienerwald. Otto had been a particular concern during the year and would shortly emerge, along with his brother Alois, as the chief source of Mahler's family worries and aggravation.

Otto Mahler was sixteen when his parents died and life up to that point had not been easy for him. Emma's birth when he was two had ended his brief tenure as the youngest in the household, at about the same time older brother Gustav had left home. Bernhard, then 48, remained preoccupied with business; and the by-now careworn Marie, at 38, was at the end of her childbirth years. Otto was doubly burdened from birth: first by constitution, second by Gustav. He had inherited from his mother's side a tendency toward depression that led to a lack of resiliency in meeting life's challenges, hence a degree of emotional instability. Otto grew up with idealized family stories about the legendary Gustav as well as his brother's actual triumphs. Drawn to follow in Gustav's footsteps yet having only modest talent, he knew of no way other than to aspire to a life in music. His father would have seen to it that Otto was offered all the opportunities Gustav had been given: gymnasium, preparation for the

Otto Mahler.

university, music lessons. Bernhard may have taken a different stance with regard to the conservatory, however, as Otto was the last son who might have continued the family business. Alois was proving to be an unreliable and therefore unlikely candidate. In any event, Otto had neither the drive to follow in his father's footsteps nor the ambitious thrust that had led Gustav to press his own case, recruiting Gustav Schwartz in his campaign. It was Gustav who guided Otto's musical education and sent him to the conservatory after the death of their parents.

With Bernhard's death, Otto, as yet uneducated and ill equipped to be on his own, had been shuffled around. At first living with Leopoldine, he was shifted rapidly from there when his sister became ill. Subsequently, he roomed with the Löhrs, where he was soon joined by the fifteen-year-old Emma in an interim arrangement. Gustav, nearly a generation older, fulfilled the role of parent to both. Otto barely knew him as a sibling and perhaps even less as a person. His mental image of Gustav was heavily weighted with legend, envy, and begrudging admiration.

The healing summer of 1890 in the Wienerwald was perhaps the first occasion in the brothers' lives for a degree of comradeship. Otto was with the Löhrs until July, when he joined Mahler. For the rest of the summer he and Gustav swam together every morning, even when it rained. They got to know each other in a new way. Much of their conversation was about music, Otto frequently provocative in his comments and Gustav lecturing away. At the end of the summer a more permanent arrangement for the family was made. Justine would set up household for Otto and Emma in Vienna. The twenty-two-year-old sister-mother-housekeeper was established in the Breitgasse with maid and cook while Gustav, now thirty, would return to Budapest alone.

Management at the opera was becoming more conservative, with Mahler now labeled a "Germanist," and a Jewish Germanist at that.[11] In any event he was already planning his next move, to Hamburg. As this final season opened, a new person came into Mahler's life, Natalie Bauer-Lechner, who had been a fellow student in the conservatory. Having recently divorced, she contacted Mahler and visited Budapest. He was "curious to find out if we shall be silent or if we shall talk"—which we may interpret to mean he wondered if there would be sexual activity between them.[12] Later developments suggest Natalie was interested. If Gustav ever entertained the possibility, his response from the outset was lukewarm at best, later quite cold. Natalie eventually settled for the friendship that Mahler was prepared to offer and became an auxiliary member of the Mahler family. In her many conversations with Mahler during the *Wunderhorn* years she became a chronicler of his life and autobiographical amanuensis, recording their talks over the course of a decade in her *Mahleriana*.[13]

Besides the strains at the opera, the new family arrangements added stress to Mahler's life, although he experienced some pride in the way he was weathering the storm. He lamented to Fritz, "I lead an existence directed entirely toward others . . . thus I have accomplished many useful things and have experienced many joys."[14] In truth, "entirely toward others" was an exaggeration, for Mahler was enjoying tremendous artistic satisfaction in his work, even recognition. Indeed, after the debacle of the First Symphony in Budapest, and despite a rabid anti-Semitism, Mahler came to be appreciated by the Hungarians before his departure to Hamburg. In the same letter to Fritz, he went on to speak of his first meeting with Johannes Brahms, who had embraced him warmly after a performance of *Don Giovanni* that he had had to be coaxed to attend. Brahms's praise was lavish. The resentment Mahler expressed to Fritz was instead attributable to the fact that he had not been able to compose for reasons both personal and practical. The *Todtenfeier* lay dormant. Gustav felt considerable financial pressure, owing to the children's needs and the upkeep of multiple households. Although his salary at the opera was generous, Mahler anticipated needing to supplement this with guest-conducting engagements and tours, which would inevitably drain his energy as well as interfere with the summer's composing and season's revisions.

Did Mahler in self-pity and masochism make a bad compromise in undertaking conducting tours? By the time of his marriage, now more than a decade away, he had indeed accumulated some degree of debt. Nevertheless, conducting engagements afforded Mahler considerable gratification and, as time went on, an opportunity to perform his own works. Moreover, valuable friendships were made, such as those with conductors Richard Strauss (1864–1949) and Willem Mengelberg (1871–1951). Through the latter, Mahler's music was embraced in Holland; and Mahler took to Holland as if it were an oasis.

To his sorrow, the control Mahler exercised so successfully in directing opera performances was doomed to fail when it came to real life. Despite the appearance of stability, things were not going well in Vienna. In particular, Otto was a source of worry. His work at studies was inconsistent and he often skipped classes at the conservatory. His grades wavered and private tutors had to be engaged—yet another expense. Nor would any kind of future be assured the boy, even if he had been an excellent student graduating with a diploma. Conservatory training was the basis for competent musicianship, nothing more. Few knew as well as Gustav that the fledgling conductor had to scrounge for opportunities in country concert halls and spas. Furthermore, the prospect of compulsory military service loomed. Mahler wrote to Fritz, "I wish from the bottom of my heart that the time were near when at long last Otto would have his examination and his year of military service behind him, so that this infinitely complicated process of providing money would become simpler for me—it is beginning to wear me down and I long for the day when I am no longer obliged to earn so much money."[15]

As the conducting season wore on, Gustav's letters to the family were increasingly demanding, critical, and complaining. Few details of life in Vienna escaped his notice and comment. His tone was biting and Otto had reason to feel hurt in light of what had been their first adult talks as potential colleagues that summer. Gustav's resentful yet self-satisfied assumption of the parental role was inevitably met with Otto's adolescent rebellion.

At the same time, Mahler had been charting his next move—to Hamburg, as principal conductor. He left Budapest at the end of the opera season in the spring of 1891. Although the new post might have appeared to be of a lesser rank, it did not involve the administrative responsibilities of the Royal Hungarian Opera. "Hurrah I am free," he wrote to Justine. "I obtained my release under extremely favorable conditions."[16] Mahler was briefly elated by the change and the cordial welcome he received in Hamburg from new friends and admirers. This was reflected in relief from the constraints on composition he had been experiencing.

An index to the occasional breaks in what was amounting to a creative block can be found in Mahler's embracing the volume of folk poetry *Des knaben Wunderhorn* by Achim von Arnim and Clemens Brentano. He had discovered the anthology in 1887, during his last year in Leipzig—"a naive medieval universe peopled by soldiers and children, animals and brightly colored saints. A universe filled with humanity, love, and sorrow, *Sehnsucht*, and eternal farewells, but filled also with a fresh humor that enchanted him."[17] The spirit of the *Wunderhorn* remained with him throughout this period, and when the urge or opportunity presented itself, Mahler would work on a vocal setting to one of the poems. As the summer of 1891 approached, Mahler hoped to begin composing again. By now Otto had become Gustav's archivist in Vienna and his older brother asked him to send the unfinished *Wunderhorn* lieder that had been Mahler's beacon these several years.

Gustav's asking Otto to send his manuscripts bespoke the older brother's success, his gifts, and his future composing plans. One such request was for the manuscript to Mahler's saga of fratricide, *Das klagende Lied*. One can only guess what effect such requests had on the increasingly tormented Otto. He, too, aspired to be a composer; eventually (in 1893) he would set to music texts by Hans Emanuel Sax, a friend of Mahler. Mahler himself, out of sympathy for Sax, who suffered from tuberculosis, had planned to set one of these poems but never quite got around to it. Otto's settings, which one of his conservatory professors evidently praised, proved to be a source of humor and derision in the nearly daily correspondence between Gustav and Justine. In a patronizing letter, Mahler wrote to Justine: "Your account of Otto's settings of Sax amused me greatly. This professor seems to have a fine, discriminating nose; I suppose Herr Schuh has a Russian potato for a nose."[18]

With summer approaching, Mahler's feelings of satisfaction and self-congratulation gave way to angry exasperation. The impulse to resume composition was dampened by the onset of a depression that he had not experienced since his melancholy summer as a tutor in Hungary and after Ernst's death. He felt depleted in every respect and far from experiencing the freedom about which he had written to Justine. That summer Gustav spent two weeks alone, wandering abroad in Scandinavia. Returning to Hamburg, no less depressed, he wrote of recent events to Emil Freund, a boyhood friend from Iglau:

> What you have gathered from my letters about my "mood" is right enough. I have been through so much in the last few weeks—without any evident material cause—the past has caught up with me—all I have lost—the loneliness of the present . . . you know these moods of mine from earlier years—when I would be overcome by sadness even while among my friends— when I was still all youth, vigor and stamina—so you can well imagine how I spend these long *lonely* afternoons and evenings here—no *one* with whom I have anything in common—whether a share in the past or shared hopes for the future.[19]

Here Mahler perceived his life in terms of "all I have lost" and consequently himself felt lost. Present, past, and future seemed empty—all signs of depression. For the first time the thirty-one-year-old Mahler spoke as if a weary old man—a theme that would recur in later years. As though becoming aware of the secret silence that depression keeps, he continued, this time to Fritz:

> [I roamed] in Norway . . . for weeks on end without speaking to a soul—and that after already having had my fill of keeping silence—and now back in this atmosphere in which I cannot get so much as a single breath of fresh air.[20]

Once again, in a retreat from life, Mahler perceived himself as an out-sider and a wanderer. But what had Mahler lost and what had he kept silent? Those dead now included Gustav's parents as well as his brother Ernst. Marie Mahler's death signaled yet again the end of childhood, par-ticularly since she was the more loved and loving parent. Beloved Ernst was in a category of his own—part vulnerable child, part companion, and from the earliest time of life, part Gustav's double. Gustav's surviving siblings—except Justine and young Emma—were burdensome.

Despite Mahler's groans to his correspondents and increasing diatribes to Vienna, he clearly could not express the extent of his rage at what life had brought him: an ironic replacement for family loss in the form of insurmountable responsibilities. Mahler's summer attempt at escape was futile for it was an attempt to eliminate feelings being generated squarely within himself. The wish to be rid of responsibilities was only a short step from the wish to be rid of the persons involved, in particular the two brothers who were the chief source of aggravation, Otto and Alois. Stifling such strivings and the rage associated with them induced a sense of suffocation: "this atmosphere in which I cannot get so much as a sin-gle breath of fresh air." The suppression of such feelings was further revealed in a portion of Mahler's letter to Emil: "Don't show this letter to Justi! I do not need to tell you that I should gladly make any sacri-fice—but I assure you I cannot bear this much longer."[21] Mahler's rage would take an uncertain course from this point on, including expressive outbursts and excessive worry.

Letters to Vienna took on the appearance of sermons as Mahler attempted to gain some distance from his emerging feelings. To Justine in October 1891 he wrote:

> Your recent letters have told me a lot of things that pleased me. I can see that you are slowly developing into a more alert human being and starting to look around for yourself. But at the same time they have given me an insight into your way of life that does not satisfy me . . . it seems to me that your mutual relationships are very confused. . . .
>
> However, there is one thing I beg of you: don't ever imag-ine that you have any knowledge of human nature! The real

deep-down truth is as follows: as long as you consider yourself to be different from the others it is all right. But if believing this you do not stop demanding from others what is possible only for yourself, everything will go wrong.

And then, the Polonius blessing:

But this might carry us too far! Please do not fight or mistrust each other. Enjoy what you have in common, don't blame what you cannot understand in someone else, and do not try to impose your laws on the "whole of humanity." . . . Try to remain united . . . and beware not to destroy this bond lightly. . . .

But I have forgotten the most essential point of my sermon: what particularly exasperates us in others is ninety-nine per cent of the time that which we ourselves are capable of. This goes for mistakes common to men as a whole: we recognize our own world in others, and this reflected image infuriates us so much that we would like to break the mirror immediately.[22]

In noting "the essential point of my sermon," Mahler acknowledged the nature of the letter. Indeed, the sermon might well have been directed to Mahler himself: it was a plea for brotherhood. But, finally, the inherent message was violent: the "breaking of the mirror." Shortly, the suppressed aggression that fueled Mahler's summer depression would be turned outward. His begrudging efforts to be the nurturing, if not exactly kindly, paterfamilias would cease, replaced by wishes to be rid of the burdens causing such pain. Fantasies of fratricide would surface.

Gustav had little time for reflection as the first Hamburg season of 1892 progressed. Adopting Gustav's stance in writing of her own privations, Justine continued to request additional money. It was likely convenient for Justi to imply that Otto was the culprit for whom all were sacrificing since at twenty-three she had little experience running a household and might thus ward off her older brother's criticism. By the spring of 1892 Mahler's bitterness had overflowed on to even Fritz Löhr, who in Gustav's view had abandoned the Viennese Mahler children for several months while traveling in Italy and whom he felt was giving up on Otto. Mahler criticized Löhr for what he believed amounted to cowardice and also blamed a friend of the family, Nina Hoffmann (who would later figure importantly in Otto's life), for spoiling him. Justine quite understandably might have been anxious to avoid the ire of a man who could so readily lash out at a devoted old friend.

Unknown to Mahler, and fearfully kept from him by Justine, was the fact that Otto had already withdrawn from the conservatory. Meanwhile, Alois—irresponsible and undisciplined—was getting into endless trouble and running up debts. Gustav had helped him make business contacts in Hamburg and by this point he was concerned that Alois might actually be sent to debtor's prison without his financial help. With increased financial burdens, Mahler had once again to renounce summer composing to go on tour, this time to London's Covent Garden. The decision proved career enhancing: Mahler was received with considerable acclaim.[23] Yet conditions had still not improved at home by fall. Alois, who had enrolled in business school (with Mahler paying the tuition), hoping this might lead to a job, developed tuberculosis. According to Mahler's upbringing, illness above all required immediate attention, although he often failed to apply this to himself. He sent Alois along with Justi to the Tirol to recover. After Justine left him there, Alois not only continued to accept Gustav's life-restoring trip but sustained debts that led to even more requests for money.

As his frustration and rage mounted, Mahler's feelings toward the relentlessly psychopathic Alois spilled over onto Otto. Gustav lumped them together in a letter to Justine in the spring of 1893:

> I am beginning to get absolutely fed up with being dragged behind, continually, through thick and thin, tied to the stirrup of my lord brothers' winged horse. . . . *I too am still young*, and not in the mood to be a grumpy moralist. I, too, would enjoy my life, and am not ready to wheeze around with the cares of a nearly dead old man.—I still have *my flight* damn it all.—I now believe that it was a *big* mistake that I was so forebearing and trusting with those two fellows.[24]

In this manner Mahler revealed the tail wagging the dog: it was he who had become the dependent, the oppressed. The master had become the servant, suffering from the sadism of fate and crying out in masochistic woe. He was the morose moralist indeed as he considered abandoning the brothers, whom he depicted as subjecting him to a primitive torture. More explicitly fatalistic than the recently criticized Löhr, Mahler wrote of Otto: "Let him face the consequences! Perhaps the only salvation for him is to find out for himself what life means and to be obliged to struggle and battle on his own."[25]

It was Alois who responded for both brothers: "I have a heart so full of bitterness that I would have to write you twenty more pages, but I shall prefer to remain silent."[26] Mahler sent Alois's reply to Justi with a note on the verso: "As you see we are thus all agreed to let Alois go his own way now."[27] Indeed, later that summer Mahler carried out his threat, writing to Alois:

> When your savings are exhausted, do not, under any circumstances, count on getting even a kreuzer from me. I assure you that I am neither in a position to support you financially, nor have I the slightest intention of doing so . . . it only remains for me to express to you my best wishes for your well-being, and my hope above all to see you yet a useful member of the human society.[28]

After this, brother Alois was scarcely mentioned in the Mahler correspondence. Emigrating eventually to the United States, he died in Chicago in 1931.[29]

That same spring of 1893 Mahler had sent Justine and Natalie (who by now was well entrenched in the family) on an inspection tour of the Austrian Salzkammergut to find a suitable place for him to work during the summer. They chose a house near the small village of Steinbach on Lake Attersee. What motivated Mahler was a compelling inner sense of generating musical ideas and the prospect of composing once again. Ridding himself of responsibility for Alois no doubt contributed to a greater sense of freedom as well. Troubling as Otto's problems were, they were of a different nature—attributable not to psychopathy but to extreme laziness and, although Mahler could not perceive it, the same tendency toward depression as his own, albeit chronic and more malignant. Moreover, whereas Alois lied wantonly, Otto tended to do so out of fear of his older brother's wrath. Consequently, for the moment Otto

Gustav Mahler, 1892.

remained a member of the family and once again summered with them all in Steinbach.

Thus the summer of 1893 found the Mahler family comfortably and tranquilly installed in five rooms of an inn by the shore of Lake Attersee looking onto gently rolling green hills against the backdrop of the Alps. For two weeks Gustav, Justi, Otto, Emma, and Natalie lived in relative harmony and order. Mahler had managed to turn the photograph of his life from negative to positive: where previously his creative energy had faltered and his emotional life had been laden with family strife and inner rage, the latter had been quelled for the moment and, as a result, creative life would burst forward.

The stage had already been set and the *Wunderhorn* lit the way. During the period of family turmoil, when Mahler was unable to compose major works, he had worked on and completed five *Wunderhorn* settings for voice and orchestra, all in the first half of 1892. The *Todtenfeier*, soon to be incorporated as the first movement of the Second Symphony, remained dormant throughout. Now, after a four-year hiatus, Mahler was ready to resume composition in earnest.

4

THE MUSIC OF FRATRICIDE

The *Wunderhorn* was more than comforting throughout the period of Mahler family crisis; it was Gustav's creative hearth, the virtual locus where new ideas were incubated. The Arnim-Brentano texts that Otto sent him inspired confidence in the composer. He wrote to Justine, "I now have the *Wunderhorn* in my hands. With that self knowledge which is natural to creators, I can add that once again the result will be worthwhile." At the beginning of 1892 he composed five songs, calling them *Fünf Humoresken* (Five Humoresques). They poured out of him, he said, "like a mountain torrent."[1] By April they were orchestrated. As the summer of 1893 approached, he would overcome the creative block that dogged him during the family crisis and make considerable headway in completing the Second Symphony—at least until he confronted its Finale. And in doing so, the *Wunderhorn* was his creative companion.

Mahler's study in Hamburg was narrow and cluttered. Two pianos dominated the room. A grand piano, nearly covered in music, fully occupied the center, while an upright, said to be Mahler's favorite instrument, stood against a wall. At his writing desk was his father's chair. Over Mahler's bed was a "faded laurel wreath with a faded olive-green ribbon on which was printed in dull gold 'To the Pygmalion of the Hamburg Opera—Hans von Bülow.'"[2] Von Bülow had presented this to him soon after Mahler came to Hamburg in 1891. Mahler rarely collected souvenirs, press clippings, or the like. But this was a special remembrance. Mahler had a rather complicated relationship with the famed Hamburg conductor and this recognition meant much to him.

On the other walls, also decorated with family pictures, were three prints: Titian's *Concert*, Dürer's *Melancholia*, and an image—most significantly—from Mahler's edition of *Des knaben Wunderhorn*. The three pictures portrayed Mahler's inner life during this period, in effect autobiography in decor. The *Concert* depicts a musician at the keyboard, head turned to catch the full illumination. His eyes are averted as if concentrating on his music and his listening ear is fully exposed. A degree of piety is represented in the slight exposure of an ecclesiastical collar under the musician's dark robe. A Hamburg friend and fellow composer who much admired Mahler, his Czech compatriot Josef Förster, regarded the Titian as Mahler's self-portrait: he was "reminded of the Italian Renaissance. Like Savonarola or Malatesta, Mahler had a hook-nosed profile, tightly closed lips, a prominent chin, and high cheekbones. No less striking were his high forehead and sharp black eyes," which, according to Förster, "glistened as though covered with dew."[3] The painting depicts two other listening figures, a man and a woman—parents, perhaps, observing their only gifted son. The woman appears younger, consistent with Mahler's mental image of his own mother conflated with the smiling St. Ursula. That Mahler identified with the monk was clear from his having told Förster, "This is a picture I could compose forever."[4]

The Dürer copper engraving *Melancholia* is a rich representation of depression, the state of mind in which Mahler's barely suppressed rage and sense of helplessness culminated. A brooding, hermaphroditic angel with a laurel wreath is seen ruminating amid a plethora of scientific instruments and symbols. Time hangs heavy with an hourglass prominently displayed. Scales of justice bespeak both guilt and judgment. These icons of depression predominate although other instruments and carpentry tools are seen at the angel's feet. The saw-toothed knife is ambiguous, representing both construction and destruction, the polar alternatives of creativity and suicide. A sun hovers in the background next to an emblem ironically engraved "melencolia"; a ray of hope escapes.

Most striking is Dürer's magic square, seen under the bell that, perhaps, "tolls for thee." The square is a rebus consisting of the numbers 1–16 arranged such that the sum of the numbers in each horizontal row,

Albrecht Dürer, *Melancholia*.

vertical column, and the two principal (longest) diagonals is the same. All total thirty-four, the age Mahler would reach on his next birthday, July 1894.

The print from *Des knaben Wunderhorn* illustrates the poem *Des Antonius von Padua Fischpredigt* (St. Anthony's Sermon to the Fish). The etching depicts a pious St. Anthony at the water's edge preaching to the fish who are gathered, wide-eyed and mouths gaping. A few laboring amphibians are on the shore for good measure, and in the background lies a simple country church. Clearly, Mahler was fascinated with the picture as well as the ideas behind it. He deeply enjoyed the ironic lesson of the *Fischpredigt*. The dumb fish, despite their receptive mouths, could no more absorb the saintly message than Mahler's critics could appreciate his new music. His arms extended as if in blessing, Anthony's stance can be identified with that of a conductor anticipating the downbeat or perhaps molding a phrase. In this comparison, the assembled fish represent a slothful audience incapable of appreciating the spiritual message being brought to them.

"St. Anthony's Sermon to the Fish" from *Des knaben Wunderhorn*.

Mahler no doubt appreciated the self-mockery the fish print also afforded him. He recognized that his family preaching in 1892–1893 was not getting him anywhere. Recalling fondly the nurturing summer of 1890, when he had reunited the family and enjoyed Otto's companionship in particular, Mahler looked forward to another such summer. He was beginning to experience the resurgence of creativity dormant since the composition of *Todtenfeier* five years earlier; its harbinger had been the "mountain torrent" of the five *Wunderhorn Humoresken*. He approved Justine and Natalie's choice of the villa at Steinbach and anticipated, at last, a summer in which he could compose in peace, without aggravation, journeys, or guests.

During the summer respite of 1893 Mahler wrote two of his most important songs and made considerable headway in the completion of his Second Symphony. One of the songs was a setting of the *Fischpredigt* for voice and piano, and Mahler was delighted with the result. He would tell Natalie,

> A somewhat sweet-sour humour reigns in the "Fischpredigt." The blessed Anthony preaches to the fishes, but his speech sounds completely drunken, slurred (in the clarinets), and confused. And what a glittering multitude! The eels and the carps and the sharp nosed pikes, whose stupid expression as they look at Antonius, stretching their stiff, unbending necks out of the water, I can practically see it in my music, and I nearly burst out laughing. Then, the sermon is over, the assembly swims away in all directions.
>
> The Sermon has pleased
> They remain as ever!
>
> Not an atom the wiser, although the saint has performed for them! Only a very few people will understand the satire on humanity in the story![5]

Natalie was by now a full member of the household and much involved in family matters. She had become a friend of Justine and exerted a tempering effect on family conflict. (Although Mahler took advantage of this mediating role, he would later criticize Natalie for assuming it.) Natalie was thus among the very few in a position to understand the irony in the

Fischpredigt: a satire of Mahler's sermons to his brothers, on whom they had no effect whatsoever.

The *Fischpredigt*, which had been some time in gestation, was endowed with an energy of its own that derived from its underlying meaning to the composer. Mahler wrote the song for piano and voice, orchestrated it, but even then the ideas behind it—both musical and poetic—seemed to have continuing momentum. Developing the piece further, he molded it into a symphonic movement, sans text, that would become the Scherzo, the central movement of the five that would comprise his Second Symphony. It was thus that his creative block was broken that summer, the *Wunderhorn* illuminating the way. With this, Mahler looked to melodic sketches he had made five years earlier in Leipzig when he worked on the *Todtenfeier*. From these, the Andante movement flowed in Schubertian fashion, and the scaffolding of the larger work took shape in the composer's mind.

It was only after Mahler solved the problem of the final—and eventually fifth—movement that he decided to interpolate the *Wunderhorn* song *Urlicht* (Primeval Light) between *Fischpredigt*, the Scherzo movement, and the Finale. Like the Andante, *Urlicht* had been written, albeit in piano score, during the surge of activity preceding the summer of 1893. Yet why Mahler chose to include it has rarely been asked. The composer's sense of form and balance notwithstanding—although clearly an important aesthetic issue—the content of *Urlicht* is revealing:

> As I came upon a broad path, an angel came and wanted to send me away. Oh no! I would not allow myself to be banished! I am from God and will return to God. Dear God will shine his light upon me and guide me to eternal blessed life!

Mahler was a Bible reader, familiar with both New and Old Testament, the latter from the compulsory Hebraic studies of his youth. The scene depicted in *Urlicht* is that of the biblical Jacob, who encounters a man with whom he wrestles the entire night, saying to him at daybreak, "I will not let you go until you bless me." Jacob realized he was wrestling with God.[6]

Mahler now turned his attention to the anticipated last movement. It would prove to be his creative Waterloo, at least for the so-far fruitful summer of 1893. The initial obstacle was one of musical invention. He told Natalie, "You can't imagine what tricks fate plays on one! Instead of the ideas in quadruple time [4/4], which I need for my Finale, I now have only ideas in triple time [3/4], which are of no use to me at all!"[7] Although Mahler would later speak of introducing a chorus and soloists in the final choral movement as a matter of course, it is by no means clear that he planned to do so that summer. In retrospect it would appear that he was avoiding this, perhaps anxious about emulating and even rivaling Beethoven. Mahler's avoidance of quadruple time may thus have been an effort to steer clear of Beethoven's *Ode to Joy*. Furthermore, the inevitable association with the theme of brotherhood would hardly have been appealing at this juncture in Mahler's life. At some point the following year Mahler finally decided to "bring in a choir," later confiding to the German author and critic Arthur Seidl: "Only the fear that it would be taken as a formal imitation of Beethoven made me hesitate again and again."[8]

With the problems of the final movement still unsolved, Mahler turned to other ideas in August. He composed a piece that would stand out among his *Wunderhorn* works, *Das irdische Leben*, this time not "Heavenly Life" but "Earthly Life." Indeed, it is a setting unique in vocal literature, as the text is about childhood starvation. Only Schubert's *Erlkönig* is comparable.

In August Mahler also spoke to Natalie about *Das klagende Lied* (The Lamenting Song), a work that he would later recognize as his Opus 1. "Gustav said to me about his 'Klagende Lied': 'This earliest composition is already completely original, but still rather inflated and overloaded.'"[9] He was considering revising it, which he did in subsequent months. However, the summer ended with the completion of the Second Symphony hanging in the balance. Yet a curious shift in Mahler's thinking occurred as he returned to Hamburg for the new operatic season. Reflection replaced invention as his thoughts turned to his own unfinished compositions. His attention refocused on *Das klagende Lied*, the underlying theme of which was fratricide. The essential plot is that of a good, fair-haired brother and an evil, dark brother who murders him for the prize the younger had won. No less dramatic is the fact that Mahler should have chosen to turn to this score at this point. In that secret stream of thought that is the source of creative content, we find erupting through the avoided and vaguely formulated idea of brotherhood, the music of fratricide.

From Hamburg, Mahler would have had to send for the score; his archivist, Otto, in Vienna, would have known just where it was. A secret communication existed between the brothers, with the music itself the message, as it had been in Mahler's earlier request to Otto for the *Wunderhorn* poems. Thus the revision of Mahler's work became at the same time an innocent instrument of aggression—at once a prize, an object lesson in creativity, and a declaration of supremacy. In any event, Mahler's attitude toward this work was revealed in another, later comment to Natalie:

> What I did later [after my student days] beginning with *Das klagende Lied*, is already so "Mahlerish," so distinctively and completely marked with my personal style, different as it is from all others, that there is no longer any connection between them and earlier works.[10]

We can only guess the effect his older brother's attitude would have had on the increasingly unstable Otto. Mahler had written both text and music when he was twenty. Unlike Otto, Gustav had graduated from the conservatory and gone on to the university. Otto, at the same age, had accomplished little. After more than three years at the conservatory and despite many tutors (paid for, of course, by Gustav), Otto's progress was shaky. Enrolled in composition class, he was not permitted to submit anything for a competition "because of his too frequent absences."[11] Soon he would drop out entirely, at first keeping this from his brother.

When Otto had been rejected for military service and wished—ever unwisely—to pursue a musical career, Gustav, using his influence, had obtained work for him in Bremen and gotten him a temporary post for the following season at the Leipzig Opera—a rare sign of promise. In May 1894 he picked up Otto there on his way to a performance of his First Symphony in Weimar. The audience's response was lukewarm and there was booing as well. Mahler summed up the experience thus: "My brother was present—quite content over this half failure as I am over his half success."[12]

After Gustav's return to Hamburg, Mahler met his new assistant, the eighteen-year-old Bruno Schlesinger (later, Bruno Walter), who was everything in music that the twenty-year-old Otto was not: extraordinarily gifted, literate, charming, and above all, highly responsive to Gustav, whom he had long admired from afar. Prior to the performance of the First Symphony Otto had ventured that "any work that won public applause must be worthless."[13] For Mahler, the young Schlesinger's unabashed admiration stood in strong contrast to Otto's resentment and was closer to heart's content in the way of everyday brotherhood—the adulation of a younger brother. Curiously, it was said that Schlesinger bore a striking resemblance to Otto, perhaps in Mahler's eyes a virtual doppelgänger. A close relationship developed between Mahler and Schlesinger, who proved to be one of several younger "brothers," fellow musicians toward whom Mahler assumed a protective and responsible attitude and served as mentor.

During the summer of 1894, Mahler finally resolved the formal problems of the Second Symphony that had stymied him at the end of the previous summer. And in finding a solution to the Finale, Mahler closed the chapter of his life that had been defined by family crisis. The story of

Bruno Walter.

the inspiration and impetus for the triumphant final movement is well known yet deserves retelling.

Mahler had by then decided on introducing a choir in the final movement. In a letter to Arthur Seidl, he wrote of the importance of "the word" as a source of inspiration: "Whenever I plan a large musical structure, I always come to a point where I have to resort to 'the word' as a vehicle for my musical idea—It must have been pretty much the same for Beethoven in his Ninth. . . . In the last movement of my Second I simply had to go through the whole of world literature, including the Bible, in search of the right word, the 'Open Sesame'—and in the end had no choice but to find my own words for my thoughts and feelings."[14]

The "word" already had a long history in Mahler's music, from the time of *Das klagende Lied*, whose text he wrote himself, to *Des knaben Wunderhorn* and his burgeoning body of songs. Curiously, no other "large musical structure" had required "the word," although the idea was prophetic: Symphonies Three, Four, and Eight would all have texts. The relationship between word and music had been inherent in the Scherzo of the Second Symphony, whose inspiration in the *Fischpredigt* resulted in the extended movement sans text. Between the summers of 1893 and 1894 Mahler not only had decided on chorus and soloists, but was reading widely in search of the text he needed. He took pains to describe the moment of clarity and insight that led to completion of this troubled work, composed toward the end of a troubled period. Both the word and the music presented themselves at once—at a memorial service for Hans von Bülow that Mahler attended in March 1894.

> The way in which I was inspired is deeply significant and characteristic of the nature of artistic creation. . . . [Hans von] Bülow died, and I went to the memorial service.—The mood in which I sat and pondered on the departed was utterly in the spirit of what I was working on at the time.—Then the choir, up in the organ-loft, intoned Klopstock's *Resurrection* chorale.—It flashed on me like lightning, and everything became plain and clear in my mind! It was the flash that all creative artists wait for—conceiving by the Holy Ghost'![15]

This episode was famously addressed by the psychoanalyst Theodore Reik. Reik's discussion leads us to Mahler's rather complex relationship with von Bülow, who had once responded to a hearing of *Todtenfeier* by holding his hands over his ears as if in pain! In Reik's death-wish formulation, "As my unconscious wish that you who rejected me as a composer should die has been fulfilled, so my symphony will be finished and will be a masterwork."[16]

It was rare for Mahler to offer explicit autobiographic exegesis and we may wonder why he did so at this point. Often, offering a single explanation detracts from several latent interpretations, all of which may be involved in an action overdetermined by multiple motivations. In this instance, Mahler's mourning of von Bülow could hardly have been unambivalent, despite the latter's eventual tribute. As a young man Mahler had implored von Bülow to take him under his wing as an apprentice: the appeal went cruelly unanswered. Thus without questioning the validity of the interpretations offered by Mahler or Reik, a further possibility suggests itself against the background of the family crisis that was only now drawing to an end.

Mahler's death wishes toward his brothers, especially Otto, had been gathering momentum prior to von Bulow's memorial service. In the course of the creative effort to find a suitable resolution to the symphony, these wishes briefly courted Beethoven's ideal of universal brotherhood as encoded in his Ninth Symphony. While emulation would have effected a psychological transformation from fratricide to its opposite in warding off unacceptable wishes, the risk of imitating Beethoven was artistically unacceptable. The fratricidal themes that had flared up in undisguised form a few months earlier during the revision of *Das klagende Lied* found compromise in a new idea, that of "resurrection." The idea literally struck Mahler like "lightning"—a powerful "Aha!" event, experienced with strong affect. Indeed, his description alluded to the creative spirit of God: "conceiving by the Holy Ghost"—the Madonna's conception through the ear! Mahler's experience was also the answer to the wish inherent in the setting of *Urlicht*: "Dear God will shine his light upon me and guide me to eternal blessed life!"

The notion of resurrection in Mahler's mind and creative hands was personal and idiosyncratic. Never one to refrain from putting his own mark on another's work, Mahler in the Finale to the Second Symphony continued Klopstock's simple verse with his own fervent commentary:

Klopstock:

> Thou shalt arise, yea, rise,
> Dust of my body, after a brief rest,
> Immortal life shall He
> Who called thee, give thee.
> Again to blossom thou art sown,
> The Lord of Harvest goes forth
> Collecting sheaves:
> We who have died.

Mahler (continuing):

> Have faith my heart, for nought is lost to thee.
> All that thou has longed for shall be thine, . . .
> Have faith, thou wast not born in vain,
> Thy life, thy suffering were not in vain . . .
> Be not afraid! Prepare thyself to live!
> All pervading pain I have escaped thee
> All conquering death, now thou art conquered.
> On wings that I have won I shall rise up again
> I die to live again.
> Thou shalt rise yea, rise My heart instantly.
> Whatever strength was thine shall carry thee to God.

Mahler's verses depart from the gentle sense of Klopstock's as if with a powerful centrifugal force. They move from self-reassurance to self-exhortation; from ecstatic escape from the inevitable—death, pain, and judgment—to the denial of death, the death of death itself. Beethoven's influence is revealed in the massive choral entry and perhaps, too, in the single word "wings" (*Flügel*). But Beethoven's reverent "All men become brothers / Where your gentle wings rest" (*Alle Menschen werden Brüde / Wo dein sanfter Flügelweilt*) is transformed by Mahler's fiercely independent "On wings that I have won I shall rise up again."

A biographical image of Mahler is invoked, on one hand guilty, on the other righteous. The reward for the heroically righteous is earned by "ardent toil and love" and won only by exertion and by struggle. Its ulti-mate form is resurrection: rebirth and a place at the throne of God. Mahler's solution in this work is at once a moving human document and a staggering musical statement—not least because of its personal flight of ideas. Psychologically, it is whistling in the dark on an epic scale.

Thus early in the summer of 1894 Mahler experienced the triumph of life over death—of creativity over aggression. Completing the Finale, he penned a postcard to Fritz Löhr on 29 June:

> Beg to report safe delivery of a strong, healthy last movement to my Second. Father and child both doing as well as can be expected—the latter not yet out of danger. At the baptismal cer-emony it was given the name "Lux lucet in tenebris." Silent sym-pathy is requested. Floral tributes are declined with thanks. Other presents, however, are acceptable. Yours, Gustav. These are my birthday greetings to you.[17]

Dürer's *Melancholia* had been prophetic: Mahler was here referring to his own thirty-fourth birthday the following week. Thus he identified himself not only as the giver of life, but as life's gift in a reenactment of his own birth: the Second Symphony, the second child.

References to Otto abruptly disappeared from Mahler's correspondence after the summer of 1893, suggesting censorship by some hand. The last reference to him dates to June of that year—a note from Mahler to Fritz from Berlin, about "meeting us at the station." A brief mention of Otto suggests he was still connected with family: "Otto will be there, to take Justi to Nina."[18] Nina Hoffmann was a friend of the family and the wife of the architect Josef Hoffmann. She was a Dostoyevsky scholar and the author of a well-received book on the writer. Increasingly depressed over the following months, Otto spent much time with her in Vienna. On 6 February 1895, Otto "turned in his ticket"—as he put it, in Dostoyevskian terms—and shot himself in her apartment. It was perhaps no coincidence that his suicide took place a month before the first (par-tial) performance of the Second Symphony in Berlin, Mahler conducting "in a half-empty hall."[19]

5

MAHLER AT MIDNIGHT

In Vienna, the night of 24 February 1901, Gustav Mahler believed that he was going to die. He was suffering from severe and neglected internal hemorrhoids and began to bleed uncontrollably. It was a condition he tended to ignore although those around him—chiefly the family, Natalie, and close correspondents—knew of his "subterranean" problems. He could not be bothered with what he considered to be minor medical afflictions and tended to work unremittingly through episodes of infirmity. He would continue to conduct long evenings of opera while in agonizing pain from migraine headaches. One of his favorite adages was *Krankheit ist Talentloskeit*—sickness is just a lack of talent. As it happened, there was considerable truth to this maxim in the opera house, where singers would cancel performances at the least indisposition or perceived slight; the freedom to do so was often written into their contracts. But Mahler applied the saying equally, and harshly, to himself.

No stranger to death, Mahler had grown up in a household in which dying and its rituals were inevitable facts of life. No one can fully grasp the meaning of death, and each person has his or her own version and iconography, particularly those with an active, creative imagination, as was the case with Mahler. For the child who experiences sibling death repeatedly throughout childhood, its serial meanings range from unawareness to bewilderment and confusion; to the mysterious and magical; to superstition and feelings of guilt; and finally to anxiety. The capacity to mourn appears only later, in adolescence, although the perception of mourning in parents and others becomes a part of the experience of death.

Mahler had witnessed childhood deaths when he was five, six, eleven, thirteen, fourteen, and nineteen. Casting a shadow over all was the legendary death of Isador before Gustav's birth, for whom he had been the replacement. But now Gustav himself had come to the brink. It was as if a nation that had formerly fought many battles on enemy and ally terrain now found itself defending its own soil.

We have seen from *Das klagende Lied*, whose text and music Mahler wrote, that ideas about death were a part of his creative fabric. Indeed, there is a strong autobiographical element in this example, relating to stages of childhood in which resentment and hostile feelings toward siblings generate fratricidal fantasies. Although these may be frightening to the daydreamer and repressed accordingly, they may, as in Mahler's case, find expression in artistic structures. The final domestic death that signaled the end of childhood for Mahler was that of his beloved brother Ernst. An interpretation of Mahler's text suggests a polarity between good and evil: the fair-haired brother, all good, may represent Ernst, whereas the bad brother incorporates all hostile and aggressive fantasies accrued throughout childhood. Putting the story on paper and, further, into music externalizes and distances the inherent wishes from their author. Nor is this process necessarily pathological. Indeed, Mahler's popular literary sources in Ludwig Bechstein and the brothers Grimm suggest the universality of the theme of fratricide.

The First Symphony, composed in Leipzig in 1887–1888, contains nothing short of an extended funeral march in its Scherzo. Mahler provided the following commentary:

> The basic inspiration for it was found by the author in a humorous engraving, well known to all Austrian children: "The Huntsman's Funeral," from an old book of fairy tales. The forest animals accompany the dead hunter's coffin to the grave. Hares carry the banner, in front of them march a group of Bohemian musicians, accompanied by singing cats, toads, crows etc. . . . The mood expressed is sometimes ironic and merry, sometimes gloomy and uncanny.[1]

Mahler had composed the funeral of the hero of his "Titan" symphony—the persona representing himself. Significantly, he is brought to the grave by "small animals," which, Freud wrote, often represent "undesired brothers and sisters."[2]

Mahler had already visited another aspect of death in his music: suicide. In 1884, the twenty-four-year-old composer wrote a song cycle—text and music—that he called *Lieder eines fahrenden Gesellen* (Songs of a Wayfarer). It was as autobiographical as *Das klagende Lied*, and in more ways than one. The texts chronicle an unhappy love affair in which the rejected lover becomes the outsider, condemned to wander the nocturnal and shining landscape, accompanied by song and sorrow. At the time, Mahler himself (then in Kassel) was breaking off a relationship with the singer Johanna Richter as he planned his next move to Prague. In the end, in Mahler's text, life is unbearable for the hero and he lies down under a linden tree and sleeps. As oblivion is represented, we realize that he has taken his own life.

Mahler would revisit death many times in his music. He himself retained rich vestiges of those successive childhood conceptions of death whose end point was anxiety. To say that Mahler simply feared death misses the complexity of his experience. More to the point, Mahler had a multifaceted psychological romance with death—not only the fear but the fascination, and despite anxiety, an underlying wish to experience death. But never had this entire complex been brought to focus as it had on the night of 24 February 1901. February 1901 was the anniversary month of the death of Mahler's father and of Otto's suicide six years earlier. It is also worth noting that on 17 February Mahler had conducted the premiere of *Das klagende Lied* at the Vienna Singakademie.[3]

Mahler had been in Vienna since the 1897–1898 season and now held the directorship of the Vienna Court Opera, arguably the most powerful and desirable musical post in all of Europe. Although family crisis had subsided, Mahler's career path had not been smooth, complicated as it was by Mahler's own restlessness and ambition. Toward the end of the Hamburg years, disaffected by conditions at the opera, he was eagerly awaiting an offer "from anyone to go anywhere." An important daily event during the summer months was the arrival of the post. Mahler would joke about expecting "the call to the God of the Southern

Vienna Court Opera, 1897–1907.

Climes," summoning him from Hamburg, in northern Germany, south-west to Austria and Vienna.⁴ A straight line would pass through the Czech lands—Bohemia and Moravia—and Jihlava, from where, in his fif-teenth year, he had first ventured to Vienna. While he longed to return, Mahler hardly waited passively for such a call. He mounted an aggressive campaign involving friends and colleagues throughout the empire that eventually succeeded in transferring him to Vienna. At first he was engaged as a conductor—kapellmeister—making his debut in April 1897. By midseason, in October, he was appointed director.

Mahler had followed the common path of assimilationist Jews, partic-ularly those who were German-speaking and university-educated: toward a dignified job, a position in the community, and a respectable income. Besides the fact that anti-Semitism was rife in Vienna, the post Mahler sought was a government position and normally open only to those who declared themselves to belong to the state religion, Catholicism. Mahler's superior, the intendant of the opera, reported directly to the emperor. Like the many Jews who were candidates for lesser government jobs, Mahler was officially baptized on 23 February 1897. His appointment arrived soon after.

That Mahler was uneasy about his conversion seems clear from his own ambiguity about the date of record. In a letter to a supporter and fellow composer in Hungary about prospects and obstacles, Mahler referred to "the fact that I was *born* a Jew" (italics mine), hardly a statement of committed identity. (In fact, the phrase was often used as an anti-Semitic barb for those attempting to pass as Christians.) He went on to reveal "as regards this point, I must tell you, in case you don't know it yet, that I was converted to Catholicism very shortly after I left Budapest."[5] This would have been some six years earlier, the distortion of time insulating Mahler from any possible reproach concerning the opportunism in his conversion. With a trusted friend, the critic Ludwig Karpath, he also avoided the appearance of opportunism in advancing the earlier date. While he in fact hid the truth, he added: "I do not hide the truth from you when I say that this action, which I took from an instinct of self-preservation and which I was fully disposed to take, cost me a great deal."[6] Hardly ever again did Mahler refer to his conversion. In this singular act he abandoned a tradition that went as far back in Bohemia as anyone in the family could remember, back to Abraham Mahler, the orthodox ritual slaughterer of the tiny village of Chelmna.

An act of reason and desperation to be sure, but at what cost? Not all sources of illness or disability are biological. Virtually all of Mahler's physical afflictions—migraines; attacks of vertigo on the podium; and the severe sore throat then called quinsy, an abscess in the tissues around the tonsils resulting from bacterial infection and usually accompanied by pain and fever—had a psychological component. There was a strong psychological element in Mahler's terminal heart disease as well. Intestinal problems of the kind Mahler suffered are commonly related to emotions, the bowel being an end-organ particularly sensitive to states of mind. Headaches, including migraines, are also frequently attributed to the stresses of emotional life.

Besides assuming directorship of the opera, Mahler accepted the invitation to become kapellmeister of the Vienna Philharmonic Orchestra the following year. It was an honor and an opportunity he could not turn down, particularly as it was a vote of confidence from the musicians of the opera orchestra, who were one and the same as the democratically organized philharmonic. Moreover, the position would facilitate performances of Mahler's own compositions in Vienna at a time when such performances were becoming more frequent in other cities. Although it became habitual for Mahler to carry on two musical seasons simultaneously, it could hardly have been comfortable.

On 24 February, a Sunday, Mahler conducted the sixth subscription concert of the Vienna Philharmonic in the afternoon; in the evening, at the Opera, a gala one-hundredth anniversary performance of Mozart's *Magic Flute*. As the performances proceeded, Mahler endured increased discomfort and eventual pain. Alma Schindler, twenty-one years old, was in the audience for both performances. She wrote in her memoirs:

> In the afternoon the Philharmonic and then, in the evening, a performance [at the Opera]. He looked Luciferlike, a face as white as chalk, eyes like burning coals. I felt sorry for him and said to the people I was with: "It's more than he can stand."[7]

That night Mahler began to bleed profusely. He called on Justine to summon a doctor on an emergency basis. As he lost more blood, the whiteness of face that Alma had noted earlier that evening became more pronounced; equally alarming was the attendant quickening of Mahler's pulse. Another doctor was called in, this time a surgeon who managed, with considerable difficulty, to arrest the bleeding. He gave Mahler to understand that he could have bled to death. Both doctors had anxiously and repeatedly listened to Mahler's heart, which the patient would later say with false bravado was "solidly installed in [my] breast and determined not to give up so soon."[8] Nevertheless, the valves of Mahler's heart had already been scarred from childhood rheumatic disease. This would have been audible to the physicians and therefore of further concern. The surgeon made clear to Mahler that he would have to undergo further surgery before too much time elapsed. He warned that without this more definitive treatment, Mahler might not survive another hemorrhage.

Whether there had in fact been a genuine threat to his life on the night of 24–25 February—and it was certainly possible—Mahler firmly believed this to have been the case. Besides hearing the physicians' words, he had read in their faces a sense beyond urgency—of emergency. It is notoriously difficult to judge quantity of blood loss when it is coming from one's own body. But Mahler was convinced that he could have died horribly, of exsanguination, the total depletion of blood. Such near-death experiences spontaneously evoke primitive fantasies of causation: "What did I do to deserve this?" In Mahler's case this took the form of joking, as lying in bed the following day he drafted his obituary: "Gustav Mahler has finally met the fate that his many crimes deserve."[9]

The experience of 24 February was intensified by when it occurred. The general atmosphere of the fin de siècle world carried with it the implied end of an era. It had been only two months since Mahler, when he dated his correspondence at all, had been writing "1901"; it was terra incognita. He had also turned forty the previous summer. Despite possessing prodigious energy for his undertakings, he considered himself to be in the autumn of his life; winter would not be far behind. His father had died at sixty-two, and his mother, with whom he more consciously identified, at fifty-two. Was he on the brink of entering the last dozen years of his own life? Or, with a reprieve for transgressions, real and imaginary, did he have at least two more decades? The fantasy and underlying fear of death at one's parents' age is nearly universal. What we call "premonition" is but an intensification of this trend. In Mahler's case, the dread of dying at his mother's age would have been uncannily prophetic: he, too, was destined to die at fifty-two.

Surgical repair required that Mahler have two operations, one shortly after the hemorrhage, in March, and a further, more definitive procedure in June. Each entailed an enforced recovery period generally inimical to Mahler. However, making the best of circumstances, he spent Easter 1901 on the Adriatic, in Abbazia, on the Istrian Peninsula not far from Trieste. An apartment had been rented for him and Justine; Arnold Rosé, violinist and concertmaster of the Vienna Philharmonic (later to be Justine's husband), joined them. Natalie, faithful as ever, came too.

Summertime convalescence had already been accounted for. In 1899 Justine and Natalie, scouting for a suitable summer rental on the Wörthersee in Carinthia for the following year, had met an architect who urged them to build a house tailored to the family's needs. Mahler needed little convincing and a telephone call sealed the deal. The architect set about designing a house and a small composing hut—what Mahler called his *Schützelputz-Häusel*, later his häuschen. It was finished sooner than expected and was ready for summer 1900, although the Villa Mahler itself was not completed until the following year. The locale was, from the first, associated with Mahler's Fourth Symphony, and in August 1900 he wrote, "This summer, for me, has been so glorious that I feel myself really and truly braced for the coming winter." He anticipated making the fair copy then and felt "this will give me a foothold in all the stress of life, a foothold such as I have needed particularly in these recent years."[10] Obsessed as ever with time as he turned forty on 7 July, Mahler had put off any celebration, holding back the clock in the hope that he might complete the symphony that summer. The urgency was

Villa Mahler on the Wörthersee, 1901–1907.

heightened as he compared himself to Mozart and Schubert, both of whom died before their fortieth birthday. He lamented to Natalie:

> The time I've lost! Until I went to Steinbach [earlier summers] I didn't know how to provide myself, during the little time at my disposal, with the peace and solitude I need. . . . Now during these few short weeks, I have to work every moment of the day, even when I'm weary and out of sorts, merely to get finished. And my work must inevitably suffer under the strain.[11]

It was "the work" that would suffer, not the person—the motto *Krankheit ist Talentloskeit* looming large. Yet only a few months later, "the strain" and "stress" on Mahler resulted in a medical emergency. Throughout the spring and summer of 1901 Mahler continued to be preoccupied with the passage of time and death's threatened imminence. As he walked on the beach at Abbazia with Natalie one moonlit evening that Easter season, he recalled two dreams. One he had had as a child of eight, its imagery so vivid that he had never forgotten it: his mother and Ernst dissolving into an image of the Wandering Jew. It seemed to him "symbolic of his wandering destiny."[12] If Mahler's dating of the dream was at all accurate, the theme of the Wandering Jew surfaced strikingly early in his life. It may have been a nightmare figure, yet also clearly represented his separateness as a Jew.

Mahler's second dream occurred during the depression and creative block of his "wandering summer" in Scandinavia a decade earlier. He was then also suffering from various psychosomatic symptoms ("stomach catarrh") and experiencing "moments of exhaustion and discouragement."[13] Mahler related the dream to Natalie in detail.

> He found himself in the midst of a large gathering in a brightly lit room, when the last of the guests entered—a large man of stiff bearing, faultlessly dressed, and with the air of a man of affairs. But he knew: that is Death.
>
> And as he drew away from the uncanny guest, fleeing ever farther toward the end of the room, the guest, whom no one else seemed to recognize, followed him as if drawn by magnetism all the way to the farthest corner of the room, behind the curtain at

the window. Here the stranger seized him by the arm with an iron grip and said, "You must come with me!" However desperate the terrified one tried to pull away, he could not tear himself loose until, by expending all his forces, he threw the nightmare off.[14]

The dream, in two parts, links past and present. In Mahler's early life, arrivals (and their opposite, departures) had been a life-and-death motif in the "large gathering" of the Mahler family. The newcomer of the dream—the "last guest," "the stranger"—is conflated with death, and his "stiff bearing" invokes one of death's stigmata: the stiffness of rigor mortis, certainly a frightening experience for a child of any age, a horrifying and guilt-inducing wish-come-true for an older sibling.

The second part of the dream plunges us into the immediate present. The dreamer no longer observes at a distance. He is pursued and seized in body and soul. The dreamer is startled and the heart skips a beat. The spirit of *Erlkönig* prevails as the dreamer falls under the threat of abduction ("magnetic power") and bodily harm as the stranger's "iron grip" parallels the stiffness of the first portion of the dream. Above all and most frightening are the sense of helplessness (trying to "flee"), abandonment (recognized by "no one else"), and loss of will ("could not tear himself loose"). The dream suggests both the underlying meaning of depression in terms of self-punishment for unacceptable wishes, and the impotence of creative block. Here we see Mahler's personal iconography of death and the extended meaning of his 24 February 1901 encounter.

The dream remained active in Mahler's memory as he arrived at the new house in Maiernigg and surveyed the woods and the lake from the attic balcony. "It is *too* beautiful," he said. "One can't allow oneself such things." Mahler had achieved another level of success—his own estate and the ideal circumstances for composition. Yet "It is a fact," Natalie wrote, "that he feels a kind of guilt in the depths of his soul for being so privileged. That he of all people, who has no material wants—the 'barbarian,' as we called him because of his distaste for luxury and comfort and the beautiful things in life—that he should be surrounded by such splendour seems to him such an irony of fate that it often brings an involuntary smile to his lips."[15]

The häuschen was perfect. In composing, Mahler required multiple zones of tranquility and silence. Foremost was inner peace. Next was the häuschen, which walled off the immediate surroundings. It served as a claustrum, insulating him from the external world while extending the space of inner life. Finally, there was his immediate environment, which Mahler strictly required be kept quiet. There are many stories about the family's efforts to keep this zone as noisefree as possible, even to the extent of bribing an organ-grinder to leave the area.

Mahler remained preoccupied with the themes of the death dream during the summer of 1901. However, they assumed another form. In August Mahler presented the summer's harvest to Natalie as a token of friendship. It was a sheaf of the seven songs composed that summer and in aggregate they comprise a unique autobiographical statement.

Among these songs was Mahler's last setting from *Des knaben Wunderhorn, Der Tamboursg'sell* (The Drummer Boy). It was as if there remained some unfinished business before completely yielding to the impulse to explore new material, moving on to the poetry of Friedrich Rückert and attendant stylistic developments. That *Der Tamboursg'sell* was imbued with unconscious sources is revealed in the curious way in which it came about. Mahler had sketched the opening bars of a symphonic idea in his notebook and hastily completed a melody. Upon doing so, he immediately realized that although the piece was unsuitable for a symphony, it was perfect for the *Wunderhorn*: it fit the opening words of *Der Tamboursg'sell* exactly!

The song is about a poor drummer boy who is being marched off to the scaffold. His crime is unspecified but some transgression is suggested by the line "Had I but remained a drummer boy, I would not lie imprisoned." Convinced of his own guilt, the drummer boy cries, "Oh gallows, you high house, you are such a dreadful sight. I will not look at you again because I know I belong there."

Had Mahler himself gone too far? He had risen from humble beginnings in a Jewish merchant family to one of the highest artistic positions in the Austro-Hungarian Empire, one open only to Catholics. He had been elevated from provincial kapellmeister to director of the Vienna Court Opera. And now, he owned a splendid country estate, the Villa Mahler. By 1901 nearly all the real and imagined rivals of Mahler's childhood and apprentice years had fallen by the wayside. His parents and brothers (save the elusive Alois, who, unbeknownst to Mahler, had emigrated to America) all were dead. Only two sisters survived, Justine and Emma. Two of his conservatory companions, Hans Rott (1858–1884) and Anton Krisper (1858–1914) had gone insane—Rott had died soon after—and Mahler was estranged from the jealously embittered Hugo Wolf (1860–1903). Gustav Mahler's was the guilt of survival on a grand scale. It was no wonder he eschewed small luxuries and felt "one shouldn't allow oneself such things" as the perfect creative space. Was survival itself among the many "crimes" Mahler joked about in his own mock obituary following the scourge of bleeding?

The gallows that figures so prominently in *Der Tamboursg'sell* had further significance for Mahler. One month after Otto's suicide, Mahler had conducted Beethoven's Ninth Symphony at the close of his second Hamburg season, 1895. Mahler had been studying Beethoven intensively and had made some alterations in the score, among them the addition of new instruments and parts. Some critics felt he had gone too far. The chorus was to be especially full, and for the occasion Mahler had the last-minute idea of constructing a large podium from which he could more effectively marshal the assembled forces. The carpenter, perhaps responding to the director's now legendary passion for precision, followed his instructions literally and Mahler was confronted with a small, one-story platform on which he had to perch as if on stilts! He experienced acute anxiety and vertigo, and only by planting his feet firmly on the platform and focusing intensely on the music could he control his symptoms. He had described the experience to the ever responsive Natalie, who commented that from such a height "he could well have broken his neck."[16]

The march to the gallows, a dirge actually, comprises the second part of *Der Tamboursg'sell*. In this valedictory slow march the drummer boy bids farewell to life in the most universal death metaphor: sleep at night. As the child may say "good night" to each member of the family in turn, and playfully, perhaps even to the objects in the room, so the singer-persona of *Tamboursg'sell* bids "Gute Nacht," one-by-one to the mountains, the hills, the officers, the corporals, and the musketeers. The song ends, "From you take my leave! Good night!" With a final four-note chromatic descent in the melody, Mahler marked the score, "With a breaking voice." A drum roll diminuendo is heard. There is no question that the *Wunderhorn* years were over.

It is but a short step from the "Gute Nacht" of the *Wunderhorn* to another of the summer's settings, Friedrich Rückert's *Um Mitternacht* (At Midnight). For, if the final drum roll is the off-stage representation of death's execution, the stroke of midnight evokes the blow—and the very instant in time. Yet even a superficial comparison of *Um Mitternacht* with *Der Tamboursg'sell* reveals its concerns to differ in nature: it is not a text of youth but rather a poem of middle age. This explains Mahler's turning to Rückert texts at this juncture in his life and also illuminates Mahler's choice of the poet's *Kindertotenlieder* (Songs on the Death of Children) in two other songs of the summer of 1901.

> At midnight I was awake
> And looked up to the heavens;
> Not one of the whole host of stars
> Smiled down at me at midnight.
> At midnight my thoughts went out
> To the bounds of darkness.
> No thought of light
> Brought me comfort at midnight.
> At midnight I heeded
> The beating of my heart: but one pulse of pain
> Throbbed, burning at midnight.
> At midnight, I fought the battle
> Of your suffering, mankind!
> I could not decide it
> With all my strength at midnight.
> At midnight I resigned all power
> Into Thy hand.
> Lord! Over death and life
> Thou keepest watch,
> At Midnight.[17]

Um Mitternacht opens with an awakening and ends with a reference to life and death. While the intense anticipatory terror and sense of helplessness with which it is chiefly concerned recalls the dream Mahler related to Natalie, here death releases its potential grip in a massive yet passive yielding. The text expresses the wish to be watched over and protected by a powerful superior being.

Other musical-biographical associations drew Mahler to this text. The states of sleep and waking and their attendant symbolism were constantly recurring ideas in Mahler's music. For example, the massive choral entrance of the Second Symphony intones the word *Auferstehn* triple-piano. When it is performed effectively, the listener may experience the sensation of shifting from a state of sleep, unawareness, to one of wakefulness. The beginning is barely audible but then sounds are dimly heard. Gradually, the volume increases and the listener becomes fully aware of the music. In *Das klagende Lied* the state of sleep is one of vulnerability to death as the younger of the two brothers competing for the queen's hand finds the prize flower and, falling asleep, is murdered by the older brother.

Above all, *Um Mitternacht* is powerfully reminiscent of Mahler's recent scrape with death. The poem is astonishing in its inadvertent biographical accuracy: The time is midnight and a sense of urgency prevails as the persona "sings" of the awareness of "the beating of my heart" and "one pulse of pain." Religion appears to be tested but the characteristics of the supreme being are unusual. Both God and Sentinel, the Lord carries musket and helmet. This cartoon of military reference, which is related to *Der Tamboursg'sell* of the same summer, must touch on some of Mahler's earliest auditory experiences of barrack and band music. In fact, in Mahler's orchestral setting of the song, he apparently recruited some semblance of a military band (sans snare drums) from the orchestra's full potential. And only in the final section did he employ the full force of the brass instruments, which bring the song to an end with a powerful "amen" cadence.[18]

Time in every respect was the preoccupation of Mahler's setting of *Um Mitternacht*. Mahler maintained strict control of it as little of tempo or rhythm is left to the performer's discretion. Indeed, the time signature is changed thirty-six times in this brief work of only ninety-four measures.[19] The germinal motifs are condensed in the first few measures, in which a microscopic image of time is created. The first is an imaginative portrayal of a clock slowed to surrealist proportions, suggesting the stroke of the hour. Within the motif, a limping rhythm recalls a heartbeat, while its immediate repetition emphasizes the passage of time.

The song outlines a fantasy in which the heart, the passage of time, the stroke of midnight, and the specter of death become discernible. A final desperately massive optimism, spelling denial in its very force, seems the purpose of the very form of the song: death itself banished. That there was a deeply personal involvement in *Um Mitternacht* is revealed by both the certainty yet the haste apparent from the manuscript. Only once did Mahler seem to falter. This was after the setting of the words "the beating of my heart." There he thinned out the scoring with the scribble of a pen. At "one pulse of pain" motion was to stop entirely—the heart standing still, but here under the tight control of the composer. Clearly Mahler took the most trouble with the portion of the text that related to personal experience and was psychically painful.

The events of 24 February 1901 powerfully affected Mahler's life course. In *Um Mitternacht*, "my thoughts went out to the bounds of darkness. No thought of light brought me comfort at midnight." As Mahler became all too aware of the vulnerability of midlife and his own fragility, he sought a solution. He found it not in religion, as suggested by the song's close, but in marriage and fatherhood. He had met Alma Schindler on several occasions but at a dinner party that autumn, he suddenly saw her in a new light: he seemed instantly to know that she was to be his wife. In an extraordinary and bold move, the obsessional conductor spontaneously invited her to a rehearsal, offered to walk her home, and, when she demurred, pressed her upon leaving the party to visit him at the opera. This must be considered a remarkable performance for the seemingly entrenched bachelor. Mahler had once said with regard to his music, "You don't have to be there when you become immortal." Suddenly, he was deeply involved in seeking the common immortality of men in fatherhood.

6

FAMILY ROMANCES

In some respects Gustav and Alma were an unlikely pair. Mahler at forty was twice her age; he a Jew in an anti-Semitic culture, she Catholic and hardly free of the prejudices of family and milieu. Their family backgrounds could not have been more divergent. Mahler had risen from his struggling middle-class and small-town origins by dint of ambition, gift, and in some measure, guile. When he fashioned his own text to the spiritual Finale of his Second Symphony, he added grandiosely to the pious Klopstock hymn, *Die Auferstehung* (Resurrection): "On wings that I have won I shall rise up again." And so he had in the temporal world. Alma, in contrast, was the pampered and cultivated child of a distinguished artistic family.

Powerful sexual attraction is perhaps the most appropriate point of entry into the puzzle of their rapidly developing relationship and strong initial bond. Physically stunning and tall in stature, Alma's looks were legendary. She was said to be "the most beautiful girl in Vienna."[1]

Mahler was drawn to attractive and accomplished Christian women.[2] Two of his most intense affairs had been with the singers Johanna Richter and Anna von Mildenburg, both handsome and talented women. To have chosen a Jewish woman would have been too close to endogamous marriage as ancient childhood prohibitions were unconsciously exerted. Yet as much as Mahler coveted gifted Gentile goddesses, he had a strong need to hold them at bay and control the terms of the relationship. In the

Alma Schindler, age nineteen.

case of both singers, it was he who broke off the relationship when the circumstances suited him.

Mahler had spelled out his personal rules of engagement in 1894: "I could not bear the sight of an untidy woman with messy hair and neglected appearance. . . . She would have to consent to sharing my company only at certain times. . . . Finally, she should not take offense or interpret as disinterest, coldness, or disdain if, at times, I had no wish to see her."[3] The occasion for this prenuptial bill of particulars was the visit of a lonely Mahler to the home of composer and countryman Josef Förster. In the course of the Hamburg years, Mahler had much admired the artistry of Josef's wife, Bertha Förster-Lauterer, whom he had engaged at the opera. He watched with envy as she now performed domestic duties as hostess. Did the thirty-four-year-old conductor really understand women so little—or himself, for that matter? Or more likely, in the agreeable company of a friend and compatriot, did he indulge in irony? For the desire revealed—and perhaps distanced with self-mockery— was not for a living human being but for a comforting mannequin that could be removed from her case at will, an erotic Olympia activated by narcissistic requirement. Possession and control are clear in this personal fable. Nevertheless, even tongue-in-cheek, a conflict of needs is revealed, if only through its denial: the wish for closeness and the fear of it. Mahler appeared to be aware of the futility of this ramble into fantasy. "In a word," he concluded, "she would need qualities that even the best and most devoted women do not possess." Despite this, he would soon be driven to test these strivings in his encounter with Alma Schindler.

As it happened, there had in fact been a woman in Mahler's life who came close to fitting the bill: Natalie Bauer-Lechner. Natalie, a violist, had studied at the Vienna Conservatory between 1866 and 1872. Her earliest memory of him, which opens her *Recollections*, set the tone for the sympathetic understanding that characterized her relationship with Mahler—that is, from her side. After her graduation, she would sit in on the orchestral rehearsals conducted by Joseph Hellmesberger (1855–1907). On one particular occasion, a work of Mahler's was to be played. "Since he could not pay a copyist, [Mahler] had worked for days and nights copying the parts . . . and, here and there, some mistakes had crept in." Hellmesberger had flown into a rage and refused to perform the work even after the parts were corrected.[4]

The year before the Mahler family crisis of 1889, Gustav and Natalie met again at the Viennese home of Mahler's longtime friend Fritz Löhr, on whom he would call for help with Otto and Emma. Mahler, then director of the Royal Hungarian Opera, had been granted free travel facilities on the South Austrian Railways. In the rare pleasure of *gemütlich* company, and elated perhaps by wine, Mahler was expansive. He offered everyone present tickets to visit him in Budapest, with the added inducement of the wonderful events he would plan for them. This was likely an overture directed toward Natalie as the Löhrs' responsibilities in Vienna were absorbing, and in any event, Fritz needed no special invitation. He had already visited Mahler in Budapest on several occasions. Natalie observed, perhaps hopefully, that Mahler "always threw himself vehemently into a friendship whenever he felt especially attracted to a person."[5] Natalie tended to have strong attachments to intellectual men and would later have an affair with Mahler's friend Siegfried Lipiner (1856–1911), a philosopher and poet.

Mahler was lonely, Natalie depressed, and the following year she took him up on the offer. Her troubled marriage had ended in divorce in 1885, and in the fall of 1890, as she put it, "I found myself at that time in the most confused and sorrowful condition, both inwardly and externally, and was very much in need of cheering up."[6] She wrote to Mahler reminding him of his invitation. Despite his favorable appointment, Mahler was feeling isolated by language and circumstance—one of his chronic "homeless" experiences. He felt unwelcome in Budapest because of his youth, criticism for the high salary he negotiated, and his double foreignness—an Austrian (as he was perceived) in an anti-Austrian environment, and a Jew. He longed to hear and speak the German language, his mother tongue. In fact, Natalie's letter coincided with the anniversary of his mother's death the previous year.

Mahler invited Natalie to Budapest, suggesting a time when he would be relatively free from duties. His response hinted at the possibility of a more than platonic reunion. "I'm curious," he wrote, "to find out if we shall be silent or if we shall talk."[7] Would "silence" imply intimacy? For appearances in entertaining a woman, he enthusiastically cleared out his apartment for her convenience and moved into a hotel for the duration of the visit. And "talk" the two did—for nearly a decade—as Natalie played an important role in Mahler's life during a major creative period, his *Wunderhorn* years.

Natalie, two years older than Mahler, was born in Vienna into the intellectual environment of a bookseller's home. Both mother and father were musicians as well and encouraged their eldest of three in her career. She became violist in a unique and well-known ensemble, the Soldat-Röger String Quartet—in the parlance of the time, a "ladies'" quartet. She was said, unflatteringly by Emma Mahler, who was in her early twenties when Natalie was a member of the household, to favor male garb à la George Sand and to have "a string of men, some married, at her feet."[8] But despite Natalie's protofeminist views, her writing style and photographs suggest a more modest nature. In a professional photograph she appears to be a stately and attractive woman in a long white gown, looking steadfastly at the camera while holding a violin (her main instrument) with an easy air of competence. Her marriage had been to an academic, the breakup of which was tumultuous in her life and had led to her overture to Mahler. There had been no children.

When Mahler retreated for the summer of 1893 to the quiet village of Steinbach on the Attersee in the Austrian Alps—a time not only for his customary work but for the regrouping of family—Natalie was invited along. It was here that she started the Mahler memoir that recorded their many hours of conversation. She would in time circulate the manuscript among friends and it was eventually published posthumously. Its content provides an invaluable account of Mahler's creative life from 1893 to 1901, a period that spanned the Second through the Fourth symphonies.

Natalie befriended the twenty-five-year-old Justine Mahler, now the woman head-of-household and sister-wife in the raising of the children, and rapidly became a part of the family. She played the role wholeheartedly, longing all the while to become a genuine family member through marriage to Mahler. To say she was in love with him is an understatement; she worshiped him. While she gave the relationship her all, her

Natalie Bauer-Lechner.

devotion may have been her downfall. Whatever slim romantic interest may have existed on Mahler's part at the outset, it was replaced with irritation before long. In September 1892 he wrote to Fritz about cheerfully putting up with a rainy trip, "urged on by never failing 'impuls' [*sic*] of our merry Natalie, who is such a dear." If nothing else, the comradely characterization suggests that any possibility of an erotic attachment had already passed, if indeed it had survived the initial Budapest rendezvous. But in 1894, by which time she had become a fixture in the family, Mahler was already writing to Justine *not* to invite Natalie to Steinbach for the summer: "I cannot stand her constant mothering, advising, inspecting and spying."[9] This was only one year into the journal-keeping period that has revealed so much about Mahler—his personality, his views on music and other topics, and above all, his method of composition.

The content of their curious intimacy was creative life on one hand and health matters on the other, including rather frank discussion of various bodily functions. Mahler found her overly "mothering"; but how was it that she knew so much about his sometimes shaky state of health if he had not confided in her or in the family of which she had so rapidly become an honorary member? Members of the family were all too familiar with the "constant and violent headaches" Mahler suffered, for example, the summer of the Third Symphony, in 1896.[10] Mahler's other chronic ailments included stomachaches and the exacerbation of his "subterranean" problems, which were especially troublesome in the summer months before the hemorrhage. Their intimacy, then, was such that Natalie was the confessor of belly and bowel but not of sex. Once during one of their walks, Mahler had a sudden physical urgency, which Natalie took charge of in maternal fashion. Explaining the situation to a woman in a nearby home, she engaged the neighbor in conversation while Mahler attended to a chamber pot that had been ceremoniously brought into a drawing room for Herr Direktor.

On more than one occasion Mahler had welcomed her advice and guidance. Absent, however, were signs of any deeper attachment that might correspond to Natalie's feelings toward him. From this perspective, it appears that Mahler largely took Natalie for granted. Her *Mahleriana* is the unique biography that Natalie of course could not have written had Mahler not responded to the adoring attendance that he would soon experience as intrusions of privacy. She craved marriage with Mahler and a family with him at its head. But for Mahler, Natalie had, in a word, become too "familiar," a situation that she herself had cultivated. The prospect of marriage with its underlying incestuous prospect was the kiss of death for Natalie.

Mahler benefited richly from Natalie's capacity to be a good, empathic listener and her relationship with him was in some respects a healing one. During the many hours they spent together the two would walk endlessly, he talking, she listening. Mahler could justify and aggrandize himself; readily ventilate the considerable rage of which he was capable; seek comfort for his psychological wounds; and repair his chronically bruised self-esteem. Many aspects of their friendship verged on psychotherapy such as Mahler would not experience until his meeting with Freud. But unlike Freud's ministrations, Natalie's "cure" was a cure by love.

Only twice did Natalie's feelings overwhelm her and lead to a spurned advance. In Berlin in February 1896, after a disastrous reception of Mahler's First Symphony, Natalie sought to console him, and perhaps herself as well.

> There [at the hotel] we all parted, and each with a heavy heart sought his own room. I alone stole a moment more at Gustav's door, and at his half-hearted "come in," I slipped into his room. . . . In a flash I seized his hand, bowed, and kissed it. And he could barely take it from me and exclaim, moved: "But Natalie, what are you doing!" when I had already hurried away to my room.
>
> Then the long built-up, powerfully suppressed agitation broke forth in a torrent of tears—and for Mahler as well; I saw it in his face the next morning.[11]

Natalie rather desperately revealed her feelings to Mahler on a second occasion at the end of August 1901. She had stayed behind at the Villa Mahler and on the pretense of something urgent arranged to come to Vienna. There she begged him to marry her and attempted to embrace him, which Mahler repulsed, responding cruelly, "I can't love you, I can only love a beautiful woman." "But I *am* beautiful," Natalie retorted, adding pathetically, if overliterally, that he should ask his friend the artist Henriette Mankiewicz.[12]

Although Natalie was blind to Mahler's disinterest, he encouraged her in a sometimes puzzling manner. Her final outburst of love was preceded by quasi-romantic scenes described in her *Recollections*. After chamber music at the Villa Mahler on a beautiful end-of-summer night, she and Mahler "happy as children" strolled in the darkness of the garden and later went to his room to look at the stars over the lake from the balcony.[13] Subsequently, when Natalie saw Mahler to the station, there was "lovely but ice-cold moonlight . . . we had to cling to each other and protect ourselves in the carriage like kittens, so that we weren't almost frozen."[14]

More than most men of his time and place, Mahler expected to be taken care of by a woman. And in his case, family adulation was considered an entitlement. There is no indication of any empathy or real concern for Natalie's needs, except insofar as they coincided with his. Was this comparable to Mahler's adolescent relationship with Gustav Schwartz—a person used and forgotten? Mahler knew that Natalie was keeping a diary of his creative life, and although he might shrug wearily when reviewers failed to understand his music, he was much interested in posterity in all its forms. As for Natalie, the journal she kept, which has proven invaluable for Mahler biographers, was the best she had of him. In Berlin, later at the Villa Mahler, and who knows where else, it was this that she took back to her room each night.

In Mahler's mock fantasy of womanhood, the Olympia would appear and disappear at will and could be taken out of her compartment and replaced after use. In fact, Natalie came closest to this. But she was omnipresent, indeed, in good measure, with Mahler's encouragement. Beyond the "sisterhood" she provided, something essential that went beyond sexual attraction was missing. The decade Natalie devoted to Mahler carried her into her forties. These were the last years that she could have expected to bear children. Instead they were spent in creative midwifery and caring for the child she found in Mahler, which he accepted. Indeed she may well have considered them the happiest years of a sad life. Mahler, too, was approaching forty and was urgently seeking to make changes in his life, fearful that it may already be too late.

Thus it was more than the physical appearance and intellectual capacity of Alma Schindler that drew him to her. She would bear his children. But had circumstances been otherwise, as Peter Franklin suggests, "[Natalie] might have become a devoted wife and assistant to Mahler and gained a quite different place in history."[15]

Natalie's manuscript ended abruptly in January 1902, its final, enigmatic entry not quite self-explanatory: "Mahler became engaged to Alma Schindler six weeks ago. If I were to discuss this event, I would find myself in the position of a doctor obliged to treat, unto life or death, the person he loved most in the world. May the outcome of this rest with the Supreme and Eternal Master!"[16] What is clear is Natalie's sense of injustice in evoking the judgment of the Almighty. And there can be little doubt that the "disease" was Alma.

It was Alma Mahler who had the last word about Natalie—a decidedly ungenerous one, referring to "Frau B . . . who although she was old and ugly was in love with Mahler and hoped for the return of her passion."[17] With this, Natalie Bauer-Lechner disappeared from Mahleriana. Certainly after their marriage, when Alma and Mahler first invited his friends to their home, Natalie was not included. There is no record of any further direct contact between Mahler and Natalie. She continued with the Soldat-Röger Quartet and her teaching; she also had affairs, but essentially was alone. Natalie Bauer-Lechner died, impoverished, in 1927.

In contrast to young and beautiful Alma, Mahler—despite his muscular effectiveness as conductor—was slight in stature and had a curiously uneven, somewhat ungainly gait. What then of the physical appeal Mahler held for Alma? At the time of their first meeting Alma was struggling with erotic feelings toward the composer Alexander von Zemlinsky (1872–1942), whom she had chosen to be her composition teacher. She had met Alex early in 1900 and her admiration for his brilliance led her to pursue him until, captivated, he agreed to teach her even as she brutally took his measure: "He was a hideous gnome. Short, chinless, toothless, always with the coffeehouse smell on him, unwashed—and yet the keenness and strength of his mind made him tremendously attractive. The hours flew when we were working together."[18]

Alma's attachment to her father was so powerful that she was drawn to men in whom she saw shadows of Emil Jacob Schindler, heard echoes of

Emil Jacob Schindler, Alma's father.

his voice, perceived familiar scents. As a child she spent many dreamy hours in his studio, rich with greenery, oriental rugs, and the odd fragrance of pigment. A giant in Alma's eyes, Schindler was in fact small in build. When he died, the thirteen-year-old Alma found a way into the locked room in which her father was laid out, "like a fine wax image, noble as a Greek statue. . . . I was astonished only by the smallness of this man who had been my father, now that I saw him in his coffin."[19]

However, what Alma perceived in her father and sought in every man who would thereafter become her intimate was genuine: a fine artistic gift fully realized, a first-class intellect, generosity as a teacher—even if it involved tolerating a bit of pedantry—and, above all, respectful (and preferably awed) attentiveness to herself. It was not merely a matter of being her father's favorite, which she was in any event. "My father," she said, "took me seriously." Unlike herself, in Alma's estimation, her mother, Anna, had had no real appreciation of these qualities in her husband. "Not until after his death," Alma wrote, "would she grasp his importance."[20] She clearly considered herself as possessing qualities that would have made her a better mate than her mother to Schindler. In fact, in Alma's view "marriage brought a narrowness into my father's life"; she would certainly not tolerate any such narrowness in a potential mate.

Despite occasional girlish uncertainties confessed to her diary, Alma did not suffer from low esteem. Armed with self-assuredness in matters of the heart that she had acquired in her earlier life with her father, Alma was confident of her own artistic and intellectual dowry as she approached marriageable age. However, among the things she inherited from her father was a tendency toward depression. Buoyed up by the attention of admirers and the singular position of her artistic family in Vienna, she had no need to convey this in her girlhood diaries. What is clear there is an intense mourning for the father who died when Alma was thirteen. Only later, in the accounts written during her marriage to Mahler and thereafter, is the tendency toward melancholy manifest.

Alma Schindler's early life fostered enduring fantasies that later dominated and molded events and choices. In her memoir, *And the Bridge Is Love*, she set forth a statement of origins that would become the theme of her life:

> I am the daughter of artistic tradition. My father, Emil J. Schindler, was the foremost landscape painter of the Austrian Empire—and always in debt, as befits a person of genius. He came from old patrician stock and was my shining idol.[21]

Thus she cast herself from the beginning as a historical figure, buttressed by superlatives: "foremost," "genius," and "patrician." This last citation emphasizes *paternal* descent, while the locale of distinction, if not the universe, was at least the empire. The single limitation, Schindler's debts, is put in an honorific context.

Alma's statement is a variant of what Sigmund Freud termed the "family romance." This is a nearly universal (although not always conscious) fantasy of origins in which the child elaborates a grandiose and idealized parental image. According to Freud, "the whole effort at replacing the real father by a superior one is only an expression of the child's longing for the happy, vanished days when his father seemed to him the strongest of men and his mother the dearest and loveliest of women."[22] Alma's family romance was paradoxical. In most instances the fantasy serves to replace the experience of mundane parentage; in Alma's case it made an already distinguished background magical and legendary. At the same time, she placed herself squarely in the picture.

Only Freud's maternal "dearest and loveliest of women" appears to have been expunged from Alma's narrative of origins. Anna Bergen Schindler came across in Alma's adolescent diaries as a rival and an obstacle to Alma's erotic strivings. Perhaps projecting her own enmity onto her mother, Alma was convinced that Anna favored her younger sister, Gretl. Even when her mother remarried and a stepsister was born, Alma, then twenty, confided to her diary that "my thoughts turned to the idea that for us the little brat will signify—a loss." The enmity of "the little brat" would later cast a shadow when Alma herself became a mother.[23]

Although Alma shunned maternal influence, it was doubtless from her mother that Alma inherited her considerable gift for music. She acknowledged in her diary the difficult life her mother had growing up, in contrast to her own. The family, living in Hamburg, was close to impoverished and, Alma noted romantically, "At eleven years of age, Mama became a ballet dancer, . . . she played walk-on parts for a whole year and became the breadwinner for the whole family."[24] Later, Anna Bergen had received her musical training in Vienna and had sung professionally in opera up until the time of her marriage to Schindler.

Freud's account of the family romance gives examples in which a child may connect him- or herself with families of "higher social standing . . . the Lord of the Manor or some landed proprietor . . . or a member of the aristocracy," employing "any opportune coincidences from his actual experience."[25] Alma's fantasy life was a matter of gilding the lily as her actual experiences in themselves had a compelling fairy-tale quality. Whatever early childhood memories she may have had of the birth of her sibling, Gretl, when Alma was two, her image of the life of a princess began before she was five. She recalled vividly the magic of travel with her family under the patronage of a wealthy collector as well as the wonders of Karlsbad and the Austrian Salzkammergut. It was during this period that the family moved into Schloss Plankenberg, a small manor at the border of the Vienna Woods. "I lived apart, like a princess," Alma wrote, "amid the beauties of nature which my father extolled. . . . Most of my childhood was spent at the Plankenberg Manor. For me it was full of beauty, legends and dread. The house was said to be haunted."[26] Carl Moll, Schindler's student, who was already a part of the household and who would marry Alma's mother after his teacher's death, further elaborated the magic of Plankenberg, an old castle that was part of the estate of Prince Karl Liechtenstein:

> A rectangular fifteenth-century building, two stories high, crowned by a gabled roof. An onion-tower with a clock in the baroque style furnished the only ornament to the façade. The two-acre grounds bore traces of their former grandeur, in particular a magnificent baroque gate, flanked by linden trees more than a hundred years old. . . . To live in the castle is to be lord of the countryside.[27]

Alma would spend hours in Schindler's studio in a dreamy state, "standing and staring at the revelations of the hand that led the brush." Sympathetic with her father, who despite improved circumstances continued to be burdened with debt, she fantasized of great wealth:

> I wished for a great Italian garden filled with many white studios; I wished to invite outstanding men there—to live for their art alone, without mundane worries—and never to show myself.

And having daydreamed of this creative harem, the exhibitionistic child in Alma added, somewhat illogically, "I loved trailing velvet gowns, and I wanted to be rowed in gondolas with velvet draperies floating astern."[28]

Emil Schindler was fifty and only just emerging from the burden of accumulated debt when he died. At the time, Alma felt "I lost my guide."[29] Years later, she still mourned on the anniversary of his death:

> It's curious . . . immediately after the death of my dearly beloved father, I was almost mad with pain. . . . And now my thoughts are with him almost daily, hourly I wish him near me. I love him more than when he was alive and mourn him perhaps more than ever, or rather: only now do I mourn him really deeply . . . I know that a time will come when I shall weep for him daily,

hourly, a time when I shall come to realize the true measure of my loss.[30]

It was natural that Alma turned to older men, in particular accomplished, mature artists who had already made their mark in their respective fields. They, too, sought her as she matured in body, mind, and seductive social graces. In truth, one aspect of Alma's seductiveness lay in a handicap: slightly hard of hearing, she tended to position herself close to others during conversation, thus conveying a sense of intimacy.

Alma doubtless was aware that her mother had carried on an affair with Moll that probably predated her father's death. By the time Alma was eighteen, Anna Schindler and Carl Moll married and the family moved to Carl's home in the Hohe Warte section of Vienna. Alma was disdainful of her stepfather, "an eternal pupil" and a "small talent" who of course could never meet the standard of her father: "It was not in him to be my guide."[31] Clearly, she saw her second-rate mother's choice to be a second-rate artist.

Moll was one of the leading spirits behind the Secession movement in reaction to Viennese academic art of the time. Alma's critique notwithstanding, he was an accomplished painter himself, specializing in household interiors that were psychologically revealing of family relationships. That many artists and writers turned up in the Schindler-Moll household seemed only natural to Alma. These visitors were among the royalty of Viennese intellectual and cultural life and constituted the manifest destiny of a princess. With her father in mind, she looked to mature, older, knowledgeable men of the artists' circle in which she was living.

Max Burckhard (1854–1912), twenty-five years Alma's senior and the distinguished director of Vienna's Burgtheater, was smitten. Shrewdly, he knew that the way to Alma's heart was through her mind. For Christmas he sent her two baskets full of books, "all classics in the finest editions." He also encouraged her musical interests. Intrigued at first, she later found his ardor "sickening." He remained a family friend and Alma's diaries contain many newsy references to pleasant outings together. But "on my side," she wrote, "our relationship lacked any erotic tinge."[32]

This was hardly the case with Moll's colleague in the Secession, and its most visible personality, Gustav Klimt (1862–1918). Klimt was a mere seventeen years older than Alma. Romantically, as she watched him during the "secret sessions" in the Moll home, she became convinced that they were made for each other: "His looks and my young charm, his genius and my talent, our common vital musicality, all helped to attune us to each other."[33] Klimt pursued Alma on a family trip to Italy, where Alma experienced her first kiss. The following day, further kissing led both to sexual arousal, to which Klimt proposed: "There is only one thing for it: complete physical union."[34] But Alma guarded her virginity. As she confessed later, albeit regarding a similar turn of events with Zemlinsky, "I was too much of a coward to take the penultimate step. . . . My old-fashioned upbringing and my mother's daily sermons had strapped me into a mental chastity belt."[35] (If sexual intercourse was the "penultimate step," what could Alma have had in mind for the ultimate?) In Alma's view, it was perennially Anna Moll who proscribed erotic encounters and thus restricted sexual pleasure. For this, Alma's own evident attractiveness to men was a source of secret pleasure and revenge.

Despite Alma's criticism of Anna and Carl and her adolescent struggle with them, the two played a sensible parental role in restraining Klimt (a delicate issue, given Moll's relationship with him), which Alma could hardly appreciate. However, even Alma acknowledged the hazards of any permanent liaison with Klimt: "We heard that he gets through quite incredible sums of money . . . we were told that five women were completely dependent on him: his mother, his sister, his sister-in-law, her sister and a young niece."[36] Nevertheless, the ancient fantasy of rescue of an impecunious artist appealed: "Poor devil! I never felt fonder of him than when I heard of his domestic plight." After her parents forbade the relationship, and as the anniversary of her father's death approached, Alma experienced a painful revival of mourning for Schindler. She had been seeking intimacy of a very different sort in her relationships with older men—reunion with her father.

In the end a residue of bitterness remained in the form of a reproach confessed to her diary: "Klimt, if much later you returned to me, I would say: 'The joys of youth you refused to share with me—keep the sufferings of old age to yourself.'"[37] Thus did Alma in her imagination construe Klimt as a heartless Eugene Onegin who, having spurned the ardent young Tatiana, at length comes to regret it in the light of her maturity. However, unlike the dignified young woman in the Pushkin narrative, Alma, privately at least, rubbed it in.

Other visitors to the Hohe Warte made their bids for Alma's favors as well. Among these were Dr. Arnold Krasny, an official at the Austrian Ministry of Railroads ("I'm beginning to loathe him . . . poor devil is madly in love with me"[38]); Joseph Olbrich, the architect and designer of monumental buildings ("hugely interesting . . . he reminds me of Wagner—his immense pride, immense vanity, immense self-assurance");[39] even Carl's married brother Ernst, a merchant ("he's warmhearted and young—very young, perhaps too young. Hanna [his wife] is older, and fish-blood courses in her veins").[40] In addition, in Alma's fecund erotic imagination, other lists were created. On the Italian family trip of 1899, when Klimt pursued her, she wrote, "I'm obsessed by three figures: my young German (whom she had "spotted" sitting opposite in a hotel restaurant—"We exchanged long glances . . . and our gaze, which initially had been merely flirtatious, grew steadily deeper, sadder, desirous");[41] Lieutenant [Schulz] ("cheerful, dashing"); and Klimt."[42]

Gustav Mahler was under the spell of his own family romance, intensified by the social and psychological distance traveled in a single generation. His father, Bernhard, had been eager to leave behind the relative provincialism of Kaliste and Marie Mahler's rural Ledec. Bernhard achieved the standing of a "burgher of the King's Mining City of Iglau"; the certificate hung among the cherished books of the former "wagon scholar." Social standing was confirmed in his status among the founders of the synagogue. While Gustav propped himself on the shoulders of his father, rivalry spurred ambition. What his son achieved went far beyond what Bernhard might have imagined when he brought the boy to be evaluated musically by Professor Julius Epstein and was told that he was a "born musician." Moreover, such a family legend lent itself to the fantasied question "Born of whom?" For nowhere visible was the progenitor of the gift that would catapult Gustav to the foremost musical position of the empire.

Mahler's family romance took the form of the self-made man, the Second Symphony's "On wings that I have won." This notion was influenced by the writings and spiritual beliefs of his friend Siegfried Lipiner, a philosopher of Jewish birth who had converted to Catholicism some years earlier. From Mahler's vantage point, Catholicism was tantamount to the higher station in life of which Freud wrote in his *Family Romances* paper. In a sense, there was a devaluation of religious origins in Mahler's conversion; if not a degree of self-loathing, rather an affiliation with anti-Semitic attitudes per se. Thus Mahler's conversion to Catholicism was more than a simple matter of politics. It was the result of unconscious elements as well as the natural consequence of an idealized self-image deemed appropriate and right even as it disavowed true origins.

The attraction to Alma was also an aspect of Mahler's family romance. She was as far as possible from the modest, lame, and worn-out hausfrau that was Marie Mahler. Inevitably, Mahler would come to wish Alma shared some of the pained and careworn features of his mother. In contrast, Alma was drawn to a man who physically resembled her father. Even as Mahler eschewed his Jewishness, she found it exotic and would prove to be nearly as philo-Semitic as she was anti-Semitic. Moreover, this difference in background appealed to her rebellious nature. Hers was the almost casual-appearing variety of anti-Semitism seen when deeply rooted in culture and family—an attitude toward the outsider who is devalued if not demonized. In her adolescent diary, for example, she and Carl joined Burckhard, who was delivering a reading of his play ("fine and effective") before a "smoke-filled room packed with working class Jews." Alma couldn't get over the fact that although the young man who introduced him spoke of the workers' "incredible thirst for knowledge," he did so "with a strong Jewish accent, in typically Yiddish slang." "Why on earth," Alma asked herself, "why did he give that reading? . . . Surely not because he cares about this degenerate race."[43]

The psychological contours of Alma's and Mahler's individual family romances were complex and more than compatible. They were complementary and compelling. They quickly led to love.

7

MAHLER IN LOVE

Alma's flair for the dramatic produced the legendary account of her first meeting with Gustav Mahler at a dinner party in November 1901. But Alma had in fact met the musician earlier, confiding her infatuation to her diary as early as December 1898: "As for Mahler—I'm virtually in love with him."[1] Shortly after the encounter, another fortyish admirer, Dr. Theobald Pollock (an official at the Ministry of Railroads), gave her an autographed photograph of Mahler. "Mahler, my beloved Mahler," Alma exclaimed.[2]

Nineteen-year-old Alma's infatuation with Mahler had actually been something of a joke in the Moll circle. Carl, his fellow artists, and various other visitors to the Hohe Warte were fond of relating to her any chance contact with the conductor, and often passed on malicious gossip. As a prank, Gustav Geiringer, a pianist acquainted with Mahler, obtained his autograph on a postcard that was then sent to Alma the summer of 1899, creating the occasion for endless teasing. Later that July, the Molls and friends were summering not far from where the Mahler family was staying; while out for a bicycle trip, they encountered a group led by Mahler. Alma related: "We met some four or five times. Each time, [Mahler] struck up a conversation. Shortly before Hallstatt he dismounted. We were pushing our bikes, and he started up another conversation, staring hard at me. I jumped onto my bike and rode off into the distance. The Geiringers were angry; they'd wanted to introduce me and he [Mahler] was expecting it too. Judging by the way he looked at me, he appears to have perceived the connection between myself and the postcard—which I found most embarrassing."[3] Alma brushed off the significance of this first meeting: "Anyway, I feel absolutely no urge to meet him." Keen to erotic nuance, she may have sensed that this was unlikely to be their last encounter. "I love and honour him as an artist, but as a man he doesn't interest me at all. I wouldn't want to lose my illusions either."[4]

Alma's preferred accounts of her first meeting with Gustav are found in her memoir, *Gustav Mahler: Memories and Letters*, and in her autobiography, *And the Bridge Is Love*. That occasion was a dinner party for Mahler at the home of the distinguished anatomist Emil Zuckerkandl. Emil's wife, Bertha, was the sister of Sophie Clemenceau, who had met Mahler at the Austrian Embassy when he conducted in Paris in 1900. Sophie was now visiting Vienna. To the invitation, "We've got Mahler coming in tonight—won't you come?" Alma claimed to initially decline. "In fact I had purposely . . . avoided meeting him that summer because of all the stories people told about him and every young woman who wants to sing in the opera."[5] In the event, the dinner was postponed a week and Alma could not resist accepting when it turned out two of her other admirers, Gustav Klimt and Max Burckhard, were also invited. Mahler would be there with his ever protective sister, Justine; the stage was thus set for high drama. In *And the Bridge Is Love*, Alma admitted finally of feeling "curiously apprehensive."[6]

Indeed, her accounts of the evening are worthy of a modern-day screenplay, with Alma sitting between Klimt and Burckhard, "laughing a good deal," and Mahler, at the other end of the table, studying her through his glasses and eventually bursting out, "Can't we all get in on the fun?" During the course of the evening Alma flirted with Mahler, casting out provocative remarks. When she finally described her teacher, Alexander von Zemlinsky, as "beautiful," Mahler could only shrug and suggest "this was going pretty far." As they distanced themselves from the group, the rest of the company may well have sensed the couple's burgeoning interest in one another. Alma described the evening as enchanted, the pair left standing "in the kind of vacuum that instantly envelops people who have found each other."[7] Mahler, too, was caught up in the experience, later writing to Alma, "Do you remember our first conversation in the presence of Burckhard? Everything I said was directed solely to you that evening. God had already willed then that we should become *one*."[8]

Alma and Gustav's courtship was as intense as it was brief. In less than twenty days, Mahler accomplished romantically what he had been unable to during the previous twenty years. Alma was caught up in the fervor and urgency of Mahler's courtship. Characteristically, once he knew what he now wanted, Mahler pursued the object of his affection relentlessly and, to a degree, oblivious to Alma's wishes. He alone knew what was best for both of them. Mahler was intolerant of ambivalence and impatient with any timetable but his own. The dinner party took place on a Thursday evening. It ended with Mahler's inviting Alma to visit him at the opera, using the pretense of showing him her songs. He already had an engagement there the following morning, having invited Bertha Zuckerkandl and her sister Sophie to the dress rehearsal for Monday's performance of *Tales of Hoffman*. Eager to see Alma again, he insisted that she come as well.

Mahler was waiting impatiently for them when they arrived and he neglected the two older women "rudely" while he helped Alma with her coat and asked how she had slept. He confided he himself "didn't sleep a wink all night." Disingenuous in her memoir, Alma had conveyed her excitement to her diary: "I must say, I liked him *immensely*—although he's dreadfully restless. He stormed about the room like a savage. The fellow is made *entirely* of oxygen. When you go near him you get burnt."[9]

Alma was thrown into emotional turmoil. Only days before, her relationship with Zemlinsky had reached a flash point of passion. As Klimt had earlier, Zemlinsky pressed Alma to act on the powerful sexual excitement she elicited and have intercourse. Although she told her diary, "I don't need to write it down," her account of her tryst with Zemlinsky a few days earlier reads like a romantic novel: "Later—he clasped my hips, I slid between his legs, he pressed me with them, and we kissed to the accompaniment of soft exclamations. He forced me onto his lap, our lips would not be parted. I sucked on his mouth . . . blessed impregnation! And then again—he forced me roughly onto a chair, leaned over me, kissed my eyes and forehead—and then on the mouth. Afterward I felt completely shattered—I could scarcely come to my senses."[10]

Mahler in foyer of Vienna Court Opera, 1903.

In parting their first evening, Mahler reminded Alma of her promise to visit him and bring her songs. "Word of honor?" he had asked and Alma had echoed the phrase responsively. The day following the rehearsal, a letter arrived for Alma at the Hohe Warte—an unsigned poem that she knew came from Mahler.

> It happened overnight.
> I would never have believed it.
> That counterpoint and the study of form
> Would once more oppress my heart.
> Thus in one night
> They gained the upper hand!
> And all the voices lead ever more
> Homophonically in only one direction.
> It happened overnight
> —I spent it wide awake—
> That, when there's a knock
> My eyes immediately fly toward the door!
> I hear, "Word of honor"!
> It rings in my ears constantly
> Like every sort of Canon:
> I glance at the door and wait!"

The music behind Mahler's poem reveals as much as its language. Although the manifest meaning of its words requires little interpretation, the music contains the latent message of *Um Mitternacht*. The repeated phrase "It happened overnight" (Das kam so über Nacht) invokes the life-threatening events of February 1901 and the song Mahler composed in response that summer. The words of *Um Mitternacht* convey a sense of hopelessness and helplessness: "No thought of light brought me comfort at midnight." Fate lay in God's hands. But "midnight" with Alma had been an enchanted evening. Marriage with an extraordinary young woman and the restitution of family would bring comfort and redemption. Thus Mahler's sleepless night of 9–10 November differed substantially from the terrifying one of February. For the first time in his life, Mahler would be putting himself in another's hands, rendering himself vulnerable. It would be in reaction to this that in the early days of courtship he would test the control that he might exert on Alma.

After the evening at the Zuckerkandls, Mahler had offered to walk Alma home. When she demurred, he walked with Burckhard instead. Conversation started casually, with a feeler from Mahler eliciting a curt response from Burckhard: "Fräulein Schindler is a bright and interesting young lady." Mahler in turn observed: "I didn't like her at first, because she seemed to be nothing but a doll. It's not everyday that one meets such a pretty young thing who's actually busying herself with something serious." When Burckhard perceived that Mahler was attempting to press him for more information, he drew himself up with, "Those who are acquainted with Fräulein Schindler know what she is. The others have no right to know." Burckhard would later tell Alma, "He was pretty wild about you the other night." Ostensibly, according to Alma, Burckhard was trying to protect her, for "Mahler, the ascetic, had the reputation of a rake, a corruptor of all the young females in his ensemble."[12] But his cutting of Mahler in this manner may have been a reflection of Burckhard's well-known anti-Semitic sentiments.

Alma showed Mahler's poem to Anna Moll, who, still unable to acknowledge her daughter's powerful sexuality, thought it a hoax. But Alma knew differently, through Burckhard's warnings and her own self-confidence. Mahler's intentions were confirmed the following week when Alma and her mother attended the performance of another opera, conducted this time by Bruno Walter. Mahler, in the director's box, was free—Alma related—"to flirt with me in a way I would never have believed so serious a man could." During intermission, he "confronted us in the lobby, asking to be introduced to my mother."[13]

Mahler charmed Anna Moll unabashedly as he offered the two women tea in his office and he soon extracted an invitation to visit. His affability and warmth toward Anna Moll at this first meeting was not insincere. It marked the start of a relationship that proved to be as complex as it was dear to Mahler. That Alma came with a family was a bonus for Mahler; and Carl Moll, too, would become an important person in his life. But at the dinner following the aforementioned performance, Moll was scandalized that his wife and his stepdaughter had compromised themselves with a visit to the office of a "rake" and a "roué," not to mention a Jew.

The jealous Burckhard weighed in as well, asking what Alma would do if Mahler proposed marriage. When she coyly replied that she would accept, he exclaimed, "But it would be a sin for so lovely a creature of such good family as you! Don't go and throw yourself away on this rachitic and degenerate Jew. Think of your children."[14]

Jews' physical traits had long been a target of anti-Semitism and indeed early in their acquaintance, Alma had expressed a degree of disgust with Mahler's body: "So many things about him annoy me: his smell—the way he sings—something in the way he speaks."[15] At the same time, Alma was drawn to Mahler physically. Although Mahler weighed only "63 kilos," Alma would cherish him; "I'll coddle him as though he were a child."[16] And children were exactly what Alma was thinking of. She had already confided to her diary her longing to bear children in her hope for "blessed impregnation" by Zemlinsky. Before long, this wish would be transferred onto Mahler.

Alma depicted Mahler's arrival at the Hohe Warte as a whirlwind. He did not come on the appointed day but rather arrived spontaneously and unannounced. He was known everywhere in Vienna and the maid rushed in excitedly, gasping, "Gustav Mahler is here!" The house was somewhat in disarray as the family had only recently moved in, and Mahler inspected Alma's unshelved books. Alma wrote, "On the whole he seemed pleased with my taste, though my complete edition of Nietzsche's works shocked him. There was a fire in the fireplace, and he abruptly asked me to feed Nietzsche to the flames. I refused."[17] This, as Alma would later recall, was the suitor's opening gambit. It invoked the requirements for a wife that Mahler had shared with Förster years before and for which he would continue to test Alma after the first days' passion. Although on this occasion, the plucky Alma resisted destroying her Nietzsche, she would soon yield on a more personal matter: her composing.

Mahler, influenced by Lipiner and Victor Adler, highly respected Nietzsche's philosophy. In fact, he had recently set a text from *Also sprach Zarathustra* as a movement of his Third Symphony, the "Midnight Song" that announces the theme of eternal recurrence. It is tempting to think that Mahler knew the edition of Nietzsche may have been a gift from Burckhard, who had earlier sent the baskets of such classics to Alma.

For him to have believed that Nietzsche was too strong fare for Alma would have been misguided and patronizing.

That afternoon, Mahler suggested he and Alma take a walk. On their way out, Anna Moll invited him to stay for dinner, adding, "We're having Paprikahendl and Burckhard." Mahler replied, "I don't care much for either," but he agreed to stay.[18] Mahler seemed to have made up his mind—indeed, made up his mind for himself and for Alma. As they returned from their stroll in the fresh snow, only nineteen days after they had "officially" met, Mahler voiced his thoughts: "It's not so simple to marry a man like me. I'm quite free; I have to be. I can assume no material obligations. My job with the opera is from day to day." Outrageous as this may seem, given his prominent position, Mahler struck a chord within Alma that revived an ancient relationship—that with her father, Emil Schindler. Drawing herself up, she replied, "To me that is only natural. . . . Don't forget, I am an artist's daughter. I've always lived among artists; I feel like an artist. I've never thought differently in these matters."[19] Alma was only secondarily seduced by Mahler's ardor. She was ensnared by her own inner strivings; by the same impulse that led her to write at the start of her memoirs, "I am the daughter of artistic tradition." This may explain the immediate "tacit agreement" Alma made with Mahler on that first visit, prior to seeking the privacy of her room, where "he kissed me and started to talk of an early wedding, as if it were a matter of course."[20]

Mahler was in love, Alma in turmoil. He sent her some of his *Lieder*, writing in his note, "All the love and loveliness continued to reverberate softly within me, even in my dreams."[21] While Alma wrote to him of "our first beautiful walk together," she confided to her diary, "Conflicting emotions are at war inside me. Here Alex, here Mahler." Both were apprehensive about Mahler's anticipated departure on 9 December—the one-month anniversary of their meeting—for a ten-day conducting tour in Berlin and Dresden. Alma had brought something entirely new into Mahler's life, an unaccustomed happiness, and his ardor only increased. Eager for her to know him, he sent her his score for *Das klagende Lied* on the eve of his departure: "Here is a 'Tale' from my youth. . . . You gave me real joy yesterday. . . . Alas, such an afternoon is dreadfully short and the coda of evening is almost mournful." Alma seemed to be working through her troubled emotions regarding Zemlinsky, powerful attraction on one hand, and guilt on the other for having drawn him into expectations she was about to dash. But by the time of Mahler's leaving she wrote, "I shan't see him for nineteen days . . . I don't know what else to write, but my feelings are *for him* & *against Alex. Never* before have I watched the clock as avidly as today. I couldn't work for sheer longing."[22]

A myth hovered commonly in the minds of the imaginative couple as Mahler perceived Alma's troubled hesitation. In a note to her before he departed, Mahler wrote, "The dearest wish I cherish before going away is that you will still be my dear comrade and help me a little to be yours too. Don't forget our favorites: Evchen—and Hans Sachs."[23] He was referring to Wagner's *Die Meistersinger*, in which the elderly Hans Sachs, although enamored of Eva and in a position to win her as the bride-prize for his accomplished singing, renounces his claim and yields instead to the younger Walther, thus facilitating the liaison of the youthful lovers. It is a somewhat puzzling reference as it would suggest the possibility of Mahler's withdrawing in favor of a man more age-appropriate for Alma— Zemlinsky or some as yet unnamed younger suitor. Alma recognized this as "an idle subterfuge." Yet the prospect of a marriage in which there was a twenty-year age difference troubled both.

Mahler shared his concern with Justine, clearly seeking her reassurance. It was also a bid for her understanding and consent, since brother and sister had shared much since the deaths of their parents. Although Mahler accepted her partnership as a matter of course and the result of necessity, the degree to which he felt she had sacrificed her youth for him was a constant source of guilt. Justine had assumed the hybrid role of sister, daughter, housekeeper, companion, and wife. Mahler's behavior toward her could be caring, encouraging, demanding, critical, and sarcastic in turn; yet he did not lack respect for her. Their correspondence was hardly limited to family affairs as Mahler habitually shared his musical experiences in intelligently detailed letters, devoid of the patronizing attitude evident in those in which he criticized her housekeeping and parenting.[24]

To a degree, Justine was also privy to Mahler's romantic life, and she was quite opinionated about whatever she could learn of it. Some women, such as Mahler's erstwhile lover Anna von Mildenburg, were her natural rivals; others, such as Natalie Bauer-Lechner, who cultivated her friendship, were warmly safe, and as much family to her as to Mahler himself. In Mahler's correspondence with Anna during the Hamburg years, Justine, then twenty-seven (four years older than Anna), and the younger Emma constantly hovered in the background: "I must drive myself constantly to make a living for my sisters and myself." A recurrent leitmotif was the figure of Justine as both helpmate and ongoing responsibility. Ultimately, this proved to be an important element in the termination of the affair with Anna. Mahler had found himself uneasily mediating between the two women. He had placated Anna, "Don't hold it against Justine if she treats you unjustly, and believe me, she doesn't think badly of you." At the heart of this triangle was a troubling dilemma for Mahler. "Do you think, my beloved," he wrote to Anna, "that I can rejoice for even a moment in my 'freedom'? How gladly I would give it up to be chained by your arms, if only I would not thereby turn another's life into a prison. . . . I know that through my own happiness, I would forever destroy someone else's (you know who that is)."[25]

Mahler knew what he was up against within his own family as he plunged headlong into his relationship with Alma. If Justine had been an obstacle and concern for Mahler when she was twenty-seven, what would he confront at thirty-three? When Mahler and Alma took their first snowy walk, they had stopped at Dobling, where Mahler intended to phone Justine that he would not be home for dinner. So set were his habits that he did not even know his own home phone number; from the public phone in the Dobling post office he called the opera house to send word. According to Alma, "No such thing had happened in their nine years of living together."[26] As for breaking the news to Justine, according to Mahler's account, he told her everything and they spoke late into the night. But Alma reported that he was loath to tell her at first "for fear of the dire effects of her jealousy."[27]

Mahler's version is the more likely, as much had happened in Justine's life since they had moved to Vienna four years earlier. Justine had met Arnold Rosé, the concertmaster of the Vienna Philharmonic. More than just a colleague of Mahler's, Rosé became a genuine supporter and friend; they read chamber music together and Rosé helped Mahler work out bowings for the string parts of his scores. Rosé rapidly became part of the small Mahler family, which then still included Natalie, and also joined the wider circle of Mahler's friends. He frequently accompanied Mahler on trips and vacations. On such occasions as well as at other social and professional events, Arnold and Justine together with Mahler and Natalie made up a pleasant foursome, at least half of which was celibate. As in some ironic short story, brother and sister were both apprehensive about the other's response should they go on with their lives in marriage.

It may be that Mahler, forever preoccupied, was the last to know how serious the other couple was, as Natalie had evidently threatened Justine with disclosure if she didn't promote the foursome, for which Natalie had high hopes.[28] Alma, in writing of Gustav's puritanical attitude, related that when he realized that what he had thought to be friendship and comradeship was intimacy of another sort, he had refused to speak to Justine for weeks and insisted that she should either break with Rosé or marry him. The result was a foregone conclusion, and in any event it is questionable that Mahler, who rarely missed anything even if he was "dead to the world" while composing, was completely unaware of the growing closeness between Justine and Arnold. And even if he felt some sense of betrayal, given his own reluctance to move ahead for fear of hurting Justine, he would very likely have felt a degree of relief as well.

Mahler's moral attitude was a matter of particular interest to Alma: "He's the purest person I've ever met—because Mahler, thank God, has had few affairs—nothing more than routine."[29] Mahler clearly had not disabused her although Alma was already well aware of the gossip.

Alma and Justine met two days after Mahler left for Berlin and Dresden. The meeting was more than civilized. It was agreeable, with Justine writing to Mahler of Alma's "warmth and gaiety"; and Alma reporting, "There's one thing I like very much about her—I recognize him in her." In her diary she could not resist a slur: "She has a slightly deflected look [i.e., a squint]."[30] They made a date for several days hence in an effort to become acquainted during Mahler's absence. Justine invited Alma to the Mahler residence on the Auenbruggergasse and showed her Gustav's room. Beneath the surface, however, they circled one another warily. Alma observed that while Justi was "exceedingly sweet and kind to me . . . she watches me like a lynx." Justine was no doubt concerned about Alma's reputation as a flirt. In any event, both women put on the best face for Mahler, who was much relieved.

In Berlin, Mahler's concern about his age surfaced rapidly with Alma's reassurance of her commitment to him. "There's only one thing that worries me: whether a man who's reached the threshold of old age has the right to tie his extreme maturity to so much youth and freshness, to chain spring to autumn, missing out summer? . . . For the time being, of course, all is well, but what will happen when winter follows my fruitful autumn? Do you see what I mean?"[31] Mahler wrote ardently of a love both unfamiliar and overwhelming, a feeling that was frightening as well: "I feel the bliss, and can say it, too, of loving for the first time. I can never be free of the dread that this lovely dream may dissolve, and can hardly wait for the moment when your own mouth and breath will breathe into me certainty and inmost consciousness that my life has reached port after storm."[32]

But with this came the now ever present specter of aging: "Oh, God, I am talking away today from sheer suspense and longing for you, like Walther von Stolzing, and never give a thought to the other half, to poor old Hans Sachs, who yet deserves your love far more."[33]

Suffused with love, Mahler remained apprehensive. Alma, who by no means had given up flirting (nor could she, it was so ingrained in her personality) was also troubled by the shadow of the double-image cast by Hans Sachs and Walther von Stolzing. She had insensitively written to Mahler of a young musician who had fallen in love with her and threatened suicide. Mahler had responded by professing his own love, but in a sarcastic and patronizing manner. The episode clearly disturbed him.

It was against this background, while he was in Dresden for the performance of his Second Symphony, that Mahler recalled the Nietzsche dispute that had marked his first private encounter with Alma. More than this, it festered, augmented by the distance now between them. With the prospect of planning marriage on his return to Vienna, only a few days away, Mahler seemed to come to his senses. "It was," Alma reported, "our first major conflict."[34] If nothing else, the sheer length of the letter he wrote to Alma betrayed Mahler's anxiety: at some three thousand words, it was the longest he ever sent her.[35]

Despite a shallow kindliness, the anger motivating Mahler's letter came through. The letter opened: "It is with a somewhat heavy heart that I'm writing you today, my beloved Alma, for I know I must hurt you and yet I can't do otherwise." The parental tone of "it-hurts-me-more-than-it-does-you" is reflected in a degree of sermonizing reminiscent of Mahler's letters to his "sibling-children" during the family crisis of 1889 and after—St. Anthony revived. The trigger was Alma's account of a conversation with Mahler's nemesis Burckhard, who had commented on the couple's relationship, remarking that two such strong personalities could never be happy together. Mahler wrote:

> First, your conversation with Burckhard—what do you understand by a personality? Do you consider yourself a personality? . . . Everything in you is as yet unformed, unspoken and undeveloped. Although you're an adorable, infinitely adorable and enchanting young girl with an upright soul and a richly talented, frank and already self-assured person, you're still not a personality.

Taking the opportunity for a slur on his rivals, Mahler added, "Not one of the Burckhards, Zemlinskys, etc., is a *personality*." Indeed, Mahler's extended and tortuous philosophical definition left little doubt whom he felt to be an authentic personality, one of those rare "supreme beings who not only shape their own existence but also that of humanity": who else but Gustav Mahler himself. It is "wings that I have won" redux; the Nietzschean "Übermensch"! Although Alma was not of this ilk, she would find her identity and influence, according to Mahler, as "in a word, my wife." Thus while it soon emerged that the issue under debate was Alma's composing—indeed, her commitment to composition—Mahler's demands that Alma be completely and entirely devoted to him were not far from the surface.

Mahler further chastised Burckhard for his pomposity and Alma for her vanity:

> They've constantly flattered you, not because you enriched their lives with your own but because you exchanged big-sounding words with them . . . because you all intoxicate each other with verbosity and because you're beautiful and attractive to men

who, without realizing it, instinctively pay homage to charm. Just imagine if you were ugly, my Alma.

Not until the second half of this lengthy letter did Mahler come to the point:

> The point that is the real heart and core of all my anxieties, fears and misgivings, the real reason why every detail that points to it has acquired such significance: you write *"you and my music"*— *Forgive me, but this has to be discussed too*! In this matter, my Alma, it's absolutely imperative that we understand one another clearly *at once*, before we see each other again! Unfortunately, I have to begin with you and am indeed, in the strange position of having, in a sense, to *set my music against yours*. . . . Would it be possible for you, from now on, to regard *my music as yours*? I prefer not to discuss "your" music in detail now—I'll revert to it later.

Mahler's requirements for his wife-to-be sounded increasingly like those he had revealed to Förster, albeit perhaps tongue-in-cheek at the time. Indeed, his very disavowal of a "bourgeois" attitude toward marriage revealed this outlook precisely:

> Don't misunderstand me and start imagining that I hold the bourgeois view of the relationship between husband and wife, which regards the latter as a sort of plaything for her husband and, at the same time, as his housekeeper . . . but one thing is certain and that is that you must become "what I need" if we are to be happy together. Would it mean the destruction of your existence if you were to give up your music entirely in order to possess and also to be mine instead?

He admonished Alma, "You, however, have only *one* profession from now on: *to make me happy*!" Mahler's narcissism gained force and became almost boundless as he criticized "the heartless way in which you treat Zemlinsky" and asked, "Could you really spend a whole afternoon with [Justine] without talking lovingly of me and about me?" And finally, the climax-cum-summary: "You must give yourself to me *unconditionally*, shape your future life, in every detail, entirely in accordance with my needs and desire nothing in return save my *love!*"

Mahler was on the brink of returning to Vienna and the powerful feelings expressed in the letter evoked a sense of urgency: "I must have your answer to this letter before I come to see you on Saturday." Alma received the letter on 20 December, scarcely six weeks since they had met. Paradoxically, the outrage she solicited in those confidantes with whom she shared the letter seemed only to increase her resolve. Thus she externalized her deep resentment, at least for the time being, and while kindling the reaction in others, pursued her romantically informed rebellion. "After all, I wanted him. I calmed down and wrote him a letter promising what he wanted me to promise."[36]

Back in Vienna the following day, Mahler drafted a further letter containing a halfhearted attempt to undo or at least mitigate the ultimatum. Its main message was what "must be decided between us. I await the answer my servant will bring in a state of suspense and anguish such as I have never known."[37] It was the first of only two occasions on which Mahler anxiously awaited a decision from Alma, his fate hanging in balance. When the situation recurred during their marital crisis a decade hence, the issues of uncompromising loyalty and devotion and the promise never to leave him were revived. But this time there was no question as to Alma's response, and she met urgency with her own urgency, running into the street to give her answer to the messenger.

By Christmas Eve, the uncertainty was over, with Mahler sending Christmas greetings "for the first and last time." St. Anthony reverted from preaching to piety as Mahler pronounced his sacred blessing: "I bless you, my beloved, my life, on this day, the children's day, in whom the seed of earthly as well as divine love strikes root wherever the seed falls. May my life be a blessing to yours."[38]

In the same spirit, late in 1901 Mahler was completing the Adagietto of his Fifth Symphony. He would later reveal to Willem Mengelberg that this was a love song without words for Alma. On his own copy of the score, Mengelberg wrote:

> N.B. *This Adagietto* was Gustav Mahler's *declaration of love* for Alma! Instead of a letter, he sent her *this* in manuscript form; *no*

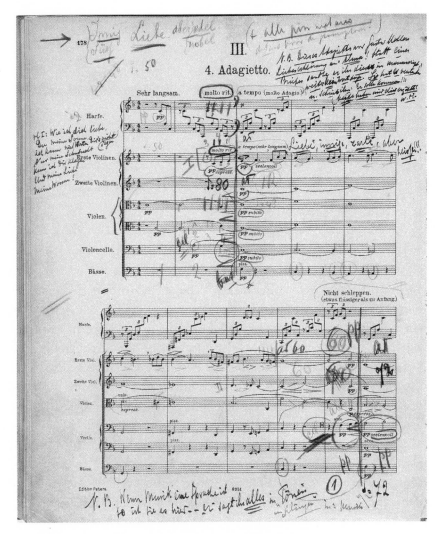

Adagietto from Mahler's Fifth Symphony, Mengelberg's score.

other words accompanied it. She understood and wrote to him: He should come!!! (*Both of them told me this!*) W.M.[39]

Over the holiday Alma and Gustav were engaged and wedding plans made. Of her promise to Mahler, Alma would write, "And I have kept my word. . . . And yet, somewhere in me a wound kept smarting."[40]

8

THE "SPLENDID" YEARS

Renouncing her artistic strivings for the moment, Alma embraced another role with equal passion: "Oh, to bear his child! My body. His soul. When shall I be his!"[1] It was, of course, her beauty that would be her contribution to the child, although her powerful eroticism may have been too much for Mahler during their first sexual embrace on New Year's Day 1902. Confiding to her diary the details ("stiff and upright stood his vigour. . . . He carried me to the sofa"), Alma indicated the session ended in failure with Mahler impotent. Alma suffered doubly, from her own frustration and Mahler's "torment." But a few days later, a single line appeared in her diary: "Wonne über Wonne" (bliss beyond bliss). And the following day too: "Rapture without end."[2] In fact, by the end of the week, "doctors' orders . . . an inflamed swelling—ice bags, hot baths, etc., etc. All because I resisted him so long—he has to suffer."[3]

Behind these words lurked the couple's private mythology: Mahler as Hans Sachs, "virginal at forty, as I was at twenty."[4] Unsuccessful under the circumstances, possibly; virginal, unlikely. The intensity with which Mahler turned to Alma suggests a degree of pent-up sexual excitement for the beautiful young woman that might well have resulted in transient impotence or, more likely, premature discharge. Mahler's earlier affairs were undoubtedly sexual in nature, in particular that with Anna von Mildenburg. Shrewdly, Mahler may have avoided telling Alma any details of his former erotic life. The gossip about it, in which Carl Moll seemed well versed, had more than a grain of truth.

Alma realized her wish sooner than expected, becoming pregnant early in 1902. Consequently, the wedding was set for March. Yet obstacles remained. Alma had to contend with gossiping family friends and an anti-Semitic family; Mahler, with his sister and old friends who had seen him through much in his life. Justine's blessing on the match posed a particular problem for Mahler after so many years of domestic partnership. Mahler doubtless knew something of Justine's growing closeness to Arnold Rosé. Indeed, Mahler appeared to have encouraged the relationship, if not for the sake of his own eventual freedom, then out of genuine concern for the needs of a woman already in her early thirties. If, as Alma suggested, Mahler felt some sense of betrayal in Justine's affection for Arnold, he was able to relinquish her in view of a more desirable replacement.

That same first week of 1902, Mahler gave a dinner at his Auenbruggergasse apartment with a guest list that spelled drama. Mahler's friend from student days, the distinguished writer Siegfried Lipiner, and his first wife, Nanna Spiegler (another Mahler family intimate), were present with current spouses, as were Justine and Arnold Rosé. Anna von Mildenburg, who had remained a friend after the affair with Mahler and was now Lipiner's mistress, was also there. On Alma's side were her mother and her stepfather, Anna and Carl Moll, and for balance, their new neighbor on the Hohe Warte, the artist and designer Kolomon Moser. The party was a disaster. Alma, tense and on display, behaved outrageously, baiting Lipiner on one of his favorite paintings ("What on earth does it represent?"). He in turn kept calling her "Mädchen," which led her to call him "the most sterile person I've ever met." When Mildenburg politely asked what she thought of Mahler's music, Alma answered, "I know very little of it and the little I do know I don't like." Mahler finally withdrew with Alma to another room, and on returning, positioned her on the sofa between himself and Anna Moll. There Alma ignored the rest of the guests for what remained of the evening.[5]

The jury did not take long to reach a verdict. A critical letter arrived the following day from Lipiner as representative of the Mahler faction. Mahler wrote back supporting Alma and counseling his friend to be more tolerant of her youth and inexperience, citing the stressful circumstances of the evening. But Lipiner was not finished. Assuming the prerogative of an old friend, he roundly criticized Mahler's character, reproaching him for his "profound, lasting and everlasting coldness." He may have struck a chord when he wrote, "You throw people away—you usually pick them up again—but not always—and everything's supposed to be all right again." No slouch at assessing character, the writer, speaking for Mahler's friends, pinpointed a trait evident as early as the days of Gustav Schwartz and, more recently, of Natalie Bauer-Lechner, who, of course, was absent during the fateful evening. Lipiner darkly hinted at retaliatory abandonment by friends in stating that Mahler could live with Alma "in splendid isolation," undisturbed by "troublesome, useless people."[6]

The disapproval of Mahler's friends dogged the marriage for years and would be reiterated in a comparable letter around 1910, when Mahler's still-loyal friends were concerned about his health and his undertaking too much in order to maintain an opulent lifestyle for Alma. But at this stage, just before marriage, Alma had the last word, shrewdly assessing the effect of this disapproval on her husband-to-be: "These people in their blindness had badly miscalculated. . . . Their plan was to degrade me in his eyes . . . and so to wound his pride. But they had not reckoned with my fierce spirit of independence or my sensitive pride. In any case, as Mahler hated nothing more than argument and thrashing things out, he simply kept more and more out of the way of his trusty old friends. They achieved exactly the opposite of their designs."[7] The bitterness of the dinner party encounter never abated for Alma. Years later in her memoir she trashed Lipiner: "He was a bogus Goethe in his writing and a haggling Jew in his talk."[8]

In fact, Alma did alienate Mahler from this circle of trusted friends and they never forgave her for it. Mahler no longer saw them informally, although there was correspondence on celebratory occasions or in the case of illness. Lipiner's letters were forceful, as one might expect from a writer of his gifts, but not to be outdone, Alma co-opted his phrase—to live with her "in splendid isolation"—for an irony of her own. In her memoirs, the chapters covering the years 1903–1906 are called "Splendid Isolation." It was, she wrote, Mahler's favorite phrase "to describe our completely solitary way of life."[9]

In a denouement perhaps more worthy of operetta than grand opera, brother and sister had close to a double wedding. Justine could not have found a better oedipal substitute for her brother than the gifted and attractive Jewish musician, Rosé; and Mahler could not have found a more agreeable and compatible brother-in-law if he had handpicked Justine's husband (which, contrary to Alma's account, may well have been the case). In Arnold Rosé, not only did Justine find a husband: Mahler also replaced a brother, having by then lost all three male siblings to whom he had an attachment. His beloved Ernst had died during adolescence; the mentally unstable Alois had vanished to America; and Otto had committed suicide six years earlier.

On 9 March 1902, a rainy day, Alma and Gustav were married in Vienna's Church of St. Charles Borromeo. The witnesses were Anna and Carl Moll for the bride, and Justine and Arnold Rosé, who were married the following day, for the groom. After Alma and Gustav's wedding, the Mahlers, the Molls, and the soon-to-be Rosés, now drawn together as family, celebrated with a quiet luncheon. Later in the day Gustav and Alma left for a conducting tour in St. Petersburg, which they resolved to make a honeymoon. Curiously, Alma said that she was relieved that she did not have to conceal her condition, although she could only have been several weeks pregnant: the child was not born until 3 November. More likely was a secret pride of possession.

Mahler was hungry for extended family. Ambivalent as he may have been after the family crisis of 1889, the losses in his own life had left a void that he hoped would be filled with marriage. He was happy to acquire Anna and Carl Moll as in-laws. Carl was actually a year younger than Mahler, the age his brother Ernst would have been had he survived. Both Moll and Mahler were deeply involved in the cultural life of Vienna, Carl as a founder of the Secession art movement, an art dealer and an artist himself. As time went on, a sense of comradeship developed in Mahler's relationship to his nominal stepfather-in-law. In later years Carl had an automobile that would be used for excursions and for the Mahlers' house hunting. At Mahler's funeral, it was he and Arnold Rosé, as the senior members of this family, who would cast the first handfuls of earth into the grave.

Carl and Anna Moll.

Anna Moll's was another story. She was about three years older than her son-in-law. From the first, Mahler took to her affectionately, soon calling her Mama. There were overtones of the solicitousness and tenderness Mahler had for his own mother and he embraced Anna as the only mother left. In his first letter to Anna Moll in December 1901, before leaving for Dresden and Berlin, he addressed her as "My dear friend," later "Mama" and eventually even "Mamatschili":

> You will, I hope, permit me to use this form of address, which I should like to claim as a delightful privilege—one, it is true, that I have not yet earned, but which has been so magnanimously conferred upon me. . . . May I confess to you that this separation seems very long and quite upsets me? I speak so frankly because I feel you will accept this confession as warmly as it is made; and that you no longer regard me as a stranger.[10]

Mahler had met Anna only days before.

Anna Moll's relationship with Mahler and the couple was a curious one. She was called on to assist when family crises arose and she was quick to respond. Mahler was grateful for this when, in later years, Alma required help and treatment in sanatoriums. At such times it was as if the two adults shared in caring for the child. Along with Carl, Anna would at length manifest strong anti-Semitic feelings. But unlike her husband, who appeared to exempt Mahler the Jew from censure, Anna's feelings ultimately emerged in dealing with her son-in-law, at least unconsciously.

Alma Mahler could measure married life in terms of symphonies. A month before their marriage and departure, on 12 February 1902, Mahler conducted the Court Opera Orchestra in the Viennese premiere of his Fourth Symphony, composed in 1892, the orchestration of which he retouched for the occasion. "It was the first time I had heard a work every day from the reading rehearsal on. . . . Thereafter I was to live with each of his works from its conception to the last time he conducted it, and those would be my most thrilling, most unforgettable hours."[11]

On a walk along the Danube Mahler told Alma, who had never heard the Fourth before, that it should be imagined as "an old painting on a golden ground."[12] The archaic scene envisioned may have been a glorious entry into heaven. For in the transition to the final movement, comprised of the *Wunderhorn* song *Das himmlische Leben* (Heavenly Life), a vibrant E major opening bursts into the cloudless blue sky of a child's view of heaven. The premiere was performed just a week shy of the anniversary of Mahler's *Um Mitternacht* experience. It had been an extraordinary year, and while recovering from the necessary surgery in Abbazia that April, Mahler had turned to this work-in-progress and developed and orchestrated its Finale.

Mahler had once again moved from darkness to light in mastering a personal crisis. In a manner comparable to the Finale of the Second Symphony, he composed himself into a landscape of paradise. Listening to the Fourth, Alma could scarcely imagine that she herself was a part of the impetus that produced the completed version of the symphony. In an initial conceptualization of the Fourth Symphony, Mahler had worked out ideas that led his early biographer Paul Bekker to suggest a program involving "a dream excursion into the heavenly fields of Paradise," progressing eventually "through a series of metamorphoses, until the last abode is reached, where all wishes are fulfilled, and where spirits dance and play and sing in everlasting bliss."[13] Despite the turbulence that Mahler himself created during courtship as well as a false start in the bedroom (at least in Alma's account), it was on this blissful note that the marriage began. With their wedding ceremony, followed by that of Justine and Arnold, which freed him from any guilt he may have felt about abandoning his longtime family companion, Mahler's ambivalence was quelled. Although his financial affairs were far from comfortable—as Alma would soon learn—his estate was established with the Villa Mahler in Maiernigg. Mahler's position at the opera was still secure, and composition would take a new direction with the summer's work on his Fifth Symphony. Now, anticipating the birth of a child, Mahler's life was as perfect as it would ever be.

A marker for all that was promising and joyful in their lives was the festival at Krefeld, a provincial industrial town in northwestern Germany, in early June 1902. There, Mahler performed the premiere of his Third Symphony. It was an unlikely place and occasion. Krefeld lacked a permanent orchestra, the organizers having assembled one for the celebration. Mahler and Alma (now well into her pregnancy) arrived after a long and arduous journey in the midst of a heat wave. But the event proved to be an early peak in their lives, a happy and special occasion that they would wistfully recall many times later. The rehearsals were held in nearby Gürzenich, where Mahler effectively whipped the ad hoc forces into shape. He was elated, and after rehearsing the first movement, called out to Alma, "And he saw it was good!"[14] Under the circumstances of his life, private as well as public, Mahler was perhaps entitled to a moment of identification with God.

Justine and Arnold were present for the performance, as was Richard Strauss (1864–1949)—colleague, rival, and sometimes friend. Strauss was president of the Allgemeiner Deutscher Musikverein, sponsor of the Krefeld Festival, and responsible for selecting Mahler's Third for the program. The performance was stunning and the audience no less enthusiastic than Mahler himself following the first movement. They broke out in a "tremendous ovation"; Alma described Strauss striding to the podium, "applauding emphatically as though to set his seal on its success." With each succeeding movement "the enthusiasm rose higher . . . and at the end the whole audience got up from their seats in a frenzy and surged to the front in a body." It was Mahler's greatest triumph to date and its effect on Alma was palpable: not only did this work "finally convince me of Mahler's greatness" but in the powerful state of excitement the occasion created, she suddenly felt the stirrings of their first child.[15]

As for Strauss, the wilder the audience became with each of the subsequent four movements, the more subdued he became, and Alma noted that during the final ovation he was nowhere to be seen. Four years younger than Mahler, Strauss occupied a special place in the Mahler household. The pair—Mahler and Strauss—both composers and among the most influential conductors of their time, were in a position to promote one another's music. Mahler and Strauss had met in 1887, Strauss writing afterward, "I made a new and very attractive acquaintance in Herr Mahler, who seemed to me to be a highly intelligent musician and conductor—one of the few modern conductors who know about tempo rubato."[16] Later, their conducting posts were nearly coextensive, Mahler's in Vienna from 1897 to 1910, and Strauss's in Berlin from 1897 to 1911. In many ways the two men represented the cities in which they presided musically: Mahler in the twilight of a great musical culture and Strauss in a city considered to be "rich . . . grandiose and sentimental."[17]

Their connection did not necessarily imply unbridled mutual admiration, however. Indeed, Alma's first encounter with Strauss and his wife, Pauline, was at the Viennese premiere of his opera Feuersnot in January, 1902, soon after she became engaged to Mahler. According to Alma, Mahler had not conducted: "He had a horror of the work," she wrote. Although this may have been the case, Mahler did indeed conduct on this occasion.[18] As a friend, Strauss could be disarmingly uninhibited about sharing his personal life. Mahler was more reserved toward Strauss, his attitude perhaps best summed up in his calling theirs "a friendship of reason." The continuation of the relationship was the more remarkable given the ingrained and seemingly casual anti-Semitism with which Strauss grew up and still shared with intimates. As for their compositions, Mahler wrote to Alma in January 1902, "My time will come when his is past."[19]

The marriage of Richard and Pauline Strauss was the subject of detailed and gossipy observations on Alma's part. Another relationship that figured in the Mahler family history, although referred to somewhat obscurely, was that of Justine and Arnold Rosé. Indeed, Gustav and Alma's marriage may be triangulated with those of the Strausses and the Rosés.

The Rosé couple had been an influence from the first, since the disastrous "full dress review" they had attended as a couple when Alma had to pass muster with Mahler's closest friends. Theirs had essentially been a five-year courtship, during which time Justine could not, from her perspective, abandon her brother until he too found a mate—an uncertainty at the time. Meanwhile, Arnold had become Mahler's friend and confidant, one of the closest friends he had made since childhood and adolescence, and all the more appreciated since the negative response of earlier friends to Alma. They frequently lunched together at the opera and were kindred spirits in musical standards and disdain for musical *Schlamperei*, or sloppiness. They also shared a moody disposition, perhaps even more pronounced on Arnold's part.[20] At the time of the double wedding, a cozy dance of musical chairs resulted in Alma's taking Justine's place in the Mahler Auenbruggergasse apartment as Justine moved several blocks away into Arnold's apartment in the Dorotheergasse.

The Rosés remained a presence from the time of the wedding lunch and the triumph at Krefeld through all the major events in the Mahlers' life. They were among the very few people Alma and Gustav saw regularly, a small circle that included Alma's parents, the Molls; the Zuckerkandls; and Klimt and Burckhard, a pair who came in time to a détente with Mahler for the sake of friendship with Alma. The Rosés were also part of a more exclusive circle of family friends from Paris that included Bertha Zuckerkandl's sister, Sophie Clemenceau, her husband, Paul (the brother of Georges Clemenceau, the prime minister of France from 1906 to 1909), and the music-loving Colonel Georges Picquart. These occasional visitors were all former champions of Alfred Dreyfus as, ironically, their hosts, the Mahlers and the Rosés, were nominally former Jews.

Curiously Alma nowhere acknowledged a major event in the lives of the Rosés, the birth of a child in 1906 named after her! It was around the time of a visit from the Parisians for performances of *Figaro*, *Don Giovanni*, and *Tristan*, an event Gustav called their "secret festival."[21] Except for Arnold's "deep brown moods," the domestic life of the Rosés appeared to be tranquil, loving, and fulfilled when at thirty-eight Justine gave birth to their Alma.

In contrast to the Rosés', the Strausses' married life was stormy, a fact that Alma made the most of in devastating vignettes. They had shared a box for the *Feuersnot* premiere, Pauline Strauss "raging the whole time. Nobody, she said, could possibly like that shoddy work." After the performance, when the foursome was about to adjourn to the Restaurant Hartmann, Pauline confronted Richard: "You thief, how dare you show yourself in my presence? I'm not coming with you—you make me sick." Mahler shooed the couple into his office, where they argued loudly. When the door was opened, Pauline emerged, announcing she was going home." Can't I take you there?" Richard begged. Her answer: "Ten paces behind me—not otherwise." At the restaurant Strauss was apologetic: "My wife's a bit rough sometimes, but that's what I need, you know."[22]

In Alma's view, Pauline had no redeeming qualities; her accounts gleefully coupled Richard's masochism with Pauline's sadism. Yet Alma knew much more about the pair that kindled her own jealousy and competition. Pauline was a professional singer and Strauss, who reputedly had an extraordinary understanding of voice, had been her teacher for five years before they became linked romantically. They married in 1894, when Strauss was thirty and Pauline thirty-two. Strauss had promoted Pauline's career before their marriage, bringing her with him to Bayreuth when he was assistant conductor there. Strauss introduced Pauline to Cosima Wagner, who favored him with advice for both teacher and pupil on the performance of *Lohengrin* and *Tannhäuser*. Later, when Strauss held a conducting post at the Weimar Opera, Pauline was brought into the company and sang roles in both of those operas as well as in Mozart operas. In effect, Strauss created her career. Pauline bore their only child in 1897, at the age of thirty-five; despite a difficult labor, she resumed her singing the following year. In contrast, Mahler not only failed to promote Alma's career; he forbade it, and Alma had agreed to relinquish her own musical aspirations in the bargain of marriage. Pauline had it all: a career in her prime as a singer, a baby, and a degree of control over her spouse that Alma could scarcely achieve with Mahler.

Another potential source of rivalry with Pauline was Strauss's financial success—and, consequently, the comfort, if not luxury, he could afford for his wife. Mahler had no such material ambitions, and from the beginning took it for granted that Alma shared his disinterest. When, on becoming engaged, he spoke disdainfully of the bourgeois custom of presenting a ring, Alma, as a "child of artists," felt compelled to agree. But in a fit of pique she would later write: "Money—vain! Clothes—vain! Looks—vain! Travel—vain! Nothing counted but the spirit."[23] And as for composing, she had buried her dream, yet there remained "a wound."[24]

Richard Strauss was unabashedly interested in money. Notoriously, while visiting America for the premiere of the *Sinfonia Domestica* in Carnegie Hall, he conducted two afternoon concerts farther downtown, in Wanamaker's Department Store! Pauline had evidently been the soloist at the Wanamaker concerts, for when Strauss later intemperately railed at another of his soloists, the singer's husband could find no worse insult than to shout, "My wife does not sing at Wanamaker's." Criticized by the German press, Strauss responded that "it was no disgrace to earn money."[25] When Pauline, having resumed her career after the birth of her child, was invited to tea by Cosima Wagner, she remarked, "Oh, my Richard is just too bourgeois for words." Cosima had responded, "Be glad of it, dear girl!"[26]

There is no doubt that Pauline was a difficult person: "temperamental, fiery, tactless, rude"—but beguiling. "Everything about Pauline Maria de Ahna was in primary colours. She expressed her views on anyone and anything without any conditional clauses." In contrast, Richard was said to be "phlegmatic and 'unflappable." He was frequently the apologist for his wife's outrageous behavior both within the family and outside. Nevertheless, others saw different aspects of the couple's relationship that eluded Alma. Lotte Lehman wrote of them in their twenty-fifth year of marriage, "I often caught a glance or a smile passing between her and her husband, touching in its love and happiness, and I began to sense something of the profound affection between those two human beings, a tie so elemental in strength that none of Pauline's shrewish truculence could ever trouble it seriously."[27] Perhaps Strauss was right when he said, "That's what I need, you know." Whatever the flaws as viewed from the outside, the couple shared an enduring attachment.

Mahler occasionally conspired with Alma in an indulgence of Strauss *Schadenfreude*. Writing from Berlin in 1907 while there for a performance of his Third Symphony, he described in detail and with obvious relish a visit to the Strausses' apartment. "*She* greeted me with: 'Sh!-sh! Richard's asleep,' and pulled me into her (very untidy) boudoir . . . and let loose a flood of nonsense about all the financial and sexual events of the last two years, rapidly interjecting questions about 'a thousand and one' things without waiting for the answers. . . . Suddenly she leapt up: 'But now to wake the brute.' Before I could stop her, she dragged me by both hands into his room, and roused him with a stentorian shout: 'Get up. Gustav's here.'" Shortly after, hurt that Strauss had not been present at a performance in Frankfurt but had nevertheless sent a card, Mahler noted, "Now that I look at it again it seems clear that Frau Pauline put her foot down!"[28]

Such exchanges implied a difference in the two marriages and, like many such instances of marital gossip, were a form of self-congratulation. Mahler did not suppress his admiration for the finest of Strauss's work, although he was sometimes bemused: "I don't know what to make of Strauss. How is one to explain his unequalness and jumbling together of good and bad?"[29] He ruminated to Alma, "A Vulcan lives and labours under a heap of slag, a subterranean fire—not merely a firework!"[30] In referring to "jumbling" and the "bad," Mahler doubtless alluded to Strauss's *Sinfonia Domestica*, among other works. Many were shocked or embarrassed by Strauss's "depiction," indeed, "exploitation . . . of his blameless Bavarian home life."[31]

Autobiographical sources were symbolized in Mahler's music rather than blatantly represented in some literal fashion. Mahler was in this sense a master of sublimation, as deeply personal sources of musical content were divested of the particular and rendered universal. Strauss's confessional tendency could literally bubble over into his music. His opera, *Intermezzo*, which had to do with a farcical marital misunderstanding, so literally represented an episode in the Strausses' married life (when Pauline threatened divorce, owing to a misinterpreted letter) that even his wife was shocked at the exposure of their private life.[32]

A prime example of Mahler's autobiographical gestures in music can be seen in his song *Liebst du um Schoenheit* (Do You Love Beauty), the last of Mahler's individual Rückert settings, composed especially for Alma. The song's underlying meaning remained private and the piece was never orchestrated. But as a love song, it can be shared and appreciated without deconstruction. In setting the words "If you love for youth, oh then don't love me," Mahler selected lines that reflected his ongoing concern with age. Indeed, the text "lists and dismisses three of the concerns that distressed the couple—his appearance, his age and his disdain for material good."[33] Stephen Hefling has explored further autobiographical meanings, including reassurance to Alma during their first summer of marriage when Anna von Mildenburg, who owned a house near the Mahlers, was nastily intrusive, tending to humiliate Alma. While an irate Mahler wished to ban Anna from the villa, Alma sensibly suggested more structured musical evenings would be better. One evening they "played and sang the whole of the last act of *Siegfried* together." When Mahler composed *Liebst du um Schoenheit*, he buried the manuscript "in between the title-page and the first page of the *Valkyrie*" for Alma to find. Alma wrote in her diary, "The song is so indescribably moving . . . it almost brought me to tears." Whether tears of laughter and relief were a part of her response is not recorded. But the message in the final strophe was an "extraordinary token of consolation and hope for renewed love."[34] Indeed, it expressed a commitment to Alma that would remain a marker for Mahler's love during their future marital crisis, in 1910:

> If you love for Love's sake,
> Oh yes, love me!
> Love me forever,
> I love you ever, evermore.

Mahler's triumph with his Third Symphony in Krefeld opened a world of opportunity. From 1902 on, interest in Mahler both as conductor and as composer increased and as a result he toured widely in Europe. The conductor Willem Mengelberg, who would become Mahler's champion in Holland, had been present at the Krefeld performance and thus began Mahler's special relationship with that country. For many years afterward Gustav and Alma would refer in their correspondence to Krefeld as one of the most important milestones in their life together.

The summer of 1902 was the first that the two spent together in Maiernigg, where Mahler set to work on the Fifth Symphony. Two movements were complete and the rest was in draft. The trumpet's opening statement suggests multiple meanings. Some hear the celebratory introduction to Mendelssohn's *Wedding March* that related to Mahler's new status in life; some a fanfare of triumph, albeit a muted one, reflecting Krefeld; but still others an omen of the future, as Mahler marked the first movement "Funeral March." All interpretations are biographically relevant at this stage in Mahler's life.

A routine was established at Maiernigg to accommodate the precious days of summer when Mahler composed. His habit was to work on new material during this period, and to revise and score at various times the rest of the year. During the many hours he spent on trains traveling to and from conducting engagements, Mahler doubtless performed mental tasks related to generating new musical ideas as well as revisions. Over the summer he usually worked with considerable speed, suggesting that much creative preparation had already been accomplished. Mahler was in a "training" mode as surely as any athlete, and life was honed to a singleness of purpose from the moment he arose. Alma reported:

> Mahler got up at six or six-thirty every day. As soon as he was awake, he rang for the cook, who promptly prepared his breakfast and carried it up a steep, slippery trail to his forest study, two hundred feet above the house. (She was forbidden to use the regular road, lest he meet her on his way up; before work he could not stand seeing anyone.) The study was a one-room brick hut with a door and three windows, a grand piano, a bookshelf with the collected works of Kant and Goethe. No music but Bach's. About noon he came down, changed and went for a swim . . . I would sit on the steps and he would climb out to chat, lie on the sun deck until his body was crimson, and jump in again . . . until he felt reinvigorated. Then we walked back through the garden . . . and sat down to lunch. The soup had to be on the table. Our afternoons were spent walking. Rain or shine, we walked for three or four hours, or rowed around the gleaming, heat-spewing lake.

Nor did Mahler stop composing during the afternoon respite:

> Often he stopped and stood with the sun burning down on his hatless skull, drew out a notebook, wrote, thought, wrote some more. Sometimes he beat time in the air before writing the notes down. This could go on for an hour or more, with me sitting on a tree trunk or in the grass, not daring to look at him. From time

to time, when an idea pleased him, he threw me a smile, knowing that nothing on earth made me happier.[35]

If life then was idyllic for Mahler, favoring his creative work, it was inevitably less so for Alma. She tried at first to resume playing the piano but Mahler, with his acute hearing, found it disturbing. As a result she occupied herself by copying portions of the symphony as soon as Mahler finished them. The Fifth Symphony was completed that summer and Mahler worked on the fair copy through the winter.

Back in Vienna, life for Alma was only somewhat more stimulating, but no less routine. She and her husband rarely went out together.

> His winter schedule was like clockwork, too: up at seven, break-fast, work, to the Opera at nine, lunch at one o'clock sharp. The Opera called when he left; when he rang downstairs, the soup went on the table in our fourth-floor apartment; the apartment door stood open, so he would not have to wait. He stormed through the rooms, flinging superfluous doors aside like a hurri-cane, washed up, and set down. As at Maiernigg, lunch was fol-lowed by a foot race: four times around the Belvedere, or all the way along the ring. Coffee and cake at 5:00 P.M. sharp. Then he went to the Opera etc.[36]

It is hard to believe that Alma's breathtaking account of daily life at the Auenbruggergasse apartment was not meant to be ironic in tone—espe-cially the part with soup on the table and the door ajar in anticipation of the arrival of the whirlwind. The same holds true of her chapter title, "Splendid Isolation." For there is no question that Alma felt isolated from the people and pleasures of her former life, above all, from a pre-occupied Mahler. In her diary she confided her growing hurt and resent-ment: "I told Gustav how hurt I am by his utter disinterest in what goes on inside me. My knowledge of music, for instance, suits him only as I use it for him." Adding insult to injury, Mahler had responded cruelly, "Is it my fault that your budding dreams have not come true?" Clearly, Alma felt that it was indeed. Mahler was not completely ignorant of Alma's situation and on other occasions a degree of empathy supervened. One day he returned home unexpectedly to find Alma in tears. He put his hand on her head, murmuring wistfully, "Dreams that never flow-ered."[37] Such episodes suggest that for Alma, a state of chronic depres-sion was already developing, as being dutiful in the role of Mahler's wife clashed inwardly with her own needs for creativity and admiration.

Of paramount interest to Mahler was the child Alma was bearing. The birth was a difficult one—a breech presentation, which Alma, no doubt recalling the hot three- or four-hour walks at Maiernigg and the after-noon "foot races" in Vienna, attributed to "overexertion during preg-nancy." Mahler was beside himself during her long labor and afterward exclaimed, "How can men bear the guilt of such suffering and go on begetting children?" He wept at Alma's bedside and later, learning of the "cross birth," roared with laughter: "That's my child! Shows the world the part it deserves."[38] The baby was a girl, born on 3 November 1902, only a few days short of a year from her parents' first meeting at the Zuckerkandls'. They called her Maria, after Mahler's mother, and gave her the nickname Putzi.

Alma Schindler Mahler and Maria (Putzi) Mahler, 1906.

A second child was conceived the following autumn, after a peaceful summer of the now familiar routine had yielded two movements of the Sixth Symphony. The birth of another girl on 15 June 1904, just before the third summer at Maiernigg, completed the Mahler family. They called her Anna, after Alma's mother, Anna Moll. Her middle name, Justine, reciprocated the Rosés' naming their child after Alma. Anna's wide-open blue eyes and unswerving gaze earned her the nickname Guckerl, after the term *gucken*, "to look or peep." Great things were anticipated, as Alma noted: "The birth, at midday, in the middle of the week (Wednesday), in the middle of the month, in the middle of the year, might have been an allegory."[39]

Mahler's gift to Alma that summer came in music form. It was the only time in his composing career that he attempted to depict a person musically: the soaring second theme of the first movement of Mahler's Sixth Symphony was meant to represent Alma, and perhaps his bursting feeling of joy at the happy events of the previous two years as well. But there was an ironic side to the "Alma" theme. Her chronic discontent had produced a marital instability that had been briefly obscured in the fulfillment of family. This very instability of love, rather than its constancy, may have led to the creation of the Alma theme in the Sixth Symphony. It is at once passionate and yearning in its first four rising pitches; then resignation follows in the descending figure.

Did Mahler owe a debt to fate for his good fortune? If Alma's superstition about Gucki was optimistic, Mahler's superstition about himself was ominous. The Sixth Symphony, completed that summer, was clouded by a musical idea contained in its fourth movement. This consisted of three "hammer blows," short, powerful, but dull-sounding strokes of a nonmetallic character. Mahler pursued its correct performance obsessively, even ordering a specially constructed drum. For all the tensions in their marriage, Alma and Mahler shared a keen sensitivity to potential musical meanings. In this instance, the portentous musical passage brought them both to tears. Mahler was said to have musically depicted the downfall of the "hero" of his symphonies. In this case, the hero was the composer himself, "on whom fall three blows of fate, the last of which fells him as a tree is felled."[40] Alma wrote, "The music and what it foretold touched us so deeply."

But 1904 was not a year of tragedy. On the contrary, Mahler was approaching the height of his career. He was in demand as a conductor and as a composer; there were increasing numbers of performances. An advertisement for the Fifth Symphony two years later boasts "20 performances in two years." If anything, a creative climax that would persist until 1907 was building and the summer of 1904 was particularly productive.

It was Mahler's very success that inwardly posed a threat. He had temporarily overcome the anxiety that had spawned *Um Mitternacht* in 1901. Life had been the answer to death and Mahler had achieved marriage and rebirth in a family. The "heroes" of his early symphonies had triumphed but had they now gone too far? The words of the last of the *Wunderhorn* songs echoed in real life: "Had I but remained a drummer boy, I would not lie imprisoned." The myth Mahler was caught up in was that of Icarus. The "wings that I have won" of the triumphant final moments of the Second Symphony threatened to disintegrate, having flown too high.

The hammer blows of the Sixth Symphony constituted a preemptive strike against fate: "You cannot destroy me; only I myself can deliver your hammer blows!" Whatever else Mahler had been credited for, he was not a prophet and could not have foreseen the blows of loss that destiny had in store for him in 1907 and thereafter. And if he had, three blows would not have sufficed. But, yielding to superstition, Mahler reorchestrated the final movement, reducing the sentence of three hammer blows to two.

What may have been behind this enactment was revealed in a strange episode in May 1906, when Mahler conducted the Sixth Symphony at a festival in Essen. He exerted special care in planning the premiere, turning down at least one offer in 1905 from Ferruccio Busoni (1866–1924) because "everything must be just right."[41] He knew that the work "would impose enigmas that only a generation that has absorbed and digested my first five can tackle."[42] Mahler arrived in Essen nine days early to refine the score, correct the parts, and rehearse the orchestra. Alma arrived two days before the concert, finding Mahler "sad and worried" in anticipating the dress rehearsal.

> When it was over, Mahler walked up and down in the artist's room, sobbing, wringing his hands, unable to control himself. . . . On the

day of the concert Mahler was so afraid that his agitation might get the better of him that out of shame and anxiety he did not conduct the symphony well. He hesitated to bring out the dark omen behind this terrible last movement.[43]

This was one of the rare times in Mahler's life when what he had encoded in his music symbolically became reality. What had been hidden in the music emerged starkly, and Mahler was confronted with inescapable and intolerable meaning: his own death. It was as if he had created a monster, comparable to Mary Shelley's *Frankenstein*. And now it led a life of its own, out of the creator's control.

Nevertheless, the creative impetus that energized the Sixth continued as Mahler turned to what seemed an unlikely work, *Kindertotenlieder* (Songs on the Death of Children). He had written three of the songs the summer of 1901, scarcely two months before he met Alma, in his sudden shift from the *Wunderhorn* texts to those of the poet Friedrich Rückert. Yet these events—the composition of songs on the death of children, and courtship and marriage—were parts of the same impulse. When Mahler's creative thinking—in word and music alike—turned to children, these thoughts were imbued with mourning. During Mahler's childhood the visit of the horse-drawn hearse had been a regular event in family life. Enduring into maturity, and now revived in his own parenthood, was Mahler's identification with grieving parents.

The immediate occasion for Mahler's turning to completion of *Kindertotenlieder* was the promise of a premiere Mahler had made to Alexander Zemlinsky and Arnold Schoenberg. They had formed a new musical group of which Mahler was the revered senior member, the Vereinigung Schaffender Tonkünstler, or the Society of Creative Contemporary Composers. A concert of Mahler's lieder was planned for the following season, when he was to be named honorary president.[44] Mahler apparently avoided informing Alma that he was undertaking completion of the song cycle, knowing that Alma would find it incomprehensible.

> I can understand setting such frightful words to music if one had no children, or had lost those one had. [Even] Rückert did not write these harrowing elegies solely out of his imagination: they

were dictated by the cruelest loss of his whole life. What I cannot understand is bewailing the death of children . . . hardly an hour after having kissed and fondled them. I exclaimed at the time: "For heaven's sake, don't tempt Providence!"[45]

The Rückert songs were too close to the bone for Alma and, understandably, she was unable to gain distance. For while the *voice* in the song is that of the father, it is the mother who is explicitly named with reference to the ghost-children. In the third of the songs, *Wenn dein Mütterlein tritt zur Tür herein* (When Your Dear Mother Comes through the Door), the father gazes upon the spot next to the mother's empty hand where the dead child would be expected. Alma remarked: "To my mind there was something eerie about it: in the garden, these two wonderfully gifted children were squealing with joy, and in his study Mahler could sing of their death."[46]

Alma Mahler with daughters.

The boundaries of music and life had intersected previously. Prior to the summer, in a letter to Alma from a conducting engagement in Cologne, Mahler had written, "I'm worried about Putzi in this weather, always wet and cold and unfriendly." In doing so, he had unconsciously quoted Rückert's words from the last of the *Kindertotenlieder*, *In diesem Wetter, in diesem Braus*: "In this weather, this blustery weather, I would never have sent the children out."[47]

Mahler responded to the illness and death of children like nothing else. In 1903, learning of the illness and death of the child of a clarinetist in the Vienna Court Opera, he wrote a condolence letter:

> Dear Herr Professor,
>
> It was only during rehearsal that I learnt of the terrible misfortune that has befallen you, and I thank you from my heart for making the great sacrifice of taking part in the rehearsal despite your great sorrow. . . . Please accept my deepest sympathy and my warmest thanks . . . I shall never forget this.[48]

"The children had a great effect on our lives," Alma wrote. "Mahler had more time for us: he could hardly tear himself away from the two

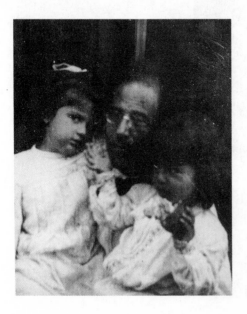

Mahler with daughters.

little girls, with each of whom he had an intimate, oddly individual relationship."[49] The portrait of Mahler as father to two young children is private and unfamiliar. Alma revealed that "for each he had a special form of entertainment—stories, jokes or funny faces. He loved telling the elder one Brentano's fairytale—'Gockel, Hinkel and Gackeleia.'"[50] Anticipating the summer of 1904, Mahler took pains to write to Alma about the placement of his daughters' play area: "The place we chose from memory is much too small. Putzi would scarcely be able to turn round." Designating a more suitable spot he had inspected carefully, he arranged to have it fenced in and filled with clean sand. "There the children will have a playground to last them for years."[51]

Success in Krefeld had had its negative side in that Mahler's conducting engagements became more frequent. Alma's perception that he had more time for family doubtless had to do with the quality of his presence. Mahler was devoted to the children, and letters expressed both his concern and regret at being apart from them. Despite the demands of both his careers, Mahler's need for the closeness of family was profound. When not distracted by frenzied activity, he did not tolerate separation well. Even in Amsterdam, which he called his "musical home," he wrote, "It's a ghastly life, waiting about in a foreign place. However kindly you're treated—but in the end it's all vexation and you feel utterly forsaken."[52] Ever mindful of his posterity, Mahler chastised Alma for her "lazy" correspondence and complained, "You never say a word of the children . . . Putzi must have quite forgotten me and Guckerl won't even know me again."[53] Mahler's sense of isolation was particularly apparent when he arrived earlier than Alma for their summer sojourn. He generally needed a break between the opera season and his summer's composing, for "all life and energy come to a stop, and it takes two or three weeks before I can rouse myself." During this period Mahler tended to struggle with fears of failing creativity before he immersed himself in work. In the interim he would miss Alma and the children terribly.[54]

Although Mahler would refer to the "children" in his letters, he would more often single out Putzi. Mahler had formed an especially strong bond with this child named after his mother; in fact, the new father had "worshipped her from the start."[55] According to Alma, Putzi was "entirely" Mahler's child. "Very beautiful, defiant and unapproachable, she promised to become dangerous. Black locks, great blue eyes." The child would seek Mahler in his study each day, emerging jam-smeared. "They held long conversations there together. Nobody has ever known what about. I never disturbed them."[56]

What the younger child, Anna, would remember from her childhood was Mahler's smile: "When he suddenly took notice of me, that complete change, and as it were a burst of warmth."[57] Anna also recalled a game Mahler played with her when she would refuse to eat: "Well—Gucki I was called—go out and send in your friend Gladys . . . and I did that, returned as Gladys . . . and sat down and said, 'Gucki's very silly, this is awfully good,' and ate it without any trouble whatsoever."[58] Anna's favorite photograph of her father was a saintly image that few would agree bore his likeness. As she described it: "Mahler as I knew him when I was a child: relaxed, delicate, good-humored, infinitely intelligent and understanding."[59]

In the middle of the productive summer of 1904, as if making himself a promise for the following year, Mahler also sketched out two of the inner movements of his next major work, the Seventh Symphony. He called them his "architect's drawings."[60] The promise was indeed fulfilled, but not without difficulty. Although Alma related that the entire work was completed "in one burst," Mahler suffered initially from a transient creative block. He feared the precious summer would be wasted as he made a solitary trip to the Dolomites in search of the rest and change of scene that might favor inspiration. None was forthcoming until his return to Maiernigg: while Mahler was being rowed across the Wörthersee, the rhythm of the oars sounded in his ear as the opening bars of the symphony's first movement.

Alma could continue to measure married life in terms of symphonies. The summer of the Seventh was their fourth in the "splendid isolation" of Maiernigg, which in truth was not quite so splendid for Alma. Mahler remained complacent while Alma, not one to suffer wordlessly, complained relentlessly. After one particularly bitter encounter, she confided to her diary, "He said he could feel that I don't love him—and at this moment he is certainly right . . . I realize that the man who has to spread his peacock-train in public wants to 'relax' at home. That, after all, is woman's fate. But it isn't mine!"[61]

One burden Alma justifiably resented involved money. Mahler had been in debt when they married and among Alma's duties their first five years together was repaying the debts Mahler had incurred during his bachelor years. For the most part these related to the family crisis and its aftermath in the support of multiple households. Alma attributed the debts from when brother and sister shared an apartment to "Justine's incredible folly." The end was now in sight but the amount had not been insignificant, some fifty thousand crowns. (This was considerably more than Mahler's annual salary at the opera during his best years.)[62] "He took it all as a matter of course. I existed only as his shadow, paying his debt, making no noise."[63]

The following year held more social stimulation. In Vienna they saw not only the Rosés but several composer friends as well. When they were in Krefeld, Alma had befriended the thirty-three-year-old composer Hans Pfitzner, who had come to see Mahler and virtually beg him to consider producing his opera *Die Rose vom Liebesgarten* (The Rose in Love's Garden). Alma, in an adjoining alcove, had been appalled at the degradation to which Pfitzner submitted himself and no doubt at her husband's lack of empathy for a fellow composer. She had revealed that she was listening and, taking the younger man's hand, interceded on his behalf. A bond was formed between the two and later Alma was instrumental in promoting Pfitzner's music with Mahler. Alma and Pfitzner had begun to correspond and the composer had dedicated a string quartet to her. Now, in 1905, Mahler was mounting his opera and Pfitzner came to Vienna for the rehearsals. Pfitzner asked Alma to play some of her songs for him and Alma was ecstatic. More than this, repaying her empathy with his own, he commiserated with her having given up composing and wished they could work together, which meant a great deal to Alma.[64]

A year earlier the Mahlers had met the playwright Gerhart Hauptmann, with whom Mahler had an immediate rapport. The two men had talked much of the night at that first meeting. A fond relationship developed between the couple and the author, and when Hauptmann came to Vienna for a performance of his plays they would dine together.

Also that year, Schoenberg and Zemlinsky founded their composers' society, with Mahler invited to be honorary president. Dinner parties were held at the Mahlers' apartment for discussion of society business. Alma served as hostess on such occasions.

After marriage Mahler had maintained professional contact with Alexander von Zemlinsky although he had forbidden Alma from seeing him. The wound Alma had inflicted in leaving Zemlinsky was slow in healing, but the business of music was another matter and Zemlinsky responded in a friendly manner to Mahler's encouragement to keep him informed of his work.[65] It was in his work, however, that Zemlinsky sought a modicum of revenge. The summer before the Mahlers met, Zemlinsky had been contemplating paying homage to Alma with a stage work in which he visualized her playing the lead. After she rejected him, he considered an opera based on Gorky's novella "Malva," a close anagram for Alma. In "Malva," "an ageing fisherman leaves his wife for a younger woman; she in turn favours his twenty-two-year-old son; conflict arises, and the tale culminates in violence."[66] Mahler was highly sensitive to the age issue and when Zemlinsky informed him of this project, Mahler was "completely opposed" to it. The project was abandoned. Through her social involvement with the Vereinigung, Alma saw Zemlinsky again and he was permitted to come to the apartment to play duets with her. Alma must have hoped to resume lessons since she offered him payment, which he refused.

As the summer of 1906 approached, Mahler had asked Alma to join him on tour to a three-day festival in Strasbourg, the first Fête Musicale d'Alsace-Lorraine. Mahler would conduct a performance of Beethoven's Ninth Symphony for which a chorus of 240 was anticipated; he would also perform his own Fifth Symphony. Strauss had been invited, too, and he conducted what proved to be a disastrous performance of the *Sinfonia Domestica*, having requested only two rehearsals to Mahler's four. Strauss's rage spilled on to Mahler, whom he felt "monopolized the whole of the rehearsal time."[67]

The Beethoven performance was attended by French friends, the "Dreyfus Four": the journalist, statesman, and leader of the Dreyfusards, Paul Clemenceau (1841–1929); his wife, Sophie, the sister of Bertha Zuckerkandl, at whose home Alma and Gustav had met; the mathematician and politician General Georges Picquart (1854–1914); and Paul Painleve (1863–1933), who was twice prime minister of France and a baron

L'Allemand. All had been involved in seeking exoneration during the Dreyfus affair that extended from 1894 to 1906 and was only now concluding. It had been in Paul Clemenceau's newpaper that the novelist Emile Zola wrote his famous letter, "J'Accuse." The Mahlers particularly admired Picquart for openly contesting the veracity of the Dreyfus accusations. Indeed, Alma found him to be more courageous than Zola since he had risked far more personally.

Summers and symphonies flowed as if they might never stop. Alma, perhaps placated by a social life that was somewhat revived if still compromised, would look back on the summer of 1906 as "our last summer of peace and beauty and content." After the uneasy fortnight he spent haunted by the fears of failing creativity that had plagued him the year before, an idea came to Mahler in a flash—the powerful E-flat major chord with orchestra and organ, and a chorus intoning the Latin hymn "Veni creator spiritus." "He composed and wrote down the whole opening chorus to the half-forgotten words."[68] Mahler telegraphed his friend Fritz Löhr in Vienna: "Very urgent!" In the message he requested a translation from the Latin poem and asked about its scanning. "It is all from 'Veni creator spiritus,'" he wrote, adding, "Please reply *at once, express*! Otherwise it will be too late. I need it both as creator and as creature."[69] Miraculously, when the complete text arrived, it exactly fit the already composed music.

In Mahler's retelling, "The Spiritus Creator took hold of me and drove me on for the next eight weeks until my greatest work was done."[70] Like the symphony, the summer's work fell nicely into two parts as the composition was interrupted by a scheduled performance of *Don Giovanni* in Salzburg midseason. Returning to Maiernigg, Mahler worked "feverishly" on the Eighth's conclusion, the setting from part 2 of Goethe's *Faust*. The passion of the "Alma" theme of the Sixth gave way to the purified and fully sublimated musical idea that ends the symphony, accompanied by Goethe's words "Das Ewig-Weiblich zieht uns hinan" (Woman eternally shows us the way). Cast in the lingua franca of the culturally educated, these words summed up the era's idealization of the feminine.[71] From a personal point of view, Mahler's experience with the everyday *Weiblich* was fulfilled. He had the rare privilege of experiencing all the primary relationships life has to offer with women: mother, sister, wife, and daughter. The successful composition of the Eighth at the height of Mahler's creative power was a harbinger of its premiere four years hence, an occasion hailed as a religious conclave for a generation. What would intervene, however, was Mahler's own *annus horribilis.*

Alma's published memoirs suggest some abatement of her by now chronic discontent. Perhaps Mahler, who tended to be more conversant with abstract symbols, had learned something more quotidian about women. He appears to have shared more with her and was tenderly solicitous on the still rare occasions when they went out to places other than the opera. She observed, "Mahler began at that time to have a new and stronger feeling for me, a conscious feeling in contrast with his earlier self-absorption."[72] Relief from indebtedness and from the pressure to manage the repayment schedule also calmed Alma.

In any case, Mahler was a devoted correspondent with his wife. In the course of his many engagements outside Vienna, he wrote to Alma regularly, sometimes more than once a day. He also kept in touch by frequent telegrams, many little more than a loving greeting. In the autumn of 1906, for example, just before leaving Vienna for Breslau, he sent the message "Another lovely morning-greeting, my love Almschili." And from Breslau later in the day an epigram, rhymed in German: "gluekliche ankunft herrliches unterkunft baldigewiederkunft gustav" (happy arrival —splendid accommodations—soon to return).[73]

The year 1906 was arguably the most gratifying in Mahler's life thus far and 1907 began on a promising note, with "beautiful productions at the opera" and "work and our peaceful routine" at home. The Viennese press complained perennially about Mahler and more than once he had threatened to resign. But, rather suddenly, the situation worsened. The season opened with a critical salvo that would be taken up increasingly during the year. The critic Hans Puchstein published a bill of particulars regarding what he believed were Mahler failures at the opera. These included not performing the works of certain composers and choosing poor assistants (especially Bruno Walter). Mahler was attacked personally as well, for his "moody character." In short, he was deemed "unfit to direct the Vienna Opera."[74] A campaign in the press ensued, the charges soon centering on Mahler's frequent absences while on conducting tours. This was particularly problematic for opera management since it made it difficult for Mahler in his administrative capacity to effectively deny the other artists leaves for performances elsewhere. Indeed, at the end of the previous year Mahler had conducted in Breslau, Munich, Brünn, and Graz, and with the start of the new year he had requested leave to conduct in Berlin and Frankfurt.[75]

There had also been a disagreement regarding the contract of a singer who had high-ranking connections. The hostility of the orchestra created further tension. In addition, the endemic anti-Semitism of Vienna now sometimes took "creative" directions. In one instance surprise was expressed at Mahler's idealism, a kind of left-handed compliment since, after all, it was widely accepted that "semites in general have a materialistic approach to life."[76]

By spring the adverse conditions at the opera had escalated and yet another element became apparent: Mahler's physical fatigue. Even under the stress of continued criticism, Mahler made prodigious conducting efforts and habitually upheld his stringent artistic principles at the opera. The tipping point, however, was his scheduling engagements in Rome for which he had not obtained permission to be away. In this act he was complicit in the decision for him to resign his post—more specifically, in the request for approval to do so from the emperor, since the position was state appointed.

Meanwhile, other opportunities beckoned, promising relief from the tensions of the year. In New York, Heinrich Conried, the director of the Metropolitan Opera, was seeking a prominent German conductor to sustain the quality of the German opera repertoire for which he was well known. Negotiations culminated in a meeting in Berlin at the beginning of June. When Mahler retreated wearily to Maiernigg at the end of the month, he had agreed to a two-month period in New York the following season, from mid-February to mid-April.

Despite a sense of betrayal by the formerly supportive management of the opera, its orchestra, and the press, which was increasingly publishing lies, Mahler was heartened by a public letter signed by seventy admirers. Included were many of the most prominent cultural figures of the time, Hugo von Hofmannsthal, Arthur Schnitzler, Stefan Zweig, Arnold Schoenberg, Gustav Klimt, and Josef Hoffmann among them.[77] But Mahler was already embarking on a new journey, once again cheating fate in personal mastery—as if reprising the Second Symphony's "wings that I have won."

Like his parents, who had sought a new life in the move to Iglau, Mahler was setting off on an adventure and a new phase of his career. In the short term he anticipated having more time to compose, and more money for a better life for himself and Alma. Yet he had sacrificed considerably. Never again would he have the opportunity to conduct operatic productions of a quality as high as those in Vienna. Nor would he ever be as effective in making his mark on a major musical institution— indeed, on the musical life of an entire city and culture. Moreover, Vienna was now as much a home as this "thrice homeless" man would ever have, and he would risk homesickness during his tours abroad. It was hardly an unblemished victory over fate.

All the details of arrangements in America were shared with Alma, who, despite her tendency to feel slighted in the course of Mahler's efforts, was very much under consideration in his negotiations. As a result of his talks with Conried, Mahler had gained some perspective on his salary in Vienna; it was low, particularly by American standards. Significantly, he would now be able to provide Alma with the higher standard of living she craved. He had tried unsuccessfully to phone her from Berlin after his initial meeting with Conried in June but settled for writing a letter, in which he enthusiastically detailed the offer in terms of money and prestige: "First and foremost he wanted me on the same footing as Caruso."[78] Alma would have known what this meant.

9

A CHILD'S DEATH

During Gustav and Alma's sixth summer in Maiernigg on the Wörthersee, in 1907, their child died.

> On the third day after our arrival in the country the elder of the two children developed alarming symptoms. It was scarlet fever and diphtheria, and from the first there was no hope. We passed a fortnight in an agony of dread . . . Mahler loved this child devotedly; he hid himself in his room every day, *taking leave of her in his heart.* On the last night when a tracheotomy was resorted to, I posted his servant at his door to keep him in his room if the noise disturbed him. . . . She lay choking, with her large eyes wide open. Our agony dragged on one more whole day. Then the end came. . .
>
> Mahler, weeping and sobbing, went again and again to the door of my bedroom where she was; then fled away to be out of earshot. It was more than he could bear.[1]

"Fate had not done with us," Alma lamented. When the hearse came to claim the body, she fainted. Dr. Carl Blumenthal, who had attended the child, was called again and Mahler, "thinking to make a cheerful diversion and distract us said: 'Come along doctor, wouldn't you like to examine me too?'" The doctor, listening to Mahler's heart, responded, "Well, you've no cause to be proud of a heart like that." Presumably he had heard the heart murmur that characteristically resulted from childhood rheumatic fever. Alma wrote: "This verdict marked the beginning of the end for Mahler."[2]

This event was hardly "cheerful diversion" by any account. Why would Mahler have presented himself thus? It was hardly an appropriate gesture even if, as Alma suggested, he wished to provide some "good news" to temper the tragic. Regardless, the heart sounds that purportedly impressed the doctor could not entirely have been news. The murmur— caused by turbulent blood flow through damaged heart valves—would have been audible to earlier examining physicians. When Mahler had suffered from hemorrhage in 1901, the attending physicians had listened anxiously and repeatedly to his heart during the course of the night. Alma herself may already have become aware of the murmur, which might have been audible when she was lying close to her husband. If so, one wonders why she did not insist on his getting medical attention earlier.

The universal symbolism of the "broken heart" may have lain in Mahler's unconscious. Perhaps, more specifically, there was also Mahler's own death wish, as in King David's biblical lament: "O my son Absalom, my son, my son Absalom! Would I had died instead of you."[3] Clearly Mahler was sufficiently frightened, as he had been in 1901, by the prospect of his death, the wish and the fear intermingled. A week after the shock of Putzi's death, he departed for Vienna to see Professor Friedrich Kovacs, a heart specialist.

This consultation would have a profound effect on Mahler's customary lifestyle. The doctor required Mahler to give up the strenuous activities that were so important to him: swimming, bicycle riding, hiking, and mountain climbing. These restrictions, according to the accepted medical practice of the time, were in fact unnecessary. Worse, they tended to induce cardiac neurosis. In Mahler's case, this would take the form of fear of sudden death. Later that summer, while out walking with Alma he would stop frequently to take his pulse and ask her to listen to his heart. He even purchased a pedometer.

A year later found Mahler both cautious and distressed at the prescribed inactivity. He wrote to Bruno Walter in the summer of 1908 of "a change of my whole way of life."

> You can imagine how hard the latter comes to me. For many years I have been used to constant and vigorous exercise—roaming

about in the mountains and the woods, and then, like a kind of jaunty bandit, bearing home my drafts. I used to go to my desk, only as a peasant goes into his barn, to work up my sketches. Even spiritual indisposition used to disappear after a good trudge (mostly uphill.)—Now I am told to avoid any exertion, keep a constant eye on myself, and not walk much.[4]

Vigorous physical activity was essential for tension reduction and creative work. Moreover, Mahler explicitly tended to develop musical ideas outdoors. Significantly, activity served to ward off "spiritual indisposition"—depression—in a kind of self-healing.

The restrictions eventually proved to be erroneous. But the relationship between valvular disease and infection of the lining of the heart was known, and for the latter (endocarditis) there was no cure. Therefore, there was indeed cause for concern.

Nevertheless, Mahler could not restrain himself completely. A photograph taken the same summer as the letter to Walter placed him in a locale (in Fischleinboden, where the Dolomites and the Alps meet) reachable only by active walking, perhaps even "mostly uphill." In the photograph he is leaning jauntily on his walking stick.

Putzi died on 5 July 1907. The bereaved family fled the scene of domestic tragedy and spent the rest of the summer seeking the beauty of the mountains of the then Austrian Tirol. At first, they stayed in the village of Schluderbach—not far from the district of Altschluderbach, where Mahler would spend the next three summers. Later they moved to Fischleinboden. He had no further need that summer of the Maiernigg häuschen, the composing hut that incubated the Fifth through the Eighth symphonies.

The flight from Maiernigg recapitulated Mahler's earliest family experience when, following the death of his infant brother, the family left for a new life in the county seat of Iglau. His parents had fled tragedy and sought opportunity. Similarly, for Gustav and Alma a new phase of life in America beckoned.

But mourning must run its course. Immediately following the child's death Alma and Mahler had clung to each other: "We could not bear being parted for an hour," Alma wrote. After her mother arrived, the

Mahler at Fischleinboden, 1907.

three even slept together. "We dreaded what might happen if any one of us left the room."[5] When death occurs so suddenly, grief is often accompanied by an unnamed terror, a sense of vulnerability to the unknown that leads one to seek the comfortingly familiar among people and places. Vigilance is another characteristic of this posttraumatic period. In this respect, Mahler and Alma had similar immediate responses. A sign that mourning was beginning, their initial dread eased as they returned briefly to Maiernigg in August to put affairs in order. To their surprise, they found that despite their decision to sell the villa, they could both still enjoy its charms. Shortly, however, Mahler returned to Vienna to pursue duties that occupied his mind so completely that he nearly forgot Alma's twenty-eighth birthday on 31 August. Already it was clear that Mahler and Alma mourned in very different styles.

Alma was soon left to grieve—with "tears and philosophy," according to Bruno Walter—along with her mother.[6] Mahler's obligations at the opera would not terminate until 31 December, after which Felix

Weingartner would succeed him. Mahler immersed himself as he customarily did, in his work. The season would start in September and a tour to St. Petersburg and Helsinki was scheduled for October. Unlike on their honeymoon trip to Russia five years earlier, Mahler went alone. Further indicating their divergent paths of sorrow, Mahler forbade Alma to wear mourning clothes: she was not to "play to the gallery."[7]

For Alma, the loss of child would serve to revive other losses: parts of her life that she had exchanged for marriage—a stimulating social life, the pleasures of celebrity (if not notoriety), and above all, her music. Thus her own grieving was not uncomplicated and a degree of bitterness was inevitable. The pregnancy with Putzi had been painful, and shortly after, Alma had been critical of herself for not loving the child properly. Furthermore, she had felt a rivalry with the children for Mahler's affection, a situation that had led her to become aware of death wishes toward Putzi—who was Mahler's favorite—as well as toward Mahler himself. In her diary many years later, Alma would write of "Ich Gettatore," the Evil Eye within her:

> As a young woman—very lonely alongside a much older husband—I once (as I was separated from Anna who was in scarlet fever quarantine), driving with Gustav in the carriage past her window, saw our older daughter, Maria (Putzi), now long passed away. At the window up above us, the infinitely beautiful dark curly head pressed against the window pane—Gustav waved lovingly up to her—Was it that? I don't know—but suddenly I KNEW: This child must go . . . AND IMMEDIATELY, FOR GOD'S SAKE! Away with the thought! Away with cursed thinking. But the child was dead a couple of months later.[8]

Moreover, in Alma's perception, Mahler blamed her for the child's death, which may not have been entirely a distortion on her part. It is not surprising, therefore, that depression, euphemized as the "nervous attacks" for which she consulted her doctor, set in. A panicky letter from Mahler in St. Petersburg has some passages crossed out but one phrase left in reads: "Be *good* [underlined] now, and don't do anything silly."[9] Henry-Louis de La Grange wonders if the problem was Alma's "budding fondness for alcohol."[10] Given Alma's tendency toward depression, coupled with her histrionic propensities, one would have to consider the possibility of a threatened suicidal gesture.

It was apparent by year's end that coming to terms with loss led Alma to seek others. Her surviving daughter, Anna, would later describe this trait as "people catching."[11] At some point, Alma's "idle emotions got entangled" with a young admirer of Mahler's, the Russian pianist Ossip Gabrilowitsch (1878–1936). The two had shared a single kiss. En route to the ship for America, the Orient Express stopped in Paris, where Gabrilowitsch met Alma and Gustav. In a private moment in the Mahlers' hotel suite, Gabrilowitsch declared his anguished love for Alma just before Mahler, seemingly unaware, walked into the room. While Alma wrote of her "embarrassment," she confided, "So I was still capable of inspiring love, not old, not ugly, as I saw myself at the time! . . . The scene stayed with me. It helped me to get over my inferiority feeling for some time to come."[12] Here one finds the same impulse that would draw her three years later, in 1910, to a liaison with Walter Gropius, which would have profound repercussions in the lives of both Mahler and herself.

Gustav and Alma were not the only ones bereaved. Putzi was the first grandchild of Alma's mother, Anna Moll, and her husband, Carl. There was also the surviving child, Anna Justine Mahler, who had reached her third birthday only weeks before and was witness to the fortnight of death agony. Describing herself as a child, Anna stated, "I was very quiet and had no need to talk."[13] In this she resembled her father. Anna was destined to become a sculptor; in her work are enduring traces of what must have been a highly traumatic childhood event. Three statues depict a grieving woman. In one, the woman is holding her hands over her eyes and face; in another, her arm is thrown over her eyes; and in the third, her face is half hidden in unfinished stone.[14]

Mahler, who had sustained so many losses earlier in his life, was no stranger to the human impulse to repeat experiences. As Alma pointedly observed, Mahler was "the perpetual grief seeker."[15] Unconsciously, he had courted loss in the very choice of Alma Schindler, whom he knew to be flirtatious and pursued by many men. In this sense, from the beginning of their relationship he had taken a high risk. For Mahler himself, mourning through music had long been the agency of mastery. In one compartment of a complex creative and emotional life, Mahler was in a

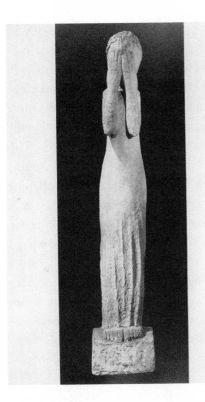

Sculpture by Anna Mahler.

state of endless mourning. The theme found its way into even his earliest unfinished opera project, *Ernst von Schwaben*, a projected heroic
memorial for beloved Ernst, one year younger than himself, who died at
thirteen. For mourning in his completed compositions, one only has to
think of *Der Spielmann*'s "O Leide, weh!" of *Das klagende Lied*; the
mourner's "Die zwei Augen von meinem Schatz" of the *Lieder eines
fahrenden Gesellen*; the "Funeral March" of the First Symphony; as well
as the *Todtenfeier*—the "Funeral Ceremony"—of the Second. The trend
can be traced to the composer's childhood, when two siblings, born in
1864 and 1865, each died a year later. The five- or six-year-old Gustav was
said to have written his first composition at that time: whether real in the
sense of scribbled or performed, or merely imagined, its title was "Polka
with Introductory Funeral March." Young Gustav was already the ironist
and the mourner.

Music then, not words, served to contain Mahler's grief. As far as is
known, he never spoke of his feelings about the death of his parents or

of Ernst, nor of the suicide of his brother Otto, except for a brief nostal-gic reference ("I had a brother once"). De La Grange cites a single pas-sage relating to Putzi's death in a letter to Hermann Behn, probably in response to his friend's earlier letter of condolence: "Forgive me for not replying to your kind letter, which meant a great deal to me. Even now you must make do with this rather summary procedure—not only because I am not yet in a mental state to talk to you about what you wish to know."[16] Others noticed, however. Bruno Walter wrote to his parents of Mahler's bereavement: "As a result he is a broken man: outwardly one notices nothing, but those that know him can tell that inwardly he is at the end of his tether."[17] No less an observer of the human condition than Arthur Schnitzler found Mahler to be so depressed that "he wondered how he was able to go on living."[18]

According to Alma, "mourning through music" began that very sum-mer of 1907. She reported that Hans Bethge's *The Chinese Flute* had been presented to Mahler by an admirer. "Now," she continued, "after the loss of his child and the alarming verdict on his heart, exiled from his home and his workshop, these poems came back to his mind; and their infinite melancholy answered to his own. Before we left Schluderbach he had sketched out, on our long lonely walks, those songs for orchestra which took final shape as *Das Lied von der Erde* (The Song of the Earth)."[19] Alma is almost certainly inaccurate here as Bethge's book was not even pub-lished until July of that year. It was the summer of 1908 that was devoted to the composition of *Das Lied*. Mahler's bypassing ordinary human emotions and being almost musically mechanical is as unlikely as it is untrue. He was unable to work the remainder of that fateful summer. Perhaps Alma's distortion of the timing of *Das Lied* reflects her sense of Mahler's turning away from her and her grief, and withdrawing into his music. As she would write subsequently, "Suffering estranged and separated us."[20]

Nevertheless, as Donald Mitchell confirms, "the poems found the composer, rather than the reverse."[21] And despite Alma's literal inaccu-racy, *Das Lied von der Erde* had been brewing before Mahler put pen to paper in the summer of 1908; even before the crisis of 1907. The loss of loved ones and the injunction to mourn were constant in Mahler's life and, as we have seen, the rites of mourning were represented in his music in many ways. Moreover, the content of such music frequently involved the symbolism of death and an array of eschatologies. *Das Lied von der Erde* is a culmination of these elements. Written following what was the most brutal loss of all, the death of his daughter, it may be viewed as an artifact of mourning and melancholia. Mahler himself called it "the most personal thing I have done so far."[22]

Mahler's mourning was transformed into high musical art, its medium the text of *The Chinese Flute*. Alma's comment on "infinite melancholy"—particularly the "infinite"—suggests that it was the final movement, *Der Abschied* (The Farewell), that caught Mahler's imagination. For it is here that the composer's own "voice" within the music is to be found: "He spoke, his voice was veiled: 'Ah! My friend—Fortune was not kind to me in this world.'"

A virtual palette of subtle shadings of melancholy (or depression) pervades both the text (as selected and modified by Mahler) and its realization in music. In the first movement, *Das Trinklied von Jammer der Erde* (The Drinking Song of Earth's Sorrow), despair is expressed in the refrain "Dunkel ist das Leben, ist der Tod" (Dark is life and death). Its music is a downward-oriented figure encompassing an octave. In this song, the singer's high pitch, against an orchestral fortissimo, vividly suggests the strain of life that makes drinking so compelling. But the music of the refrain tells us that in the end no soothing is possible, neither chemical nor spiritual; there is no consolation for one's own anticipated death. Where spring is evoked, it is disinterested, of which human nature is revealed as envious. There is neither the nostalgia of true mourning nor the promise of redemption. Rather a sense of bitterness pervades for the "rotten trifles" that life begrudgingly provides. Mahler painted this point of decay musically in the accompaniment with a dissonant chord.

Paradoxically, the beginning of this initial movement sounds almost triumphant, with its horn call thrice sounding the interval of a fourth while it (and the orchestral texture) stakes out the territory of the C major pentatonic scale that would later figure prominently at the end of *Der Abschied*. This is a masterstroke in the psychology of musical composition. For in its manic exhilaration, the music opens with powerful defensive denial of the prevailing despair.

Another song of drinking, *Der Trunkene im Frühling* (The Drunkard in Spring)—the fifth movement—conveys other depressive signs in its text, namely, apathy, oblivion, and withdrawal. And here, too, the vigorous introduction belies and denies the underlying pessimism. Wisely, Mahler marked this *allegro*, "*keck*," "bold," with its implication of brazen abandon. When, in a middle interlude, spring arrives with a promise of redemption, and the words are tenderly realized in the music, there is little interest. A comparable vocal figure soon carries the action of refilling the cup. Mahler's characteristic *Naturlaut*, nature sounds, are discernible in the orchestral accompaniment expressing a degree of nostalgia for past seasons, which is disavowed by the singer. The jagged vocal line suggests inebriated swagger and the final words tell us that there are but two alternatives: drunken song or sleep, the latter equated with the oblivion of death.

Sleep, "death's brother," and the change of mental state from wakefulness to sleep had long been a theme in Mahler's music. In *Das Lied* we encounter sleep in several guises. Besides the intoxicated sleep of *Das Trinklied*, another variant occurs in *Der Einsame im Herbst* (The Lonely One in Autumn), the second movement, which captures yet another melancholic shading in both word and music: "My heart is weary. My little lamp / has burnt out with a splutter; it puts me in mind to sleep." The vocal line is reminiscent of the descending figure that characterizes Mahler's Rückert song *Um Mitternacht* and the rhythmic motto of the latter is heard in the last unaccompanied section.

In *Der Einsame*, the scalar constriction of the opening ostinato figure mirrors the narrowed affective life of the depressive. Its "somewhat dragging" character (as Mahler wrote) reflects the characteristic slowing down of mind and body technically called "psycho-motor retardation." Once again, Mahler, the psychologist-in-music and no stranger to depression himself, marked the score "as if tired." Here one finds the ultimate weariness of giving up. The particular affect represented musically here is perhaps best seen in the physical depression accompanying terminal disease: a massive depletion of energy is experienced along with a complete yielding, associated with a withdrawal of interest in the world and its objects and an acceptance of death. In *Der Einsame* a longing for death is implied: "Autumn in my heart is lasting too long." Here, too, spring is referred to briefly, but with no sense of mourning for the past: "The sweetened air of flowers has vanished." There is, however, a flash of nostalgia: "Sun of love, will you never more shine to gently dry my tears?"

In *Der Einsame* we find Freud's death instinct writ large and set to music. The voice drops out eighteen measures before the song's ending. As Donald Mitchell indicates, in the coda "the protagonist is absent."[23] Also noteworthy is that Mahler changed the feminine voice of the original (*Die Einsame*) to the masculine.

These, then, are Mahler's melancholic movements. True to the self-preoccupation of melancholy and its pathological narcissism, Mahler's selection of poems contains hardly a mention of another living being. The profound isolation of depression becomes explicit in *Der Einsame*.

Only in two of the inner movements (the third and fourth), in contrast to the melancholic sections of *Das Lied*, do we encounter true mourning in music. In *Von der Jugend* (Of Youth) and *Von der Schönheit* (Of Beauty) we observe masterpieces of transformative art and the sublimation of the particular. That is to say, the gestures of mourning are realized in musical form: idealized images of a poetic and auditory nature and fabricated memories are suffused with a sense of pastness and loss while encoding the affect of nostalgia. The specifics of personal loss are effaced in favor of more universal ideas and images, as suggested by the titles themselves. Such sublimations may occur in the service of denial as well. And certainly the selection of Chinese texts favors distance of both time and place.

Typically, in mourning one psychologically revisits lost persons, past times, familiar places formerly animated with humanity, and even cherished non human objects—all in the process of giving them up. The warmth of *Von der Jugend* lies in the persons recalled and their community—and the enduring stability of a setting that is as static as the following movement, *Von der Schönheit*, is kinetic. In the "youth" pavilion are "friends . . . beautifully dressed, drinking, chatting." It is perhaps in the passage "Several are writing verses" that the author of the music in his own youth may be found. (In this fleeting reference to creativity one finds a musical counterpart to Yeats's *Lapis Lazuli* and the enduring joyfulness of art.) At the close, the vocal afterthought following a measure's rest, and Mahler's harmonically indecisive ending suggest a wish that this perfect moment might go on forever. This sublimation—an idealization in mourning of a personally lost yet eternal youth—is cut off from its autobiographical moorings. It does not even come as close to literal "personal" reference as the mourner of *Kindertotenlieder* despite Mahler's statement that *Das Lied* was the "most personal" of his works.

Like *Von der Jugend*, *Von der Schönheit* opens and closes with a section of stable and eternal tranquility. But in contrast, distinct and powerful feelings penetrate the vivid scene of maidens, lads, and steeds. *Sehnsucht*, or the sense of longing, is explicit as the movement ends with the desire of "the loveliest of the maidens" for the "handsome lad," whose horse "whinnies joyfully . . . and tears away." Both text and music exude eroticism as all the senses are evoked. More than this is the potent expression of sexuality—in both masculine and feminine aspects and, again, in text and music alike. The masculine aspect is explosive as in the second "march" of the movement, the passion of the lad is displaced onto his joyfully runaway horse, which is just barely in control as it tramples the flowers: "Look at its mane flapping frenziedly, its nostrils flaring." At this point, the music literally brings him up short as if to say, "simmer down." The feminine aspect is equally intense but more intimate. The maiden, the youth's deflowering not withstanding, meets him "in the darkness of her passionate glance" and love is aroused.

With respect to sexuality, one may seek some biographical reference to the composer's life. As the seasons turn in *Das Lied*, the flowers and "golden sunlight" in *Von der Schönheit* suggest the metaphoric potency of spring and summer. Mahler had been apprehensive about marrying Alma when he was—as he put it—in the autumn of his own life. In this respect *Von der Schönheit* may be viewed as an artifact of mourning that looks back vividly on a more potent time of life.

Mourning often dictates a diminution of sexual activity. However, it is natural that as mourning progresses, a desire for replacement of that which is lost takes hold. Perhaps, as suggested by the powerful equine sexual force of the music, Mahler and Alma were drawn to one another sexually after the loss of their child. Alma may have had more than one miscarriage during this period.[24]

In *Das Lied*, the significance of the appearance of human objects in addition to oneself, such as the friends of Youth and the lads and maidens of Beauty, lies not only in loss—that is, in the passing of youth and its beauty—with its imperative of mourning, but in separation from love objects. While both loss and separation require a degree of resignation, they are quite distinct human, and hence affective, situations. In separation the beloved is still alive, not only in the mental life of the beholder but in reality as well. Thus a sense of longing and the latent wish for restitution and reunion in the world of the living may persist. Although in such instances hope is kept alive, there may be endless grieving.

At the heart of both loss and separation is the human need for attachment that pervades life from its beginning until nearly the end. A degree of detachment from lost objects is part of the work of mourning, "the work of severance," as Freud put it.[25] Strikingly, a parallel exists in Eastern religion and mystical tradition in which entry into the desired state—whether inner life, afterlife, or nirvana—must be prepared for by detachment from worldly matters. This is confronted extraordinarily in the words and music of *Der Abschied*. There, the promise of what lies beyond remains ambiguous in terms of life and death, but implies rather some third state of being. However, its achievement requires the detachment characterized by the parting of friends and the retreat from humanity to nature.[26]

In *Der Abschied* one finds both the culmination and terminus of all the Mahler eschatologies noted previously. The ultimate "place," the end point of human destiny has been transformed from the "heavens" of the Second and Fourth symphonies, the Mutter Haus of *Kindertotenlieder*, and the occasional moments of grace in the lieder to a unique "place" never before articulated in music. At the same time, musical acts of mourning evident earlier find a point of resolution and comfort beyond mere resignation in the last moments of *Das Lied*.

In this final movement boundaries dissolve between the living and the dead; the human and the nonhuman; the organic and the inorganic. By the same token, music, poetry, and philosophy merge in a confluence of meaning that none could adequately elaborate singly. The truly engaged listener is drawn into the amalgam in such a way that there is a commingling of music and self.

The work's final words are "The dear earth everywhere / Blossoms in spring and grows green again! / Everywhere and eternally the distance shines! / Bright and Blue! Forever . . . forever." That much has been written about these last moments of *Der Abschied* bespeaks the richness of Mahler's musical symbolism, that it can cogently support multiple yet not necessarily contrary interpretations. Among multiple creative sources, one stands out because of its near uncanny correspondence in prose to Mahler's musico-philosophical achievement in tone. That is the "pan psychic" philosophy of Gustav Theodor Fechner, in particular, his *Little Book of Life after Death*.[27] Fechner was said to have been "Mahler's favorite philosopher."[28] William James, in his introduction to the American edition of Fechner's book, elaborated Fechner's view "that the entire material universe, instead of being dead, is inwardly alive" and animated by consciousness. Consciousness "and the physical universe are co-eternal aspects of one self-same reality." Fechner embraced the "idealistic notion that it is inner experience that is the reality, and that matter is but a form in which inner experiences may appear." Experience, when it passes away, leaves "a memory of itself," and "when we die . . . the whole system of our outlived experiences . . . [are] impressed on the whole earth-mind as memories." There, "they lead the life of ideas and realize themselves . . . along with all the similar vestiges left by other human lives, entering with these into new combinations, affected in turn by experiences of the living, and affecting the living in their turn."[29] Thus in Fechner's view, there exists what he called a "third stage" of human existence. It was this "third stage" of neither death nor life as we know it that Mahler reached for in the final, "ewig" (eternal) passages of *Der Abschied*.

In what Fechner called the "daylight view of the world," one finds that notion of Eastern philosophy embraced by transcendentalism, among other intellectual movements, namely, according to Fechner, "that we are ourselves a breath emanating from the divine Being, a tiny particle [of God]." In this final movement of *Das Lied*, Mahler created the sense of detachment from persons that characterizes mourning, in tandem with the worldly detachment that marks Eastern philosophy as he understood it. In doing so, he reconciled East and West as relatively static "Eastern" passages, marked by sparse orchestration, harmonic pedals, and silence itself, alternating with surging symphonic "Western" sections.[30] The patches of *Naturlaut* observed in the earlier movements reach full expression here. Beyond that, there is a different concept of time itself, the difference between being and becoming.

The manner in which Mahler realized the final moments of *ewigkeit* musically is nothing short of miraculous. In these last measures not only is there no resolution on the singer's part (as the sixth on A is famously added to the C major tonic chord) but the D is firmly in the ear as well, owing to the repetitions of "ewig." Thus all of the notes of the penta-tonic scale are sounded, as if encompassing the entire universe forever in an aesthetic statement of endlessness.

When Mahler revised Hans Bethge's rendering of "The Parting of Friends," he changed a central moment in the drama. Bethge had writ-ten of the friend, "I asked of him where and why he wished to journey." Mahler changed the text to "He asked him where he was going, and also why it had to be." In this Mahler placed himself equidistant between the one who left and the one who remained behind, identifying with both. And in answering his own question—*warum es müsste sein*, why it had to be—in *Das Lied von der Erde*, Mahler mastered his all-too-human loss, creating his personal artistic vision of "world without end."

10

OLD WORLD, NEW WORLD

When the Mahlers were about to leave for America in December 1907, a committee spurred by composer Anton von Webern (1883–1945) circulated an invitation for a "final farewell."

> Dear Friend,
>
> The admirers of Gustav Mahler are assembling to take their leave of him on Monday the 9th, before 8:30 A.M. on the platform of the West Station, and invite you to attend, and to inform all like-minded people.
>
> As this demonstration is intended as a surprise for Mahler, it is of importance not to confide in persons who are close to the press.[1]

More than two hundred people responded, representatives of Vienna's cultural and intellectual elite. Among them was Gustav Klimt, who, as the train pulled away, was heard to sigh, "Vorbei"—it's over.[2]

Klimt's remark was wise and perhaps prophetic. Mahler's departure was considered a tragedy by some in the cultural life of Vienna. No successor of Mahler's stature replaced him and shortly Vienna (along with Berlin) would relinquish its musical hegemony in Austro-German classicism. Mahler's leaving, then, heralded the passing of an era.

Klimt remained connected to Alma's parents, the Molls, through the continued activities of the Secession and would thus have known about the Mahlers' domestic trials. He himself had recently sustained some artistic reversals, and had withdrawn somewhat to an increasingly narrow circle of admirers and friends.[3] Thus his saturnine "vorbei" reflected personal pessimism as well as his response to Mahler's departure. The two men's artistic endeavors had tracked each other although in no simple way. Some have seen parallels between the glowingly decorative art nouveau style of Klimt and the transparent chamber-music qualities of Mahler's orchestra. But most strikingly, where their interests and ideals converged, one found Beethoven: both artists had famously contributed to the continued posthumous Viennese Beethoven saga and its artistic canon. In the 1902 Secession celebration of Beethoven, Klimt had painted his controversial *Beethoven Frieze*, in which the brotherly kiss for all the world was transformed into the erotic embrace of lovers. This, along with some of Klimt's frescoes for the university, had incurred public opprobrium.

For many of his friends, intimates, and even casual observers, a mythology developed regarding Mahler's health and vulnerability. This may initially have been fostered by Alma, a concerned witness to Mahler's frequent bouts of sore throat. Certainly, after Mahler's death she tended to emphasize his health problems. In any event, he had been deeply affected by the summer diagnosis and restrictions placed on him. His friend and colleague Alfred Roller (1864–1935), the stage designer, observed that the "effect on Mahler was severe and disabling . . . the long, happy rambles had been replaced by careful little strolls." Soon he tried taking longer walks and "ignored the doctor who had sent him so much into his shell."[4]

In view of recent events, Klimt's "vorbei" may have connoted his friends' concerns that Mahler would not survive the strenuous transcontinental commute he was embarking on, or what may have seemed up front to be an arduous conducting schedule. Mahler conducted his last opera in Vienna on 15 October, Beethoven's *Fidelio*. A fitting end to his sometimes conflicted relationship with the Vienna Philharmonic took place in November with a farewell performance of his Second Symphony.

Anticipating the uncertainties of the coming season, Gustav and Alma decided to leave three-and-a-half-year-old Gucki with Carl and Anna Moll. This was a strange decision for the still mourning couple. One would think it would have been comforting to have their remaining child with them, painful to be separated from her. Furthermore, the decision completely ignored the child's feelings. Besides having witnessed the death of her sister just months before, she would now suffer the loss of her parents, as she might experience it, for an unspecified period. Surely practical matters, such as the cost of passage and the hiring of a governess, could easily have been overcome. Indeed, the following year, the Mahlers did bring their daughter. Nevertheless, the couple felt happy as they left Vienna behind. Alma wrote, "We did not miss our child . . . in spite of all, one thing had us both in its grip—the future."[5]

To question the family's rationale in leaving Anna in Europe is to wonder what compromise this represented beyond any reasonable practical consideration. Neither parent had bonded with this child as intensely as they had with the elder. Putzi, as Alma had remarked, had been completely Gustav's; and Alma herself had confided to her diary her ambivalence and rivalry, a revival of her hostile feelings toward the half sister born to the Molls when she was already an adolescent. A major factor in Mahler's acceptance of Conried's offer had been the money involved. This would not only facilitate spending more time composing but also provide a more commodious life for Alma. Mahler was not unaware of his wife's chronic dissatisfaction in their marriage, in particular the relatively modest manner—as she saw it—in which they lived. He wished to be able to afford the luxuries that would gratify Alma and compensate for what she had relinquished. He knew also that she longed for a more stimulating social life and was perhaps concerned that the still-attractive Alma would seek satisfaction with other men. Surely, the voyage to the new world would be another honeymoon, comparable to the first in 1902 in Russia, exotic and exciting in nature.

Thus in December Alma and Gustav set sail from Cherbourg on the *Kaiserin Auguste Victoria* (understandably recalled as *The America* by Alma) and arrived in New York on 21 December, awed and elated by the sights and sounds of the harbor. They took up residence in a corner suite on the eleventh floor of the Majestic Hotel on Central Park West, where they faced their first Christmas in the city alone. Their arrival "so took our breath away that we forgot all our troubles," wrote Alma, "but not for long." Any expectation that they would experience different feelings in New York was soon dispelled as they confronted loneliness and loss, exacerbated now by self-imposed—albeit temporary—exile. Alma wrote:

> Our saddest evening of all was Christmas Eve, the first we had spent separated from our children [sic] and in a foreign country. Mahler did not want to be reminded it was Christmas and in the desolation of loneliness I wept without ceasing all day.[6]

Characteristically, Mahler had proceeded thoroughly and cautiously in opening up opportunities for himself in the new world. Sometime during 1907, Mahler had been approached by Conried, the director of the Metropolitan Opera in New York. A contract had been signed on 10 June, less than a month before Putzi's death at Maiernigg. Although the announcement in the American press cited him as the forthcoming "musical director," Mahler's duties and authority would be considerably less than at the Vienna Court Opera. The season was well under way as Mahler headed to the Metropolitan offices the morning after their arrival. There he confirmed that he would make his debut conducting *Tristan und Isolde* on 1 January 1908.

Mahler's abbreviated season was a success from the beginning, and deemed a fitting final achievement by Conried, whose last season this was. The premiere was received ecstatically by the New York critics, some of whom found the performance revelatory. Even Henry E. Krehbiel of the *New York Daily Tribune,* soon to become Mahler's critical nemesis, wrote of the "strikingly vital reading . . . admirable . . . eloquent . . . rich in color, elastic in movement and always sympathetic with the singers."[7] Mahler, who claimed to be unmoved by critical comment, was pleased by the performances and "swam in bliss," according to Alma. In all there were five performances of *Tristan* during January and early February and performances of *Don Giovanni, Die Walküre, Siegfried,* and *Fidelio* followed. Mahler's honeymoon with reviewers was over quickly, giving way to their criticism of his innovations, tempos, and staging. But assessment at the end of the season placed Mahler as "one of the most interesting figures of recent years at the Metropolitan." In particular, "fine and subtle feelings dominated Mr. Mahler's readings of the Wagnerian music dramas."[8]

With Conried's resignation, speculation regarding his replacement was followed by confirmation that this would be Giulio Gatti-Casazza of

La Scala Opera in Milan. Rumor also had it that Mahler had been offered the post but turned it down. An article in a Viennese newspaper revealed how the monetary rewards of the new world were inflated by Europeans: Mahler was said to have declined $120,000 to be director of the Metropolitan Opera! As it was, his earnings were not inconsiderable, especially in contrast to his Viennese post. His contract for the three months' work at the Metropolitan was 75,000 kronen (about $15,000), more than three times his annual salary at the Court Opera.[9]

Life in New York that first brief season provided much in terms of the excitement and celebrity that Alma craved. At the opera she and Gustav encountered the legendary singers of the time, among them Chaliapin and Caruso, with whom Mahler had already worked in Vienna. The playful tenor drew a caricature of Mahler. There were dinner parties and there was travel, with opera performances in Philadelphia and Boston. Isabella Stewart Gardner held a luncheon in the Mahlers' honor. Among the appealing new people, as well as those who provided a private laugh for the couple, they met Dr. Joseph Fraenkel, who would prove to be an important friend at the time of Mahler's illness. "He was a genius both as a man and as a doctor, and we both fell in love with him the day we first met him," Alma recalled.[10] This was at the home of Otto Kahn, the financier and one of the major supporters of the Metropolitan Opera.

It sometimes happens that some extraneous and even indifferent event, often lasting only seconds, can assume monumental importance and grave implications. This, of course, is the result of private meanings brought to bear on the occasion in question. Thus a scene Gustav and Alma witnessed during the first New York season, recorded by Alma, became a powerfully charged memory for the couple and eventually assumed legendary status. It occurred while the couple was in their eleventh-floor apartment at the Majestic and is here quoted in full:

> Hearing a confused noise, we leaned out of the window and saw a long procession in the broad street along the side of Central Park. It was the funeral cortege of a fireman, of whose heroic death we had read in the newspaper. The chief mourners were almost immediately beneath us when the procession halted, and the master of ceremonies stepped forward and gave a short

The Majestic Hotel, scene of fireman's funeral, 1908.

address. From our eleventh-floor window we could only guess what he said. There was a brief pause and then a stroke on the muffled drum, followed by a dead silence. The procession then moved forward and all was over.

They had watched from adjacent windows and the scene had "brought tears to our eyes." Alma looked anxiously at Gustav, still leaning out; "his face was streaming with tears." Alma noted that "the brief drum-stroke impressed him so deeply that he used it in the Tenth Symphony."[11]

The mourning process seizes every opportunity for emergence and expression, the element of surprise often serving as trigger. Public grief may elicit a measure of personal mourning, which might never be complete. The encrusted layerings of loss and grief in Mahler's life were thick. Undoubtedly both he and Alma were confronted with recent memories of Putzi's death, which silently haunted these present months in spite of the attractions and distractions. For Mahler, the past opened up as surely as in the resurrection images in which the graves of the dead open. Beyond this, however, lay anxieties about the future. Despite his medical prognosis the previous summer, Mahler continued to test the proscription given to him. Alfred Roller quoted Alma as saying that her husband's initial resigned state of mind gave way in the last years to "a crazed hunger for life and a terrible fear of death."[12]

Superstition played a powerful role in the Mahlers' minds. Inevitably, the muffled drum would recall to both the frightening hammer blows of the Sixth Symphony. Mahler had long since taken himself as the subject of his symphonies—the hero-persona. This is perhaps one of the reasons why, at a certain point, he eschewed written programs: falsification no longer satisfied, for the truth was too personal. The Finale of the Sixth contained the prophetic hammer blows that Mahler had found so frightening at its premiere. Alma, too, was swayed by magical notions of destiny, believing Mahler's *Kindertotenlieder* to have been prophetic.

As the summer of 1908 approached, Mahler was already planning creatively for his next, ninth "symphony." This, of course, turned out to be *Das Lied von der Erde*, which had been germinating since the end of the previous summer. Nine was an unlucky number; neither Beethoven nor Bruckner lived to create a tenth symphony. Like the accused who exults in a temporary reprieve of punishment, Mahler believed that in calling the new symphonic work *Das Lied von der Erde* rather than the true Ninth Symphony, he had averted the fatal decree. Later, in the unreason of superstition, Mahler having survived, his named Ninth Symphony would *really* be his tenth symphonic effort.

Mahler had made his mark on New York—at least in the operatic world. And New York had left its imprint on him. He wrote to Willem Mengelberg, "I am quite entranced with this country."[13] But Mahler's presence in New York was too tantalizing for his artistry to remain confined to opera. There were two symphonic orchestras in the city at the time, the New York Symphony, founded by Leopold Damrosch in 1878 (and from 1885 conducted by his son Walter), and the New York Philharmonic, which was essentially a cooperative of its musicians. Neither measured up to the preeminent Boston Symphony Orchestra. Indeed, many felt that New York had enjoyed its halcyon days a decade earlier, when the likes of Antonín Dvořák and the conductor Anton Seidl dominated the musical scene.[14] Anticipating that Mahler would return the following season, one person—Mary Seney Sheldon—saw an opportunity.

In today's relatively informal social ambience, the name Mrs. George R. Sheldon (as she was uniformly referred to in all written references) conjures up the Hollywood image of a wealthy corseted dowager with more money than good taste, let alone a sense of humor. This hardly described the forty-five-year-old Mary Sheldon. A daughter of the American Revolution in the best sense, she came from a distinguished background in which philanthropy and patronage of the arts were highly valued. Her father, a prominent banker, gave half a million dollars to the Methodist Hospital in Brooklyn, New York, the same year that he gave away eighteen-year-old Mary in marriage. George R. Sheldon, a Harvard graduate, headed his own banking firm and was active enough in Republican politics to claim partial credit for the election of New York's governor in 1906 and Presidents Theodore Roosevelt and William Howard Taft in 1904 and 1908, respectively. Thus Mary understood how to raise money, spend it for common good, and exert the power this conferred.[15]

In April 1908, a few days after the Mahlers arrived back in Vienna, reunited with Anna after a four-month absence, the *New York Times* reported:

> "Mr. Mahler's influence has been deeply felt at the Metropolitan Opera House this winter," said Mrs. Sheldon last evening, "and we have to thank Mr. Conried for bringing him over. While he is here it would be a pity if he should not have a chance to conduct purely orchestral music with an orchestra of his own."[16]

Mary Sheldon was an ambitious and capable woman. Her estate was secure, with a home and yacht in Glen Cove, Long Island, and a house in New York's fashionable Murray Hill. Her two daughters were of marriageable age. She herself now needed to create something enduring while carrying on family tradition. It was in her nature and heritage to think big. For Mary Sheldon (and Gustav Mahler, for that matter) neither the New York Symphony, effectively controlled by Damrosch in any event, nor the faltering Philharmonic in its present state would do. Her project would be on the artistic level of the mighty Metropolitan, which aspired to equal the preeminent Boston Symphony Orchestra. Like the Boston orchestra's legendary founder Henry Lee Higginson some twenty-five years earlier, she would be its guiding spirit.

Mrs. Sheldon assembled a committee to revitalize the Philharmonic, essentially to recreate the orchestra for Mahler. Despite its name—the Ladies' Committee—the founders included three men, the guarantors who were committed to underwriting the endeavor in its early years. Mrs. Sheldon's personal contacts and the committee members who became contributors to the Guarantors' Fund included some of the wealthiest and most influential Americans, such as John D. Rockefeller, J. P. Morgan, and Joseph Pulitzer. The stage was set for Mahler's return the following season, which would include the first concerts of the newly constituted New York Philharmonic as well as performances at the Metropolitan. A contract had been signed before Mahler left New York. At last, he would have his own orchestra.

Meanwhile Conried became ill and was forced to retire from director- ship of the Metropolitan. Giulio Gatti-Casazza had been offered the post to be shared with the singer and Metropolitan business manager Andreas Dippel. Gatti-Casazza accepted but brought with him from Italy his own favored conductor, the forty-one-year-old Arturo Toscanini. Thus the seeds were planted for the inevitable turmoil of a divided directorship the following season.

It was perhaps this outcome as well as his authority over Mahler that led Alma to a decidedly ungenerous assessment of Conried, whom she found to be a man of "utter innocence of culture." She could not resist describing his den, in which "there was a suit of armor which could be illuminated from within by red lights." After attending a luncheon in his flat, the Mahlers burst with laughter on the street outside his home. Further, Alma hinted at the reason for Conried's deteriorating health and resignation: "a cripple from tabes . . . unmistakable signs of megalomania." She was referring, of course, to syphilis.[17]

Alma tended to be as sensitive to physical handicaps as she was to attractive features of the young and handsome. This perhaps explains her depicting her husband as sickly. Disembarking from the voyage home in May 1908, the customs inspector mistook Mahler for Alma's father. She was disturbed more than he because in her eyes he did in fact look "so aged and ill."[18] This was not the only hint of the toll life in the new world might have been exacting. Alfred Roller noted:

> From his first visit to America [Mahler] had returned not exactly aged but nevertheless very much changed. I was taken aback when he stood there before me in the dim light of the station forecourt. The easier workload over there and the reduced amount of exercise had thickened him up.[19]

Mahler immediately immersed himself in conducting engagements on his return to Europe. In May he conducted his First Symphony in Wiesbaden and proceeded to perform ten concerts in Prague with the anticipation that after the summer he would return for the premiere of his Seventh.

Meanwhile, Alma was commissioned to seek a suitable summer house. She recalled making the trip with her mother, although more likely Justine, whom Mahler continued to trust in such decisions, was her companion. There was still snow in the Tirol and the women trudged their way through many properties before settling on the farmhouse near

Villa Trenker at Altschluderbach (Toblach), 1908–1911.

Toblach where Mahler would spend the final three composing summers of his life. The return to the Tirol revived the atmosphere of the previous summer as well as the Mahlers' grief. Gustav, predictably, turned to composition, and it was here, during the summer of 1908, that he composed *Das Lied von der Erde*. Engrossed as never before, he worked, Alma related, "at white heat all summer."[20] But 1908 was "the saddest summer we had ever spent together . . . his long bicycle rides, his climbing and also swimming under water, to which he was so passionately attached. There was nothing of that sort now. On the contrary, he had a pedometer in his pocket. His steps and pulse beats were numbered and his life a torment."[21]

Alma for the moment appeared to be in equilibrium, which may have been attributable to Mahler's attention and dependence on her. A vacation in Salzburg was planned at the end of the summer, "a holiday—a thing we had never done before during our whole married life."[22] They both looked forward to the second season in New York with pleasure, Mahler anticipating that he would spend the next few years in America. This time the couple would stay at the Hotel Savoy, where many artists from the Metropolitan Opera resided.

Oddly, Alma has virtually nothing to relate about this second season in America, satisfying herself with the comment that "they were days of blissful repose."[23] This time they brought little Anna along with a governess, and domestic life at the Savoy was tranquil; Anna Moll made a visit. It was a pivotal season in which Mahler fulfilled obligations for guest concerts with Damrosch's New York Symphony before resuming at the Metropolitan and later taking up the baton with the newly organized New York Philharmonic. The Mahlers had disembarked in New York scarcely a week after Arturo Toscanini had conducted his concert debut at the Metropolitan with Verdi's *Requiem*. Polite on-the-record exchanges between the two conductors had been made public. In an interview in *Musical America*, Toscanini stated, "I am content. I am certain that we shall agree, for he is a great *maestro*. Only the small, incompetent ones are contrary and cautious."[24] Mahler's private correspondence contains a single reference to Toscanini, in a letter to Alfred Roller in which Mahler returned the compliment: "A very well thought of conductor."[25] Toscanini's own correspondence reveals him to have been less generous, expressing pungently to a friend: "Believe me, Mahler is not a genuine artist. His music has neither personality or genius."[26] As for Mahler's compositions: "I was nauseated by Mr. Mahler, director of the Vienna Opera with his symphony no. 5. If he conducts the way he writes, oh what a trivial conductor he must be."[27] Only in the last months of his life, in 1956, did Toscanini demonstrate any positive response to Mahler's music, telegraphing Kathleen Ferrier: "I was moved by your beautiful performance of Mahler's symphonies and lieder."[28]

Collision between the two autocrats was inevitable with the dubious plan, as Mahler saw it, to appoint Toscanini to "take charge of Italian opera, and hand, as it were, German opera over to me."[29] Nonetheless, Mahler's political antennae told him that his proprietary *Tristan* was endangered and he fought for what he called his "intellectual property" before the term became legal tender. By the same token he had early on sensed tensions in the administration, "a noticeable cooling off of the powers that be."[30] True to form, Mahler already had his next move charted with the reorganization of the New York Philharmonic. The first concert at the end of March was well received by the critics; another, however, held the following month, suggested a rift in what had been critical acceptance if not acclaim.

Perhaps Alma's speaking of a blissful period reflected Mahler's satisfaction with the season's prospects. He wrote to Guido Adler of the fulfillment of a "lifetime wish" in finally having his own orchestra. "Why has not Germany or Austria offered something similar? Can I help it that Vienna threw me out? Further: I need a certain luxury, a comfort in the conduct of life, which my pension [from the Vienna Opera] could not have permitted. Thus it was a more welcome way out for me that America offered an occupation adequate to my inclinations and capabilities, but also an ample reward for it."[31]

Mahler embarked on shaping the orchestra, hiring a new concertmaster and others, and eschewing public criticism of American musicianship. Privately he confided to fellow conductors such as Willem Mengelberg and Bruno Walter: "My orchestra here is a real American orchestra. Untalented and phlegmatic. It's uphill work."[32] But one wonders in retrospect whether this attitude bled out to a degree. Some of Mahler's seemingly optimistic public pronouncements might have been construed as having a distinctly "un-American" quality that would come back to haunt him. To some, and possibly to an influential few, he may have come across as arrogant, patronizing, Teutonic.

"It will be my aim," Mahler related to an interviewer, "to educate the public . . . and that education will be made gradually and in a manner which will enable those who may not have a taste for the best to appreciate it."[33] The following season, true to his word, he would institute a quasi-educational "historical cycle" as well as a Beethoven cycle, increasing the number of concerts considerably. The problem was, the public did not respond. In his history of the New York Philharmonic, Howard Shanet cites newspaper accounts from the period that read, "probably the smallest [audience] that ever attended a Philharmonic concert in fifty years," "perhaps the smallest in number ever gathered at a Philharmonic concert."[34] By the following season, lack of public response was only one problem. Trouble was brewing with the guarantors as well. Finally, after an initial honeymoon, there were adverse reactions from the press. Pro-Mahler and anti-Mahler factions developed. Leading the latter was Henry Krehbiel, music critic of the *Tribune*.

Krehbiel was also the Philharmonic's program annotator. His critiques, even at their best and most favorable, often had a bite, an archness bordering on sarcasm. Even when he had been favorably impressed the first year, he had found Mahler "more inciting and exciting than satisfying." The performance of Beethoven was a particular source of contention. Regarding a well-known oboe cadenza in Beethoven's Fifth Symphony, Krehbiel wrote, "Mr. Mahler phlebotomized it." Krehbiel's review of the final concert of the 1909 season, Beethoven's Ninth, was a harbinger of what was to come. He wrote: "Those who think Beethoven wished to have the ears of his auditors assaulted as they were last night by the kettledrum player must have been delighted by the bombardment to which they were subjected; others must have felt outraged."[35] Krehbiel was yet to reveal the full extent of his own outrage. A serious musical scholar, he considered himself the arbiter of standards. His interest in the Philharmonic had a proprietary ring. More than this, he was an American chauvinist who was quick to take umbrage at any perceived superior or patronizing old-world attitude. That Mahler would be so arrogant as to "educate" his public flared Krehbiel's own arrogance. In Vienna, Mahler had been an outsider by dint of the city's resident anti-Semitism. In America, there were two sides to his foreignness: the attractive aspect, embraced by Mrs. Sheldon and her cohorts, and the offensive, attacked by Krehbiel.

Life in New York was otherwise enriched by growing friendships and social engagements. The Mahlers got to know both the city and an odd assortment of its occupants, ranging from the artists of the Metropolitan to the socialites who supported symphony and opera; to the reclusive (and "addicted," according to Alma) Louis Tiffany. They toured the city's ethnic quarters, among them an underworld Chinatown with an opium den, and a teeming Lower East Side Jewish quarter whose inhabitants Mahler could scarcely see as "our own sort of people." "Are *these* our brothers?" he asked Alma. "Can it be that there are only class and not race distinctions?"[36]

A curious episode prefigured the return to Toblach and the superstitious resumption of the Ninth Symphony, now of course (with *Das Lied von der Erde* completed) the actual Tenth. After dinner at the home of the millionaire Otto Kahn, Dr. Fraenkel led an adventurous group to a séance by the famous medium Eusapia Palladino. While all were holding hands in a circle in her studio, the physician counted her racing pulse as her trance approached its climax. The participants felt they were being touched and "Palladino commanded Mahler to look into the alcove behind her and murmured that he was in danger. She summoned him almost compassionately to sit beside her." Predictably, the experience affected Mahler, who superstitiously perceived danger in many quarters—in his own music, for example, in the hammer blows of the Sixth Symphony. "We went away in silence, pondering deeply," Alma commented. For some days Mahler was preoccupied with the experience, recalling numerous details. "After a week Mahler said: 'Perhaps there wasn't any truth in it and we only dreamed it.'"[37]

As it turned out, Alma was the one in peril. She had become pregnant at the beginning of the year and now miscarried. In a letter to Carl Moll in March, Mahler wrote, "She has been relieved of her *burden*. But this time she actually regrets it."[38] Both phrases are cryptic. Why a "burden"? Would she, and Gustav as well, not have desired another child to replace the one who had died? Had they moved on, adjusting all too well to the life of relative luxury about which Mahler would soon write to Guido Adler? "Regret" is understandable, especially since Alma slipped into a depression as the summer began. But what of regret "this time"? Had there been other miscarriages, and if so were any of them not spontaneous, but rather induced abortions?

On return to Europe, the Mahlers enjoyed a reunion with their "Dreyfus" friends in Paris. Mahler had plunged himself into a concert tour after the previous return from New York. Not so this time and Alma's enthusiastic response suggests that the holiday was at least in part for her benefit. They were entertained lavishly not only by their old friends the Clemenceaus but by other Parisian notables. Carl Moll had commissioned Rodin to sculpt a bust of Mahler and Sophie Clemenceau flattered Gustav, indicating it had been Rodin's own desire to undertake the work, so inspired was he by Mahler's head. Colonel Picquart was then minister of war and when the Mahlers visited him at the ministry, he had gleefully arranged a royal welcome: "The gates opened and a guard of honour drawn up to left and right in full-dress uniform presented arms as we walked through."[39] To Picquart, who was a great admirer of Mahler, they *were* royalty. For Alma this was all a dream come true but the Parisian excursion from reality set her up for the depression that followed.

The summer of 1909 was that of Mahler's Ninth Symphony. When he returned to Toblach he returned to the atmosphere of *Das Lied von der Erde*, to preoccupations with mortality and to ever present mourning. Sometime earlier in the year he had purchased a cemetery plot in Grinzing, a country suburb of Vienna. In July Putzi's body was transferred to the site where Mahler anticipated that he, too, would be interred. He had asked Bruno Walter to arrange a meeting with his old friend Siegfried Lipiner, from whom he had been estranged since marriage. (Alma had nothing but contempt for him.) Mahler had been fascinated by the scholar's ideas about death since discussions with him at the time of his hemorrhage in 1901, and he now felt compelled to learn more.[40]

Few of Mahler's symphonies have been subject to the debate over meaning that the Ninth Symphony has. From the first, responsive auditors have heard it as Mahler's farewell. Among these was Mengelberg, who wrote of "departure from all that he loved—and from the world." Alban Berg sensed "an unheard-of love for this earth, the longing to live in peace upon her . . . before death comes. This entire [first] movement I based upon a presentiment of death."[41] From the same inner source that produced the music came verbal comments, which Mahler inscribed on the orchestral sketch. They are like intimate program notes. In the first movement he wrote: "O days of youth! Vanished! O Love! Scattered" and "Farewell! Farewell!" (Leb' wol! Leb' wol!).

These remarks accompany a seemingly unlikely musical quotation from a waltz by Johann Strauss Jr., *Freut euch des Lebens.* Despite Mahler's occasional vernacular music, the likes of this Strauss were another story. Alma related how early in their marriage on a rare night out they had attended a performance of Lehár's *Merry Widow.* Trying to reconstruct the music on the way home, they stopped in a music shop where Mahler engaged the proprietor while Alma sneaked a look at the musical score. Both considered it beneath them to actually purchase such music. Yet, in the first movement of the Ninth Symphony, nostalgic regret and resignation are musically conveyed through the Johann Strauss quotation. Mahler doubtless knew the music of *Freut euch des Lebens*—Let life be full of gladness—from his student days.[42] (It was a Viennese version of the Latin student song *Gaudeamus Igitur.*) But there is a cryptic message inherent in the music. Typically, the larger form of such waltzes consisted of an introduction, followed by a string of five waltz tunes (and a coda in which the first might be reprised). Where he wrote "O days of youth! Vanished!" Mahler was musically quoting the last waltz.

After taking Gustav to Toblach, Alma retreated on doctor's orders to a sanatorium, taking Gucki with her. For her, grieving was becoming indistinguishable from depression. Although it is questionable whether mourning a child can ever be complete, hers was approaching a chronic state with idiosyncratic markings. The wound of losing her child commingled with those of other losses. Thus grief merged with grievance as Alma sank into a state of melancholy. The exchange of daily letters with Gustav was no comfort to her as she perceived him to be in his "abstract" mode. Indeed, Mahler's empathy often left much to be desired. For example, in attempting to console Alma and sympathize with her depressed moods, Mahler assured her that he himself ("this may surprise you") had gone through "the same thing a thousand times over"—an effort sure to alienate the individual sufferer.[43] Moreover, helpless in light of Alma's moods, Gustav reverted to the kind of philosophical verbosity that characterized his earlier, frustrated letters at the time of the family crisis. "Abstract" indeed, Mahler ended his "sermon" to Alma with a series of rambling admonitions perhaps stemming from Lipiner's influence. (And, if Alma had gotten wind of their source, they would most certainly not have been helpful.) Perhaps applicable to himself, they were unlikely to comfort a woman who longed for a kind of love that Mahler could no longer satisfy in spite of his otherwise quite affectionate letters. Fantasies that would make her ripe for an affair when the time came were revealed in her desire for renewed love. And like many a depressed person, Alma wished that fate might deal her a new hand. "I longed to

Alma Mahler, 1909.

plunge myself into love or life or anything that could release me from my icy constraint."[44]

Mahler, strongly experiencing the passage of time, made the most of this summer of 1909. In the past, even in the face of blocks or melancholy, he could indulge the luxury of spending multiple summers on a work. Not so now. He had written to Bruno Walter earlier in the year, "I am more avid for life than ever, and find 'the habit of being alive' sweeter than ever. The days of my life just now are like the Sibylline Books."[45] Mahler demonstrated his classical gymnasium education in citing from Livy the story of nine oracular books that were offered by a prophetess for a sum that was initially rejected. Only after she burned three and then three again, each time offering those remaining at the identical price, was her offer accepted; thus the increased value of what remained. The preciousness of time remaining never left Mahler's mind.

The summer's final task was putting the finishing touches on *Das Lied von der Erde*. For this, Mahler in a sense went home. He completed the work in Moravia, staying with friends in Göding (now Hodonín), at the border of Moravia and Austria about one-and-a-half hours from Vienna. In the course of this remarkable summer Mahler even found time to consider the following New York season, actively pursuing plans for the reconstituted New York Philharmonic. Among the visitors to Toblach was Richard Arnold, the Philharmonic's former concertmaster and now its administrative manager.[46]

Alma faced two tasks before returning to America. A tonsillectomy had been recommended. This was performed (along with one on Anna) at a sanatorium in Vienna while Mahler was away. It also fell to her to arrange for the dismantling of the Auenbruggergasse apartment, which they no longer needed as they now foresaw regular seasons in New York and summers in Toblach. Following the holiday in Paris, Mahler and Alma were thus separated during a significant portion of the summer.[47] Although Mahler had not scheduled conducting engagements initially, he embarked on a tour of Holland while Alma was tending to the apartment in Vienna. They reunited early in October for their third voyage to New York.

The contract that Mahler signed with the guarantors was described by Alma as "by no means exacting," and elsewhere she commented that that season "the work he was called upon to do was child's play compared with his official duties in Vienna."[48] Anticipated was a workload of forty-three concerts over a twenty-four-week period, in addition to demanding rehearsal time and travel to half a dozen cities outside the New York area. Some writers, most prominently Zoltan Roman, perceive significant overwork during the pivotal 1909–1910 season.[49] Furthermore, Mahler could not completely give up what opportunities remained at the Metropolitan Opera, where he rehearsed *Pique Dame* for its four performances. Since he was no longer on regular contract with the Metropolitan, he had to endure Toscanini's ascendancy and, worse, enthusiastic reviews at a time when critics were increasingly polarized with regard to his own performances, and generally negative toward his own compositions.

Henry Krehbiel in particular continued to be a thorn in Mahler's side. The two locked horns when Krehbiel requested a "programme" for his notes on the December performance of Mahler's First Symphony. Mahler had long since given up providing such information, preferring that music be heard on its own. Krehbiel wrote an extensive and scathing review, arguing that Mahler had essentially written program music from which the program had been removed. He called Mahler "a prophet of the ugly." Evidently smarting from Mahler's declining to provide a program, he wrote, "The symphony has no justification without a programme . . . Mr. Mahler's refusal to take advantage of his opportunity presents him in the light of a composer convinced that his music carries its own message; it compelled a multitude of his hearers to wonder what he bases his conviction on."[50]

Krehbiel had marked Mahler as an enemy of music, if not his personal enemy. Despite the detail of Krehbiel's critiques—or perhaps because of it—one wonders at the source of the critic's outrage. Only after Mahler's death would the full force of his animosity become apparent in the obituary he wrote. There, he took the occasion to reopen the "programme" issue. Further, the fact that Mahler was a foreigner continued to rankle. Krehbiel was speaking for himself when he wrote, "It is a fatuous notion of foreigners that Americans know nothing about music in its highest forms."[51] One is left with the impression that if Krehbiel could have resurrected the dead Mahler in order to destroy him, he would have done so. In fact, the obituary was so inappropriate in its perverse criticism of both the man and his music ("It is a harsh thing to say of a dead man, but . . .") that a lengthy rejoinder was published as an open letter by Ossip Gabrilowitsch, who wrote of Krehbiel's "language full of hatred."[52] Mahler, certain of his own worth and constantly forward-looking, paid little heed to such criticism; nor was he overly grateful for favorable comments from such quarters.

Before leaving for what would become the most challenging summer of his life, Mahler had to contend with the guarantors' committee, whose members were by no means as complimentary as before. There were some problems with his contract for the following year. A new manager had proposed sixty-five concerts, an increase of twenty-two performances! Mahler had requested "for this colossal increase in output a small increase in my honorarium," and did not have the committee's response prior to leaving New York in April.[53]

The outlay of money inevitably entailed a degree of power and control, and the committee members were feeling their oats. When one of the members, Mrs. Samuel Untermeyer, remarked, "I do nothing but give money," Mahler, who seemed genuinely fond of her and her husband, felt compelled to respond with a friendly note: "Yesterday I did not understand its full implication. But now I feel obliged to tell you that you *do a great deal more* than 'give money'! (Which in any case is much needed)—I am very much in need of you."[54] Mahler shrewdly understood the implications of Mrs. Untermeyer's remark and took pains to keep cordial relations with the members of the committee.

On another occasion, in a friendly letter to Mrs. Untermeyer while she was away, Mahler wrote, "I miss your presence very much at the rehearsals and performances."[55] Although a gracious attitude toward having strangers present at rehearsals seems unlikely on the face of it, the committee's growing power and their surveillance at rehearsals might have left Mahler feeling that he needed an ally. Once, while he was rehearsing a piano piece with Busoni, Mahler put down his baton to discuss the score with the pianist. A guarantor in attendance interpreted the interruption as a work break! A dispute followed in which the committee informed Mahler that "his behavior would never do."[56] Soon other demands would be made on his return—in particular, control over programming. Alma had assessed these wealthy women astutely, and claimed that she had counseled Mahler that this was coming: "When the committee was formed I warned Mahler not to allow these ladies too free a hand in the choice of programmes. He laughed and said he did not mind being relieved of the burden."[57] But of course Mahler minded greatly and had taken it for granted that his accustomed autonomy in such matters would not be challenged.

The excitement of the spring of 1910 was another trip to Paris, this time for the French premiere of the Second Symphony; then on to Rome for a pair of concerts. But most important was the awaited premiere of the massive Eighth Symphony in Munich on 12 September. The demands on Mahler's energy were enormous as he embarked on the most strenuous summer of his life. He looked forward to working on his next major composition, and although there were as yet no sketches for the Tenth Symphony, Mahler was preparing himself mentally for the initial uncertain weeks in Toblach that would eventually yield the first musical ideas. Preparations were also already under way for the September premiere, which would require rehearsals of several choral and orchestral components in different locales. In May and June Mahler conducted preliminary rehearsals—the Choral Unions (*Singverein*) in Vienna and Leipzig, and orchestral sessions in Munich. Bruno Walter meanwhile had selected the soloists and was rehearsing them. The impresario Emil Gutmann, without Mahler's approval, announced the Eighth as the "Symphony of a Thousand."[58]

By now Mahler's anxieties about his physical condition seemed to have been forgotten in the face of compelling events and precious time. He felt fit as he readied himself for his busiest summer ever.

11

ALMA AT TOBELBAD

An exchange of letters between Mahler and his old friend Guido Adler (1855–1941) tells the story of the tensions Mahler was experiencing during the New York years. The relationship between the two men reflects Mahler's profound need for close companions with whom to share ideas and ideals. Their thirty-year relationship stemmed from conservatory days in Vienna. Although Adler was also born and raised in Iglau, in a Jewish family, he and Mahler were not childhood friends. Mahler had gone on to become the eminent Austrian conductor; Adler had become the preeminent Austrian musicologist instrumental in creating and naming his field—*Musikwissenschaft*, the science of music.

From the first, there had been conflict between Alma and Mahler's friends. Some did not see her as a suitable mate, and she resented sharing him with them. In Alma's view, "The few people that Mahler had dragged around him like leg-irons from his early youth were completely alien to me and must always be so." Lipiner particularly irked Alma. At the unfortunate gathering of friends to introduce Alma, he had been "very condescending, call[ing] me 'girl.'"[1] As a result, Mahler dropped many friends, but not without regret since he missed both the camaraderie and the intellectual stimulation. He wrote to Bruno Walter sometime in 1909: "I often find myself thinking of Lipiner. Why do you never mention him in your letters? I should like to know whether he still thinks the same way about death."[2]

Guido Adler.

A decade into the marriage, compromises had been made on all sides, but from time to time the old issue would flare up. Sometime the previous summer Adler must have written to Gustav of his sense that Alma had alienated him from old friends. For Alma, in a letter to Adler ("Most esteemed friend"), attempted to undo any such behavior, pleading their "chain of sorrows" and apologizing that "we seemingly neglected you and your dear wife." She conveyed Mahler's invitation to visit him in Toblach. This document of reconciliation—the only extant one in Alma's hand—suggests a domestic dispute, the outcome of which was for Alma, as the party responsible for the rift, to reassure Adler.[3]

Later in 1909 Mahler had occasion to write to Adler about life in New York, noting almost as an aside, "This year in the summer I wrote my 9th."

> Here real American turmoil prevails. I have daily rehearsals and concerts. Must conserve my strength a great deal, and after rehearsals generally go to bed, where I take my midday meal. . . . If I survive these two years without injury—then, I hope, I can settle down to enjoying everything and perhaps also creating "con amore."[4]

Adler found Mahler's letter alarming as it reinforced his suspicion that Mahler was under considerable stress and physically vulnerable. He shared his concern with other friends of Mahler's and a flood of letters from Vienna ensued. Mahler replied to Adler with the frankness befitting their long relationship; although Adler's letter no longer exists, Mahler's prompt response makes clear its content. Adler doubtless had much to say about Mahler's exertions and, like a concerned parent, sought to lay blame externally—in this case, on the trials of artistic life in America. But in particular, Adler apparently had much of a critical nature to say about Alma, which represented not only his own views but those of Mahler's well-wishers in Vienna. In addition, and in view of other justifying remarks Mahler made, Adler had been against Mahler's going abroad to begin with.

Mahler wrote at length. He defended his taking to bed after rehearsals as salutary, reinforcing his argument with the provenance of this "hygiene": none other than Richard Strauss. Writing further of his plans, Mahler spoke of his active conducting as a necessary "counterpoise" to creative life, and of his need for "a certain luxury . . . which my pension . . . could not have permitted." In sum, "America not only offered an occupation adequate to my inclination, and capabilities, but also an ample reward for it."

"And now," continued Mahler, getting to the heart of the matter and clearly the purpose of his letter, "most closely connected with this situation, I come to speak of my wife, to whom you with your views and utterances have done a great injustice."

> You can take my word for it that she has nothing other than my welfare in view. And just as, at my side in Vienna for eight years, she has neither allowed herself to be blinded by the outer glamour of my position, nor allowed herself to be seduced into any luxury, even one quite appropriate to our social position, in spite of her temperament and the temptations to do so from Viennese life and "good friends" there (who all live beyond their circumstances), so now also her earnest endeavor is nothing but to put a quick end to my exertions (which, by the way, I repeat, are not over-exertions, as in Vienna) for my independence, which should make it possible for me to create more than ever. . . . And are we perhaps obliged to eat the charity bread of the Vienna Court

Opera in a garret in Vienna? Should I not, inasmuch as it is offered me, in a short time earn a fortune in honorable artistic work? Once more I assure you that my wife is not only a brave, faithful companion, sharing in everything intellectually, but also (a rare combination) a clever, prudent steward, who, without regard for all the comfort of bodily existence, helps me put by money, and to whom I owe well-being and order in the true sense.[5]

Mahler was perhaps protesting too much. Not only did he defend Alma but, remarkably, there is not a trace of ambivalence toward his wife. However, a good deal of Mahler's striving at this juncture had a dual purpose—not only to provide himself with the leisure to compose but to make life more comfortable for Alma, now and in the event of future contingency. He was careful in his letter to write of his own need for "luxury," not Alma's, although in truth this was of little consequence to him personally. His concern that he had "a short time" remaining had been well ensconced in his mind since the summer of 1907; it had been part of the background to the Ninth Symphony. But Mahler's own reading of Alma—her chronic discontent and depression, her wishes for material comfort and longing for social stimulation—remained private. His loyalty to Alma was absolute.

For Alma, return to Europe followed the pattern of the previous year. Once again, the spring found them in Paris, this time for the French premiere of Mahler's Second Symphony at the Concerts Colonne and a pair of concerts with the Accadèmia di Santa Cecilia in Rome. The excitement provided by the concerts, Parisian friends, and the two cities themselves distracted Alma from her melancholy, but disappointments in Paris and Rome left both her and Mahler in bad humor. During the course of the rehearsals of the Second Symphony, they were entertained warmly by Gabriel Pierné and other French composers, including Debussy. This made an incident occurring at the performance all the more painful, as Alma reported:

Suddenly, halfway through the second movement, I saw Debussy, Dukas and Pierné get up and walk out! They said later that they had found the music too Schubertian and that

Schubert, also, was alien to them—too Viennese, too "Slavonic"
. . . the enthusiasm of the audience could not compensate Mahler for the bitterness of being so grossly misunderstood by the
leading composers of France.[6]

In Rome, the undisciplined "job-lot" Italian orchestra was barely adequate. Gustav was not in a position to buoy Alma up to a degree that
might have helped her, and with the prospect of a long summer with
Gustav further preoccupied with preparing for the Eighth Symphony in
Munich in September, depression engulfed her. With the April concerts,
rehearsals in Vienna nearly all of May, and travel in June to prepare various components of his massive September performance, Gustav would
not even get to Toblach until early July.

These undertakings were the natural consequence of ideals and ambitions seemingly unrelated to Mahler's desire for a more luxurious lifestyle
for himself and Alma. He, too, would feel that he had overexerted himself conducting when, in Munich, before he retreated to Toblach, he
injured his arm. Regaining his energy to an unusual degree, and in good
spirits, mortality nonetheless touched him as he approached his fiftieth
birthday on 7 July. Max Burckhard, the former director of the Vienna
Burgtheater, was immobilized with a painful terminal illness. He had
been Alma's intellectual guide, probably the person who had given Alma
the edition of Nietzsche that Mahler had asked her to destroy. Burckhard
had remained a friend to Alma, as he had been to the Molls, and by
extension a tolerated acquaintance to Mahler. Alma believed Mahler
remained jealous.

Alma and Mahler had felt it their duty to visit Burckhard when he
became ill two years earlier. On the occasion he had remarked to Alma,
"I must be in a very bad way for Mahler to let you come and see me."[7]

In late May Emil Zuckerkandl died. Alma and Gustav had met at the
home of Emil and Bertha, and only weeks before they had visited in Paris
with Bertha's sister, Sophie Clemenceau, and her husband, Paul. Both
Burckhard and Zuckerkandl were of an older generation. The illness of
Siegfried Lipiner, only four years older than Mahler, struck especially
close to home. Lipiner, too, was in considerable pain and thought to be
terminal.

Mahler's own chief health concern, however, was with Alma, whose depression deepened during the month of May. "I was really sick, utterly worn out by the perpetual motion necessitated by a giant engine such as Mahler's mind. I simply could not go on. . . . I went with little Gucki to Tobelbad, a small Styrian spa in a wooded, mountain-ringed valley."[8] Neither she nor Mahler was in a position to understand her depression. Mahler's efforts were tinged with denial as he could only intellectualize and thus spare himself any true empathy that might have come from memories of his own severe depression in 1889. In addition, he would have had to examine his own behavior. Inevitably, despite his attempts to pay more attention to Alma's needs, the requirements of his two careers would be perceived by her as neglect of their marriage. Bewildered by Alma's moods, Mahler veered between declarations and demonstrations of heartfelt love and the abstract philosophizing of which Alma complained. She, in turn, would use this as rationalization for seeking love elsewhere; her anger at her husband and the self-loathing of depression would have tended to neutralize his genuine ministrations. From her point of view, Mahler was the entire problem and she accorded herself no responsibilities for the choices she had freely made. Yet Alma could not have been completely aware of the depth of her resentments or the demands of her own narcissism.

There is an important element in the way Alma understood her condition at the time. De La Grange suggests that in speaking of her "schwere Hysterien"—severe hysteria—in one of her diary entries, Alma was "certainly alluding to her state of sexual frustration."[9] Freud had published his *Studies on Hysteria* (along with Josef Breuer) in 1895, and although Alma would not have been aware of it, the term "schwere Hysterien" is found there.[10] Strongly implied and later asserted by Freud was the sexual origin of the condition. By 1910, to the chagrin of the first generation of psychoanalysts, the popular press had reduced psychoanalysis to the sexual origins of the conditions it undertook to treat. Mahler himself "shunned such concepts" as Freud's oedipal complex.[11] In any case, Alma's correspondence in the following months tended to corroborate the notion that she considered sexual deprivation to be a cause of her problem, and hence sexual gratification the implied cure.

A single reference in otherwise "edited" correspondence suggests decreased libido on Mahler's part, if not impotence. In a letter to Alma later in the summer, anticipating his visit to Tobelbad, where Alma was in a sanatorium, Mahler wrote, "I am looking forward with joy, my darling, to hold you soon in my arms. But for heaven's sake, I implore you, be sensible. And don't demand symphonies from me—for they have to come of their own accord, otherwise they don't come at all, or else they are suites."[12]

Beyond this, there was likely a hereditary component to Alma's depression. Alma's father, Emil Schindler, appeared to have been a chronically pessimistic person, whose frequently jaundiced attitude toward life rendered him subject to moodiness. Characteristic of his tendency toward depression is the self-denigration and sense of depletion found in his journals, as the nearly forty-year-old Schindler wrote: "The life of the spirit exists no more for me . . . I make myself a laughing stock in front of others. Why couldn't I have died two years ago?" On the birth of Alma herself, Schindler confided in his diary, "On 31st August I became a father, a natural consequence of my marriage. My Anna was a martyr, and I felt only indifference towards the child. Even now I can't say I like it much. . . . I tell Anna so as not to hurt her, that I love it, but really I feel nothing."[13]

In the beginning of June, Mahler, on the advice of Alma's doctors, interrupted his preparations for the fall premiere of the Eighth Symphony to take Alma to Tobelbad, a fashionable spa for the treatment of nervous conditions and female disorders. The spa was said to offer new treatments in addition to the traditional warm water baths. The emperor himself went there. Alma was accompanied by Gucki and her English governess, Miss Turner, who had been employed in New York. It was planned that Mahler would visit at the end of the month and that later, Anna Moll would as well. Mahler hoped that Alma would spend sufficient time there to effect a cure. Writing to her immediately after leaving Tobelbad, Mahler observed, "You were so sad before we left," and begged her for details of the spa.[14]

It was at Tobelbad, on 4 June 1910, that Alma met Walter Gropius. The twenty-seven-year-old architect had only recently begun his independent practice, the stresses of which served as rationale for a rest cure.

Walter Gropius at his desk at the Bauhaus, Dessau, 1925.

Beyond this was a custom that almost amounted to hygienic discipline as, with the onset of summer, educated persons of the upper class, emulating royalty, would retreat to a spa. Such establishments offered treatment for what would now be considered psychosomatic disorders, depression, and the manifold symptoms of the popular diagnosis, neurasthenia. More than this, individuals sought physical and psychological renewal with the imprimatur of medical treatment. At Tobelbad, Alma lived on the lettuce and buttermilk diet and "bathed conscientiously in the hot springs—although the very first time, I promptly fainted and had to be carried back to bed."[15]

Alma soon felt quite isolated; Gucki could hardly fill the role of companion by dint of her age; Miss Turner, by her station. Alma met Gropius one month before the anniversary of Putzi's death. Thus a double void in her depressed inner life made her all the more ready for restitution. And what a restitution it was! She depicted herself as quite passive when the doctor in charge indicated she should have some companionship on her heretofore solitary walks—no less than "doctor's orders." As Alma and Gropius sat by a brook in the moonlight, they talked well into the night. And the youthful Gropius—said by his biographer to have been relatively inexperienced—obliged, soon falling in love with her. Clearly, the attraction was mutual and powerful, and the now thirty-year-old Alma was eager for the relationship. For three or four weeks they saw each other every day.[16]

Thus Alma led a double life that summer, for as she continued to write melancholy letters to Gustav, she pursued an ecstatic affair with Gropius. Three interlocking triangles eventually emerged among the summer drama's personae. The first was that of the lovers and Gustav Mahler. The second included the lovers and Anna Moll, who would shortly become Alma's confidante and accomplice. Anna would be privy to all, while Mahler was kept in the dark, trusting Alma and grateful to Anna for what he perceived to be her unstinting familial help. Thus the third triangle, of Mahler, Alma, and Anna Moll, was marked by deception and betrayal. The ever shifting interplay among these four individuals would continue for the remainder of Mahler's life and formed a hidden layer to his final illness and death scarcely a year later.

While Alma and Walter were finding each other, Mahler, who was spending the month rehearsing in Vienna, Leipzig, and Munich, confided to Alma feelings that would be intensified later in the summer. Soon after leaving her, he wrote, "This time I had a hard time separating from you."[17] Ironically, Mahler sounded the theme of separation and implied abandonment virtually at the moment the lovers met. He went on: "One day I would love to settle down with you, not work, and relax in a completely calm and joyous way. . . . But for that to be you must be in good health. Maybe in September if all goes well. For the moment, I live in your small room and think always of you."[18]

Alma documented her experiences with Gropius in a kind of "triple-entry" bookkeeping, writing in her published memoirs of dancing with Gropius at the sanatorium and "talking" through the night; and in a private diary of "a certain x" who unfortunately fell in love with her during their walks.[19] But elsewhere she recorded their passion in spending the night together making love. Later, letters between Alma and Gropius dwelt in considerable detail on their sexual relationship. Their liaison was consummated soon after meeting, with Alma confiding ecstatically in her diary of three glorious nights.

Meanwhile Mahler's letters revealed a loneliness and longing for Alma despite his frenzied rehearsal schedule. Early in June he was rehearsing in Vienna and staying at the Moll villa. On a Sunday, sitting by the window of Alma's old room in order to feel closer to her, he fell into a reverie in which he achieved a soothing merging of self with his mental image of Alma. Listening to the sounds of the spring day, he thought back to his childhood and felt comforted by the fused imago of a maternal Alma and his own beloved mother.[20] This wistful letter was written two days after Alma had met Gropius.[21]

Mahler was frustrated not only by the separation itself but by Alma's lack of response to his letters. She had never been a very good correspondent, a frequent cause for complaint when Mahler was away on tour. Now nearly all available energy for relationships was absorbed by her adulation of Gropius. Even Gucki was hardly mentioned in what correspondence she did carry on with Mahler, although some of the child's drawings were sent. Astonishingly, given the amount of work Mahler undertook, he always somehow found time to write letters filled with everyday personal details, news and gossip, and accounts of his work of both an artistic and political nature. Thus connections by letter were of more than casual importance to him, the more so now, given his concern for Alma's state of mind when he left her. During his first days in Toblach, Mahler's letters to Alma comprised what de La Grange calls an "intimate journal" of his inner and outer life: his feelings and perceptions on one hand and the events of daily life at the Villa Trenker, which they had rented, on the other. Alma's unresponsiveness soon became a source of anxiety. Mahler worried about Alma and her condition, while he himself began to experience incipient feelings of loss and abandonment.

In the absence of any news, Mahler's concern grew more serious. Toward the middle of June, he wrote: "It worries me today to have no letter from you after your so sad one of yesterday. Are you hiding something from me? For I feel there must be something to read between the lines."[22] What were Mahler's antennae searching for? During an earlier episode he had cautioned Alma not to do anything "silly." Was he again worried about suicide? Or was it Gucki who concerned him? It seems unlikely, given the perception of withdrawn depression Alma created at this time, that Mahler was consciously suspicious of infidelity. Later, however, Mahler's "between the lines" sensibility suggested some awareness of the affair between Alma and Gropius. In mid-June he wrote to Anna Moll from Munich, where he was rehearsing for ten days. Addressing her as "Dearest Mama," he revealed: "I am so perturbed by Almschi's letters, which have such a peculiar tone."[23] Mahler sought Anna's advice as to whether he should go see Alma before he settled down to the summer's composition in Toblach. He also asked Alma herself, although he had already purchased his ticket through to Toblach and needed "to regenerate and air myself." Moreover, the trip would require eight hours of train travel. "So think it over, my dear. If you're experiencing unrelenting loneliness and want me now *immediately*, it's no problem and I will simply forfeit my ticket to Toblach."[24] He did in fact do so, and it was while en route to Vienna to make the connection that he wrote Alma the letter about not expecting "symphonies."

It should be noted that in the context of the varied letters Mahler wrote—encouraging, loving, exhortatory, newsy—St. Anthony still lurked. Mahler could scarcely avoid sermonizing and, worse still under the circumstances, philosophizing. The above letter was so full of allusions to Aristotle, Plato, and Christ that one can readily see how Alma might complain of having an "abstraction" for a husband, although no one knew better than she that was hardly all Mahler was. In fact, Alma was in part responsible for Mahler's occasional extended discourses as she raised philosophical questions in her letters that then elicited his responses. To some extent, this reflected her sense of intellectual inferiority. In June 1910, however, Mahler's unsolicited philosophical treatises could serve as rationalization for an entitlement to the fulfilled physical life she was enjoying with Gropius.

The ironies of betrayal are best viewed in retrospect. Mahler had confessed his loneliness for Alma at the exact moment that she was embarking on the affair with Gropius. Furthermore, Mahler offered to relieve *her* loneliness, although it would involve an exhausting trip. Meanwhile, Mahler was writing to Anna Moll, signing himself with "Love, my dearest little Mama, to you and Carl," yet Anna would soon be privy to Alma's love affair and become her confidante.[25] Concurrently, Mahler was undertaking, in addition to a strenuous rehearsal schedule, the husbandly duties of house hunting for the following season. Having given up the Auenbruggergasse apartment the year before, Mahler, with the help of Carl Moll (and Carl's newly acquired automobile), was seeking a suitable house in the suburbs of Vienna. A ten-hour excursion warranted a detailed report to Alma.

If Mahler's suspicion of Alma's "hiding something" was allayed during his visit to Tobelbad, it spoke for Alma's skill in deception, what with Gropius on the scene; and her ability to convey that the "cure" that seemed to be working was that of the spa's regimen rather than the affair. In any case, the joy Alma was experiencing with a new lover and the renewal of sexual life was not completely suppressed, as Mahler found her state of mind encouraging. He wrote to Anna Moll, "I found Alma much fresher and fitter and I am firmly convinced her cure here is doing her a great deal of good."[26] As for "symphonies" or even "suites," the visit was uneventful and there was no indication of any breakthrough on this account. Conditions reverted quickly, however, as a few days after no word from Alma, Mahler wrote irritably, "Don't you have five minutes?"—the "for me" implied.

Anna Moll arrived in Tobelbad 4 July, the eve of the third anniversary of Putzi's death. If indeed it had been arranged so, there was no acknowledgment on anyone's part. Anna soon learned of her daughter's affair with Gropius and enlisted herself as an accomplice, promoting and facilitating the relationship. From what is known of Walter Gropius's tendency to be interested and involved in his lovers' families, Anna likely met Gropius during the course of this visit.[27] Soon after, when Gropius left the sanatorium before Alma, she wrote to him of her desire to meet *his* mother. From this point on, Anna remained devoted to the lovers, all the while maintaining an apparently warm family relationship with Mahler.

After Anna returned to Vienna, Mahler continued to correspond with her, particularly regarding Alma's status. Later, during the last season in America, there would be more letters. More than merely looking to her for the kind of help that might be forthcoming for a sick member of the family—and a daughter at that—Mahler had a genuine affection for Anna Moll, apparently viewing his mother-in-law as if a revenant of his own mother.

In a letter to Anna in July, after receiving a birthday greeting from her, Mahler revealed much about his feelings toward his mother-in-law. He addressed her with the same kind of loving diminutive he sometimes used for Alma—"My dear Mamatschili"—commenting parenthetically, "Good heavens, isn't it hard to find a pet name for you!" Here Mahler was remarkably empathic with Alma's condition: "I am terribly sad about the recurrence of this tormenting ailment—I live here, as you know from my letters to Alma, much occupied with you all in my thoughts." He continued:

> How lucky we are to have you!
>
> And I don't say that out of egotism, for [if], instead of so sweetly helping us, you were yourself in need of help, it would be a joy to both of us to give back to you all that we ceaselessly receive from you—and I should ever and again say: How lucky we are to have you.
>
> But now everything possible must be done to get Alma well and strong again! I had completely forgotten about my birthday and only your letters reminded me of it so suddenly that I couldn't help smiling at the thought of how unimportant that day seems to me and yet how lovingly you all remember it. Thank you a thousand times for your sweet words, and always remain what you are to me, friend and mother (as dictated by a peculiar whim of fate).
>
> Your old
> Gustav[28]

Indeed, a mother never forgets a child's birthday; but no greeting or gift arrived from Alma on Mahler's fiftieth birthday, 7 July 1910. Nor did he hear from her in the days leading up to or following that date.

When Mahler returned to the Villa Trenker in Altschluderbach, he was not yet in his häuschen, the composer's hut that he had built on the property. While he appears to have been engrossed in multiple activities, these may be properly viewed as preparation for the resumption of creative life. The piano—one of three that were sent to him each spring—had been installed in the twelve-by-twelve-foot "Schützelputz-Häusel" (as he had affectionately called his private creative space earlier) in mid-June but the weather remained chilly. More to the point, Mahler required a breathing space during which musical ideas sparked, germinated, and coalesced to a point of urgency, at which time häuschen, piano, pen, and paper were not merely necessary but essential. He was moving toward that point even as he answered the deluge of birthday greetings and engaged in full-scale correspondence with New York regarding the following season. Of more immediate concern were details of the premiere of the Eighth Symphony in Munich, now only two months away. In addition, the "intimate journal" of letters to Alma continued, despite Mahler's anger at his wife's sporadic silences. He urged her now to stay in Tobelbad at least past her "monthly indisposition," which Alma was inclined to do, as Gropius would remain there as well. The outpouring of affection for Mahler from friends and other well-wishers and the warmth of his relationship with the Molls, particularly the duplicitous Anna, could hardly compensate for the loss he was experiencing with regard to Alma.

Meanwhile, Mahler was living with the Trenker family, who owned the villa and were doing all they could to attend to his comforts. The ten-room apartment on the second floor of the villa was commodious and boasted an enclosed veranda. Mahler habitually arose before 6 A.M. and would start the woodstove downstairs himself, even before the family was awake. All the fixings of his breakfast had been made ready, especially the fresh butter that he craved, as well as honey, eggs, pastry, and fruit.

Mahler's only complaint was the perennial one—the noise. Referring to the youngest of the Trenker children, not without amused affection, he wrote: "On the ground floor, below me, there lives a tiny citizen of the world who passes the greatest part of the day howling." The country folk would remember the composer fondly and with humor. Another Trenker child later, in her adulthood, recalled his stay in Altschluderbach: "The rooster woke his morning slumber with 'Kikiriki.' 'How does one teach the rooster not to crow?'—asked the Director. To that Herr Trenker replied that one just chokes him. Gustav Mahler didn't want to know about such things." On another occasion, "a vulture chased a raven into the 'Arbeitskabinett' where Mahler was working. Director Mahler was upset and went to old Trenker and complained bitterly about the intrusion. Trenker laughed at him to his face, and Gustav Mahler had to laugh as well." Mahler was respected by the Trenkers, did not put on airs, and seemed comfortable in the company of a large family. He was described as "warm and friendly" and during his stay with them often spoke of his own modest background and family.[29]

Sometime during the two-week period between his birthday and the end of Alma's "cure" in Tobelbad in mid-July, Mahler almost certainly resumed composing, starting work on the Adagio, the first movement of the Tenth Symphony. The intensity and gravity of the first theme—angular in contour and anguished in affect—does not bespeak the joy of reunion. Nor does the fifteen-bar introduction of the solo viola of the desolate-sounding Andante added later.[30]

Alma's return to Toblach began the most troubling of all the crises in Mahler's life and one in which the music concurrently composed—destined to remain unfinished—sonically encoded its autobiographical sources.

12

MARITAL CRISIS

Anna Moll more than blessed the liaison between Alma and Walter Gropius; she encouraged and enabled it. In her view it was a match between an unfortunately love-starved woman and a painfully impassioned man. Between Alma's leaving Tobelbad (either alone or, as may have been the case, with her mother) and her return to Toblach, the lovers secretly met in Vienna. The event was somehow insinuated into the gap between departure and arrival and hidden from Mahler, who was by now engrossed in creating the Tenth Symphony. The rendezvous was facilitated by Anna. In a "thank-you" letter to Anna dated 17 July, Gropius assumed a pious tone as he wrote, "I dedicated my brief stay here in the St. Stephen's Cathedral, since it appeared to me to be the only place worthy of my serious thoughts. Now I am more placid and can breathe again. . . . My [own] mother couldn't have let me go more filled with love."[1]

Anna was as if mother to them all, but in differing ways, and trusted by each of the three: Alma, Gropius, and Gustav. In participating in the illicit liaison, Anna was reliving her past, just as Alma, in turn, was psychologically tracking the life of her mother. The now fifty-three-year-old Anna had had an affair with Carl Moll when she was about Alma's present age; he had been a seemingly devoted student of her husband, Emil Schindler.[2] Thus Anna Moll, too, had been involved with two creative men, both artists. Anna had other affairs as well, one having produced an out-of-wedlock child Gretl, Alma's half sister, by an allegedly syphilitic lover.[3] On the occasion of her mother's marriage to her stepfather, the precocious Alma proved herself to have been well aware of the sexual nature of their relationship when she cleverly remarked that her mother had married the pendulum when before she had the whole clock!

Now it was Alma's turn. Just as Anna's duplicity in the past had enabled her to carry on as wife to Schindler and lover to Moll, she seemed to be able to comfortably divide her maternal affection between Gropius and Mahler. This split in Anna's mind may have been informed by the different esteem in which she held the two men. Whereas Mahler was at the peak of his career and Gropius just starting his own, the younger man was physically quite attractive, and Anna was hardly past appreciating him sexually, if vicariously. But beyond this he was German and a Christian; Mahler was a Jew. Anna's anti-Semitism appears at first to have been conventional for the time and place during the decade she knew Mahler and, accordingly, exceptions could be made for her Jewish son-in-law. Later—especially during the Hitler years—Anna, along with Carl, revealed the full extent of a fierce anti-Semitism. In this light, it seems likely that the Jew, devalued, could justifiably be betrayed and the Aryan favored.

Anna's involvement in Alma's love affairs was nothing new. The adolescent Alma, flirting with Klimt, complained to her diary that "day after day she [Anna] broke her word of honour . . . and thus kept track of the stations of my love. And in Genoa—oh horrors!—she read that Klimt had kissed me."[4] Alma did not mention that the diary had been left available for her mother to read. But by now Alma shared confidences of her love life with Anna, and her mother enjoyed the gossipy pleasure of viewing her own erotic life replayed by her daughter. Only one person was hurt by this enactment, Gustav Mahler. With no apparent sense of guilt or remorse, Anna Moll blithely carried on as an involved family member and Mahler's surrogate mother, and he seemed to respond reciprocally and ingenuously. But the correspondence with Anna waned with Gropius's ascendancy in the triangle. Mahler initially appeared unsuspecting; by the time he was likely to have had suspicions, he was already a sick man, which may explain a degree of submissiveness. By then he wanted "Mama" by his bedside.

Although Alma, in what ensued, may have unconsciously savored her power, she nevertheless feared hurting Mahler and felt guilty at the prospect. Thus while she returned to Altschluderbach refreshed, and speculated that the young man's infatuation had "restored the equilibrium of my self-confidence," she was "looking forward to the future and not eager for any change."⁵ But a correspondence began that would continue well into Alma's widowhood. For what remained of the summer, Alma asked Gropius to send his letters to *postlagernd*—general delivery to be called for personally.

A fortnight later, Alma discovered with horror that Gropius had not only failed to send a letter as she had requested, but addressed it to "Herr Direktor Mahler"! When Freud heard the story, it would certainly have elicited a chuckle. A decade earlier, he had published his *Psychopathology of Everyday Life*, a treatise on just the sort of slips of the pen Gropius appeared to have made.⁶ Years later, in her memoirs, Alma speculated, "I was never to find out whether the youth had gone mad or had subconsciously wanted his letter opened by Mahler himself."⁷ At the time, struggling to understand and troubled by the pain the affair would cause Mahler, she wrote to Gropius, reproaching him for having revealed "all our secrets and love nights":

> The only thing that lets me believe that you addressed the letter on purpose to Herr Mahler is the passage in your letter of today "Has your husband noticed anything yet?" Write me soon, I always want to understand you rightly.—otherwise I would have to consider some kind of craziness on your part. . . . Because it was revealed to him by accident and not by a frank confession on my part, he has lost all trust and faith in me.⁸

Alma again instructed Gropius to send his letters only to the designated box and, suspicious of his overture to Mahler, feared he would attempt to visit. She implored him not to do so, adding, "With feverish yearning I wait for your letter in which you must explain yourself." Clearly, Alma was not inclined to end the relationship despite the domestic disaster that had been set in motion, for she added, "I hope that you can say something to save me and you."⁹

Gropius soon answered, "Your letter gives me horrible anxiety for you both. No tragedy! I'll go out of my mind if you don't call me to come over. I want to justify myself before you both and clear up the mystery."¹⁰ What could Gropius have had in mind regarding the "mystery" (*Ratsel*)?

He was unquestionably confused about his own motives. Even if the address had been an unconscious slip, other processes of which he might not have been conscious were at work. His biographer, Reginald R. Isaacs, notes a pattern in Gropius's choice of women. They were usually older and "married or otherwise 'taken.'"[11] Moreover, Gropius would often contrive subsequently to have contact with their husbands or lovers. Thus an element of homoeroticism emerges, of a type that is inhibited sexually: a pattern of idealization of the man and consuming passion for the woman. The letter proved to be only the first of Gropius's several contacts with Gustav Mahler. Why he wrote "No tragedy!" confounds the riddle and suggests that Gropius was so involved with his own needs and gratifications that he was unable to recognize the gravity of his enactment in the lives of the Mahlers, or to empathize with the turmoil he had unleashed in writing the letter.

And in the Mahler household, tragedy it was. Alma related

> Mahler read it sitting at the piano. "What's this?" He cried in a choked voice and handed me the letter. He was, and remained, convinced that my admirer had addressed it to him on purpose— "to ask me for your hand," as he put it.[12]

The specter of *Die Meistersinger* had returned. Dormant these many years, Mahler's worry about their disparate ages resurfaced. He continued to be haunted by the story of Eva, the youthful Walther von Stolzing, and the elderly Hans Sachs, who had won her through his prize-winning song; a story that ended with Sachs's generously yielding his prize to the younger man. Ironically, the young lover was now another Walther and the old man, as Mahler was perceived, an acclaimed musician at the height of his creative powers while his sexual potency declined. Whether the content of the letter (no longer in existence) was explicit in this regard or not, Mahler found this myth as compelling as Gropius did, perhaps more so. In any event, the letter locked Mahler into the triangle with the lovers from sources within himself:

> Now—at last—I was able to tell him all.
> I told him I had longed for his love year after year and that he, in his fanatical concentration on his own life, had simply

overlooked me. As I spoke, he felt for the first time that something was owed to the person with whom one's life has once been linked. He suddenly felt a sense of guilt.[13]

As we have seen, Mahler had increasingly become aware of Alma's needs as time went on. The boldness of Alma's response lay not only in the degree of triumph it conveyed but in the lack of insight into her own narcissism, put shamelessly here as her sense of entitlement to a debt that must be paid. Nor did she make explicit here, or in other passages of memoirs, her own "sense of guilt" for the affair, although this may have convinced her that she could never leave her husband. Treated as yet another reversal of fate (like Putzi's death), the "tragedy" occasioned summoning Anna Moll to pick up the pieces— the very pieces, of course, of that which she had colluded to destroy. "Until she came," wrote Alma, "we could do nothing but walk about together all day long in tears."[14] Thus the composition of the Tenth Symphony was put aside.

Mahler was deeply shaken by Alma's betrayal. Perceiving the magnitude of his reaction, she attempted to undo her actions in words while continuing them in letters to her lover. The "elemental feeling" that she could never leave Mahler did not imply that she would relinquish Gropius. But when she reassured Mahler of this, "His face was transfigured. His love became an ecstasy. He could not be parted from me for a second."[15] Mahler left a note by her bedside: "Remember what you said to me yesterday and say it again today."[16]

Mahler's jealousy and clinging, described by Alma in a somewhat self-flattering light, was hardly the excessive romantic sentiment Alma construed it to be. Rather, it revealed the depth of a disturbance in which he could not tolerate separation without experiencing intense anxiety. The doors of their adjacent rooms had to be open at night so that he might hear her breathing. He attempted to continue working but at times, when Alma would come to fetch him for meals, she would find him on the floor weeping. He told her that he felt thus "nearer to the earth," an indication that his thoughts were about death.[17]

Mahler left poems and letters around the house for Alma to find as if he and she were far apart and communication required the written word. Anxiety bred worship as Alma found by her bedside the following:

> My breath of life!
> I've kissed the little slippers a thousand times and stood by your door with longing. You took pity on me, glorious one, but the demons have punished me again, for thinking again of myself and not of you, dearest. I can't move from your door; I'd like to stand there until I've heard the sweet sound of your living and breathing.[18]

On another occasion:

> My darling, my lyre,
> Come and exorcise the spirits of darkness, they claw hold of me, they throw me to the ground. Don't leave me my staff, come soon today so that I might rise up. I lie here and wait and ask in the silence of my heart whether I can still be saved or whether I am damned.[19]

The themes of abandonment and death in these notes disclosed the content of Mahler's inner suffering. In the emotional state that had been set off and was now running its course, reassurance of Alma's love had only a temporary effect; anxiety would soon reemerge begging for more. In another note after Alma offered reassurance, "I believe there can never now be a moment when I do not feel the happiness of knowing: she loves me! That is the whole meaning of my life. When I cannot say that, I am dead!"[20] Alma intuitively understood what Mahler was saying and this led her to live the lie she felt their marriage had become. She grasped the suicidal meaning of his communications, and warded off the potential anger obscured in her husband's excessive adoration.

At this point Mahler himself was suffering not only from depression but from a "decompensation" of his accustomed mental functioning (which was normally excellent), commonly called a nervous breakdown. The episode proved to be brief but intense and involved severe anxiety, distortions of reality, and even frank suicidal ideation.

As the episode reached its climax, Mahler's behavior became increasingly strange to Alma. He was insomniac and paced the house at night.

Once, she woke to find him standing at her bedside gazing at her. Another time, he fainted on the stairs, a lighted candle at his side. Finally, after several days had passed, Mahler developed a severe sore throat, which was always a hazard given his cardiac condition. Indeed, emotional stress and its psychosomatic sequelae would set the stage for the onset of a potentially fatal organic disease.

Alma's admonition to the impulsive Gropius not to visit Toblach fell on deaf ears as Gropius was experiencing the urgency about which he had written earlier to Alma: "I'll go out of my mind if you don't call me to come over." One afternoon, while riding through the village with Mahler, Alma spotted Gropius lurking under a bridge. When they arrived home, Alma told Mahler, who responded, "I'll bring him here myself." He found the young man and said simply, "Come."

> Nothing more was said. Night had fallen in the meantime; wordlessly they walked the long way, Mahler ahead carrying a lantern, the other following in the pitch darkness. I stayed in my room until Mahler came in, very serious, and asked me to see his rival.
>
> Reluctantly I agreed to have a talk with him, but after a few brief minutes I broke it off in sudden fear for Mahler. I found him pacing the floor with a book in his hand. Two candles burned on his desk. He was reading in holy scripture.
>
> "Whatever you do," he said, "will be well done. Choose!"[21]

Drama aside, this is a puzzling account. The walk from the village of Toblach to Altschluderbach on its outskirts was not short, as Alma indicated. A pleasant rural stroll would have taken half an hour; in darkness, more. One can only imagine the unspoken tension as the two men walked, one behind the other as Mahler held the lantern. One knows what Gropius wanted: Alma. But what could Mahler have been thinking? There is a cautionary tale about a lover who requested of a husband to sleep with the man's wife. The moral of the story is that, the moment one even engages in such an outrageous discussion, half the battle is lost. Here we find Mahler deeply engaged in the triangle as commerce with the lover replaced what would expectably be confrontation with the spouse. As far as we know, at no point did Mahler challenge Alma; he was clearly in no position to do so given his anxiety. Nor did he behave as if

Gropius's intrusion was offensive. Rather, in his present state of mind, perspective was lost and reality distorted in the direction of grand opera that he had many times directed: Walther was asking Hans Sachs for the hand of Evchen! The new plot twist was that Eva was given the choice and old Sachs-cum-Mahler had more than a fighting chance.

In fact, the outcome of this episode was anticlimactic as Alma observed wearily, "What choice did I have?" As Mahler had led Gropius to the villa by lantern light, he escorted the younger man to the edge of the property "hat in hand," that is, politely and respectfully.[22] Alma went to Toblach the following morning to see Gropius off at the train. In keeping with the somewhat unreal tenor of the previous night, Gropius wrote Mahler a rather bizarre thank-you note before leaving:

> Unfortunately we saw each other so little—it hurts me, that I can only cause you pain. Let me at least thank you for the "Noblesse" with which you approached me, and let me for the last time shake your hand.[23]

Gropius's insertion of French in his German text suggested his idealization of Mahler as virtual royalty. Although this was the last time he actually shook Mahler's hand—consistent with the civilized meeting and departure the previous night—it was hardly the last of Mahler in Gropius's life. Gropius followed Mahler's career avidly and attended whatever performances of his music he could. Deeply moved by such occasions, he would share these experiences with Alma in his letters.

On the train from Toblach, Gropius wired Alma from every station along the way and Alma related cagily in her memoir that "for weeks I kept getting entreaties by mail, by telegraph, by telephone."[24] (Interestingly, Mahler would follow suit when some weeks later he was en route to visit Freud.) In the weeks following, Alma and Gropius resumed their correspondence, now more passionate than ever. In all, there were about two dozen letters attributed to the summer and its aftermath, and an equal number the following winter.[25]

That Mahler was able to achieve as much as he did under the circumstances of the summer of 1910 was a miracle of creativity. Returning to Europe from America that spring, he had been much involved in preparing for the premiere of the Eighth Symphony in Munich from the beginning of May to the end of June. He only reached Toblach for the anticipated composing summer on 3 July. It is unlikely that any actual work had been done on the Tenth Symphony except for preliminary mental preparation. Meanwhile, Alma had been at the spa since early June and had begun the affair with Gropius. With his birthday on 7 July and time then spent answering greetings, Mahler didn't get to work composing until shortly before Alma's return to Toblach. According to Alma, it was about a week after her return that the infamous letter arrived and the emotional disruption ensued. Thus by then Mahler had scarcely two weeks remaining to work on the score.

Mahler probably wrote the first two movements—or at least sketched them—before the Gropius letter as they are considered the strongest and most complete, and do not contain "highly emotional superscriptions."[26] During the subsequent marital crisis, he did not enter the häuschen; Alma noted relief when he eventually did return there. The central, third *Purgatorio* movement was likely written then. The last days of August and the beginning of September were filled with other things—the visit to Freud, finishing touches to the Finale of the Ninth Symphony, and

The häuschen at Altschluderbach.

further preparation for the premiere of the Eighth. Mahler was accustomed to composing rapidly during the summer months and he did so when he was able to in 1910. Scholars have judged that Mahler accomplished what he did on the Tenth Symphony in five or six weeks.[27] The work, in five movements, remained incomplete at the summer's end and when Mahler left for his final season in America, he did not bring the unfinished score. Nevertheless, entire movements had reached an advanced stage and other portions existed in reduced score or sketch, such that other hands were ultimately able to render performing versions from the material Mahler had left.[28]

There is tragic autobiography encoded in the Tenth Symphony. The chronology of Mahler's life that summer, and the course of the work's composition, strongly indicate that these intensely personal portions of the music were written after the catastrophic events, indeed, as a direct response to them. Representative of the period of turmoil were verbal exclamations scrawled on the manuscript pages of the third, fourth, and fifth movements in seven separate locations. These were written spontaneously during the crisis or shortly thereafter, in the overflow of emotions and as personal verbal associations to the musical passages. But why did Mahler leave them instead of creating a clean copy? Indeed, in one instance where there is another copy of a preliminary sketch (to *Purgatorio*), the verbal statement is not only repeated ("Tod! Verk!") but clarified ("Todesverkundigen" —a reference to the *Todesverkündigung* of Wagner's *Die Walküre*).[29] Was it simply that the crayon Mahler used to dash these statements on the manuscript page could not be readily deleted? Or did he intend to remove these emotional superscriptions later, lacking the time during the summer? Alternatively, it is an intriguing possibility that Mahler meant music and word together to stand as an autobiographical statement, that there was something he wanted Alma and the world to know. For Alma would certainly have understood the occult musical meanings; and she is specifically addressed in several of these outpourings. As for Mahler's posthumous audience, many seemingly personal diaristic entries fairly beg the future reader to bear witness to his suffering.

Mahler's exclamation "Tod! Verk!" had long been thought to relate to Richard Strauss's *Tod und Verklarung* (Death and Transfiguration).

David Matthews clarifies that this verbal outburst "refers to the so-called *Todesverkündigung* (Annunciation of Death) scene in Act II of *Die Walküre*, in which Brunnhilde appears to Siegmund to tell him he must die."[30] A passage over which Mahler's superscription reads, "Have Mercy!" (Erbarmen!) follows. This too is a Wagner reference, "the cry of the wounded Amfortas in Act I of *Parsifal*, the climax of his lament when he is called upon . . . to perform the grail ritual."[31] In the end Amfortas begs for death but is healed by Parsifal, who proclaims himself king of the grail. The "Have Mercy!" passage of Purgatorio is associated musically with a striking moment in the first (Adagio) movement; the intense and dissonant outburst of the "*Neuntonklang*" or nine-note chord. Matthews, who concurs that these were conscious connections on Mahler's part, writes of this "potent symbol of pain and anguish, the nine-note chord," and infers a "psychological link between *Parsifal* and the Tenth Symphony. For Mahler, surely, felt wounded by Alma's betrayal, and cried out for his wound to heal."[32] Besides *Die Meistersinger*, then, other Wagner operas that Mahler had conducted remained active in his imagination and lent a layer of meaning to his experiences.

Two further superscriptions in the *Purgatorio* movement are biblical: "O God! O God! Why hast thou forsaken me?" (O Gott! O Gott! Warum hast du mich verlassen?) and "Thy will be done!" (Dien Wille gesche!).[33] Perhaps these were the passages Mahler had looked at while reading the Bible during Gropius's visit. According to Alma, Mahler had said to her, biblically, "Whatever you do will be well done." Identifying with Christ, Mahler expressed despair in terms of the dramatic moment of the Passion when faith wavered for a God who abandoned. This is hardly the only indication of Mahler's messianic identification, the earliest of which harks back to childhood when at the age of four or five he was asked what he wanted to be. "A martyr," he replied.[34] That Mahler viewed Alma as the powerful abandoning goddess was apparent in his poems and letters to her.

Probing *Purgatorio* more deeply, one finds an association from the past written musically. The title page under "Nro. 3" reads "Purgatorio oder Inferno," with "Inferno" crossed out. What else might have been on this page is a mystery, as the lower half has been cut away, probably by Alma, as David Matthews suggests, "because she did not want us to see what

Mahler had written there."[35] But the figuration that initiates the *perpetuo mobile* of the movement—what some have called "the mill of life"—is strongly reminiscent of a singular song in Mahler's vocal works, *Das irdische Leben* from *Des knaben Wunderhorn*. As stated earlier, this song is unique in vocal literature as it deals with childhood starvation. Unlike Schubert's *Erlkönig*, which this piece clearly emulates, the psychological issue is not seduction, abduction, or bodily harm, but rather absolute annihilation! And the human stage of life that it limns is not merely child-hood, as in the Schubert song, but specifically its earliest stage, when the helpless infant is completely dependent on his or her caregiver and the threat of abandonment portends the loss of life itself. The two songs do have in common, however, the issues of childhood death and the perils of delay. (Indeed, the original title of the *Wunderhorn* poem is *Verspätung*, meaning delay.)

In the successive strophes of *Das irdische Leben*, a child cries for nour-ishment: "Mother oh mother, I am hungry, give me bread or I shall die" (Mutter ach Mutter, es hungert mich, gib mir Brot, sonst sterbe ich). The mother's seems responsive at first, with a lilting cantabile melody urging the delay and tolerance of frustration that the child must learn in life: "Wait a little darling child! Tomorrow we will quickly bring in the corn" (Warte nur, warte nur, mein liebes Kind! Morgen wellen wir erten geschwind). But when in subsequent stanzas the child becomes increas-ingly agitated (and his vocal line more jagged) and the mother responds in the same singsong fashion (and tonality) for the child to wait while the corn is successively harvested and threshed, she appears by turns unre-sponsive and wooden. When the bread is finally baked, the child is dead; the mother who had seemed to be good enough has turned into the bad mother.

In the performance indications on the score, Mahler had written "uncanny," an affect conveyed in the Tenth Symphony's *Purgatorio*. Mahler's intense response to Alma's betrayal as revealed in his notes to her sounded the alarm of threatened abandonment. When the familiar becomes unfamiliar—as when the beloved suddenly becomes the betrayer; or as in the song the good and trusted mother becomes the starving mother—the affect of the uncanny prevails. As Alma herself noted, Mahler could not bear separation from her without experiencing anxiety. It is in the music of *Purgatorio* via *Das irdische Leben* that this feeling is most poignantly encoded. And while Freud would shortly relate Mahler's anxieties to his attachment to his mother as the source of neurosis, Mahler himself made the association here in music.

The texts of these verbal outcries have all the earmarks of a suicide note: a death is announced; an unbearable wound is exposed begging mercy and release; the despair attending perceived abandonment is bemoaned; and a final resignation is reached: "Thy will be done." In the exclamations on the score of the E minor Scherzo movement, the wish inherent in suicide is explicit: "The Devil leads me in a dance. Madness seizes me, Curses! Anihilate me that I may forget, that I am! That I may cease to be" (Der Teufel tanzt es mit mir. Wahnsinn, fass mich an,

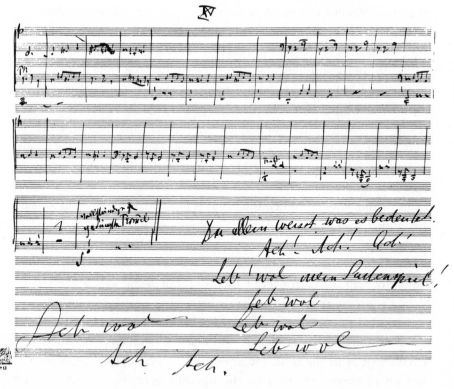

Mahler's Tenth Symphony, end of fourth movement.

Verfluchten! Vernichte mich dass ich vergesse, dass ich bin! Dass ich aufhore, zu sein dass ich ver). In a suicidal communication, the victim turns passive into active as the fear of annihilation becomes the wish to be no more.

The suicidal communications are addressed to Alma. A drum stroke ends the movement in which Mahler explicitly wrote, "You alone know what this means" (Du allein weisst was es bedeutet). And indeed, Alma would have known that Mahler was referring to the fireman's funeral that had moved them so deeply the year earlier from their apartment high in the Majestic Hotel. The odd event had held some vague portent at the time and now Mahler spelled it out in a private communication to Alma: he believed himself to be under sentence of death. The note continues, "Oh! Oh! Oh! Farewell my lyre! Farewell, Farewell, Farewell" (Ach! Ach! Ach! Leb'wol mein Saitenspiel! Leb' wol, Leb' wol, Leb' wol). The despairing message is completed in the superscriptions of the Finale: "To live for thee! To die for thee! Almschi" (Fur dich leben! Fur dich sterben! Almschi).

Suicidal ideas do not necessarily imply suicidal intent let alone suicidal behavior. Moreover, although Mahler's experience was intense, it was short lived. (Some transient disturbed states, where acute, may result in self-destruction.) But Mahler was too connected to his multiple lives to contemplate actually ending them. If hopelessness engulfed him in feeling abandoned, the promise of creative fulfillment in the premiere of the Eighth Symphony and the next New York season lay on the horizon. Mahler's acute breakdown occurred within a matter of little more than a week or ten days, while its consequences and vicissitudes persisted at least to the end of the summer, and beyond that to the end of his life, now less than a year away.

Mahler's scribblings on the manuscript of the Tenth Symphony comprise a symbolic suicide, at once expiating guilt, discharging aggression, and satisfying the atonement he perceived to be required by Alma. One would expect then that the renewed energy of rebirth would ensue. The superscriptions of the Tenth are reminiscent of Beethoven's *Heiligenstadt Testament*, which Maynard Solomon has read as symbolic suicide after which the artistic breakthrough of the *Eroica* occurred and changed musical history. "Beethoven," Solomon writes, "here enacted his own death in order that he might live again."[36] We can only speculate what innovations Mahler's next symphony might have contained.

Alma seemed intuitively aware of the issues that had emerged for Mahler and of their potential dangers. In a letter to Gropius after his visit, she wrote, "On my side I experienced something that I thought not possible. Namely, Gustav's love is so boundless—that my remaining with him—in spite of all that has happened—means life to him—and my leaving—will be death to him . . . Gustav is like a sick magnificent child."[37]

Indeed, Mahler became more loving and attentive toward Alma. The jolt had been powerful, its meaning augmented by Mahler's underlying fears of abandonment and annihilation. That these had never before come to the surface reflected Mahler's aloof and controlling attitude even when he was most in love. In the past, he had been the one to terminate liaisons, frequently in a calculating manner and conveniently concurrent with a change in his conducting post. He always had the next step in mind. But never before had he been so committed hence so vulnerable. As in all marriages, he and Alma shared a common history; theirs included triumphs such as that in Krefeld and tragedies such as the death of their child. Thus even as anxiety distorted Mahler's perceptions and behavior, a part of him truly valued Alma and would experience the loss of her as bereavement as well.

Beyond this, however, Mahler also exhibited uncharacteristic behavior that reflected remorse and the need to appease. Alma related:

> One day during this time of emotional upsets I went for a walk with our little Gucki. When we were nearly home again I heard my songs being played and sung. I stopped—I was petrified. My poor forgotten songs. I had dragged them to and fro to the country and back again for ten years, a weary load I could never get quit of. I was overwhelmed with shame and also I was angry; but Mahler came to meet me with such joy in his face that I could not say a word.
>
> "What have I done!" he cried. "These songs are good— they're excellent. I insist on your working on them and we'll have them published. I shall never be happy until you start

composing again. God, how blind and selfish I was in those days." And he played them over again and again.[38]

Mahler had brought many a singer to tears, frustration, and murderous impulse by his exacting standards. Not infrequently, he confronted musicians in a humiliating manner. Mahler contained his private judgment of Alma's songs. In this instance he suspended his critical faculties in keeping with the idealization of Alma that resulted from the summer's events. Alma, of course, did in fact have some training and had a degree of competence. In an assessment of her work, Susan Filler remarks perhaps generously, "Alma was a good composer who happened to marry a better one."[39] It might more accurately be said that a would-be composer married a musical genius. In any case, it is not at all clear that Alma would have had any sort of career nor was her impulse to create pressing. Once released from Mahler's constraints, and even encouraged by him, she did not resume her composing career to any degree. Nor, according to Filler, had Alma's style developed after the ten-year hiatus. As for potential rivalry with Mahler, competition had already ended in disaster when Otto had attempted to follow in his brother's footsteps. Otto's life ended in suicide. But Mahler would not let anything close to this come to the fore. Before the end of 1910 he saw to it that five of Alma's songs were published.

During a night of insomnia, thinking of the forthcoming premiere of the Eighth Symphony, Mahler decided to dedicate the work to Alma. It was something of a momentous decision, fraught with superstition, and Mahler had always avoided it in the past. In some sense it also involved sharing honors and deflecting attention from himself as sole creator. He had written to his publisher at dawn and now stood by Alma's sleeping bedside asking, "Would it give you a little pleasure if I dedicated the Eighth to you?" Alma, by this time alarmed at Mahler's atypical behavior and wary of its further consequences, responded, "Don't do it. You've never dedicated anything to anybody. You might be sorry later."[40]

The intensity and rigidity of Mahler's feelings about Alma's music emerged later that summer during a rare visit by the conductor (and champion of Mahler's music) Oskar Fried. Mahler was recovering from the sore throat noted earlier and, except for the hours composing in the häuschen, spent the rest of the day in bed. Anna Moll, who had been summoned during the domestic crisis, was still visiting, and she was sitting with Mahler, at the edge of his bed. He called out to Alma to play her songs for Fried, and after the first he impatiently asked the conductor what he thought of it. Unlike Mahler's, Fried's critical faculties were compromised only as far as a guest's tact might dictate. He answered, "Very gifted," or "Very nice," which Alma considered "impudent." Mahler flew into a rage and it was all Anna could do to restrain him from jumping up and abusing Fried to his face. Alma could hear his tirade through the walls. Calling Fried an idiot, Mahler said he'd be lucky to compose anything half as good. Fried heard this and since Mahler had not calmed down by the end of the day, the evening meal was strained. The next morning Fried sounded out Anna with "Frau Moll, I think I'd better go, eh?" She replied, "I think so too, dear Fried."[41]

At some point after Mahler resumed composing, the idea of a consultation with Sigmund Freud was raised. The impetus likely came from Alma for several reasons. Her cousin Dr. Richard von Nepallek (1864–1940) had often served as family consultant in medical matters and it was he who played the role of liaison in contacting Freud. A doctor of laws and medicine, Nepallek was a practicing physician and forensic expert. He was also an early adherent of psychoanalysis and would become a member of the Vienna Psychoanalytic Society the following year, recommended by Alfred Adler. Alma did not share Mahler's initial bias against psychoanalysis because of its reputed sexual content. To the contrary, what she took from popular accounts of Freud's early theories would have related to the effects of sexual frustration. And the self-cure had proven effective. This was reflected in some of the intimate passages in her correspondence with Gropius, where she wrote of their relationship being the only "healthy" thing in her life.[42]

The urgency that Mahler felt to appease Alma—operative in the dedication of the Eighth as well as in the promise to publish her songs—would in itself have motivated him to seek a meeting with Freud, if that were Alma's wish. But his procrastination in setting an appointment with Freud in Vienna was not simply psychological resistance. It may well have stemmed from the impetus that was by now driving Mahler to complete the symphony. He abhorred wasting time during the precious summer days and having resumed composing he would have been loathe to leave the häuschen.

According to Freud, Mahler made and broke two appointments by telegraph before accepting the third, which by then had to be in Holland, where Freud was vacationing with his family. Mahler's procrastination not only meant having to squeeze the visit to Freud between composing in Toblach and rehearsals in Munich, but necessitated a twenty-hour train ride to Holland. With matters thus arranged, the arduous trip had an element of expiation. Mahler left Toblach on 25 August for the consultation the following day. En route to Freud, Mahler telegraphed Alma a goodnight greeting from a stop at Innsbruck, only a short distance away: "All good and evil powers accompany me; you sit throned in triumph. Goodnight, my lyre, I feel only joy and longing."[43] His adoring tribute suggests that the trip to the doctor was something of a royal command performance. Mahler strolled during a two-hour wait in Cologne for the connecting train that would take him to Leiden. Anticipating Freud, he telegraphed Alma, "Hope to find a precious word early tomorrow."[44]

13

THE WALKING CURE

The city of Leiden in southern Holland is situated in such a manner that two separate branches of the Rhine enter from the east and unite in the center, where an old castle once stood. Intersecting the broad quays of the river were numerous canals and tree-lined streets. In 1910 Leiden was a tranquil town of fifty thousand and perhaps the perfect walking place, particularly on a quiet Friday afternoon. It was there that Sigmund Freud and Gustav Mahler strolled on 26 August. The two men were engaged in a peripatetic psychoanalytic consultation, even more unusual then than it would be now. Like the branches of the Rhine, each had entered the city by a different route. Freud had arrived on the small steam trolley that connected Leiden with the seaside resort of Noordwijk, less than ten miles away, where the Freud family was vacationing. The trip took a little less than an hour. Mahler, having changed trains in Cologne, had come in from the south. He had stayed overnight at the Hotel Lion d'Or, expecting to meet with Freud the following day.

As prearranged, they met not at Mahler's hotel, as Freud would later recall, but at a café, In den Vergulden Turk, the Golden Turk, on the Breestraat, Leiden's main street. There, under the sign of the Turk, each respectfully tipped his hat and shook the other's hand. Thereupon, doctor and patient embarked on a four-hour *Spaziergang* that took them through the maze of the ancient city and through the web of Mahler's troubled mental life. Neither could have been unaware of the meaning of the word *leiden* in their native tongue: to bear pain, to suffer.

Freud's steam trolley: Noordwijk to Leiden.

Like Mahler, Freud was at the end of a demanding season—the psychoanalytic "year" that mirrors the academic. And important events had taken place in the new world for Freud just as they had for Mahler. He had been in the United States in September, where an honorary doctor of law degree had been conferred on him by Clark University in Worcester, Massachusetts. It was a singular occasion for Freud, who, through the many trials of the decade that followed, would remember it as "the realization of an incredible daydream." In particular, he contrasted the unprejudiced and open acceptance of psychoanalysis in America to its reception in Europe, where, like the patient he was about to meet, he often felt like an outsider. "In Europe," Freud wrote, "I felt like someone excommunicated."[1] As for the Viennese, Freud later that autumn wrote to Carl Jung, who had been with him in America, "I sometimes get so angry at my Viennese that I wish them a single rear end, so that I could thrash them all with one stick."[2] Shortly before the summer, he had convened an international congress of psychoanalysis in Nürnberg, a major achievement that for him marked the end of "the

Breestraat.   LEIDEN.
„IN DEN VERGULDEN TURK",
Grand Café Restaurant.

At the sign of the Golden Turk, August 1910.

childhood of our movement," although it controversially diluted Vienna's seminal influence.[3] The internationalization of psychoanalysis at Nürnberg was for Freud what the premiere of the Eighth Symphony in Munich would be for Mahler.

The consultation in Leiden was necessary for Mahler but considerably less than convenient for Freud. He was exhausted by the strain of the Nürnberg congress and was only just recovering from a bout of colitis that had followed earlier in the summer. His mood was not his best. He had noted his pattern of experiencing the "real misery of exhaustion that . . . goes along with the end of the work year" only weeks into his vacation.[4] Moreover, the course of the rest of the summer was uncertain since his mother-in-law, Emmeline Bernays, was slowly dying of a terminal cancer in Hamburg, and Martha, Freud's wife, could be called away at any time. Finally, this vacation was particularly important for Freud as the two previous summers had left something to be desired. He was

Sigmund Freud, c. 1910.

corresponding with his colleague Sándor Ferenczi about a proposed trip together and wrote, "The vacation this time is very important to me as well. The last two summers I, too, did not have the fairy-tale feeling of living in freedom and beauty."[5] Freud's life in Vienna was parceled by the clock; "points of importance" in psychoanalysis, as he would write, are issues of "time and money." He would "lease a definite hour" for the patient's use.[6] Only in the summer did he have the freedom to reclaim this time for himself.

However, Freud could not turn down Mahler's request even if the latter had inconvenienced his erstwhile psychoanalyst by his double cancellation. Like Mahler, the moralistic Freud was contemptuous of those he considered "worthless" and, accordingly, he could not refuse a man of Mahler's reputation. As Freud said, "I made an exception by receiving someone during my vacation, but a man like Mahler!"[7] This in itself would be healing for Mahler's fractured esteem.

The Freud family was spending August in Noordwijk, on the North Sea, at the Pension Noordzee. The location, which had to be within a day's journey to Hamburg, had been selected with the help of some Dutch patients. Freud had arrived with his two youngest sons, Oliver and Ernst. The first evening of vacation, he had exulted at the "glowing red sunset from the breezy balcony of our apartment." He would walk briskly on the beach, poking seaweed with his ever present walking stick. When asked by a visitor what he expected to find, he replied characteristically, "Something interesting. You never know."[8] But he missed his womenfolk: his wife, Martha, and her unmarried sister, Minna Bernays, who had long been a member of the Freud household.

Martha Bernays would follow her husband shortly; she had gone from Vienna to Hamburg, along with Minna, to visit their mother. In contrast to the Mahlers', the Freuds' marriage was conventional for that time and place. Martha's role was never in question. As Peter Gay puts it, "Martha Freud was the complete bourgeoise."[9] She ran the household at 19 Berggasse in Vienna efficiently and with good cheer, and bore six children in the first nine years of marriage. She would have preferred three.

In courtship the young Freud had found Martha "sweet, generous and reasonable"—sobriquets that compensated for the fact that, as he had "candidly told her, she was not really beautiful in the literal sense."[10] It would be hard to imagine traits of greater contrast than Alma Mahler's seductiveness, narcissism, and duplicity. Like Mahler, Freud could be quite possessive. During courtship, he demanded that Martha renounce her attachment to her family—and with it, traditional Jewish customs. He wrote to her: "If you can't be fond enough of me to renounce for my sake your family, then you must lose me, wreck my life, and not get much yourself out of your family."[11] Although there was no messenger to urgently convey her affirmative reply, as there was with Alma, Martha answered in terms of her devotion. She adored Freud and idolized him to the degree that she naively wondered why they had to search for a summer house each year. Why had not some admiring benefactor offered one?[12] Even now, Martha would leave her dying mother's bedside in Hamburg to be with her husband in Noordwijk. As for their sexual life, desire diminished for Freud from the time he was thirty-seven. After the family was completed, intercourse between husband and wife was sporadic and by the time Freud met Mahler, he himself had experienced episodes of impotence.

Sister-in-law Minna Bernays, four years younger than Martha, was almost a marital counterpart, "the intellectual sister, known for her witty remarks and capable of following Freud's imaginative flights at least some of the way."[13] In a sense, Freud had courted Minna as well as Martha, writing her affectionate letters ("My Treasure") and signing himself, "Your Brother, Sigmund." Tragically, Minna's fiancé had died young, and encouraged by Freud, she embraced a role in the Freud family that was mutually gratifying. Minna was the secret sharer and Freud told a later confidante, Marie Bonaparte, that while he had been working on his early theories, only Minna and his Berlin colleague Wilhem Fliess had believed in him. Martha went unmentioned in this regard. A rumor that Freud and Minna had had an affair had no basis in fact.

In giving Mahler a last chance to see him that summer, Freud was anticipating the end of the family's vacation by the sea, and plans that he had for the following weeks, before returning to Vienna. He was awaiting Sándor Ferenczi, his colleague and disciple, and the psychoanalyst he had deputized to propose the international organization at the Nürnberg congress. Shortly after the congress, they had begun to plan a trip together to Italy. Although it would inevitably be something of a working vacation, Freud's chief objective was travel to new places with an agreeable companion with similar tastes and with whom he could share experiences of art, culture, and interesting sights. Martha Freud did not fit this bill and, besides, her duties lay elsewhere. Minna Bernays might have been a candidate, but this would not have been seemly. Besides, by 1910, Minna had become singularly unattractive, looking older than her trim older sister. In mid-August Freud wrote to Ferenczi eagerly, "It would be nice if you came here soon. Every day earlier means a possibility to see more and to move about freely."[14] The trip would take the two men via Paris, Florence, and Rome to Naples, where they would board a ship for their ultimate destination, Sicily. But more than this, it would be an opportunity for bonding; Ferenczi was destined to become one of Freud's closest and most important colleagues at that time. Anticipating the trip in their lively correspondence, Freud had written, "I am looking forward to a friend and traveling companion between whom and myself not a hint of discord is possible."[15] Meanwhile, the August sojourn over, Martha would move the household to The Hague for a further fortnight, before returning to Vienna to await her husband.

Mahler and Freud's session was an agreeable experience for both men, associated by each with collegiality, friendship, and problem solving.

Freud was then informally analyzing the first generation of psychoanalysts on such walks, during which he would also listen to their respectful analyses of his own motives. Mahler, too, customarily used such walks in the company of intimates to work through personal conflict as well as creative problems. During his *Wunderhorn* years (up to 1901, when Mahler met Alma), Natalie Bauer-Lechner had filled this role: Mahler talking, expressing, ventilating, revealing and concealing, justifying, reviling, pontificating; Natalie, walking quietly at his side, questioning, eliciting, but above all, *listening*. For the past three years, however, strenuous exercise was officially forbidden Mahler. Normally, Alfred Roller wrote, "Mahler was incapable of strolling. . . . Uphill he would go far too fast; I could barely keep up with him."[16] The four-hour walk with Freud was leisurely, the two men pausing from time to time to reflect while looking out at the canals or to sit at a bench or perhaps a café. In any event, with Freud—a physician, after all—Mahler would have felt a sense of freedom, loosened of constriction, and safe passage.

Mahler was fifty at the time, Freud fifty-four. Rapport was fostered by the striking similarities in the men's lives, their experiences and personalities, even their ways of thinking. The two spoke the same language— German, of course, but with the regional coloring, idiomatic expressions, and obligatory quotations of educated men who shared the same socioeconomic, historical, and cultural background. But beyond this, they "spoke the same language" in another way: a kind of congruence of cognition that facilitated an immediate connection.

Both avid readers, Mahler and Freud shared a keen sense of irony, an appreciation of humor, and a knack for turning a pithy epigram. Irony was Mahler's métier and he had a rare gift for encoding the ironic in music. One example is that called "progressive tonality." Just as the hero of a drama may end up in a place other than one might anticipate, so do many of Mahler's works begin in one key and, contrary to classical custom, end in another. A disproportionate number of texts that Mahler selected for musical settings involve irony. Moreover, life itself had been an exercise in irony: summoned to Vienna to an exalted lifetime position, his tenure was now in New York; having married to have a family, he was bereft of a child and marriage itself was faltering.

On an everyday level, Mahler's turn of phrase was often cast ironically. "Who hath brought me into this land?" he would say.[17] And his elated sentiment "How blessed, how blessed—a composer to be" would become "Oh blessed, oh blessed a modern to be."[18] Later, with mock helplessness at musical incompetence:

Motto: How blessed, how blessed

A barber
Waiter
Tenor
Rentier
Member of the Committee of the Universal German Music
   Society to be[19]

But the humorous could become vitriolic, as Mahler's brothers well knew—"those winged stallions, my noble brothers."

The philosophical implications of Mahler's progressive tonality would appeal to Freud, who knew only too well "from the couch" that the fate of dreams, strivings, and wishes traverse a circuitous route in life, and rarely is the outcome straightforward. As his experience might have dictated, the ironic in life is the rule rather than, as in common wisdom, the exception. But more cogently, the very notion of the unconscious, the fundamental principle of psychoanalysis, involves the ironic: things are not what they seem or what they seem to mean; there are multiple and hidden meanings, the emergence of which often take one by surprise. Indeed, not infrequently, psychoanalytic interpretation is the very praxis of irony. When Freud noted during their session that Alma unconsciously equated Mahler with her painter father, who was "ein Maler," he was interpreting in the ironic mode.

Freud, who wrote a treatise titled *Jokes and Their Relation to the Unconscious*, was an inveterate collector of Jewish jokes and had once hoped to publish a collection. One of the bases for Jewish humor is irony, which Freud noted to be "very close to joking."[20] Where irony, humor, and modes of thinking converge, we encounter important aspects of Jewish identity.

Both Mahler and Freud were Jews although "unbelievers"; they were what Peter Gay calls "Godless Jews."[21] What yoked them both to

Jewishness is best expressed in Freud's *Address to the Society of B'nai Brith*:

> What bound me to Jewry was (I am ashamed to admit) neither faith nor national pride. . . . But plenty of other things remained over to make the attraction of Jewry and Jews irresistible—many obscure emotional forces, which were the more powerful the less they could be expressed in words, as well as a clear consciousness of inner identity, the safe privacy of a common mental construction.[22]

As Josef Yurushalmi comments, Freud seemed to believe that "the character traits embedded in the Jewish psyche are themselves transmitted phylogenetically and no longer require religion in order to be sustained."[23] It was precisely this "safe privacy" that formed the virtual walls of the consulting room that was Leiden. More than this, the same "mental construction" that fostered rapport between the two men richly informed the work of each. The key was interiority. Freud's was the science of inner life. Mahler's music, with its well-formed musical and verbal associations and its eclectic breakthroughs, mirrored mental process. Indeed, when Mahler was the butt of anti-Semitic musical criticism, the diversity within was perceived as mongrel and labeled "cosmopolitan," a euphemism for Jewish. According to Alfred Roller, Mahler was "not a card-carrying Jew and at times more attacked for not being so than he was from the other side." With characteristic irony, Mahler said during his final period as director of the opera, "It's a funny thing, but it seems to me that the anti-Semitic newspapers are the only ones who still have any respect for me."[24] The designation "Godless Jew" does not completely account for the complexity of Mahler's musical thought. Bruno Walter called him a "seeker after God."[25] In his music, one finds "a constant search for the divine."[26] This is most apparent in the fervent words Mahler wrote for the Finale of the Second Symphony, which ended: "you will be carried to God" (Was du geschlagen zu Gott wird es dich tragen). But it was not a Jewish divine.

Ancestors of Mahler and Freud had followed the same upwardly striving migratory path from province to Vienna. The significance of the Mahler family's move from Gustav's birthplace in Kaliste to Iglau, only twenty-two miles away, was that Iglau was midway between Prague and

Vienna. It was situated on the railway to the capital and was therefore squarely in the worldly current. A more direct route of family migration was followed by Freud's father, Jacob, who moved the family directly from Freiberg (now Pribor) to Vienna when Sigmund was three years of age. A victim of geography rather than a beneficiary, as Bernhard Mahler had been, Jacob's textile manufacturing business faltered when the new railroad to Vienna bypassed Freiberg. With the Mahlers, it remained for Gustav to continue the historical family passage when Bernhard sent him to Prague to attend the supposedly superior gymnasium there, and when, at age fifteen, he convinced his father to permit him to enter the Vienna Conservatory.

Like many Jews who had embarked on this ancient procession from province to capital, neither Mahler nor Freud was observant. They perceived affiliation to be secondary to ambitions for professional success— as well as a potential obstacle. Unlike many nonbelievers, neither observed the Jewish High Holidays. However, the Freuds celebrated Passover and Purim, chiefly at the behest of Martha and as an occasion for family dinners. Mahler observed none of these; his holidays were all secular, with Christmas predominating.

In 1910 Jews comprised 8.6 percent of Vienna's population.[27] In effect there were two Jewish communities, one populated by the Polish, Galician Jews and one by the German-speaking Jews, who often looked down on their eastern brethren. Both Mahler and Freud identified themselves as German-Austrian. Mahler was always taken aback when, in the course of his travels, he inevitably encountered what he considered to be the worst Jewish elements. Typical was his writing to Alma from Lvov (Lemberg) in 1903, "No effort of imagination could conjure up a dirtier creature than the Polish Jew of these parts."[28] A younger Freud shared Mahler's contempt so graphically that his biographer declared that "a professional Jew-baiter could hardly have expressed it more forcefully."[29] However, with respect to connections with the Viennese Jewish community, there could hardly have been a greater contrast between the two men. The Jewish communities of Vienna sustained an astonishing number of organizations—religious, fraternal, political, and philanthropic. Mahler belonged to none of them. Freud was proud to belong to the B'nai B'rith, whose very name means "Children of the Covenant."

In a model statement of roots in his *Autobiographical Study*, Freud wrote: "I was born on 6 May, 1856, at Freiberg in Moravia, a small town in what is now Czechoslovakia. My parents were Jews, and I have remained a Jew myself."[30] In contrast, Mahler remained evasive, remarking only that he was "born a Jew." His conversion, an act that he said he undertook "from an instinct of self-preservation," had cost him "a great deal." In an earlier chapter this "cost" was considered in terms of the shame, guilt, and attendant stresses that underlay psychosomatic illness. Mahler claimed he had converted, a year or two after the deaths of both his parents, prior to his engagement in Vienna. If so, he had probably avoided telling his parents. Nevertheless, such breaks with the parental past take an emotional toll.

Both men paid the price of being Jews in the world in which they lived. But besides costs were benefits that, articulated by Freud, applied to Mahler equally. In the same B'nai B'rith address he spoke of his perception "that it was to my Jewish nature alone that I owed two characteristics that had become indispensable to me in the difficult course of my life. Because I was a Jew I found myself free from many prejudices which restricted others in the use of their intellect; and as a Jew I was prepared to join the Opposition and to do without agreement with the 'compact majority.'"[31] Mahler's independence of spirit, uncompromising ideals, and innovative nature would have been seen by Freud as reflecting the same Jewish background that was his own. No doubt such were the qualities Freud had in mind when he made an exception to see a man of Mahler's worth. The "Opposition" cited by Freud was of course the anti-Semitic establishment—the scientific establishment in Freud's case, the artistic in Mahler's; both suffered for their eventual acceptance. In Vienna, the Jew was the perennial outsider.

Mahler's version of the "outsider" was that of the wandering, homeless Jew; the Jew not as chosen but as exiled. This informed his fear of abandonment and the banishment he now feared at Alma's hand. The theme of Ahasuerus, the Wandering Jew, had been with him from as early as he could articulate it. A depressed and lonely Mahler writing to his adolescent friend Steiner conjured up a dream-image of "Ahasuerus (the Wandering Jew) with all his sufferings." Scorned by an angel and denied redemption, he "takes up his staff and goes on his way with tears, eternal, immortal."[32]

The Jew as outsider had important political implications for the founder of psychoanalysis. Most of Freud's analytic colleagues were Jewish and, predictably, he was most comfortable in their company. Sándor Ferenczi, for example, was a Hungarian Jew. But the discipline Freud developed was too precious, and as yet too fragile, to be tainted by its Semitic origins and thus become a target for anti-Semites. Fearing that his work would become known as a Jewish science, he cultivated Carl Jung and advanced Ernest Jones, both Gentiles. Nevertheless, in 1912 when Freud formed a secret committee dedicated to the promotion of psychoanalysis, all but one member (Jones) were Jewish;[33] Ferenczi's father had changed the family name from Fränkel and Otto Rank had been born Rosenfeld.[34] By then Jung was not to be trusted.[35]

Neither Mahler nor Freud admitted any knowledge of Hebrew from their early years. Freud's disavowal was explicit if untrue. In Mahler's case, it was taken for granted, although like Freud, he had had early experiences in the synagogue and completed the obligatory religious studies in gymnasium. Nevertheless, both were well acquainted with scripture—the Old and the New Testament. Mahler once told his friend Natalie:

> A magnificent symbol of the creator is Jacob, wrestling with God until He blesses him. If the Jews had been responsible for nothing but this image, they would still inevitably have grown to be a formidable people—God similarly withholds his blessing from me. I can only extort it from him in my terrible struggles to bring my works into being.[36]

Thus Mahler identified himself with Jacob—as he had in the setting of the *Urlicht* of the Second Symphony, confronting the Angel who would block his way to God. But in the conversation with Natalie, the Jews were still "they."

Freud wrote, "My deepest engrossment in the Bible story (almost as soon as I learned the art of reading) had, as I recognized much later, an enduring effect upon the direction of my interest."[37] Indeed, Freud's profound identification with the biblical Joseph prefigured his discoveries in *The Interpretation of Dreams* and was in turn reinforced by it. Leonard Shengold, who has written on this aspect of Freud's life, justly emphasizes Freud's ambition as a youth, his drive for power, and his identification with conquerors such as Hannibal and Napoleon. He states, "Freud, like Joseph, perceived that the ultimate secret of power was not force but understanding."[38] The aspect of the Joseph-in-Freud that would soon become relevant to Mahler's plight was that Joseph's legendary power lay precisely in his demonstrated ability to predict the future. It was this, rather than any psychoanalytic interpretation, that proved to relieve Mahler of the anxiety he was suffering.

The life histories of Mahler and Freud reveal many other parallels. They were both favored by their mothers, of which Freud wrote: "If a man has been his mother's undisputed darling he retains throughout life the triumphant feeling, the confidence in success, which not seldom brings actual success with it."[39] Self-confidence propelled both throughout their lives and was a means of tolerating the loneliness of the innovator. Mahler never doubted his worth as a composer. When his esteem was shattered, it was by the threat of losing Alma. Both Mahler and Freud were their mothers' first children and they experienced the existential trials of early life when siblings were born. But Freud had two-and-a-half years of his mother before the next birth whereas Mahler had scarcely a year. Much of their respective characters was formed in this context—not exclusively rivalry, however, but caring as well.

The early life of both Mahler and Freud had been clouded by the death of a younger brother. The infant Isador Mahler died before Gustav's birth and the deaths of four infant brothers followed before Mahler was fourteen, when his beloved brother Ernst died. Freud was able to recall his satisfaction at the death of his seven-month-old brother, Julius, who was born seventeen months after his own birth, with "malevolent wishes and genuine childhood jealousy."[40] "His death," Freud wrote to a colleague, "left the germ of guilt in me." An unconscious sense of guilt pervaded the mental lives of both men—the guilt of the survivor. Freud's oblique reference to his own rivalrous, fratricidal fantasies mirrors the universal human situation that forms the essential contours of Mahler's *Das klagende Lied*.

Both had surpassed their fathers in distinguished and visible ways and survivor guilt would only increase after Bernhard and Jacob died. At the time of their respective fathers' deaths, Mahler was twenty-nine, Freud forty. In his self-analysis Freud discovered that "it is as perilous to win one's oedipal battles as it is to lose them."[41] Mahler was a survivor on a grand scale, having outlived—and outdone—parents, multiple siblings, and youthful companions who had died, gone mad, or otherwise fallen by the wayside.

Both were creative geniuses and at the pinnacle of their careers, although Mahler more so than Freud at the time of their meeting. The year of Mahler's official conversion, 1897, marked a particular professional high point for each of the men. Mahler, at thirty-seven, had achieved the directorship of the Vienna Court Opera, the most influential artistic post of the Habsburg Empire. Freud, just past forty, was on the brink of his greatest discovery, which would be published two years later as *The Interpretation of Dreams*.[42] Looking to the cachet of the twentieth century, it was postdated to 1900. Years later, Freud would consider this "the most valuable of all the discoveries it has been my good fortune to make." Insight such as this, he said, "falls to one's lot but once in a lifetime."[43] Yet another similarity may be noted between the men. Work, for both, was autobiographical in significant ways. Mahler avowed this early on, when he equated his music with his life: "My whole life," he wrote, "is contained in my two symphonies."[44] Virtually all of Freud's major discoveries were the result of his self-analysis, among them the oedipal complex he would evoke in his consultation with Mahler. And in his masterwork, a number of the dreams purported to be those of patients proved to be his own. Interestingly, in the pursuit of career both had recently been in America—Mahler for his third season in New York, Freud lecturing at Clark University in Worcester, Massachusetts. Freud was catching up to the international reputation that Mahler already enjoyed.

It was in the spheres of art and science that they diverged, the very domains of the other's achievements. Freud, although highly responsive to nearly every form of art, was not musical, a condition anomalous for a Viennese of the time. Yet there is no reason to assume that everyone is equally endowed with a potential for this medium of expression. Freud's style was such that the auditory mode and its representation in time (that is, the essence of music) was far less cultivated than the visual— this despite his "talking cure" and writings on psychoanalytic listening. It is no coincidence that his greatest work should have been

The Interpretation of Dreams, in which he revealed a stunning sensibility in the visual sphere of perception, comparable to Mahler's in the auditory sphere. Although Mahler's "table talk" reveals a lively interest in contemporary science and philosophy, he was cool to psychoanalysis as science and treatment—a paradox, since his works fairly breathe psychological meaning.

Freud wrote of his scientific journey from the time of his revelation on hearing Goethe's beautiful essay on nature read aloud at a popular lecture. The "turning point" of his career was the abandonment of a theoretical career in favor of clinical medicine.[45] (He wrote ironically: "My teacher . . . corrected my father's generous improvidence by strongly advising me, in view of my bad financial position.") But any musical interest he may have had was limited to opera, and only a few "safe" operas at that: three by Mozart, including *Don Giovanni*; Wagner's *Der Meistersinger*; and Bizet's *Carmen*.[46] It was only the connection of the word to music that enabled Freud to enjoy these to any extent. It is reasonable to say that he did not know Mahler's music since he virtually never attended concerts of this kind. However, he may well have been present at an opera conducted by Mahler.

In turn, Mahler's interest in science was not casual. Bruno Walter recalled:

> Friends of his, professionally occupied with natural science, were hard pressed by his deeply penetrating questions. An eminent physicist whom he met frequently could not tell me enough about Mahler's intuitive understanding of the ultimate theories of physics and about the logical keenness of his conclusions or counterarguments.[47]

But it was "natural science," to be sure, that fascinated Mahler, not the science that Freud had discovered. Psychoanalysis was by now elaborated to the degree that it would serve as theoretical background to effective clinical work in which Mahler would shortly engage. In spite of Mahler's bias, Freud would find him psychologically minded.

The source of this psychological attunement in Mahler was related in part to a common cultural background. Both Freud and Mahler were steeped in the philosophy of Schopenhauer and Nietzsche; Mahler had set Nietzsche's "Midnight Song" from *Also sprach Zarathustra* in his Third Symphony. Freud acknowledged his debt to both philosophers, who had preceded him in understanding many of the basic tenets of psychoanalysis, in particular, the unconscious.[48]

Mahler read widely for a man of his double profession, Freud wider still as a man of letters and science. Another common literary locus was Dostoyevsky. Mahler was passionate about the Russian's writings; and Alma had described him as a "disciple," citing his frequent quoting, "How can one be happy while a single being on earth still suffers."[49] Mahler's friends admired his "Dostoyevskian love of humanity."[50] Shortly, while in America for the final season, Mahler suggested Alma reread *The Brothers Karamazov* while he was on tour. Having done so, she wired, "Splendid journey with Aliosha." Mahler wired back, "Journey with Almiosha much more splendid."[51] Mahler considered Dostoyevsky "the greatest psychologist in world literature." Ironically, Mahler shared his admiration for Dostoyevsky with brother Otto, whom Alma considered a "fanatical disciple" who philosophized about his imminent suicide in the manner of the Russian writer.[52] Freud was yet to write his study *Dostoyevsky and Parricide*, in which he distinguished four facets of the writer's rich personality: "the creative artist, the neurotic, the moralist and the sinner."[53] As in many of his formulations, Freud no doubt saw these traits in himself. The first three characteristics would have been evident to him in his observation of Mahler; the sinner existed in Mahler's fantasies as survivor, as it did in Freud's.

Neither man was free from neurosis or superstition; and both suffered from psychosomatic disturbances, the result of character, heredity, and aspiration played out under circumstances of adversity and tension. In both cases these took the form of migraine headaches and gastrointestinal problems. Curiously, there were other symptoms each had suffered as well. Freud experienced agoraphobia—the fear of open spaces—even after his self-analysis, whereas Mahler had transient fears of height. But Freud never suffered from the degree of depression Mahler experienced when he was blocked in completing the Second Symphony; nor had he ever experienced the breakdown of function that brought Mahler to see him. Both were obsessional in character and symptomatology, euphemized as the "minimal price" one has to pay when striving for excellence in one's field. Freud, in describing "an ideally 'normal' person," was probably writing of himself when he cited "a mixed type, [with] narcissistic, obsessional as well as hysterical layers to him." This was also likely the diagnosis he silently made during his consultation with Mahler. He would approach Mahler from the vantage point that "psychoanalysis has demonstrated that there is no fundamental difference, but only one of degree, between normal people, neurotics and psychotics."[54]

Both Mahler and Freud had a morbid fear of death. If a single theme can be said to pervade Mahler's works from the beginning ("Funeral March with Introductory Polka," age five) to the incomplete Tenth Symphony, it is death. Freud's romance with death was every bit as rich and creative as Mahler's. As his biographer Ernest Jones wrote, "the theme of death, the dread of it and the wish for it, had always been a continuous preoccupation of Freud's mind as far back as we know anything about it."[55]

Mahler's superstitions, such as avoiding naming his Ninth Symphony, are well known, Freud's less so. Mahler feared tempting fate by giving the symphony a number that the likes of Beethoven and Bruckner had failed to survive. Freud, too, was preoccupied with fateful numbers. When in 1899 he was assigned the telephone number 14362, he took the "43" as confirmation of the age at which he would publish *The Interpretation of Dreams*, whereas the ominous "62" represented the death knoll.[56] It was the equivalent of Mahler's "Tod! Verk!" on the manuscript of the Tenth, the announcement of death. Freud had initially harbored the fantasy that he would not live beyond the age of fifty-one, an anniversary he passed in May 1907. Subsequently, his sixty-second birthday had loomed. Beyond that, he feared the eighty-first, the age at which both his father and an older half brother died. These superstitions were fueled by survivor's guilt. The image of the guilty self appeared in the dreams of both men, from which, Freud wrote, "one is bound to emerge as the only villain among the crowd of noble characters who share one's life."[57]

At the time of their meeting, fifty-four-year-old Freud was safely past the dangers of this fifty-first year and not yet under the cloud of the sixty-second. Mahler had just passed his fiftieth, and Freud, noting Mahler's attachment to his mother, could not have failed to be attuned to its fantasied perils. Marie Mahler had died at fifty-two. As fate would have it, Mahler died before this birthday.

Had Mahler and Freud ever encountered one another earlier? Possibly a rare opera Freud attended had been conducted by Mahler, although frequently Gustav was in attendance supervising the performance while others conducted. However, in his very first season as director, Mahler conducted a performance of *Die Meistersinger* featuring his erstwhile paramour Anna von Mildenburg, which Freud may have attended. It is intriguing to consider that once before the two men had shared the story of Walther, Hans Sachs, and the bride-prize.

Beyond this, since they had resided in the same city for nearly fifteen years, Mahler and Freud had acquaintances and places in common and the tracks the two made were rife with coincidence. Both were avid walkers in the city but their paths had never crossed. Surprisingly few people bridged their two lives. One was the writer Arthur Schnitzler, who had been deeply moved by the Finale of Mahler's Sixth Symphony, leading Mahler to exclaim, "This Schnitzler must be a splendid fellow."[58] It had been Schnitzler who, after encountering Mahler sitting on a bench after Putzi's death, wondered in a letter "how he was able to go on living."[59] On another occasion Schnitzler had watched Mahler walking for fully five minutes, fascinated by the strangeness of his gait. An admirer of Mahler, he would attend the coming premiere of the Eighth Symphony in Munich. But Mahler was not the avid reader of Schnitzler that Freud was. In an admiring letter to him, Freud had written of his envy for Schniztler's "secret knowledge" of the human heart.[60] Indeed, Freud considered Schnitzler to be his own doppelgänger.

As it happened, Mahler had visited 9 Berggasse, the location of Freud's home and office, more than once, albeit in his student years. When he first came to Vienna, Mahler was a member of a loosely organized socialist-vegetarian group more or less headed by Victor Adler, the social democrat. Freud had once heatedly debated Adler in his own student days. Adler occupied the ground-floor apartment at 19 Berggasse until 1892, when Freud took it over for use as his first office for a number of years.

The person who formed the closest bridge between the two men was Max Graf, a music critic and member of Freud's circle. Although Freud was no habitué of cafés, preferring to take his leisure in domestic quarters except for his regular walks, Graf and Mahler could be seen regularly at the café of the Hotel Imperial, only a hundred yards from the opera. Graf was a supporter of the new music Vereinigung formed by Schoenberg and Zemlinsky, of which Mahler was a senior member. In his writings he sympathetically cited the difficulties Brahms, Bruckner, and others had had with Viennese audiences.[61] But he was no uncritical champion of Mahler. He had mercilessly weighed into the Viennese performance of Mahler's Fifth Symphony with "no less than twenty-three quotations from famous writers . . . all of which were meant to show the fatal weaknesses Mahler had displayed."[62] Yet in his final assessment of Mahler in each of two books written after Mahler's death, he was admiringly appreciative, assigning Mahler an important place in the history of Viennese music. Of Mahler's symphonies he wrote there: "They are huge symphonic mystery plays, starting from earth and climbing to heaven, where choruses of angels and the light of the Almighty hail the newcomer, while in the depths Death plays on a strident violin and hell screams."[63]

At the time of the walk in Leiden, Graf was a regular member of the Vienna Psychoanalytic Society and the first to apply psychoanalytic concepts to music and musical creativity.[64] Freud, despite his musical deficit, was said to have "collaborated" with Graf in such theoretical works as a study of Richard Wagner. *The Minutes of the Vienna Psychoanalytic Society* reveal Freud's lively interest in Graf's work and his input of ideas. In psychoanalytic circles, Graf is perhaps best remembered as the father of "Little Hans," the subject of a famous case of Freud's. Referred to anonymously in the study, Graf wrote weekly accounts of the child's treatment and progress, Freud in effect supervising the case.[65]

But the most striking connecting link between Freud and Mahler came from an unexpected quarter: Bruno Walter. Toward the end of 1906, when Walter was "second-in-command" at the Court Opera, he developed a troubling symptom, a paresis or weakness of his arm. "Medical science called it a professional cramp. It looked deucedly like an incipient paralysis," wrote Walter.[66] It had progressed to the point where he had to cancel conducting appearances and his wife had to serve as amanuensis for his correspondence. The disability reached alarming proportions as "the rheumatic-neuralgic pain became so violent that I could no longer use my right arm for conducting or piano playing. I went from one prominent doctor to another. Each one confirmed the presence of psychogenic elements in my malady."[67]

As a result, Walter continued, he consulted "Professor Sigmund Freud, resigned to submit to months of soul searching."

> The consultation took a course I had not forseen. Instead of questioning me about sexual aberrations in infancy, as my layman's ignorance had led me to expect, Freud examined my arm briefly. . . . [H]e asked me if I had ever been to Sicily. When I replied that I had not, he said that it was very beautiful and interesting, and more Greek than Greece itself. In short, I was to leave that very evening, forget all about my arm and the Opera, and do nothing for a few weeks but use my eyes. I did as I was told.[68]

Walter left soon after, but on his return he was still ailing and resumed sessions with Freud, who advised him to return to conducting. Walter recounted the following dialogue:

> WALTER: But what if I can't move my arm?
> FREUD: Try it, at any rate.
> w: And what if I should have to stop?
> f: You won't have to stop.
> w: Can I take upon myself the responsibility of possibly upsetting a performance?
> f: I'll take the responsibility.

> And so I did a little conducting with my right arm, and then with my left, and occasionally with my head. There were times when I forgot my arm over the music. I noticed at my next session with Freud that he attached particular importance to my forgetting. I tried once more to conduct, but with discouraging results . . . I also tried to familiarize myself with Freud's ideas and learn from him. . . . So by dint of much effort and confidence [in Freud], by learning and forgetting, I finally succeeded in finding my way back to my profession.[69]

Although the cure was not magical, the treatment certainly would have seemed so to an observer such as Walter's superior at the opera, Gustav Mahler. Freud's words, demonstrating his authority yet flexibility, had been the turning point in Walter's affliction. After all, the psychoanalysis of the time was not about forgetting but about remembering. It was just such a word that Mahler hoped for when he telegraphed Alma on the way to Leiden: "Hope to find a precious word." There are few better recommendations for a physician than that of a close friend who has gotten relief from painful symptoms on that doctor's advice.

And so Mahler and Freud began their *Spaziergang* in Leiden. In the ancient university town they would have attracted little attention that Friday afternoon, despite Mahler's erratic step-and-stop gait. Freud, with his walking stick and student's stoop, might have appeared to be one of the professors. A casual observer could have thought them to be two academic colleagues engrossed in discussion.

14

THE PRECIOUS WORD

The septuagenarian Sigmund Freud was reclining in the desk chair of his antiquity-cluttered consulting room at 19 Berggasse, his chow Tofi curled on one of the oriental rugs scattered throughout the room, the most notable of which covered the analytic couch. It was fifteen years after the walk in Leiden as he reminisced to his erstwhile patient Marie Bonaparte, now colleague and confidante: "I once analyzed Mahler. . . . I was vacationing in Holland, at Noordwijk by the sea, near Leiden. There I received a telegram from Mahler, who was then in the Austrian Tirol. 'May I come to see you?' I answer, 'Yes.' . . . So then he comes to Leiden to meet me at a hotel. I go and we walk all over the village for four hours, he telling me his life."[1]

In Freud's circle, Marie Bonaparte (1882–1962) was known as the Princess. She was royalty by both heredity and marriage: her great-grandfather was Napoleon's brother Lucien, and her husband, Prince George of Greece. But the sobriquet was not without irony. She was a favorite of Freud's—in particular among his women disciples—and the natural subject of gossip. Freud's own modest family background hardly inured him to the gratifications of association with the great, the near great, and the aristocrats of art and science. That her Lucien Bonaparte had been reduced and exiled by Napoleon in disapproval of his marriage mattered little—the name remained and Marie favored it. In any event, she currently held the title of Princess George of Greece.[2] Beyond this was the issue of a person's worthiness. The same impulse that had generated the Mahler consultation ("but for a man like Mahler!") led Freud to inquire about the princess as a person before he agreed to her treatment in 1925.

An immediate rapport developed between Marie and Freud as she underwent six-day-per-week psychoanalysis. Within weeks Freud had begun talking to her about himself, speaking of his suffering from the cancer that was by then barely under control and the losses in his life. He warned her of the perils of excessive attachment as well as the limitations he detected in himself: "I am seventy. I was in good health, but there are a few little things that don't work anymore. . . . I must also add that I am not a connoisseur of human beings." Bonaparte protested and Freud repeated, "No, I'm not an expert. I offer my trust and later I'm disappointed," adding, "You may disappoint me too." The princess extended her hand behind the analytic couch; Freud took it. "My dear friend," she dared to say, tears in her eyes, "No, I will not disappoint you."[3]

Nor did Bonaparte disappoint. She was to become devoted to psychoanalysis as analysand and later as practitioner; she was active in the psychoanalytic movement in Vienna and Paris and was a translator of Freud's works. She also became involved with the Freud family, who, paradoxically, became her own chosen royalty. Later, she worried about them as conditions in Vienna deteriorated with the war, and following the *Anschluss* of 1938, she was instrumental in achieving safe passage for the ailing eighty-two-year-old Sigmund and his family. It was in the trust and intimacy of this unique relationship that Bonaparte had learned of Mahler's consultation with Freud.

By the time of Marie Bonaparte's psychoanalysis, Mahler, dead fourteen years, had become a legend in Vienna, and his wife, Alma Mahler, long since a popular subject of gossip. Indeed, the trajectory of Alma's life had always been closely followed: there had been marriage to Mahler, motherhood, bereavement, and widowhood; affairs (Walter Gropius and Oskar Kokoschka); a second marriage, to Gropius; motherhood again; divorce and a custody battle; and a third marriage, to Franz Werfel. Soon there would be a second bereavement, with the death of the child Manon Gropius, and later, widowhood once again, following Werfel's death. At the center of her life was Vienna, where Alma made her home until, like

Freud, she left in 1938. Little wonder that Marie Bonaparte's curiosity was aroused on learning of Mahler's visit to Freud during the summer of 1910.

"What was he like?"

Mahler gave me the impression of being a genius, yet at the same time somehow curiously apelike. He has been dead a long time so I suppose I can tell you something about him. He came to see me because of his marriage. He had married a woman quite a bit younger than himself. At the time the marriage was not going well although he was a normally potent man and loved his wife.

"Was he faithful to her?"

Aside from her he had only had a few love affairs. Yes, he was faithful to her. But she no longer excited him. On our walk he spoke to me of every possible thing. And, as it turned out, after this analysis their relationship was happier. He demonstrated an intuitive understanding of analysis. He didn't know much about me and had not had analysis before, but right away he was in his element. What impressed him greatly was when I said to him, "Your mother's name was Marie?" "But how do you know!" he exclaimed. Of course, I could see it from what he was telling me—he had an enormous fixation on his mother. "But how was it," I asked him, "that you could marry a woman whose name was not Marie?" "But," he exclaimed, "she is called Alma-Marie!" As it happened, names were significant for his wife as well. Her father was the Emil Schindler, the famous Viennese painter whose statue is in the public gardens. So that she fell in love with a man called Mahler. [*Maler* means painter in German.]

But here's what I want to get to: Suddenly Mahler cried out, "Now I understand something about my music. I have often been criticized for crude changes from the noblest melody to one that is banal. And he told me the following story: His father was a peculiar person who harassed his mother with irrational, pathological jealousy. Young Mahler had often to witness such scenes. One day, while sitting in his room, he heard his father in the next room engaged in a violent scene with his mother. He eavesdropped by the door until he could bear it no longer, and then ran out into the street. There was a barrel organ playing a well known tune: "Ach, du lieber Augustin, Augustin," an old Viennese melody.

(Marie Bonaparte, in an aside: "Freud hummed the melody rather out of tune.")

The boy Mahler heard this and for the rest of his life he reproduced in his music the strange contrast of a common hurdy-gurdy tune alongside one reminiscent of the violence of his father in the scene between his parents.

(Marie Bonaparte herself commented here, suggesting some familiarity with Mahler's music, and perhaps a notion of creativity, shared by Freud at the time, that would eventually become controversial: "That's precisely the character of Mahler's music. Perhaps for a genius neurosis is essential. If Mahler had been analyzed and cured of his neurosis, his work would probably have been very different.")

"What was the name of that town where you said you saw him?" It was Leiden. We were staying by a lake not far from Leiden. It must have been somewhere between 1910 and 1912. The year of Mahler's death [*sic*].[4]

Marie Bonaparte drew out Freud on his session with Mahler. She kept sporadic notes on her analysis in 1925, Freud permitting her to do so during their sessions. Freud at this time could hardly have been called "Freudian" in its later, anachronistic sense. Although he published the rules of psychoanalytic engagement that would become dogma for the next generation (particularly in America) he himself adhered to them irregularly. In fact Freud preferred to call them "recommendations" rather than rules, and thought it well advised to avoid their unconditional acceptance.[5] These guidelines related to the anonymity and neutrality of the psychoanalyst, and the confidentiality of the psycho-

Freud and Marie Bonaparte in Freud's consultation room, London, 1938.

analytic exchange between analyst and analysand. It was precisely these that Freud took liberties with in many of his cases. Certainly with Marie Bonaparte anonymity and neutrality were blown to the winds, as the first psychoanalyst was seduced by both the warmth and the demands of his patient. As for confidentiality, Freud "supposed" that he might tell Bonaparte, about Mahler, although clearly he was aware of exempting himself from his own recommendations. What went into this supposition? And what may have made Freud treat Bonaparte in this special manner?

"On the couch" a different atmosphere prevailed with the princess than with many of Freud's other patients. She demanded confidences, for one. But Freud, too, had private inner demands and he responded from emotional needs of his own. He was well aware of the fantasy of the family romance that he had written about in 1909.[6] In this universal fantasy of origins, humanity strives retrospectively to associate its frequently humble past with the great and noble of civilization. The wonder of it!

The child who was born in the small Moravian town of Freiberg, the son of a poor Jewish textile merchant, was destined to have commerce with a descendant of Napoleon Bonaparte, one of Freud's early heroes! The unconscious would hardly recognize the fact that royalty had been revoked and that Marie was a Bonaparte by marriage. Freud's "family romance" with Bonaparte was the counterpart of Mahler's with Alma.

Before long, their roles were reversed, or at least reciprocated. What would later be delineated as the boundaries between patient and therapist were transgressed and the distinction between transference (the distortions of relationship that the patient brings from the past) and countertransference (the equivalent on the therapist's part) blurred. And thus Freud, the first psychoanalyst, who had only himself as analyst and hence a necessarily flawed one, confided in his patient. Soon after they began to meet, he unburdened himself of the grief he was experiencing at the death of his first grandchild, Heinele—the five-year-old son of his favorite daughter, Sophie, who had herself died four years earlier. Together, the two deaths constituted the greatest sorrow of Freud's life. On a more daily basis, he also spoke a good deal about money. In any case, it was in the context of this relationship and the privacy that insulated Freud from his own technical recommendations that Bonaparte led Freud to speak of his encounter with Mahler fifteen years earlier.

Freud later gave two additional accounts of his session with Mahler. The same year of Bonaparte's notes on the meeting, 1925, Freud had championed a younger Viennese colleague, the psychologist Theodore Reik. Reik had been summoned before the city magistrates for practicing without a medical license; the occasion had prompted Freud to write his seminal paper *The Question of Lay Analysis*.[7] Reik, unlike Freud, had a sensitive musical ear and was steeped in musical understanding. There was much about music in the autobiographical memoir from his subsequent years of practice, *Listening with the Third Ear*.[8] Reik was an admirer of Mahler and his music and had planned to write "a psychoanalytic study of the obsessional trends in [Mahler's] personality."[9] Only recently, while visiting Holland from America, where he had emigrated, had Reik learned of Freud's consultation with Mahler. He wrote to Freud early in 1935 with New Year's greetings to his mentor and a query regarding the meeting with Mahler. Freud replied:

> Dear Doctor,
>
> Thanks for your New Year's letter which at last brought the news so long expected by me, that you have settled down in the foreign country, are entering into good social connections and earning what you need. . . . Some stability and security seem to be a requirement for our difficult work. . . .
>
> I analyzed Mahler for an afternoon in the year 1912 (or 1913) in Leyden. [It was, of course, 1910.] If I may believe reports, I achieved much with him at that time. This visit appeared necessary to him, because his wife at the time rebelled against the fact that he withdrew his libido from her. In highly interesting expeditions through his life history, we discovered his personal conditions for love, especially his Holy Mary complex (*Marienkomplex—Mutterbindung*). I had plenty of opportunity to admire the capability for psychological understanding of this man of genius. No light fell at the time on the symptomatic façade of his obsessional neurosis. It was as if you would dig a single shaft through a mysterious building.
>
> Hoping to hear good news from you, with cordial wishes for 1935.
>
> Yours, Freud[10]

Freud was nearly eighty at the time, approaching the dreaded anniversary age of his father's death, and within four years of his own. As for Mahler's "withdrawal of libido," what Freud actually wrote was "seiner Libido von ihr auflehnte"—referring to averting or alienating the sexual drive. He was not necessarily referring to sexual impotence. He had told Marie Bonaparte a decade earlier that Mahler was a "normally potent man" although his wife "no longer excited him." The term "libido" was caught up in the American medicalization of psychoanalysis and, extending to other medical specialties, became a euphemism for the capacity for sexual excitement and performance. Freud's final definition of "libido" (in 1924) was not a physical designation at all, but rather an entirely "hypothetical" *mental* construct, "the force . . . of the sexual instincts . . . which enable the doctor to deal with the analytic material."[11] Freud made a point of trying to recall anything related to Mahler's "obsessional neurosis," since Reik was planning a study of it. His metaphor of the single shaft of light conveys the wonder of mental life that Freud experienced to his dying day, as well as the literary prowess that earned him the Goethe prize. For the rest, he considered Mahler "a man of genius," as he had observed previously to Bonaparte, and was somewhat self-congratulatory regarding the therapeutic result, although he offered little detail about the session itself.

In fact, Freud's note to Reik was nothing more nor less than a brief communication to a fellow psychotherapist, providing in shorthand diagnosis ("obsessional"), psychodynamics ("Holy Mary complex"), and outcome ("much achieved"). It also reveals how the aging clinician in Freud would recall a case many years after the actual details had faded.

When the case had been fresher in Freud's mind, he had been more tightly bound by confidentiality, particularly while Mahler was still alive. As he told Bonaparte, "He has been dead a long time so I suppose I can tell you something about him." Freud doubtless would have discussed the recent consultation with Sándor Ferenczi on their voyage to Sicily but there is no trace of it in their subsequent correspondence. Neither were notes routine; Freud wrote the case histories he would eventually publish after the day's work.

As for the more intimate details of Mahler's life, Freud generally believed that outside the consulting room a gentleman tactfully forgets what is confided within. Could Mahler have failed to mention Gropius, the affair, the letter, the visit? The pain, grievance, and anxieties attending these events were so recent and so germane to Mahler's mental state that Freud would unlikely have failed to deal with these raw feelings during the course of a four-hour session. But even letting down his guard as he was warmly encouraged to do in the company of Marie Bonaparte, Freud (at least in her account) made no mention of such details. Conceivably, some of their conversation was, by agreement, expunged or "off the record."

So we are left with only two remaining accounts, both from Alma Mahler and essentially identical. One appeared in her memoirs, *And the*

Bridge Is Love; the other, in *Gustav Mahler: Memories and Letters*. This second contained somewhat more elaborated detail:

> [Mahler] . . . was churned to the very bottom. It was at this time that he wrote those outcries and ejaculations addressed to me in the draft score of the Tenth Symphony. He realized that he had lived the life of a neurotic and suddenly decided to consult Sigmund Freud (who was then on holiday at Leiden in Holland). He gave him an account of the strange states of mind and his anxieties and Freud apparently calmed him down. He reproached him with vehemence after hearing his confession. "How dared a man in your state ask a young woman to be tied to him?" he asked. In conclusion, he said: "I know your wife. She loved her father and she can only choose and love a man of his sort. Your age of which you are so much afraid is exactly what attracts her. You need not be anxious. You loved your mother and you look for her in every woman. She was careworn and ailing, and unconsciously you wish your wife to be the same."[12]

Alma concurred, "[Freud] was right in both cases."

The question underlying Mahler's visit differed little from that of anxious patients consulting a physician: "Will I live or die?" Mahler's messages in the Tenth Symphony, which Alma so clearly understood to be directed toward herself, were unmistakable: life and death hung in the balance. God had forsaken Mahler as he pleaded, "Erbarmen," mercy. Would Alma abandon him too? At the death knoll of the muffled drum in the Finale, Mahler had written, "You alone know what this means." And what it meant was death—the cry of despair that precedes the suicidal threat, "Oh! Oh! Oh! Farewell my lyre." And finally, "To live for thee! To die for thee! Almschi."

As a psychotherapist, Freud could play the roles of magician, soothsayer, and predictor of the future with conviction. As magician with Bruno Walter, Freud prescribed Sicily as if introducing a deus ex machina alien to the realm of medical discourse. In Walter's case, the implicit promise of cure was in fact eventually fulfilled. Walter feared failure and humiliation should he be unable to conduct during performance. It was too much responsibility, yet given that music was his entire life, he found the thought of not conducting unbearable. Recognizing this, Freud the soothsayer relieved him of his burden, saying confidently, "I'll take responsibility." But, in truth, what kind of "responsibility" could Freud have assumed if his patient flopped? Freud had confidence either in Walter's recuperative power or—more likely—in his own power of persuasion. What Freud did *not* do was seduce himself into accepting an interesting patient for a lengthy treatment when a shorter one might be accomplished. Remarkably, the doctor who not long before had discovered that neurotics suffered from repressed memories, urged his patient to forget!

If Freud failed to formulate his reminiscence of his session with Mahler to Reik in terms of the threatened loss of the maternal object or her love, it does not mean that he failed to deal with this interpretively. Freud was already well aware of the potency of the maternal relationship and its vicissitudes throughout life. In one of his dialogues with Princess Bonaparte, she commented, "Man is afraid of woman." Never one to underestimate the power of a woman, Freud responded: "He is right!"[13]

From all accounts, it would appear that Freud's psychoanalytic "base of operations" was the oedipus complex. He cited Mahler's "Holy Mary complex" and *Mutterbindung*—mother fixation. If nothing else, the plausible narrative he was capable of elaborating had in itself an organizing quality; there was hope in meaning itself, however inexact. Freud may later have taken a somewhat different view of Mahler's case. A tract not yet published in 1910, *Inhibitions, Symptoms, and Anxiety* (1926), contains Freud's great conceptual sweep relating the history of anxiety from cradle to grave.[14] Here he spelled out the nature of separation anxiety and traced its human history "from the loss of the mother as an object" onward as the root cause of anxiety.[15] "The final transformation," wrote Freud, "is the fear of death (or fear for one's life) which *is* the fear of one's own superego projected on to the powers of destiny."[16] Although clearly separation anxiety—a preoedipal issue—was at the root of Mahler's conflicts, Freud, curiously, did not mention that in his 1935 letter to Reik. Although the oedipal interpretation may have had a calming effect, such that in the midst of psychic chaos some understanding could be reached, the plausible narrative might not in and of itself have accounted for the favorable therapeutic outcome. This likely came from elsewhere.

If Freud had been soothsayer to Bruno Walter, he was the predictor of the future with Mahler. His identification with the biblical Joseph was powerful. And in each of his cases, he proceeded with authority. He reassured Mahler that Alma would not leave him. In today's psychological parlance such measures would be called supportive rather than interpretive or expressive.[17] However, this does not mean that Freud was unaware of a deeper meaning to the abandonment Mahler feared. For, Freud's prediction answered Mahler's urgent question as to whether destiny decreed life or death.

Alma's account of the meeting suggests a different Freud, no doubt the one she hoped would be her advocate in giving her husband a good talking-to. Although Freud did not eschew giving advice or indulging in gratuitous remarks in his work with patients, sermons were not his métier and lectures were reserved for colleagues and larger audiences. Not surprisingly, the narcissistic Alma remembered, or perhaps invented, Freud's purported analysis of *her*: "I know your wife. She loved her father and she can only choose and love a man of his sort." The histrionic Alma took to the oedipal like a fish to water. What is relevant and important is that since Alma could only know what Freud said secondhand from Gustav's report (and therefore her story is doubly distorted), she seems to have had to agree with their acceptance of a simple fact. Not only would Alma not desert Mahler (as she herself asserted later) but—with the imprimatur of the highest psychological authority—she was constitutionally incapable of leaving him!

It was thus that Alma's own enduring oedipal strivings (the childhood love of her father) would serve as a balm for anxieties that stemmed from a period much earlier in Gustav's life. Just as Freud took responsibility for the advice he had given Bruno Walter, his authoritativeness proved reassuring. Alma already knew she could not leave Mahler. "Freud was right," she said. "I always looked for a small, slight man, who had wisdom and spiritual authority, since this is what I had known and loved in my father."[18] Nevertheless, at this point in their relationship Mahler could not live with the doubt elicited by the affair and required some external force to bind her to him. It was as if the child in the man had cried out: "She will abandon me; I am terrified; I am sentenced to death"; to which some powerful authority had answered: "I assure you that such a thing cannot possibly happen and I take responsibility for this assertion. You need not fear; you shall live and not die." The "precious word" that Mahler sought and found in the journey to Leiden to see Freud was thus "life."

Mahler left Freud relieved, no longer feeling divided or tormented within himself. He turned southward toward Munich and the resumption of rehearsals for the premiere of his Eighth Symphony, now only three weeks away. En route he sent Alma a few lines of verse:

> Night terrors were scattered by one powerful word,
> The torments that plagued me were silenced.
> At last, united in a single harmonious chord
> Were my timorous thoughts and raging feelings.[19]

The metaphorical "single harmonious chord" of the poem has been related to the musical moment in the Adagio of the Tenth Symphony in which Mahler inserted an anguished dissonance created by nine notes— the *Neuntonklang*, the nine-tone chord. The "single chord" whose elements are "united" in the poem remains an unresolved dissonance in the score-sketch. Far from the poem's "harmonious chord," Mahler may have wished this extreme musical expression—like the suicidal expressions on the autograph score—to be a part of the human document that is the symphony.

Ironically, Mahler may have been *too* reassured by Freud's words. He was not suspicious by nature and did not display the vigilance of a jealous husband. Accordingly, as time went on and Alma's affair with Gropius continued with both love meetings and the exchange of letters, there is no evidence that Mahler was aware of continued betrayal. If he harbored suspicions, he kept them to himself. He may have reached a compromise in his own mind in which, supported by Freud's belief that Alma would never leave him, he came to accept the affair, tolerant of Alma's needs that he could no longer satisfy.

Touching home at Toblach, Mahler set out for Munich within a few days, accompanied to the station by Alma; it was the first time in years that she saw him off on tour. The session with Freud had given Mahler new life. From Munich he wrote to Alma of his joy in receiving the piano score to the soon-to-be performed Eighth Symphony with its dedication: "It gave me a peculiar and exciting feeling to see the sweet, beloved name on the title-page for all the world to read as a joyful acknowledgement. . . . Does it not make the impression of a betrothal? Doesn't it seem more like the announcement of an engagement?"[20]

Regarding his recent visit with Freud, Mahler had written to Alma, "Freud is quite right—you were always for me the light and the central point! The inner light, I mean, which rose over all; and the blissful consciousness of this—now unshadowed and unconfined—raises all my feelings to the infinite."[21]

Two other documents relate to Mahler's consultation with Sigmund Freud, both curiosities in their own way. Although during Mahler's lifetime Freud was under constraint not to reveal what had been told to him in confidence, following Mahler's death he was more open, at least to a degree, albeit at first only among his followers. The Wednesday evening discussions of the Vienna Psychoanalytic Society were intellectually free-wheeling occasions that provided an opportunity for its members to try out ideas with colleagues. Surprisingly, Mahler's name came up at the meeting on 17 May, the eve of his death, at a time when the progression of his fatal illness was being reported daily in the Viennese newspapers. In the context of a discussion of symbolism, Max Graf remarked that "what was actually a sign of genius in Gustave [*sic*] Mahler was his ambition." With no corroboratory evidence whatsoever, and probably repeating gossip, Graf stated that "this agrees very closely with the fact that as a child of nine he suffered night after night from eneuresis." Paul Federn, not to be outdone, chimed in that he also "knew of that fact," yet, as the *Minutes* recalled, "he would not for that reason deny Mahler his genius." Federn added that "Mahler was also a fanatical swimmer, which was partly responsible for his later heart disease."[22] It was an odd moment. Graf was a musicologist but Federn was a physician and should have known by then that strenuous activity in itself would not induce heart disease. As frequently occurred in the Wednesday meetings, eyes turned toward Freud, the more particularly in this case since it was rumored that he had treated Mahler. The *Minutes* reported: "Prof. Freud could—if medical discretion did not prevent it—enlarge this brief analysis in several directions." (Tantalizingly, this entry did not mean that Freud failed to pursue these directions among intimates.)

By the following Wednesday evening, Mahler was dead and buried. Dr. Hugo Heller, who was the publisher of the first psychoanalytic journals and a patron of young poets and writers, was speaking of "premonitions of death," citing a recent article on a writer's early death and "his unconscious wish to die." He recalled "a seemingly paradoxical remark of Freud":

> Man does not actually die from illness; it is the will to die in the unconscious that brings about death. This view makes it possible to understand the puzzling forebodings of death: the will to die anchored in the unconscious, is transported into consciousness in a distorted form: "I am going to die," instead of "I want to die."[23]

During the ensuing discussion, Dr. Maximillian Steiner, who would shortly publish a book on the disturbances of male potency, commented that "cases are known in which a psychic influence has hastened death." He cited Gustav Mahler and Federn again "corroborated." Heller went on to say that "What is striking in this context is the comparatively large number of people of genius, especially creative artists, who die at an early age." Once again Mahler was mentioned in this regard. This time Freud spoke up. The *Minutes* read:

> Professor Freud is able to readily confirm the validity of the assumption expressed about Mahler's death, for he knows that Mahler was at a turning point in his life at which he had the alternative of either changing, and thereby giving up the basis of his artistic power, or of evading the conflict. With regard to this communication, discretion is especially requested.[24]

The members of the Vienna Psychoanalytic Society were approaching an elaboration of what Freud would later term the death instinct, cases in which "a psychic influence has hastened death." The implication was that Mahler, recently deceased, had yielded finally to a death wish.

Although these early psychoanalysts did not know about Mahler's early and ongoing experiences with death (they were wrong about eneuresis), this sort of intellectual play characterized the group. Translated into biography, it would suggest that in some of the crises in Mahler's life, most notably the mortal crisis of 1901, the fear of death harbored the wish. Freud did not seem interested in pursuing this line of inquiry, however, and had something else in mind regarding Mahler—that is, a choice that Mahler had to make, presumably between his continued creativity and a harmonious marriage.

Dr. Emanuel E. Garcia, in an article titled "Gustav Mahler's Choice," writes, "We know that Mahler changed, and we have evidence to assume that the basis of his compositional artistic creativity was extinguished simultaneously."[25] Further, "he began a life of diminished gloom, greater equilibrium, but *relative creative inactivity* shortly cut off by death" (my italics).[26] Garcia emphasizes the "startling implication," according to Freud (per Dr. Heller), "that with the extinction of Mahler's creativity came the extinction of his physical life."

The "evidence" of extinguished compositional creativity is weak. Although Mahler may have been superstitious about the Tenth Symphony, as Alma related, he did not bring the sketches to New York because another task took precedence in his customary winter's work: the revision and scoring of the Ninth Symphony, the manuscript of which he did have with him. Moreover, the six months between the visit with Freud and Mahler's final New York concert were consumed by the premiere of the Eighth Symphony in Munich and preparation for the augmented New York season that Mahler had not anticipated. Subsequently, orchestral politics became as demanding as they were debilitating. Contrary to the connection Garcia proposes between the wish to die and Mahler's creative inactivity, the wish had been active throughout Mahler's most creative periods—and endowed the content of the music itself.

Nevertheless, it is possible that the Freud of 1911 may have endorsed the formulation that Mahler was confronting a "choice" between his beloved Alma and his beloved music. After all, Freud himself had relinquished his own sexuality after Martha's childbearing period, when he was only in his early forties; a most creative career ensued.[27] If Freud did indeed view the sexual and creative impulses as mutually exclusive, this has not been borne out in the intervening years. Admirable as Freud's clinical intuition may have been in his wise and timely interventions with both Mahler and Bruno Walter, one may perhaps venture that the inspiration of "Mahler's choice" was not Freud's finest hour. Freud had a long theoretical path before him in his construction of the human psyche. Following his writings on the ego of 1920 and 1923, he would doubtless have taken a more flexible attitude.[28] As Garcia acknowledges, Freud was later of the opinion that "psychoanalysis as treatment would heighten the artist's capacity for achievement."[29]

Famously, in his 1928 paper on Dostoyevsky, Freud wrote, "Before the problem of the creative artist, analysis must, alas, lay down his arms."[30] But this should not be taken too seriously, for Freud never did surrender in this endeavor and it was he himself who paved the way to the discipline of applied psychoanalysis—that is, the method of psychoanalysis applied to art and literature. Noteworthy, however, is that Freud never ventured to apply psychoanalysis in any systematic way to music, which may have been wise since, as we have seen, he was distinctly unmusical. His bias toward the visual has marked psychoanalysis forever, giving us the basis for understanding dreams and, with this, the richness of the entire panoply of human mental life.

The final document in the Freud-Mahler saga concerns the bill for services rendered. Somewhere along the line Freud submitted a statement to Mahler, which went unpaid during the latter's lifetime—something to ponder. Owing to a simple mistranslation when the receipt was offered in auction, it was called the bill. But it indicated that payment was made five months after Mahler's death, in October 1911, by his old Iglau friend and executor, the lawyer Emil Freund. Freud's "honorarium" was 300 crowns, about $60 in 1911.

15

TRIUMPH AND DESPAIR

Following his consultation with Freud, Mahler did not fail to remember Alma's birthday on 31 August with a gift that Carl Moll helped select. Curiously, Alma made no mention of it in her writings. Rather it was overshadowed by the bitter memory of Mahler's earlier attitude toward such gifts: "Some people give each other rings, but I am sure that this kind of lack of taste displeases you as much as me." Alma had agreed at the time but harbored resentment through the years.[1] Her wedding, she reminisced with some rancor, "came, but no wedding present." What she did recall was a gift a friend and admirer of both of them, the physicist Arnold Berliner, had given her in Munich. In the midst of the celebration and adulation of Mahler, he had paid particular attention to her, saying, "Alma, everybody's paying tribute to Mahler. But you've suffered for the Eighth and you deserve something too." The baroque pearls she selected at the atelier of a stylish craftsperson were "the first piece of jewelry I had ever received in my life."[2] Here Alma was almost certainly exaggerating, as more than one photograph shows her wearing jewelry. Later in life she habitually favored long strings of pearls.

The purchase of a gift by another man put Mahler in bad humor and he attempted to pay Berliner for the pearls, which Alma would not permit. Could Mahler's anger have been informed by a nagging doubt as to whether the affair with Gropius was truly over? Despite protestations to Mahler, writes Gropius's biographer, "Alma and Gropius remained in communication with each other." Alma was in a constant state of anxiety regarding their correspondence, however—a state that may have been communicated to Mahler. The lovers devised various ways to keep their secret. Anna Moll served as go-between, receiving and redirecting letters. Discreet locations were chosen for their trysts, the times and places selected according to Mahler's commitments. Alma and Walter used pseudonyms when booking hotels and trains. Above all, they agreed "to always play dumb whenever the conversation turns to us."[3]

After Mahler's departure for the Munich dress rehearsals on 3 September, Alma wrote to Gropius to meet her there. She had already responded to Mahler's plea that she return to New York with him the following month, so time was short for the lovers. After Alma and her mother arrived at the Hotel Continental on 9 September, Alma met Gropius whenever Mahler was rehearsing; he awaited her at the Hotel Regina, where he was staying and they could meet relatively discreetly. Alma considered her professed devotion to Mahler to be both sacrifice and compromise. In her letters to Gropius she continued to rationalize her passion as a necessary remedy for what she construed to be Mahler's sexual failures:

> I feel that for my heart and all my other organs nothing is worse than enforced asceticism. I mean not only the sensual lust, the lack of which has made me prematurely into a detached, resigned old woman, but also the continuous rest for my body.[4]

Meanwhile, the stress of travel and the intense four-hour session with Freud took their toll on Mahler as he developed one of his dreaded throat inflammations. He had felt it coming on when he wrote Alma the ecstatic letter redolent of rebirth. Now, in another letter to Alma, he confessed to feeling "very worried." At least part of the worry stemmed from the fact that sometime after summer's end Mahler had had his tonsils cauterized to stave off future infections; this latest sore throat was thus a troubling disappointment. Concerned about the arduous schedule and performance of the coming days, Mahler climbed into bed and summoned a doctor, who observed a "festering white spot and a very bad inflammation."[5] Engaging the Munich impresario Emil Gutmann as "chief bather," Mahler swaddled himself in heavy blankets, sweating heavily for three hours while Gutmann sponged his face and eyes with a towel. In the evening, he was able to rehearse. Writing the following day, Mahler was almost desperate to reassure Alma about his health: "My Almschi, don't worry. I'll be very, very good when you get here, I will be completely cured." Once again, he missed her letters: "I worry about you so much! It's no life when I don't see your eyes and don't hear your voice. And you don't need me at all; otherwise you would feel compelled to write me!"[6] The recurrence of Mahler's sore throat in Munich was ominous, the second of the summer, and likely caused by the endemic streptococcus that would ultimately inflame his heart valves, wreaking mortal damage.

The premiere of the Eighth Symphony was now only days away, with two performances scheduled for 12 and 13 September. Letters to Alma just before her arrival expressed elation as Gustav awaited her and her mother. When the women arrived at their suite in the Hotel Continental, they found it filled with roses that Mahler had ordered. The piano score to the Eighth was on a table in Anna Moll's room, with the dedication "To our dear Mammerl, who still belongs to everyone and who gave me Almscherl, from Gustav whose gratitude will never die."[7] The intensity of Mahler's welcome more likely suggests relief from the recent life-and-death issues rather than the suspicion of a continued affair; Mahler was deeply preoccupied with marshalling forces for the Eighth, the "Symphony of a Thousand."

In the days before Alma's departure for Munich, now only three months since her meeting Gropius, her letters, via Anna's "clearing-house," took on an erotic tone that was the result of sexual urgency and continued fantasy. "When will there be a time," she asked Gropius, "when you lie naked next to me at night, when nothing can separate us any more except sleep?"[8] By now Alma was signing her letters as "Your wife"; clearly what was "separating" them was Gustav!

Alma was no stranger to death wishes. In 1920, looking back on her life, she confided to her diary a recollection of when she had been "very lonely alongside a much older husband." Putzi had been in quarantine for the scarlet fever that caused her death and Alma had seen her at the window. There had then flashed to mind the thought that troubled Alma many years later: "Suddenly I KNEW: This child must go . . . AND IMME-DIATELY, FOR GOD'S SAKE!" She tried to disavow the thought—"Away with cursed thinking"—but added, "Gustav's death—I wanted that too."[9] In addition to his age, Mahler's physical vulnerability was now advancing Alma's fantasy of a time after Mahler's death, when she might in fact be free to marry Gropius.

Just as Alma had longed for a child by Zemlinsky and later Mahler, she wished for a child from Gropius:

> My Walter, from you I want a child and I will cherish it and care for it until *the* day comes when we, without regret, secure and composed, sink smiling and forever, into each other's arms. Wire me, Walter, whether this wish is still as strong in you as a month ago.[10]

Walter responded:

> On my knees I lay before you, truly and have thankfully looked up to you . . . you gave the wish of life renewed nourishment— fresh beautiful life do I see blossoming out of our pain . . . what we experience together, is the highest and best that human souls can encounter. . . . My Alma, may God protect you, that you can bear your heavy burdens and stay well.[11]

Gropius's biographer notes the "stilted" style of his letters to Alma, the result of multiple drafts before he sent out the final copy.[12] Alma's love prose, in contrast, is redolent of Richard Strauss and Wagner. The merging of lovers in eternal bliss is one of the themes of the *Vier Letzte Lieder* (Four Last Songs) and of *Tristan und Isolde*, the final *Liebestod* of which echoes Alma's "smiling and forever": "Mild und leise" (Gently and softly he is smiling).

But it was the spirit of *Die Meistersinger* that returned to tragically haunt. The "detached, resigned old woman," as Alma bitterly described herself, was, after all, only thirty-one and still of childbearing age—as she would later prove. Mahler, who had been virile enough to father two children when they married ten years earlier, was aging rapidly. The Eighth Symphony, which was shortly to be performed, was hardly a work of the *Wunderhorn* years, as were the four symphonies completed at the time of their marriage. The Eighth displayed powerful maturity— although not yet the valetudinous senescence of the Ninth. The work was in a sense an artistic precipitate of Mahler, man and artist, at the height of his musical potency. When he wrote it in the summer of 1906, the "creative spirit" had come to him so powerfully and urgently that the opening music had virtually written itself from a text subconsciously remembered: "Veni creator spiritus." Mahler's greatest triumph was awaiting him in a few days in Munich on 12 September 1910.

But the man himself at fifty was no longer in his prime physically. Alma would remain with Mahler as duty and conscience dictated, but far from being the self-pitying "old woman," she would not yield her relative youth. The only compromise acceptable to her was to maintain the marriage and at the same time continue her affair with Gropius through letters and visits. The premiere of the Eighth provided such an opportunity. Inevitably, she would wonder what the effect of a six-month separation from Gropius would be; and by the same token, with Mahler's recent illnesses and the coming pressures in America mounting, how long he might last physically and emotionally. Mahler had always appeared invincible but the summer of the visit to Freud, he revealed a fragile side that was shocking to all. As rehearsals progressed, many noted Mahler's paleness and apparent weariness.[13]

Mahler found his strength during the course of the final rehearsals. He took particular pleasure in the enthusiasm of the children's chorus and they seemed to adore him. When in one passage they responded to his shout above the orchestra to sing so that "the angels in heaven will hear them," Mahler was so joyful that he could be seen wiping away "the tears of joy" that ran down his face.[14] Paul Stefan, who would become Mahler's first biographer, described the scene:

> He conducts but he is still tired, sick and each time exhausted by his work and by his own passion. He sweeps everyone away with him. Little by little the ensemble builds before our eyes. The orchestra, the soloists and, finally, the members of the chorus join in one by one.[15]

Meanwhile, guests began to stream into Munich for the event. Among them were the playwright Gerhart Hauptmann, the novelist Thomas Mann, and the writer Stefan Zweig. From Paris came the pianist Alfredo Casella and the diplomat Paul Clemenceau; from Holland, the conductor Willem Mengelberg and the composer Alphonse Diepenbrock; from

Berlin, Richard Strauss, Max Reinhardt, and Lilli Lehmann. There was an especially large contingent from Vienna; indeed virtually all the persons who peopled Mahler's biographical world were present—singers and other associates from Mahler's opera years such as Anna von Mildenburg (and her husband, Hermann Bahr); Selma Kurtz; the set designer Alfred Roller; and old friends such as Guido Adler and Rudolf Krzyzanowski from conservatory days. Mahler's cousin and boyhood companion, Gustav Frank, traveled the furthest distance, arriving from St. Petersburg, where he held a diplomatic post. Mahler's two sisters, Justine and Emma, and their musician husbands, the brothers Arnold and Eduard Rosé, of course attended the premiere, as did Anna and Carl Moll. Gropius, too, likely remained in Munich for one of the performances. Only Mahler's companion of the *Wunderhorn* years, Natalie Bauer-Lechner, and Mahler's brother Alois, who, unknown to him at the time, had emigrated to America, seem to have disappeared completely from his life.

The premiere was Mahler's moment of triumph, the peak experience for which artists wait a lifetime but which few achieve. There were more than a thousand performers from three cities and the audience numbered three thousand. On Mahler's appearance, all rose. He seemed relaxed as he surveyed the concert hall filled with admirers. A camera panned the scene, as did his gaze, and would register cumulative biography. The tension of anticipation in the audience broke briefly as Mahler shouted, "Hello!" to the children, and they answered back. Mahler poised his baton and gestured the downbeat, unleashing the massive, orchestral and choral incipient E-flat major chord, triple-forte. Never in the history of music had there been an opening such as this. Its power, augmented by the organ vibrations that filled the hall, thrust each of the listeners into an altered and elevated state of consciousness that would be sustained throughout the colossal work. At the end, silence hung for several seconds before the ovations burst forth. These lasted thirty minutes, as the orchestra stamped and performers waved their scores.

The concert proved unforgettable to the many who wrote about it. Mahler was variously depicted as an artist, a magician, a charismatic leader, a god, a priest. Indeed, the entire event was like an awesome religious ceremony for a generation. The feeling among those who attended was summed up by Thomas Mann, who, along with other distinguished

Premiere of the Eighth Symphony, Munich, September 1910.

guests and members of the Mahler circle, attended a supper after the performance. That evening he told his wife, "It was certainly the first time in my life that I had the impression of meeting a truly great man."[16]

Mann transformed what he perceived in Mahler into the fictional composer Gustav Aschenbach the following year, when he wrote *Death in Venice*:

> Gustav Aschenbach was a man of slightly less than middle height, dark-haired and clean shaven. His head seemed a little too big for a body that was almost dainty. His hair, combed back, receding at the top, still very full at the temples, though quite grey, framed a high, furrowed, and almost embossed looking brow. The gold frame of his rimless glasses cut into the bridge of his full, nobly curved nose. His mouth was large, sometimes relaxed and full, sometimes thin and tense, his cheeks were lean and hollow, and his well-proportioned chin was marked by a slight cleft. Important destinies seemed to have played themselves out on

this long-suffering face, which he often held tilted somewhat to one side. And yet it was art alone, not a difficult and troubled life, that had taken over the task of chiseling these features.[17]

The novelist was perhaps prescient in selecting a fictional name into which the word for ashes (*aschen*) was incorporated, recalling the biblical "You are dust and to dust you shall return." Or had the perceptive novelist detected something sickly in Mahler's pale complexion that evening? "Aschenbach" might also be interpreted as the Bach of Ashes.

Several observers wrote about Mahler's special rapport with the children's chorus during the rehearsals and performance, and the pleasure he took from them. Mahler displayed a remarkable capacity for sublimation—in this instance, freedom from the bonds of mourning and elevation of the object of bereavement into art. Putzi would have been almost eight years old at the premiere of the Eighth Symphony, the age of many of the children participating. It was as if Mahler encountered the spirit of the beloved child writ large in the chorus. At the end, Bruno Walter recalled, "Hundreds of small white hands were extended toward the great artist who shook them while walking along the row. And these cries of enthusiasm from hundreds of little voices! This scene moved thousands in the audience."[18]

And it most certainly moved Mahler. One witness observed that when the conductor came out for his third bow, three children walked up to the podium and presented him with a beautiful crown of laurel from the whole chorus.[19] Genuinely surprised—it was just the sort of tribute he had always eschewed—he accepted this gift from the children with visible joy and reached out to touch as many of their outstretched hands as he could. Alma, whose two accounts neglect to mention such details, continued to pursue her own path of mourning, finding new loves—most immediately and passionately Walter Gropius.

The next major event in Mahler's life was of a different order: the return to America and the day-to-day work of conducting in New York and on tour. Early in the summer Mahler had attended to some of the details of the forthcoming season with the New York Philharmonic and his fourth sojourn to America. Conditions were beginning to change as the Ladies' Committee—$100,000 in deficit for the previous season—thought it prudent to hire a business manager, Loudon Charlton. It was a poor choice, as they later discovered, since his position as head of an artist's agency implied a conflict of interest. Mahler had agreed to forty-five concerts (originally forty-three) with a contracted fee and was deeply dismayed to learn that the new manager, without his consent, had scheduled sixty-five concerts. Mahler complained to his concertmaster, Theodore Spiering, of the "vast increase in the workload . . . a colossal amount of extra work."[20] Ignoring the potential strain, instead of attempting to modify it, Mahler requested additional payment. This issue remained unsettled until well into the season, and resolved only after arbitration by Samuel Untermeyer, who ruled in Mahler's favor. Mahler had asked for an additional $5,000 and compromised at $3,000. But by 1911, Mahler's relationship with the management and the women of the guarantors' committee had become frayed. The high-handed scheduling prior to the season was not a good omen.[21]

In accepting the more demanding schedule, Mahler had been imprudent, denying the effects of the strained summer months and the potential for physical illness. Several observers at the premiere perceived Mahler as sickly: "M[ahler] looks so ill we hardly knew him," one English critic wrote in his journal.[22] Once again, Mahler's friend Guido Adler appeared as witness and self-styled guardian of Mahler's health. Writing of Mahler's "last disastrous voyage to America," Adler depicted him as an "almost mortally exhausted man driven by others for the sake of the mammon that he scorned."[23] Here Adler was back at work on Alma, conflating wife and mammon, and not too subtly at that. However, the bias of an old friend in his sensitivity to Mahler's condition is worth noting and perhaps comparable to Thomas Mann's aschen/Aschenbach/Mahler association. Adler wrote, "He came to me, pale, with weary eyes [and] at that time I obtained his promise: 'Gustav, you must never again go to America.'" This commentary, written after Mahler's death, ended ironically, "He promised, and kept it, as in life every promise was sacred to him."[24]

Adler may have had further reasons to distrust Alma. He was in the gossip stream of Mahler's circle in Vienna—current friends as well as those who considered themselves neglected by him after his marriage.

However discreet Alma and Gropius may have been at their romantic meeting in Munich's Hotel Regina, the risk of disclosure and rumor was great. Any hesitation they may have had was trumped by desire. At the time visitors, particularly Viennese, were already arriving in Munich for the premiere and hotels were filling. Mahler, as one observer would comment, "seems to have been as noted for his wife as for his music."[25] Gropius was not yet well known, but he was handsome and he was young. Tongues would wag.

It was characteristic of Mahler to ignore signs of fatigue and replace them with vigorous activity and future plans; he masked depression the same way. Yet on the brink of the final season in New York, elated by the triumph in Munich, he appeared neither depressed nor preoccupied with death. And if he was troubled by suspicions of the ongoing affair between Alma and Gropius, he did not reveal it. In correspondence with Carl Moll from Munich, Mahler asked him to bring his "gigantic American trunk" to serve as a wardrobe for Alma in what he considered to be their smallish bedroom at the Hotel Savoy. In thinking of the coming season, he was eager for an extended visit from Anna Moll for Alma's sake and his own, constituting some semblance of family life in the midst of a nomadic sojourn. Ever forward-looking, Mahler, with Carl's help, had been looking for a site to build a new home after selling their Vienna apartment. Meanwhile, when in Vienna he and Alma stayed with the Molls. Earlier that spring the search had proven successful and Carl was now making the legal arrangements for the purchase of a plot of land in Semmering. The land, wrote Mahler, was to be registered "in both our names, Alma and Gustav Mahler."[26]

Alma and Mahler set sail for the anticipated five-month tour in America from different ports. Gustav departed from Bremen on 18 October on the *Kaiser Wilhelm II*; Alma boarded the same ship at Cherbourg the following day. Alma had arranged it thus so there could be a farewell rendezvous with Gropius in Paris. It was she who took the initiative and made the carefully thought-out arrangements.

> I shall leave Friday 14th October at 11:55 on the Orient Express from Vienna. My coupe-bed Number 13 is in the second sleeping car. I have not been to town and so I don't know your answer

yet. I write and hope into the blue. I advise you (if you are going) to take your ticket in the name of Walter Grote since Gustav leaves two days later and might have the lists of travelers shown to him. Please answer soon.[27]

While the lovers were in Paris, Mahler, on his way to his port of embarkation, stopped to see Oskar Fried, with whom he had apparently reconciled after the fracas about Alma's music. Fried wrote poignantly of this last visit, "Not a word was spoken of either his or my plans for the future. He merely played in the garden with my child."[28] Fried painted a picture of a subdued Mahler at this point and it is tempting to conclude that Mahler agreed to Alma's strange and impractical travel arrangements knowing of—or at least suspecting—the affair. If so, he was coming to terms with it, having experienced the depths of his anxiety should he lose her completely. The attention to her wardrobe and the projected Semmering house (which in fact Alma would enjoy after his death) may have been part of the appeasement of Alma already seen in the publishing of her songs and the dedication of the symphony.

Nevertheless, the seven-day voyage was a blessing, at least for Mahler, as it provided a complete rest—or nearly complete. He had agreed to perform in a charity concert while on board the *Kaiser Wilhelm II*. He accompanied the singers, including the tenor John McCormack. Arriving in New York 25 October, and settling once again in the Hotel Savoy, Mahler had little time before the start of another strenuous season.

Alma could hardly wait to contact Gropius: "Don't waste your lovely youth, which belongs to me. I got dizzy when I saw and felt the one thing that makes me so infinitely happy. I love you! It is as though I were your wife—were going on a trip, and were waiting for you. Stay healthy for me—you know why."[29] Walter responded in kind, and Alma reminisced, "Those days in Paris—wonderful, full of untroubled atmosphere. Never was there a bad feeling in our love, only that you poor fellow always have to wait so long for me."[30] The theme of waiting was a delicate one, virtually code, as its unspoken meaning was the waiting for Mahler to die. Anna Moll would shortly imply that more clearly. Meanwhile, what Alma awaited impatiently were the letters Gropius sent in care of a New York post office general delivery.

Alma related that Mahler's workload was actually lighter this year—perhaps defensively avoiding responsibility for his working more for more money. This proved not to be the case. And although for the sixteen-week season the number of concerts per week averaged three plus rehearsals, they were unevenly spread. In January alone, for example, there were fifteen concerts, a few requiring travel to Philadelphia and Washington.

During the course of the season the orchestra was also on tour in Pittsburgh, Cleveland, Buffalo, Rochester, Syracuse, Utica, and Hartford. Critical commentary was highly favorable, ranging from the thoughtfully appreciative to the ecstatic. "Little Mahler, the giant!" exclaimed the Cleveland critic. "His gigantic power makes the other conductors seem like pygmies."[31] In New York, there was a perceptible decline in the number of concerts reviewed; Mahler's personality and the drama of his arrival in the new world was no longer news. What would get the press going again were the alienating tensions among Mahler, management, and the guarantors, and the gossip regarding whether he would be reengaged for the following season.

Mahler held up remarkably well, although while on tour he needed to rest in bed prior to conducting in the evening. Anna Moll was not scheduled to arrive until after the new year, but Gustav and Alma, in typical fashion, welcomed a few New Yorkers into the family circle. Among these was the forty-three-year-old Viennese-born physician Joseph Fraenkel (1867–1920). The Mahlers had met Fraenkel during their first winter in New York at the home of Otto Kahn, the financier and patron of the Metropolitan Opera. Alma wrote of him:

> Fraenkel had a great influence on both Mahler and me during the years that followed. He was a genius both as a man and as a doctor, and we both fell in love with him the day we first met him. He was a complete entertainment in himself; dazzling in his wit and a daring thinker—a little splenetic perhaps, but always original. . . . Mahler finally fell so entirely under his sway that he would unquestionably have done whatever he told him.[32]

Joseph Fraenkel was a graduate of the University of Vienna Medical School. Evidently unsuccessful in his early years of practice, he emigrated to the United States in his mid-twenties, traveling steerage. In a

Dr. Joseph Fraenkel.

rags-to-honors story, the engaging doctor was by now a distinguished physician and neurologist who for half a dozen years had been medical director of Montefiore Hospital in the Bronx. He joined the Mahlers in many social activities (it was he who accompanied them to the séance at Eusapia Palladino's in 1909) and sometime during the summer of 1910 he had visited them in Toblach.

By now social life in New York was richer than it had been and Mahler saw to it that Alma did not feel isolated. The Mahlers enjoyed a box at the Metropolitan Opera, where they entertained a growing circle of friends and acquaintances. Although Alma underscored Mahler's attraction to Fraenkel, she downplayed her own. Fraenkel was charming and, although scrawny, possessed distinguished good looks. For Alma, he provided warm friendship and lively distraction. For Mahler, he was like a lifeline—a doctor in the house—and Fraenkel would prove himself as friend and as physician when the time came.

Although nothing more developed between Joseph and Alma at the time, Fraenkel was clearly taken by Alma. After Mahler's death, he would present himself as a suitor; she spurned him. In the fall of 1910, Alma remained obsessed with Gropius, idealizing him passionately as letters continued: "You float like a spirit, made of light before me—most beautiful young man—and know what I need."[33]

In November, as the holidays approached, separation was more painful for the lovers. Alma must have written to her mother of her difficulties and perhaps depression for in a letter to Carl, Mahler sought to reassure that Alma appeared to be "in good spirits and full of hope."[34] To Gropius, Alma wrote: "When will I have you physically in front of me again? When will I see you again, like a god . . . I want to take in your beauty."[35]

That same month Anna Moll wrote to Gropius:

> That is the sadness that one cannot do anything at the moment; one has to leave it all to a development over time—I believe firmly that with both of you, your love will last beyond everything. . . . I am firmly convinced that you like my child so much that you will do everything not to make her more unhappy.[36]

There is no question that Alma, Gropius, and Anna were waiting for Mahler to be out of the picture. At the same time, Mahler was writing warmly to Carl Moll: "We were overjoyed to hear that you are now fully reconciled to dear little Mama's coming to stay with us here for a while. God bless you for it, dear Carl."[37]

Mahler, by now awakened to Alma's need for gifts, saw to it that this Christmas would be a high point in her life in America. And if Alma were overwhelmed, all the better; since the trials of the previous summer, Mahler continued to take every opportunity to please and appease. When Mahler left the apartment one day with his checkbook, Alma knew something was afoot, something she had "missed so sorely for ten years." The surprise was unveiled on Christmas day, a table full of "lovely things he had thought of without any regard for his own likes and dislikes."[38] There were also two "promissory" notes:

> Bon
> To the value of $40

> For a fine spree
> along the Fifth Avenue
> For Herr Gustav Mahler on a country ramble with his Almschi
>
> Bon
> For the purchase of a
> Solitaire
> Worth over $1,000
> Gustav Mahler
> New York, Christmas 1910

"The whole room was soon full of pink roses," Alma wrote. "We spent this Christmas—by our own choice—quite alone."[39]

The signs of trouble that holiday season had to do with Mahler's health. Just before Christmas Mahler had a transient "septic throat," in retrospect a grim reminder as well as a harbinger of what Anna and the adulterous lovers awaited. Beneath the surface of holiday cheer lay a sense of time-on-loan, a feeling of the fragility of all the pleasures and accomplishments of the year. This was poignantly revealed on New Year's Eve as the Mahlers celebrated with Fraenkel:

> New York stretched on out of sight in a milk-white haze. Sirens opened up . . . the bells of all the churches united in an organ-note of such awful beauty that we three who loved each other joined hands without a word and wept. Not one of us—then—knew why.[40]

This experience shared on the ninth floor of the Hotel Savoy overlooking Central Park was the counterpart to the fireman's funeral at the Majestic the year before. That had been the moment of the muffled death drum that Mahler had incorporated into the E minor Scherzo of the Tenth Symphony, the manuscript of which bore the inscription "You alone, Alma, know what this means."

In January, Gropius attended a performance in Berlin of Mahler's Seventh Symphony. Mahler had long since figured prominently in his exchange of letters with Alma, although the issue of his death remained a matter of restraint, alluded to only in the code of "waiting." A part of Gropius's attachment to Alma encompassed a strong interest in Mahler and his work as a fellow creative artist.

> I am just coming out of Gustav's 7—exhausted—in turmoil.
> Listen to my impressions, because I feel the need to get this off
> my chest. I feel like someone who has to hold on tight in order
> to not be thrown off course or seduced away from my ideals, like
> someone who enters a new land in awe . . . previously in Munich
> there were too many other streams of feelings in my breast. . . .
> Today everything seemed new and strange—a strange distant
> Titan has rattled me, tore me away with a colossal impulse, all
> the valves of my heart touched by demonic and emotional child-
> like innocence. The sincere effort, the lonely search for God in
> this work has grabbed me, but, I am afraid before this strange
> strength, because my art grows from a different earth.[41]

If Mahler was aware of the betrayal of his womenfolk, there is no
record of it. But then, to whom would he have revealed any perceptions
or suspicions he might have had? Other than Alma, there was no intimate in his life in whom he might have confided. Estranged on this level
from concerned friends such as Guido Adler, Mahler had long taken the
position of defending Alma to them. Natalie Bauer-Lechner, the chronicler of his *Wunderhorn* years, had been out of Mahler's life since Alma
entered into it. Justine was no longer as attached to her brother as
before each of them had married. She herself had accomplished a separation from a relationship that had perhaps been too stifling for her and
she now had a family of her own. Mahler's relationship with his brother-
in-law Arnold Rosé, albeit close, was more collegial and political than
intimate. Mahler left no autobiographical writings, save those encoded
in music; and there were no new works after the sketches to the Tenth
Symphony.

Mahler had to a considerable degree shifted his attachments to his
wife's family. Indeed, when not abroad, he was now living with the Molls
in a new house in the Hohe Warte. He depended on Carl Moll for companionship, advice, attention to legal matters, and the disposition of his
manuscripts while he was on tour. And he adored his "little Mama." As
Freud noted, Mahler was close to his own mother and he "sought her"
in other women. Mahler acted as if he truly felt that he had found her
again in Anna Moll.

Alma was the curator and gatekeeper of Mahler's biography. If there had been any friction in the marriage caused by her ongoing relationship with Gropius, it would have met the same fate as their meetings and correspondence—which went unmentioned in her memoirs, only to be unearthed many years later by Gropius's biographer. In Alma's accounts, the affair with Gropius was closed with Mahler's session with Freud. She had a knack for spinning a plausible narrative with omissions neatly sealed over.

After the first of the year Mahler wrote "My dear little Mama" in anticipation of her visit. Once again, there was reassurance regarding her daughter, suggesting that in their correspondence Alma had revealed to Anna her underlying depressed mood and its sequelae in a degree of lethargy, drinking, and perhaps uncharacteristic lack of attention to her appearance. For Mahler went on to tell "the best of news about Almscherl. She is really blossoming—is keeping to a splendid diet, and has entirely given up alcohol, looking younger every day. She is hard at work and has written a few delightful new pieces that mark great progress."[42]

But betrayal was brewing from another quarter, the Philharmonic Ladies' Committee. Curiously, it was Mahler's former champion, Mary Sheldon, who, in the context of supporting Mahler in an interview with the *Musical Courier* at the beginning of the new season, issued the threat of his departure from New York.

> We have given New York one of the best orchestras ever heard here or anywhere, and if the musical public does not support this work, the orchestra will be disbanded. . . . Should Mr. Mahler return to Europe next season this country will find out what it has lost. He is a wonderful organizer and a great conductor. New Yorkers never heard such programs as Mr. Mahler has planned for the season.[43]

By year's end Mahler wrote to Emil Gutmann begging him to respect that June through October was Mahler's "close season"—that is, reserved for composition. As for New York, he added, "it is as good as certain that I shall return here next season."[44] The guarantors in fact wished to reengage him, but Mahler himself was undecided, thereby stimulating rumors about a successor. The committee needed a strong candidate, particularly for fundraising, as the initial endowment was dwindling. Consequently, they may have been considering other conductors. They may have leaked information, despite self-righteous disclaimers by Mrs. Sheldon to the effect that "We do not feel called upon to give private matters to the public."[45] Manager Loudon Charlton was instructed to approach Mahler "unofficially" and ask his terms. The minutes of 11 January recorded that "Mr. Mahler has expressed his willingness to conduct 90 to 100 concerts for $30,000."[46] Yet earlier that season Mahler had bridled at the increase from forty-five to sixty-five concerts. This latest increase was clearly an effort to generate more income for the committee, although Mrs. Sheldon acknowledged that it would never be sufficient and that the guarantors' support would have to continue. When the offer was officially made, Mahler felt compelled to accept. By the end of January he had signed a contract, although he wrote cagily to a correspondent, "As the dice appear to have fallen here, I may well become my own successor next season. With their love and determination, the people here are making it virtually impossible for me to leave them in a bind. And thus I am half decided to return here next winter."[47]

Although Mahler appeared to be enchanted with Americans, at least at times, he could be tactless and patronizing toward musical America. He was widely held as arrogant. Unlike Dvořák before him, Mahler was hardly an enthusiast of native American music, whether folk or art music. Critics such as William Henderson of the *New York Sun* and Arthur Farwell of *Musical America*, a composer himself, were sensitive to any perceived slight of cultural America. Thus Mahler was the unfortunate inheritor of the long-standing tension between Europe and America.

The year prior, Mrs. Sheldon had stood up, if not for Mahler personally, then for her Philharmonic, stating in an interview, "There are critics in this city whose interests in other institutions and organizations are so great that they cannot afford to write as they must feel concerning the magnificent work of the orchestra."[48] She was not too subtly referring to Krehbiel and Henderson, both of whom held posts at the Institute of Musical Art (later Juilliard) and who considered themselves to be curators of everything American.

Despite performances that year of works by George W. Chadwick and Edward MacDowell, Mahler was perceived as giving short shrift to American composers. For this, Arthur Farwell, who had been a pupil of Humperdinck in Berlin and was an avid proponent of indigenous American music, struck back in a scathing review of Mahler's Fourth Symphony: "What can be said of musical qualities where none can be detected, and why should one go into detail concerning the orchestral mask, where there is nothing behind it?"[49] The redoubtable Henry Krehbiel continued to be a hostile critic as well, working up a lather of antagonism that remained undiminished after Mahler's death. The response of the press was only one of the stresses that preyed on Mahler during the 1910–1911 season.

A simple entry into the committee minutes during negotiations proved to be ominous, and for Mahler, inevitably inflammatory: a resolution to form subcommittees, one of which would be an executive committee, chaired by Mrs. Sheldon, charged with supervising the Philharmonic programs.[50] Mahler's authority in this regard had never been challenged. For ten years in Vienna he had been sole arbiter of what and whose music would be performed at the opera. As Alma would later say, in Vienna even the emperor did not dictate the music to be played. In New York Mahler had enjoyed to date the autonomy of choice that led him to perform not only "historical concerts" of worthy classics but "moderns" such as Richard Strauss, Ferruccio Busoni; Americans such as MacDowell and Chadwick; and, of course, himself. Complacent at first, he did not foresee the imminent conflict.

While the resolution was taking its course, trouble was brewing in the orchestra. Although in general Mahler was admired by the musicians he had forged into a unique instrument, gossip and intrigue were a regular part of orchestral life. Their chief subject was inevitably the man who stood before them and commanded strict attention and response. One Thomas Johner, a second violinist, fomented distrust on both sides and had taken in Mahler in a manner unprecedented in the conductor's experience. Johner served, in effect, as a spy, and Mahler, though annoyed, was complicit. Perhaps Mahler felt of uncertain in his control over a non-European orchestra. Certainly Alma portrayed him as pitiably isolated: "J[ohner], he said, was his only friend. If he lost him he would be alone among enemies, for the whole orchestra hated him."[51] The situation escalated when the orchestra realized what was happening and complained to the Ladies' Committee, which demanded that Mahler dismiss Johner. Mahler's refusal to do so created ill feeling at a time when he needed all the goodwill he could draw on.

Mrs. Sheldon and the Ladies' Committee had moved in a direction perhaps predictable in the life of institutions and the human nature that animates them. The New York Philharmonic endeavor had been worth the effort and the money; the honeymoon season of 1909–1910 had gone well. Now, against the background of the current season, Mahler's initial demand for more money for more concerts, and his refusal to fire his orchestral confidant, friction was developing regarding who controlled programming. Money had backed the orchestra; the power money commanded, and the participation it warranted, were now being asserted. Increasingly, committee members began to attend rehearsals and in one aggravating example, after one of Mahler's symphonies (probably the Fourth), one woman "could not refrain from remarking that she thought he had played the first movement much too slowly. . . . [Mahler], utterly exhausted from the long, grueling rehearsal, simply turned away from her in silence."[52] But Mahler's frustration and rage at the challenging of his autonomy was gathering force. Alma related that the committee began to dictate programs that Mahler "had no wish to perform and they did not like it when he declined." In addition, "J[ohner] had set the whole orchestra by the ears and they were so refractory that Mahler no longer felt secure in his position. His habit of shutting his eyes to what was unpleasant prevented him from seeing his danger."[53]

At a committee meeting convened in mid-February at Mrs. Sheldon's home at Twenty-four East Thirty-eighth Street, Mahler was confronted. The timing was unfortunate, as Mahler's unstinting supporters, Minnie and Samuel Untermeyer, were away. In the past they had helped resolve any disagreements with the committee. Samuel had brokered the compromise earlier that season, in Mahler's demand for more money. In a departure from the artistic control to which he was accustomed, Mahler was told in no uncertain terms what he could and could not do. The discussion, heated at times, ratcheted up as the guidelines covered were put in the form of a legal document. It had been drawn up by a lawyer who, unbeknownst to Mahler, was listening on the other side of a curtain. In Alma's version:

> [Mahler] found several of the male members of the Committee there and was severely taken to task. The ladies had many instances to allege of conduct which in their eyes was mistaken. He rebutted these charges, but now at a word from Mrs. Sheldon a curtain was drawn aside and a lawyer, who (as it came out later) had been taking notes all the time, entered the room.

Mahler returned home trembling with fury. To add to the debacle, the committee, responding to a unanimous resolution of the orchestra, summarily dismissed Johner in midseason, an act that Mahler took as a further personal affront. Alma recorded, "Mahler went on conducting, but with rage in his heart against the orchestra and the Committee."[54]

Mahler did not go on conducting for long. Within days he was febrile once again, with a sore throat, and this time he did not rebound so readily. The program for the week had been printed, announcing the concert on the evening of Tuesday, 21 February, and the repeat performance the following Friday afternoon. Despite his fever and Dr. Fraenkel's misgivings, Mahler insisted on conducting the evening concert. He said he had done so many times before with such a fever. Besides, he had an almost magical faith that Fraenkel would see him through this episode.

On the program that evening was a work that had revived an ancient aching for Mahler. This was Busoni's *Berceuse Elégiaque*, the "Cradlesong at the Grave of My Mother." In his program notes, Krehbiel, who had been so bitter at Mahler's refusal to supply a program to his music, published the text that had inspired Busoni and been printed in the score:

> Schwingt die Wiege des Kindes,
> Schwankt die Wage seines Schicksals,
> Schwindet der Weg des Lebens,
> Schwindet hin in die ewigen Fernen.
> [The child's cradle rocks,
> and so do the scales of fate.
> The course of life also swings
> and dwindles in the endless distance.]

Ferruccio Busoni, *Berceuse Elégiaque*, 1909, cover.

Busoni himself commented on the score from which Mahler conducted that evening:

> The title page bears a picture of a mother at her child's cradle and, in the background, a man following a coffin. The man sings to his dead mother the same song which he had heard from her as a child and which had followed him through a lifetime and undergone a transformation.[55]

Mahler himself could not have chosen a more characteristic text to set, combining as it does the naivete and lyricism of the *Wunderhorn* and the gravitas of *Das Lied von der Erde*.

Nor could there have been a more fitting prologue to the beginning of the end. At the intermission, Mahler was exhausted and his head ached, but he completed the concert that would be his last.

16

MAHLER DYING

Early in 1911, Mahler had written to Anna Moll, enthusiastically anticipating her proposed visit to America and their subsequent return to Europe together after the season ended in March, "in posh cabins on the finest ship in the German merchant navy." "I shall probably be returning here for another year," he added. "Thank God I can now sense the first breaths of spring."[1] By May, however, Mahler was dead.

The new year began on a happy note for Alma. The singer Frances-Alda Gatti-Casazza (1883–1952) paid a visit to the Savoy—surprisingly for Alma, not to see Mahler but her. The singer had read through Alma's published songs and wished to perform one of them at an approaching concert. Mahler was ecstatic. He wanted all five to be performed: "Let her leave out something else!" One song was agreed on, which Mahler carefully rehearsed. "Is this how you want it?" Mahler asked repeatedly. Alma was too excited to think straight. "We were in close harmony then," she wrote.[2] In that moment Alma lived a long-suppressed dream: to be respected as a composer and to share music with Mahler as a colleague. Mahler finally realized this, as he had recognized her need for gifts and tribute under the threat of losing her the previous summer. His continued excessive enthusiasm for her music was a part of this.

Despite the renewed intimacy with Mahler, as plans for leaving New York and returning the following year were being considered, Alma wrote to Gropius of their anticipated March return date. Her song *Laue Sommernacht* (Mild Summer's Night) was almost an echo of the summer past: "In the starless summer night, deep in the darkness of the faraway forest we sought and found one another" (am Himmel stand kein Stern, im weiten Walde suchten wir uns tief im Dunkel und wir fanden uns). But the pace and ardor of correspondence with Gropius had diminished for the moment and Alma seemed more content. By the time of the concert, Mahler was sick in bed. He listened to the accompanist discussing the song with Alma but was too weak to attend the event. Alma, who by now was constantly close to her husband's bedside and would remain so to the end, nearly gave up hope of attending the performance. But by now Joseph Fraenkel was a frequent presence in the apartment and he took Alma to the concert.

After Mahler's near collapse on 21 February, Dr. Fraenkel had come home with them and had been there ever since, following Mahler's condition. Deceptive improvements recurred several times, only to finally disappoint on each occasion. A gifted clinician, Fraenkel understood what this meant although he did not convey it in words. Rather, when Alma called him in at the end of the first week, following a recrudescence of symptoms, she read the signs: the next morning, she wrote, Fraenkel's hair had turned gray. "Thus Mahler and I saw with our own eyes that hair can turn white in a few hours."[3] Although this was highly unlikely in any literal sense, Fraenkel's message was clear: Mahler was under sentence of death. Later, Fraenkel told Alma that "that night he had buried Mahler."[4] The clinician already knew his friend was terminal. He would ordinarily shield patients from knowledge of a situation's gravity but he was evidently unable to do so with someone he loved and idealized. Fraenkel would, however, go beyond the physician's duty to not abandon the patient or (as he saw it) deprive him of hope. He would be like a benign master of ceremonies at Mahler's death.

Fraenkel was equally concerned about Alma. She had begun to nurse Mahler, who was not a person to be left alone. He could be demanding, quite aside from sickbed requirements, and Fraenkel already knew that they were only just embarking on a long journey with a predictable outcome. He called in a friend as a consultant for Alma, Dr. Joseph Brettauer of Mount Sinai Hospital, a distinguished gynecologist and chief of the department.[5] Besides his medical qualifications, the German-speaking Brettauer came from Graz, Austria, and was trained at the University of

Vienna. He had also known the Zuckerkandls well enough to recommend young American physicians to the anatomist Emil Zuckerkandl, who had died the previous year.

Dr. Brettauer was a great favorite among the Mount Sinai interns and residents. He was of good humor and worked agreeably with the tyro surgeons. They, in turn, were somewhat protective. Legend had it that when Dr. Brettauer doffed his operating gown and dressed in his characteristically natty manner, he would often neglect to button his fly. The young doctors would monitor his departure and, if necessary, remind him, often having to do so as Brettauer walked briskly down the corridor.[6]

There is no evidence that Alma needed anything other than a comforting hand, which Brettauer, just three years older than Mahler, was able to provide in a fatherly way. By urging her to get more rest, he gave her permission to do so, when her feelings of guilt as to the proximate cause of Mahler's physical breakdown may have driven her to the detriment of them both. The death wish toward Mahler, the Evil Eye ("Gettatore") later confided to her diary but which she could not have failed to be aware of at this time, drove her to compensate.[7] Soon she herself collapsed with exhaustion and stress. At this point both Fraenkel and Brettauer urged her to send for her mother as soon as possible. In a moment of joy in the midst of troubles, Mahler was delighted at the prospect.

Fraenkel was also responsible for requesting a consultation with the master clinician, Emanuel Libman.[8] Dr. Libman was chief of medical service at New York's Mount Sinai Hospital, and associate director of laboratories. Dr. Libman's life paralleled the scientific development of bacteriology, a field to which he contributed significantly. In the days before the compartmentalization of medicine into science and practice, Dr. Libman combined both brilliantly. Indeed this is why Fraenkel called him in on the case. He was aware of Libman's research into what was then called subacute infective endocarditis, a disease of the lining of the heart and, in particular, the heart valves. Libman had almost single-handedly developed the technique of blood cultures, now a regular feature of medical diagnosis. In this test blood from the patient is layered on a nutrient gel in petri dishes and incubated. If bacteria are present, the naked eye may detect clumps, but more diagnostic, the microscope will reveal the

Dr. Emanuel Libman.

specific type of bacteria. Dr. Libman first reported his findings in 1906; the year before he consulted on Mahler, in 1910, he had refined the technique thoroughly and written extensively on its applications.

This was up-to-date medicine and Fraenkel wished to leave no stone unturned. He knew that despite more accurate diagnosis than had ever been possible before, there was as yet no definitive cure for infective endocarditis. Should the microscope confirm the diagnostic impression, Libman would know if palliative treatment existed anywhere. He was a force and a resource in the city and in constant touch with clinicians and investigators throughout the world. Alternatively, if the test was not positive, then perhaps he could come up with an alternative diagnosis. Known for his diagnostic acumen, Dr. Libman had the legendary knack for the *Augenblick Diagnose*, diagnosis made by simply observing; frequently, he did so as the patient approached, before even being seated in the consulting room. Libman was on call for diagnosis in at least twenty hospitals in the metropolitan area.

Emanuel Libman was something of a maverick and even in the home he owned and shared with his sister's family at 180 East Sixty-fourth Street he was quite private. He took his meals separately, served by his chauffeur, and lived chiefly in his well-appointed office on the ground floor or in his bedroom on the third. He would sometimes meet there with visiting scientists or occasional guests—but never women. A nephew, Dr. George Engel, speculated that Libman was homosexual in an age when disclosure would have been perilous to his standing. The rare times he entertained, he took guests out to dinner at a favorite restaurant, often the old Lindys; he was said to be quite a gourmet.[9]

Paradoxically, despite his pursuit of privacy, Libman was well known as a raconteur. He was a great lover of music, mainly symphonic music, and had his record collection (78 rpm at the time, of course) in his bedroom, as well as the most up-to-date recording equipment. He himself played the piano but would do so only in the living room, when no one else was occupying it. However, it is doubtful whether he was a devoted concert-goer, hence any knowledge he may have had about Gustav Mahler probably came from conversation or gossip, and the newspapers.

There was also a small laboratory in Libman's home, where he carried out some of his research. Mount Sinai was then only three blocks away, at Sixty-seventh and Lexington, and he might be found working there at any hour. Although not as popular as Brettauer with the house staff, Libman was highly respected and held in awe on three accounts. First were his scientific accomplishments, despite the fact that Mount Sinai, then a small and not very famous Jewish hospital, was not yet a teaching and research institution. Second was his astonishing success as a doctor. His patients included both the rich and the famous: Sarah Bernhardt, Queen Maria of Romania, the popular Fanny Brice. Third was Libman's power in the medical community. It was said that if one could become associated with Libman and get in his favor, then one's career (provided one had the capability) would be assured.[10]

There was perhaps another reason in the back of Fraenkel's mind for consulting with Libman about Mahler. Dr. Libman had a truly fabulous reputation for his knowledge of outcome in disease, a reputation he enjoyed indulging, particularly the theatrical effect of his expertise. Famously, in 1923, the fifty-one-year-old Libman had attended a dinner party at the White House during Warren G. Harding's tenure. The following day, tongue-in-cheek, he telephoned one of the other guests in Washington, asking, "Who was that fellow yesterday who is vice-president?" "Why, Calvin Coolidge, of course," came the answer.

"Well, tell him," responded Libman, "that in eight weeks he will be president." On schedule, so the story goes, Harding died of a sudden thrombosis, and on 3 August 1923 Coolidge, who was visiting his family in rural Vermont, received a message informing him that he was now president. It was said that Coolidge's father, who was a notary public, administered the oath of office by the light of a kerosene lamp.[11]

The Mahlers had become like family to Fraenkel. And with Mahler's developing illness, he may have permitted himself in the recesses of his mind to think of Alma as his future wife. However opportunistic that may seem, Fraenkel was by now warmly attached to Mahler as well and committed to seeing his illness through. If he was terminal, as Fraenkel suspected, there would be much to do in what might be little time. When it came to support from family or close friends, Alma was virtually alone in the new world. Bags had to be packed—forty of them!—transfers arranged, and passage booked. Above all, if on Libman's consultation it emerged that there might be any hope of treatment in Europe, this too had to be arranged in advance.

Dr. Libman's chauffeur drove him to the Hotel Savoy, where he examined Mahler at length and consulted with patient and wife. In performing a physical examination Libman would note a number of telltale signs that he had been observing in similar cases. Besides the loud murmur of the mitral valve that other physicians had heard earlier were the pallor of the skin, a result of anemia; and petechiae, tiny accretions of blood on the skin's surface. Libman was meticulous in examining the conjunctival tissue adjacent to the eyes, for involvement of these was diagnostic. There was a palpable enlargement of the spleen. Obvious to Libman but never noted by Mahler or Alma was the insidious "clubbing" of the fingers and toes, a curved, almost clawlike elevation of the nail beds. "Weakness," Libman would write, "is usually an early and prominent symptom"; this was the extreme fatigue Mahler had experienced during his last concert. And the malaria-like intermittent fever, from which Mahler was suffering, was likewise described by Libman in minute detail. Mahler's illness was recorded anonymously in medical history, one of the many patient histories classified in Dr. Libman's landmark monograph *Subacute Bacterial Endocarditis*.[12]

The diagnosis, made clinically, was clear in Libman's mind. It was consistent with the history of familial heart disease; the likelihood of "St. Vitus Dance," known as the chorea of childhood; the frequent sore throats in childhood; and the recent bouts in Toblach and Munich (called "angina"). Libman's diagnosis required only laboratory confirmation, which was now possible as a result of his research. He telephoned his assistant Dr. George Baehr to join him at the hotel to perform the test. Baehr came cross-town immediately, lugging his black doctor's bag containing the necessary paraphernalia and culture media.[13]

Twenty-four-year-old George Baehr was a fortunate man among Mount Sinai's younger doctors. Like his mentor, Baehr was headed toward a career in medicine that combined the clinical and the investigative. He would inherit a leadership position as chief of medicine at a time when Mount Sinai was in the process of becoming one of the great teaching hospitals of New York. A young man of his aspirations was expected to engage in some scientific *Arbeit*. Baehr's choices led him to become a leading authority—indeed, a definer—of the entity now known as collagen disease.

As fellow in pathology and bacteriology, essentially Libman's resident, Baehr enjoyed the privilege of following the master's patients. In return, his duties included performing those menial medical tasks that many an attending physician, having similarly paid his dues, assigned to assistants. It was thus that in late February 1911, Baehr was called to the Hotel Savoy to draw Mahler's blood for culture. Actually, Libman, whose life *was* blood, would not necessarily have considered this task beneath him. But the truth of the matter provided delicious gossip among the Mount Sinai house staff: in performing venipuncture, Libman had trouble finding patients' veins! In his hands, they would "roll" and he would sometimes bloody the bedclothes.

Baehr approached the bed and withdrew 20 cc of blood from a vein in Mahler's arm. He squirted the blood into several boullion flasks before pouring the mixture onto petri dishes. As Baehr later recalled, "After four or five days of incubation in the hospital laboratory, the Petri plates revealed numerous bacterial colonies . . . of the organism *Streptococcus Viridans*." He continued: "As this was long before the days of antibiotics, the bacterial findings sealed Mahler's doom. He insisted on being told the truth and then expressed a wish to die in Vienna." It was extremely unusual for Dr. Libman to countenance telling a patient of a fatal diagnosis. It was his rule never to do so, in order not to remove a degree of hope. Revealing a fatal diagnosis also made life more difficult for the clinician. Libman either made an exception for Mahler—as had Freud in consulting with him—or was moved by Mahler's insistence. Libman allowed that a very small percentage of patients improved spontaneously, although this outcome was extremely rare at such an advanced stage.

Mahler's wish to die in Vienna was more than a matter of geography. His desire to return home was spiritual. Putzi was buried in the suburb of Grinzing, and Mahler wanted to be buried beside her. Indeed, in one of Alma's accounts, she noted Mahler's wish to be buried "in the same grave" as their daughter.[14] The fantasied reunion with the child named after his mother would close the circle of Freud's *Mutterbindung*, and restore the maternal security Mahler craved. Once again, as in Mahler's retouching of the text of *Kindertotenlieder*, the grave was equated with the womb or mother-house: "Frightened no more by storms, protected by the hand of God, they are resting as if at home with Mother" (Von keinem Sturm erschrecket, Von Gottes Hand bedecket, Sie ruh'n, Sie ruh'n wie in der Mutter Haus).

When psychoanalyst and medical educator Dr. George Engel reviewed the life's work of his uncle, Emanuel Libman, he noted something extraordinary: case histories prior to 1899 often began with references to life settings associated with illness and were presumably believed to be connected with its development.[15] Such observations, usually psychological in nature, yielded to the fascination with new scientific methods around the turn of the century. By the same token, in the absence of medical technology, clinicians depended on the observational data from all five senses in determining diagnosis. Above all, they were willing to use their ears to listen not only to the heart sounds but to the story of the patient's illness. Many years later, Libman's assistant, George Baehr, now distinguished professor emeritus, recalled vividly his visit to Mahler's bedside. In reciting the case history, true to his traditional medical heritage, he began with the relevant antecedent life events and psychological state of his patient.

As I understood the history from (Dr.) Libman, Mahler had lost a daughter from scarlet (fever), a streptococcus infection of the more acute type. As I understood the history of the case I got from Libman, he became very depressed and rightly or wrongly, that made me believe that his depressive states were due to the memory of this daughter. I also learned that he had been told by his doctor long ago he'd had a heart lesion and that he must not tax it and get rest. So that I didn't know to what degree his depressive states were involved.[16]

What Baehr noticed, and what his mentor Libman ignored completely in his detailed monograph, published much later, was Mahler's mental state. Mahler was clearly depressed during the examination and although fatigue may often mask depression—indeed, may constitute one of its signs—there can be little question that Mahler was suffering from clinical depression at the time. More than this, as Baehr suspected in eliciting the story of Putzi's death, Mahler's state of mind was not exclusively of recent origin, although one might expect that the onset of illness and an interruption of career such as Mahler experienced could bring on melancholy.

Dr. Nicholas P. Christy and Beverly M. Christy have made a notable contribution to Mahler studies in researching and documenting his diagnosis.[17] Had an autopsy been performed at Mahler's death, it would doubtless have revealed the fibrous clumps colonized by blood-borne bacteria on the heart valves. But this is not the whole story. In a monograph titled *The Psychological Autopsy*, psychiatrists Avery Weisman and Richard Kestenbaum write:

> The somatic autopsy does not answer all the questions. Autopsies do not always disclose the cause of death, nor do they invariably demonstrate why people die when they do. *What people die with is not the same as what people die from.* Furthermore, what prompts a person to become ill, enter the preterminal phase, and die at a particular time and in a particular way cannot always be ascribed entirely to a [somatic] disease process. The final illness is a psychosocial as well as a medical event.[18] [italics added]

If Mahler died *with* bacterial endocarditis, what did he die *from?* The terminal illness was more than an affair between the bacteria and the lining of the heart. One of the themes throughout the present book has been Mahler's lifelong romance with death. In Mahler's mental life, death was not only the opposite of life but its reciprocal, death and life equated. More than this, death was conflated with afterlife in the form of musical ideas of resurrection (the Second Symphony) and eternal life (*Das Lied von der Erde*). On the other end of the spectrum, death was abandonment (the Tenth Symphony); death was terror (*Das irdische Leben*). At the root of all were Mahler's early and constant experiences of familial deaths at ongoing stages of life, and the consequent and varied forms wishes for his own death assumed.

Although multiple examples could be cited, one in particular stands out as Mahler's signature representation of death, his setting of the Rückert text *Ich bin der Welt abhanden gekommen* (I Am Lost to the World) composed at the time of the mortal crisis of 1901. At the words "I live alone in my heaven, in my loving, in my song" (Ich leb' allein in Meinem Himmel, in meinem Lieben in meinem Lied), Mahler created a cessation of music, of time, of life itself, that blended into eternal silence. In this he depicted musically a personal nirvana consistent with Freud's death instinct: a blissful end to motion, emotion, and consciousness itself.

More immediately, the events leading up to Mahler's final illness comprise an account of repeated stresses and assaults on the psyche. The events of 1907 figured heavily in this, particularly the death of the child mentioned by Dr. Baehr in his report. Even three and a half years later, Mahler was still in mourning in his own way. Bereavement is a singular human experience that tends strongly to precede the onset of illness. In this sense, Mahler may be said to have been at risk in the ensuing years. Clustered around the same time were difficulties with the Vienna Court Opera, the anti-Semitic critics, and Mahler's resignation; as well as the diagnosis of his heart disease. While Mahler was able to master these traumas and go on with creative life, they took their toll mentally and physically. The coup de grace, however, was delivered by Alma in her affair with Gropius. Briefly, Mahler fell apart. His resistance lowered; by the end of the summer he experienced a recrudescence of sore throat and fever, a medical omen for what would follow. He righted himself even before his visit with Freud but in his marriage he was never the same again. His anxieties about Alma led to chronic worry that she would leave him; he tried to appease her with gifts, the dedication of his music, and the promotion of her own music. His efforts to placate her and pay tribute were transparent, as she had changed into a powerful and dangerous force in his life.

The visit with Freud promoted the self-healing that had already begun and Mahler clung to the hope held out to him that he would not and could not be abandoned by Alma. But shortly after, in Munich, he once again demonstrated growing physical vulnerability in the febrile episode that he "sweated out" before Alma's arrival. And again, another "septic sore throat before Christmas." Only in retrospect did Alma realize its implications: "It passed over very quickly and did not alarm us. But it might well have done [so]."[19]

The most recent stresses were the growing animosity of the New York Philharmonic and the humiliation before the Ladies' Committee. Musically, Mahler continued to be the master in musical peformance. His conducting, before the last in February, had not declined either in quality or in his demands on the orchestra. But the otherwise cogent score-sketches of the Tenth Symphony showed evidence of transient mental deterioration in the scrawlings on the manuscript page. Similarly, there were distortions in the way he was experiencing events and making judgments. Suspicious and feeling vulnerable before the orchestra, he had sanctioned what in effect was a spy and let the affair escalate to unanimous open opposition. At that point, Mahler felt let down by what he perceived as desertion.

The assertion of control and power by the Ladies' Committee was too close to the bone to be managed in Mahler's previously habitual cool and politic manner. For the issue, as Mahler viewed it, was that which had been uppermost in mind during this period: abandonment and desertion. This issue was still raw; it was "Alma" displaced and writ large. Once again, Woman could withdraw unstinting love and admiration yet require submission. More than this, Mahler experienced a degree of mortification that was totally foreign to him. He had always been in the superior position; nor had he avoided the humiliation of others who had not met his standards, rationalized as being in the service of art. Unaccustomed to being on the receiving end, Mahler was overcome by a sense of helplessness. Such was the state of mind that favored the onset of illness.

"I looked after him now just as if he were a little child," Alma wrote. "I put every bite into his mouth for him and slept in his room without taking off my clothes." In the natural regression of severe illness Mahler appeared to be uncharacteristically dependent, saying to her, "When I'm well again, we'll go on like this. You'll feed me—it's so nice."[20] Mahler was impatient for the arrival of Anna Moll, who had been cabled soon after Mahler's collapse. She left Vienna the same day she was summoned and took the speediest boat. Consulting the newspaper, Mahler counted the days. Theirs was a curious bond. Despite her betrayal in fostering of Alma's affair, Anna demonstrated a strong maternal attachment to Mahler. That there was an inherent contradiction in her side of the bond did not seem to deter her. She apparently lived comfortably with this split in consciousness.

For Mahler, who had been deeply attached to his own mother, Anna was all the mother he now had, at least of her generation. Alma played a maternal role toward her sick husband, but his need was extreme. If there had been any suspicion of Anna's loyalty earlier—or Alma's, for that matter—necessity made the issue moot. Anna was perhaps Mahler's greatest comfort. In motherly fashion, she would cook his favorite dishes on the tiny improvised kerosene stove in their elegant hotel suite. In the short time he had left, Mahler tended to spurn members of his own family. As Alma perceived it, "Mahler was no longer blind. On the contrary he now watched feverishly whether or not I was shown enough warmth and respect."[21] When both women were exhausted and male nurses were hired, Mahler became so irritable that at length a female nurse was engaged, although in attending to his needs she had to avert her eyes.

On several occasions, Mahler perked up, and one almost thought the dreadful episode was over; that he would be the exception of which Dr. Libman had spoken and recover spontaneously. He would suddenly experience a surge of energy accompanied by an optimistic outlook and an appetite as regressive symptoms of his illness seemed for the moment to vanish. However, Dr. Libman did not share the relief and rising hope of Alma and Anna. Scientist to the core, he would eventually describe an unusual behavioral feature in his patients in which they would suddenly experience a paradoxical sense of wellness. He termed this heartbreaking false hopefulness *spes endocarditica*, the deceptive hope of endocarditis.

By the second week in March Alma realized that Mahler had been ill for three weeks. Writing to Gropius of this, she asked him to keep the information between themselves for the moment. Two weeks later, she communicated to him all the details, including the diagnosis. In describing her exhaustion since the earlier letter, she wrote: "To my great surprise I was able to do more than I ever thought I could. I did not change my clothes for 12 days. I was nurse, mother, wife, everything, and above all full of sorrow, fear and worry." The letter began with "My Love" and closed with "Your Bride." In the last paragraph she implored her lover passionately: "At the moment I am numb, but I know when I see you, everything in me will become alive and blossom. Love me with those feelings which have made me so tremendously happy. I want you! But you? Do you want me also!"[22] Confiding in her lover, Alma looked to her future with Gropius now that Mahler's impending death was certain.

And so began the long voyage home to Vienna and to Grinzing. After Anna Moll's arrival Dr. Fraenkel had remained involved. He served as the conduit for recommendations from Libman and other colleagues as to doctors abroad who might conceivably salvage a hopeless situation. They all knew it would be in the nature of a miracle and none truly believed in miracles. Fraenkel provided a long list of famous European physicians, including two who would play a role in Mahler's final days: the bacteriologist Andre Chantemesse (1851–1919) of L'Institut Pasteur in Paris, and Franz Chvostek (1864–1944) in Vienna, chosen because of his work in the developing specialty of hematology. Others were chosen from the European medical centers in Lyon, Berlin, Heidelberg, and even England. Meanwhile, passage had been booked for 8 April on the SS *Amerika*—the "finest ship" with "posh cabins" about which Mahler had happily written to Anna only months earlier.

From the moment the Mahlers left their suite at the Hotel Savoy until their arrival in Vienna on 12 May Mahler was the object of public curiosity as well as private concern. Fraenkel smoothed the way in their departure from the hotel, seeing to it that the large lobby was deserted as the elevator descended. Mrs. Untermeyer's chauffered automobile was waiting at a side entrance and Fraenkel drove with Mahler to the pier while Alma settled accounts. Alma recalled: "When I arrived on board Mahler was already in bed and Fraenkel was at his side. He gave me his last instructions and warned me not to call the ship's doctor. Then he bade Mahler a brief and sad farewell. He knew that he would never see him again."[23]

The voyage took ten days. It was a comfort to all to have the good-hearted Ferruccio Busoni as shipmate. He loved Mahler and Mahler appreciated the younger man's warmth and good humor. He would send Mahler "crazy specimens of counterpoint to amuse him."[24] The boat's captain maintained the respectful spirit shown by the hotel staff in New York. He saw to it that there was time and privacy in the boarding of the tender.

By the time they reached Vienna, only days before Mahler's death, journalists had been meticulously and intrusively charting the course of

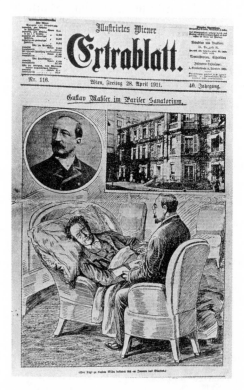

Engraving in a Vienna newspaper accompanying an article on Mahler's illness, April 1911.

his illness and the daily progress of the morbid procession. They followed the Mahler entourage from the time of disembarking in Cherbourg, to the clinic in Paris, to the journey on the Orient Express from Paris, through Munich and Salzburg, and home to the final destination, Vienna. By then the redoubtable satirist Karl Kraus wrote of the Viennese, "Now that it is already very late, they are trying to right the earlier wrongs. The patient receives addresses and wishes for his recovery which he probably does not read. Now people remember he 'was one of us.'"[25]

On arrival, the scene at the quay had been dreadful with the confusion of baggage, customs, and getting a sick man onto the train. The group reached Paris at 5 A.M. on 18 April. Carl Moll had boarded the train at an earlier stop to help settle everyone at the Hotel Elysées, which was run by Viennese. Later in the morning all were astonished to find Mahler fully dressed and shaven, sitting on the balcony and ringing for his break-fast, saying, "I always said I should recover as soon as I set foot in Europe. I'll go for a drive this morning." Alma and the Molls wept for joy. Was this the miracle for which they had been hoping? As Mahler impulsively ordered a car, Alma felt "a pang of dread." Soon her premo-nition turned into harsh reality: "He got into it as a man recovered, and got out, after an hour's drive, as a man at death's door. He got paler and paler from the moment we reached the Bois." Put straight to bed, he had a shivering fit. "Then a collapse."[26] Once again Mahler—and his family—had experienced the merciless *spes endocarditica*.

When it came to getting medical help in Paris, the Mahlers experienced the chaos more ordinary families frequently encounter when a member becomes sick over a holiday. It was Easter. The doctors Fraenkel had recommended in Berlin and Lyon could not be reached but Dr. Chantemesse was contacted. Alarmed at Mahler's condition, he insisted that the sick man immediately enter what was considered to be the most up-to-date clinic in Paris. Mahler did so three days after arrival in Paris. Although it was situated near the Bois de Boulogne in a mag-nificent park of its own, Alma found the facility primitive compared with those of Vienna. And since it was lacking in nursing staff, she and Anna were once again called on to care for their patient.

The family would remain in Paris—actually, at Dr. Defaut's clinic in Neuilly—for nearly three more weeks while Dr. Chantemesse attempted an experimental treatment that Mahler's doctors in New York had been loathe to try. This was the preparation and injection of a serum in a procedure that had been described in an American journal three years earlier. The bacteriologist prepared a vaccine in which antibodies to the specific toxic bacteria had been formed. The first injection was disastrous—not only painful, but further debilitating to the dying patient.

The deceptive surge of energy in Paris may not have been Mahler's last since he had tolerable days despite inexorable decline. The Viennese newspapers covered Mahler's progress avidly, responding to their readers' demand for news, good or bad. The *Neue Freie Press* had been granted an interview and reported a different Mahler than the one who collapsed in Alma's account:

> When Mahler arrived in the sanitorium Chantemesse was already waiting for him to begin the serum treatment as soon as he had examined him again. I spoke to Chantemesse after his visit. He found Mahler better than yesterday, and in particular he confirmed the satisfactory activity of the heart. . . .
>
> I had a chance to see Mahler when he was brought to the sanitorium. He does not look bad. His lively gestures and his fiery eyes confirm the reports from those around him that as a result of the long fever Mahler has lost nothing of his sharpness of mind, his remarkable will power or his feeling for life.
>
> Mahler was said to have spoken a long time in this interview, about an opera he was interested in producing, "until his wife, who watches over him with touching care, made him rest."[27]

Twice—at the very end of April and again on 1 May—Alma wrote to Gropius from Neuilly. Assuming at that point that she might remain in France for some period, she asked him to come to her. She shared the details of Mahler's suffering with Gropius: "Such a dignified human being is now laid low." But at the same time she longed for the "warm, soft, dear hands" of her lover. Walter replied by telegram, later sending her a photograph of himself that she hid in her room at the sanatorium. In her thanks to Gropius she ended, "strong, dear being—hold me—I kiss your hands as your lover, Alma."[28] She again instructed him to send his letters addressed to Anna Moll.

At the sanatorium in Neuilly and later in Vienna Mahler read works of philosophy. It had seemed almost humorously unempathic years before, when Alma had been in labor, that he attempted to read to her from Kant. But such readings really did settle Mahler. He now read Eduard von Hartmann's *The Problem of Life*, tearing the pages from the binding as he lacked the strength to hold the entire treatise. The book became like a clock, as page after page was torn off to read and Mahler's own life waned.

Dr. Chantemesse's serum treatment had failed and Mahler was worsening. As Chantemesse now busied himself with the novelty and fascination of the blood culture, quite forgetting his patient, Alma resigned herself to the fact that diagnosis promised no treatment. Panicked, she telegraphed Dr. Chvostek in Vienna and asked him to come immediately. He arrived the following morning.

Dr. Chvostek, like his American colleagues, was not one to reveal a terminal diagnosis. His attempts to be cheerfully merciful and hold out hope for the doomed man earned him a parody of deception in Alma's memoirs. He boldly encouraged Mahler: "Shall I ever be able to work again then?" "Of course. Why not? Keep your heart up, that's all. This evening we'll be off to Vienna together." To be fair to the physician, given Mahler's now fragile state, he may have been trying to shore him up for the journey to Vienna. For at this point all agreed that the wish that would be his last, to die in Vienna, must be granted. Knowing that time was short, Chvostek acted rapidly, making arrangements for a transportable bed, an ambulance, and a train for the immediate return to Vienna. That night, en route home, Alma was with Mahler when Chvostek called to her and motioned Carl to take her place. "No hope," he said solemnly. "And may the end come quickly."[29]

The date was 11 May and the *Neue Freie Press* carried the story:

> This afternoon Mahler left Paris; he is traveling on a stretcher accompanied by his wife, by Herr Moll and by Professor Chvostek. At his own specific request he is being brought to

Vienna. Professor Chvostek agreed with Chantemesse's treatment, but neither of the doctors could refuse the sick man's request to be taken to Vienna. . . .

The latest examination, which took place in the afternoon before Mahler's departure, revealed that his condition is very serious and that there is nothing to lose by the journey.[30]

The journey was like that of a dying king. Journalists crowded at every station as the Orient Express sped through Germany and Austria that night. Arrangements had been made for Mahler to enter Dr. Anton Loew's sanatorium and at 5:30 A.M. the ambulance pulled up to await the train's arrival. Despite the keen interest of the public, people had respected the wish of the doctors and family not to crowd the station. There was only a small group of family and friends that included Justine

Arnold Schoenberg, *Burial of Gustav Mahler*, c. 1911. Oil on canvas.

and Arnold Rosé and Bruno Walter. (Walter, devoted to Mahler to the end, had visited for a few days in Paris.) The newspaper reported:

> A few minutes before 6 the Orient Express arrived. From one of the sleeping cars, which was located in the middle of the train, Herr Moll, Gustav Mahler's father-in-law, alighted first. Friends went up to him. Herr Moll said to them: "The journey was reasonable. The patient is very weak."[31]

Mahler's dying was the news of the day in Vienna and newspapers printed every scrap of information that could be gleaned about the progression of Mahler's terminal state. Proverbially, the Viennese were said to have loved a beautiful corpse, no less did they savor a man dying. Dr. Chvostek issued reports regarding his patient's vital signs and status. On 8 May: "pulse 120; temperature 37.3; mood (*Stimmung*) better; night status bad—fever." Remaining faithful to the end, Chvostek applied supportive measures as they became necessary in the final days: morphine, oxygen.

Gustav Mahler died on Thursday, 18 May 1911, at midnight. When the final agony began, Alma was banished from the room. Carl Moll was with him to the end and watched the spirit that animated the man gradually ebb and pass. When the face was fixed, he made the death mask.

17

FOREVER ALMA

After Mahler's death Alma wrote, "I wanted to follow him," quickly adding, "But I was thirty then and I recovered."[1] (Actually, she would shortly be thirty-two.) And recover she did, soon "surrounded by outstanding men, as before." For the next thirty years, extraordinary men came and went in her life, and there would be second and third marriages. Only in her final years was Alma without a man and by then she enjoyed the career of eminent widowhood as the curator and arbiter of the memory of Gustav Mahler. She played a similar role for Franz Werfel, her third husband. Anticipating correctly that it would be of interest to many, Alma titled her memoir simply *My Life*.[2] Its English edition came out as *And the Bridge Is Love*.[3] The bridge had many paths.

In her account, Alma leapfrogged over her continued relationship with Walter Gropius. Or rather, she substituted other suitors who occupied her first year of widowhood. The first was Dr. Joseph Fraenkel, who had fallen in love with her during the New York years. As medical adviser to the couple during Mahler's final illness, he dared to hope that, with the tragic inevitability he foresaw, Alma might one day be his. After a decent interval, he came to Vienna twice to woo her and to press his case. He took Alma on a romantic trip to the island of Corfu on the Adriatic that turned into a disaster for Fraenkel. He was seasick in his stateroom during the voyage while Alma flirted with an interesting Albanian.

There is little question that each of Alma's affairs was sexual and that with Fraenkel was no exception. It also set a pattern that would tend to recur later, namely, an initial warm attachment followed by an interval of cool appraisal. Having made a decision to break off a relationship, Alma would wait to do so until the next suitor in line was promising if not secure. And even afterward, there would inevitably be letters to and fro. Fraenkel evidently did not measure up sexually and could not pass muster on intellect alone. "I always though of Fraenkel as sheer intellect, and embodied brain," Alma wrote. And preserving bragging rights for her own intellect, not to mention her sexuality, "He was one man for whom even I was too earthy."[4] In her distinctly unsentimental farewell letter, she summed things up for the spurned suitor, "My watchword is: Amo— ergo sum. Yours: Cogito—ergo sum."

While Alma accorded Fraenkel a degree of respect, acknowledging his friendship through recent years and his devotion to both herself and Mahler, she by now saw him as "an elderly, sick little man quite unheroically nursing a fatal intestinal ailment," surely a distortion as Fraenkel was only forty-four and would live more than a decade.[5] She was gratuitously contemptuous, writing in her letter to Fraenkel, "When it comes to living you're a miserable failure. At best men like you are put between book covers, closed, pressed, and devoured in unrecognizable form by future generations. But such men never *live*."[6] Thus Alma revealed the dark side of mourning. For it was Mahler she had bitterly complained was an "abstraction" and Mahler to whom she had given her best years; it was he who would inevitably become apotheosized by generations to come, the person having become the music. The secret anger of the bereaved became articulated in the uncalled-for tirade against Fraenkel, who additionally, as physician, failed to save Mahler after all. Alma, the survivor, ended her letter to him on a note at once narcissistically ecstatic yet curiously practical: "Today I know the eternal source of all strength. It is in nature, in the earth, in people who don't hesitate to cast away their existence for the sake of an idea. They are the ones who can love. I go on living with my face lifted high, but with my feet on the ground—where they belong."[7] With this, Alma Schindler Mahler declared her entitlement to love.

Alma moved on to an affair with the Austrian composer Franz Schreker (1878–1934), who was enjoying considerable success as "one of the leading composers in Germany," and who had just been appointed

professor of composition at the Music Academy in Vienna. The relationship followed an emerging pattern: "For a while we saw much of each
other, but he played no part in my life; I walked beside him for a stretch
and left him at the right time."[8]

The "right time" hardly squared with Alma's resolve to keep her feet
"on the ground," as her next lover was the biologist Paul Kammerer
(1880–1926). In calling him "one of the oddest individuals I ever came
across," she was certainly on target. The appeal was his encouragement
to engage Alma, the child of artistic tradition, in an entirely different
field, as she tried on new roles. He offered her a voluntary job as assistant in his laboratory at the recently formed Institute for Experimental
Biology on the Prater in Vienna.[9] It may have been Kammerer's passion
for his scientific work that led Alma to write in her letter to Fraenkel that
the people who can love live exclusively "for the sake of an idea." As for
physical love, Alma denied the least attraction: "As a man I always found
him disgusting."[10] Nevertheless, their relationship was a cause for gossip
and some—Kammerer's wife, for one—believed "that the experiments
continued in the bedroom," although Alma loudly protested otherwise.[11]

Kammerer's other passion was Gustav Mahler and his love of the man
serves as a paradigm for the several men whose adoration of Alma was
informed by their affection—in varying degrees of intensity—for her late
husband. Kammerer had alienated Mahler in life by his intrusiveness after
a cordial exchange of letters had piqued Mahler's curiosity about what
sounded like innovative scientific work. In fact, an invitation to visit
Toblach ended in a debacle when it became clear that Kammerer was
pathologically obsessed with Mahler's music and nearly worshiped the
composer. Kammerer attended Mahler's funeral and let it be known to
his wife—who restrained him—that he intended to kill himself on
Mahler's grave in order to join him in the afterlife. This from a scientist![12]
As for Kammerer's scientific work, Alma noted that the conscientious
records she kept for his experiments annoyed him. Shrewdly she
detected, "Slightly less exact records with positive results would have
pleased him more."[13]

Before the first of the year, Alma had moved out of the Molls' house
on the Hohe Warte and into an apartment of her own. She was in the
process of building a house in Semmering on property Mahler had

purchased before his death. At the time, Kammerer was experimenting with praying mantises, lizards, and salamanders. To enable Alma to work at home instead of going to the Prater for long periods each day, Kammerer set up a large terrarium in the apartment, which frequently leaked reptiles that escaped down the stairway. Gucki, who was with Alma, was delighted. At first Alma tolerated this absurdity out of pride in what seemed to be a useful and increasingly responsible job. No doubt the worship that Kammerer lavished on her was flattering up to a point as well. Soon a sense of uneasiness supervened and, finally, fear. "Every day he wrote me the craziest letters; every other day he would run out of my house threatening to shoot himself—preferably on Gustav Mahler's grave." As far as is known, he never threatened Alma personally although his entreaties to her, the intensity of which was ultimately frightening, were tantamount to harassment. The solution, however, had always been close at hand and was finally exercised by Alma: she simply let his wife know of his behavior and he was reined in, at least temporarily. Assuming the moral high ground, Alma loftily wrote, "'Thank God,' I told her, 'that he brought his lonely heart to me—for I don't want him, and so you have not lost him.' . . . Frau Kammerer thanked me profusely."[14]

In retrospect, Kammerer doubtless suffered from a variant of erotomania, which also manifested itself serially in a passion for all five sisters of an artistic Viennese family.[15] It was said that his suicide occurred after the last of the sisters refused to accompany him to Moscow, where he had been invited to create a program at the Pavlov Institute. At the same time, however, an article had appeared in the scientific journal *Nature* in which it was revealed that Kammerer had faked certain experimental results.[16]

"Thank God," of course, equals "Thank Alma." In widowhood, a markedly self-inflating quality surfaced in Alma's personality, an erotic grandiosity that seemed to give her license to do as she would with lovers. She more than simply bore the name of Mahler; rather, she seemed to have coopted its distinction and power as well. Alma took it as a providential sign that Mahler died on Walter Gropius's birthday—his twenty-eighth. During the first days after Mahler's death, the exhausted Alma had taken to bed, where she wrote to Gropius often. And concurrent with the Fraenkel, Schreker, and Kammerer affairs, Alma and Walter continued their correspondence. Gropius's condolence letter had a ring of intimacy—as if the three had shared much in the past, which of course they had, although not the way Gropius construed it. "I am mourning Gustav with a sincere heart. As an artist I did not know him well enough, and as a human being he approached me in such a dignified way, that the moment is forever etched in my memory."[17] In June, on the anniversary of their Tobelbad adventure, he wrote to Alma from a vacation on the North Sea, "I am thinking with longing of you and Gustav and everything that has happened. If only I could take care of you here! You would get well. Today it's been one year since I first laid eyes on you."[18]

Gropius came to Vienna later in the summer, staying in a hotel where he and Alma met frequently. With renewed intimacy and expecting an empathic response, Alma related Mahler's last days and how "she had given herself totally to Gustav Mahler's strong need for love and tenderness in the last days of his life."[19] Gropius, who was naive enough to believe that the terminal Mahler had demanded sex with Alma, took this as a confession. Rather irrationally, he accused Alma of infidelity, revealing his ambivalence toward Mahler and competitiveness with the dead man. "When did you become Gustav's wife again?" he wrote from his hotel. Consistent with the triangle in which he was involved and equally illogically he continued, "The only comfort that I can hang on to is that I have helped two such wonderful people."[20] Licking the imagined wounds of a lover betrayed, Gropius seemed to be saying goodbye. But Alma would have none of this, at least for the moment, and no sooner had Gropius returned to Berlin than she appealed to him, "Please write me in your loving way."

Gropius was confused, undecided, and unable to bring his mixed feelings to a single focus. A proposed September rendezvous in Berlin was cancelled as he reflected on his behavior and experienced "a hot shame [that] rises in me, which won't let me alone." He confessed to feelings of guilt as well, "for the sorrow that I brought to you and Gustav out of lack of mature forsight."[21] Suddenly, Alma had to contend with a new turn of events: the youth, at twenty-eight, was growing up. As for her own desires, she was not at all sure that she wanted him now, although neither was she quite ready to give him up. A December trip to Berlin proved disappointing. She liked neither the city nor Gropius's family—his mother and sister, both Manon. Nonetheless she wrote at the beginning of 1912, "Are you still being faithful?" His answer came in the form of an exchange of letters that dwindled as the year wore on. Meanwhile, Alma's house in Semmering had been completed and she was happy there. Yet she wrote to Gropius in the spring that she "needed his protection." As his pulling away from her became more apparent, she asked, "Why such reticence, when are you coming to Vienna?"[22] Writing to him on the first anniversary of Mahler's death, 18 May 1912, the day Gropius turned twenty-nine, she failed to send birthday greetings.

This story was not told in Alma's memoirs. Similarly untold was the fact that she was already involved with the artist Oskar Kokoschka (1866–1944) even as she pressed Gropius in vain for a response. By the year's anniversary with Gropius, the relationship with Kokoschka was well on its way. The propitious timing was likely the work of Alma's guardian angel, Anna Moll, who, as perennial confidante, may have been alarmed at the increasing craziness of Paul Kammerer and the diminishing prospect of Walter Gropius. Carl Moll had been involved in introducing Alma to Oskar, whom he considered to be a young genius, and he had arranged for him to paint Alma's portrait. They met at a dinner party at the Molls' home on 14 April 1912 and it was passion at first sight. "After that evening," according to Kokoschka, "we were inseparable."[23] Predictably, there are two versions of their meeting. Kokoschka contended, "She enchanted me! . . . After dinner, she took me by the arm and drew me into an adjoining room, where she sat down and played the *Liebestod* on the piano for me."[24] Alma recalled, "After a while I told him I could not stand being stared at like this, and asked whether I might play the piano."[25] Writing later, Alma could not restrain herself from observing that while he was drawing her, he was interrupted by coughing spells and tried to hide his handkerchief, which had spots of blood on it, implying tuberculosis. (Actually, Kokoschka never had the disease. But by that time he had joined the ranks of rejected lovers who, like Fraenkel and Kammerer, were deemed to be diseased in some way.)

Kokoschka was captivated and proposed in a letter the following day: "If you will be the woman who gives me strength, and will thus help me out of my spiritual confusion, the beauty we honour, which is beyond our understanding, will bless us both with happiness."[26] Within days, he wrote, "Dear Wife, as you want to be. Make me the only man you love."[27] By then the two were sleeping together in her flat, although she would not let him stay the night and, for the sake of appearances, insisted on separate rooms when they traveled.[28] On these occasions it was Alma who paid the way for the as-yet impecunious artist. In response to his wish to be her "only man," Alma complained of Kokoschka's jealousy. At the time they met, Kokoschka knew that she was still working for Kammerer but she kept her correspondence with Gropius secret. Hovering over all was Gustav Mahler. His memory was everywhere in Alma's home, Rodin's bust of Mahler and the death mask prominently displayed. When Alma invited Kokoschka to the premiere of Mahler's Ninth Symphony in Vienna, he declined, writing, "Alma, I cannot be at ease with you as long as I know another resides within you, whether alive or dead. Why have you invited me to this dance of death?"[29] If Alma received a guest late in the evening, he would stalk the house weeping with rage. "I am a jealous God," he wrote to her.

Secure in the liaison with Kokoschka after only a week, Alma left to spend several days in Paris with a lesbian friend, Lili Leiser, leaving her new lover pining for her and writing as many as three letters a day. He complained, as Mahler had, about her not writing back. Alma was perhaps trying on new sexual roles. In her memoirs she mentioned another trip to the resort at Scheveningen, Holland, with Gucki and the same but here unnamed "woman friend who cherished me but did not suit me."[30]

Meanwhile Kokoschka, like Mahler and Gropius, before him, rapidly developed a warm relationship with Anna Moll, whom he was soon calling Mama. He was also charmed by the child Gucki and became one of her soon-to-be serial "Papas." During Alma's several trips without Kokoschka, he remained close to her family. In this sense, he readily fit into Mahler's place in the family. Curiously, Kokoschka's father had been named Gustav, as had an older brother who had died in infancy before Oskar's birth. He himself remained deeply attached to his own family and, in spite of financial straits, assumed responsibility for them.

Consistent with this, Kokschka longed to start a family of his own. He was elated when, in July, he learned that Alma was pregnant with his child and he hoped that this would lead to marriage. "If it should be that you do have a dear child from me, then it means that Nature, great and good, is also merciful and sweeps away everything terrible and will never tear us apart again, since we find rest in each other and sustain each other."[31] Nevertheless, he continued to be haunted by Mahler's presence in Alma's home and her veneration of him. Alma herself described her personal shrine: "Wherever I lived after Mahler's death I would put on his desk his music and his pictures from childhood through the last years."[32] "In the end, no love could have withstood such an atmosphere," Kokoschka reminisced, "and Alma was unwilling to give an inch. Furthermore, she was expecting a child. There was a moment when I even began to imagine that it would turn out to look like Mahler . . . in which case I'd have preferred it not be born."[33]

In October 1912 Alma entered a sanatorium to undergo an abortion. Unspoken in her memoirs, it is alluded to in her diary only in her rationale before the operation and in a fragmented and troubled passage afterward. She erroneously dated her decision to the receipt of Mahler's death mask, which shocked her on a return from a trip. The "smiling, forgiving, distinguished face" that she perceived suggested guilt, and she became hysterical, calmed only by Kokoschka's permission "to have the child taken away. He gave it—but he was not to recover from that blow."[34] Clearly, Alma had made her decision about a life with Kokoschka, although the affair lingered for nearly three years. Her language about "the child taken away" has overtones of the private death wishes she had harbored toward Putzi: "this child must go."

But the decision to let go of Kokoschka was unlikely the whole story. Alma had not given up on Gropius, to whom she wrote the following month on the pretext of asking him to return some magazines she had lent him. Appealing for a response to the love she still felt for him, and wondering if it might yet grow, she asked, "Aren't we people who understand each other fully?" In his reply, the fullest since he had left Vienna, he answered, "You have gone too far away from me and therefore mutual trust had to suffer. . . . No, it cannot be as before."[35] But the final break made by Gropius (at least for the moment) did not occur until early 1913, when Kokoschka exhibited the *Double Portrait of Oskar Kokoschka and Alma Mahler* in Berlin. Ostensibly Gropius had not known about Alma's relationship with Kokoschka—just as Kokoschka did not know about

Alma's with him. One can only imagine Gropius's response when he saw the portrait. It was typical of Alma to want to have her cake and eat it too. For despite the burgeoning relationship with Kokoschka, it proved difficult for her to forget Gropius. She, who had signed her letters to him "your bride," now wrote self-pityingly, "Alma Mahler (and nothing else anymore in this life").[36]

By this time, and until the end of their relationship, Alma was the central theme of Kokoschka's art as she was in his life.[37] "I witnessed his rise," Alma wrote.[38] And indeed the years from 1912 to the beginning of 1915 saw the creation of some of his greatest works, with increasing exhibitions and acclaim throughout Europe. Among these was the famous *Tempest* of 1913, called *Die Windsbraut* (The Bride of the Wind), originally to have been called *Tristan und Isolde*. There can be no question what it depicts: "We look very strong and calm in our expressions, holding each other's hands." And on the separately represented seven illuminated fans Kokoschka created as gifts for Alma, is the story of their affair.[39]

World War I was decisive in the fates of Alma, Kokoschka, and Gropius. Both men served in the war, Kokoschka in the exclusive Fifteenth Regiment of Dragoons, a mounted Austro-Hungarian regiment and a decided reach for him; he had to purchase a horse and an elaborate uniform. Perhaps sensing a degree of alienation on Alma's part, he needed to be a hero and hoped to become an officer. Gropius joined the Ninth Wandsbeck Hussar Reserve regiment as sergeant major and saw action almost immediately. He was later promoted to lieutenant. Both men would be wounded in the war and Gropius was awarded the Iron Cross. While attending the rise of Kokoschka, Alma had followed that of Gropius as well, to whom she remained attracted despite a long year of no contact. By this point she had clearly made her decision: exchanging letters with Kokoschka as he was awaiting orders to the front, she boldly contacted Gropius. She confided in her diary, "Oskar Kokoschka has slipped away from me. He is no longer within me. . . . We set each other's nerves on edge. . . . We were not good for each other. 'Who can say he understands the heart?' Yes, who indeed!"[40]

Now, feigning that contacting Gropius had not been her initiative, Alma attributed the idea to Bertha Zuckerkandl, at whose home she had met Gustav Mahler. Bertha, by this time a writer and critic, had attended an exposition in Cologne where she had seen Gropius's work enthusiastically received. "There is a young architect in particular who has had an enormous success, a certain Walter Gropius."[41] Thus the excuse for renewed contact was a letter of congratulations. Indeed, by the spring of 1914 Gropius's reputation had grown considerably. Alma told him she was lonely and suggested a meeting.

A reply was long in coming since Gropius, a casualty of the war, was on convalescent leave in Berlin. In the exchange of correspondence, Gropius, now more responsive, invited Alma to visit and a reunion was planned in February. It lasted two weeks and their old passion was revived. When they met again a few weeks later, Alma suspected that she was pregnant. She suggested that she come that summer to Strasbourg to be near him "and we will get married there, whether it is necessary or not."[42] Although it proved to be unnecessary (raising the question as to whether Alma was in fact pregnant to begin with), they were secretly married in August 1915.

Kokoschka, also wounded in the war, as well as by Alma, did not take his leave quietly; it took him many years to regain his equilibrium and even to eventually resume a cordial relationship with Alma. In 1918 he ordered a life-size doll constructed with Alma's features, and took great interest in collaborating with a famous Munich dollmaker on the details. He made many pen-and-ink drawings of the doll and in the end threw the effigy in the trash. Like many creative artists, Oskar Kokoschka grazed the borderline between creativity and madness. But he emerged squarely on the side of reality and grew into a mature man and artist, one who took a moral stance at the time of the Third Reich. He was twenty-eight when Alma married and would outlive Alma and all her other lovers. He died at the age of ninety-six, productive to the end.

Walter and Alma's wedding was secret because his family vigorously opposed the marriage—especially his mother, Manon. After Gropius returned to the front and Alma to Vienna, she complained about his family in her letters. When Manon eventually succumbed to the entreaties of her son, who was still in the war, Alma arrogantly rejected her letter: "Tell her that the doors of the whole world, which are open to the name Mahler, will fly shut to the totally unknown name, Gropius. . . . There are a thousand *Geheimrate* around but there was only one Gustav Mahler and there is only one Alma."[43] Increasingly self-aggrandizing, Alma here demoted her husband in citing Gropius's academic position before the war. Throughout the war, Gropius, often at the front and exhausted, had to mediate between these natural enemies, mother and wife, so alike in their "strong sovereign manner," as he once described Alma.[44]

In February 1916 Alma discovered once again that she was pregnant, the result of Gropius's furlough at Christmas, which had been spent in Vienna. The child, a girl, born in September, bore the names of the family battlefield: Manon Alma Anna Justine Caroline (this last after a Gropius ancestor and successive Carls).[45] Gropius obtained a hurried leave to see the child. Alma reported, "When I saw him grimy, unshaven, his uniform and face blackened with railroad soot, I felt as though I were seeing a murderer."[46] She refused to let him hold the baby. With the birth of her third daughter, Alma began to hope for a boy next time.

The war wore on with increasing duties for Gropius as he was promoted to adjutant of the regiment. Leaves were rare and he did not see his child again until she was six months old. Alma did not do well under conditions of deprivation. She was impatient and in her letters complained of the hardships war imposed in Vienna, such as limitations on food. Although Gropius shielded her from the risks and privations he experienced and the gruesome details of war he shared with other family members, Alma did not hesitate to let him know of her continued attractiveness to other men and the gay times she enjoyed to assuage her loneliness.

By Christmas 1917, when Gropius again obtained leave, Alma was already embarked on an affair with the poet and novelist Franz Werfel (1890–1945), whom she had met in October. Still engaged at the front, Gropius was unaware of this despite the gossip in Vienna and Berlin. When Alma learned in March that she was pregnant again, both felt weary and neither could experience joy. Strangely, a letter Alma wrote to her mother-in-law, Manon Gropius, with the news (there was some détente if not reconciliation) suggests a confession: "As happy as I was the first time, as desperate I am now. . . . The endless war . . . and the fact that Walter is not with me has resulted in my concentrating more on myself. This is sad for both of us."[47] On the occasion Gropius wrote to his mother, "About Alma's new condition I cannot feel joy yet. The conditions are too desolate and I am afraid about the future."[48]

Alma had good reason for not being quite so happy. Since Gropius had been on leave for Christmas, and Werfel, who was also in the service, had been on leave in January, when Alma realized she was pregnant she was initially uncertain which was the father of the child. She concluded finally from the dates that it was Werfel. As with Gucki, she was anticipating a breech birth. Meanwhile, mother-in-law Manon had responded immediately to Alma's troubled letter with an invitation to Berlin. Alma declined as she was planning a reception for forty people at her home in honor of the Dutch conductor and Gustav Mahler's champion Willem Mengelberg.

The house that Alma was having built on the property Mahler had purchased in Semmering, two hours from Vienna, was now complete; she called it Haus Mahler. Franz Werfel and Alma spent the summer of Alma's confinement there. After one particularly aggressive lovemaking session, Alma hemorrhaged and as a result would deliver her child prematurely. After four weary years, the war was still not over for Gropius although it was nearing its end. He was once again wounded in combat, buried alive in the collapse of a fortification and the only survivor of his group. Recuperating in a field hospital, he learned that Alma was anticipating a difficult delivery and was able to obtain a transfer to a military installation in Semmering in July 1918. When he learned of the emergency he rushed to the sanatorium with a specialist in tow. Thus, when Alma was giving birth, both "fathers" were present.

To complicate matters further, Gropius, an upper-class German, was typically anti-Semitic for the time and place. It was an attitude shared with his mother, to whom he wrote from the front: "We can fight battles as much as we want to but the weaklings and pigs at home will destroy everything we achieved. The Jews, this poison which I begin to hate more and more, are destroying us. . . . They are the devil, the negative element."[49] At the sanatorium, Gropius discovered that Werfel was the newborn baby's father when he overheard Alma speaking endearments to him on the phone. Reenacting his own version of the encounter with Mahler eight years earlier, Gropius first confronted the couple, demanding a confession, and later visited Werfel at his home. Alma attempted to justify her behavior with Werfel by Gropius's absence, as if he were responsible for it, not the war. Implausibly, she rebuked Gropius for not sending Werfel packing. Even stranger was the purpose of Gropius's visit to Werfel when the latter was not at home. Gropius left a note, "I am here to love you with all the strength at my command. Spare Alma. The worst might happen. The excitement, the milk—if our child should die."⁵⁰ "Our child" indeed! Gropius made a pact with the very devil he had cursed in the letter to his mother, the Jew Werfel. The boy was named Martin Johannes Gropius, probably after Gropius's great-uncle, an architect who had been a childhood hero. His acceptance of the child as his own suggests that Alma may not have completely disabused him as to fatherhood.

By the fall of 1918, much had changed. The war ended in the armistice and Gropius was mustered out a lieutenant in November. That same month he requested custody of his daughter, Manon Gropius, and proposed that Alma, Werfel, Gucki, and the infant Martin remain as a family unit. Gropius had no question about the paternity of his daughter, Manon. That the infant Martin was not thriving only reinforced for him the fact of Jewish paternity: a defective child. Gropius's suggestion would have been a neat solution but Alma said no. Citing her concern that Martin was mentally retarded, and cognizant of the relationship that had grown between Gucki and her half sister, she was unwilling to relinquish Manon.

Within weeks Alma became frightened when she noticed the increasing enlargement of the infant Martin's head. This ushered in a messy year of separation from Gropius, miserable letters by both, keeping the truth from Gropius's mother, and the deterioration of Martin's condition. Meanwhile Alma resumed her social life in Vienna and Gropius his career; in spite of all, they still had hopes of salvaging the marriage, at least for the children. There were occasional visits to Weimar, where Gropius announced the school he founded there in the *Bauhaus Manifesto*. But the town was not Vienna and Alma could not bring herself to spend time there, repeatedly breaking her promises to visit with their daughter. In correspondence with her mother-in-law she played the devoted wife and mother while at the same time continuing her affair with Werfel. Entries in her diary had a familiar ring: "A glorious night. Werfel was with me. We clung to each other and felt the deepest oneness of our loving bodies and souls."⁵¹

For the last three months of his life Martin Gropius lay in a sanatorium in Vienna, where he died in May 1919. Martin's death marked the end of the marriage, at least for Gropius; in November he finally asked Alma for a divorce. Confused and still unwilling to give him up, Alma made a bizarre suggestion. She would spend half the year with him and half with Werfel. Gropius sensibly declined. Astonishingly, there continued to be a community of Alma's lovers. Werfel weighed in, sharing his concern about Alma. In a letter to Gropius, Werfel declared his affection for *him*. No man in his life had ever been so "very dear and close." Gropius was for him "a natural blessing."[52] Gropius did not reply, although he filed away the letter. As he continued to press Alma for a divorce, she seemed increasingly entrenched, by turns recriminating, self-accusing, cajoling, seductive. A brief reconciliation in Weimar failed and meanwhile another woman entered Gropius's life, the beautiful Lily Hildebrandt—thirty-one-years-old and married. Alma and Gropius's divorce was eventually realized in October 1920, a decade after the couple had met in Tobelbad. The child Manon Gropius would remain with her mother. And by now Werfel was an affectionate and agreeable paternal presence in the family if not yet officially stepfather.

Franz Werfel was eleven years younger than Alma. When she met him, in late 1915, Werfel, like Kokoschka and Gropius, had been in the army, recently assigned from a field artillery regiment where he was a platoon leader (not considered to be a high rank for a gymnasium-educated man) to the Army Press Section. By now Alma was living in a spacious apartment not far from the Ringstrasse in Vienna. Despite her complaints of privation, she had occupied herself in Gropius's absence by cultivating a salon that was beginning to rival that of her friend—now competitor—Bertha Zuckerkandl. And despite the shortage of food in Vienna, she managed to entertain generously, attracting prominent figures in government and the arts. It was thus that Werfel came to a reception at her home when on leave. "She is tremendously warm and alive, a woman of quality," Werfel wrote to a friend.[53] Alma, who not only shared her ex-husband Gropius's attitude toward Jews, but elaborated her own version of anti-Semitism, wrote in her diary, "Fat, bow-legged Jew . . . thick lips . . . liquid-slit eyes."[54] Absent Mahler, Jews such as Fraenkel, Kammerer, and now Werfel were tainted with disease or deformity. Nevertheless,

Werfel cast a spell, as had Mahler. Werfel "was eminently musical," and the association with Mahler was powerful: "He loved Mahler's music and said he had wanted to make my acquaintance for that reason. He had a beautiful speaking voice and a fascinating gift of oratory. . . . He was the most extraordinary reciter, lecturer, and storyteller on any subject."[55] She would soon come to call him "my child-man" and was genuinely affectionate, although anti-Semitic remarks and comments on Werfel's overweight would become a regular feature of her exchanges with him.

The passion kindled in Werfel that afternoon would burn for thirty years. However, Alma did not grant his fervent wish to marry her for nearly half that period. With the war over, it was Werfel's habit to retreat to Semmering to write since Alma was often preoccupied with her salon in Vienna. He was enormously prolific and increasingly successful with his plays, poems, and novels. Alma soon became somewhat of a collaborator in a manner different than she had wished to be with Mahler (she only copied *his* music); and an inspiration different than she had been with Kokoschka. (She had never been involved to any degree in the work of Gropius.) With Werfel, Alma would hear and critique works in progress and exert the power of veto on projects of which she disapproved. She also solicited anecdotes from a variety of people they met, which would turn up as material for Werfel's novels. When inspiration flagged, or when life was too hectic in Vienna, Alma would send Werfel off to Haus Mahler to write in solitude. In addition, the couple did an enormous amount of traveling together, so much so that when they eventually left Vienna in 1938, Werfel could truthfully say that they could live anywhere comfortably. A favorite place was Venice, where, in 1922, Alma purchased a palazzo with a garden not far from the Grand Canal.[56]

In 1929, as she approached her fiftieth birthday, Alma agreed to marry Werfel on one condition—that he renounce the Jewish faith. He did so in an official manner, duly sworn and witnessed. Alma was moved by his desire to be declared stepfather to the fourteen-year-old Manon Gropius.[57] The following year saw the beginning rise of the Nazis and increased anti-Semitism. While Werfel (and possibly Alma) knew that his renunciation of Judaism was socially and politically meaningless, they would ignore the prodromal signs of the incipient storm and Hitler's rise until it was quite nearly too late. Werfel would even ignore the burning of his own books a year or two later. The couple were too preoccupied with Werfel's work and Alma's increasingly talked-about salon. At the start of the following year, while Werfel was away on a lecture tour, Alma purchased a luxurious villa on the Hohe Warte in Vienna, not far from the Moll home where she had grown up. She built a working studio for Werfel and glass cases for Mahler's manuscript scores.[58] Salons were now more famous than ever and had become Alma's midlife career. Throughout her widowhood Alma never did return to composing, which she had bitterly resented giving up in marrying Mahler. She did, however, maintain considerable skill on the piano.

The year 1932 saw Alma's return to Catholicism, an event that, characteristically, involved a man. This time, it was the priest Johannes Hollnsteiner, the thirty-seven-year-old canon of the St. Florian Monastery, whom she had chosen as religious councilor. Hollnsteiner was a frequent participant in Alma's salon, to which he also introduced Kurt Schuschnigg, who in 1936 would become chancellor of the incipient fascist Austria. Alma's friendship and spiritual relationship with Hollnsteiner was said to have teetered on the edge of becoming a sexual affair a year after Alma's renewal of Catholic vows.[59] According to biographer Susanne Keegan, on evidence from interviews with Alma's daughter Anna Mahler (who disliked Hollnsteiner intensely), the pair met in a small flat that "Alma rented for their assignations," where they "consumed the champagne and caviar and other delicacies the professor was unable to afford for himself."[60] Alma was fifty-four when she confided to her diary, "Johannes Hollnsteiner is thirty-eight-years-old and thus far has not yet met Woman."[61]

On the infant Martin's death, Alma had written, "I loved Franz Werfel but the powers of light and darkness were ranged against us. Our punishment was hard and deserved."[62] She had already lost one child she had made with Mahler and now the one with Werfel. As if fate decreed a tragic symmetry, she was soon to lose Manon, the child with Gropius. In 1934, when Alma and Werfel returned to Vienna after a stay at the villa in Venice, the eighteen-year-old Manon remained behind and contracted polio. She died after an arduous and heartbreaking year. Professor Hollnsteiner delivered the funeral oration. In a reenactment of the selling of the house at Maeirnigg after Putzi's death, Alma and Werfel went to Venice to sell the villa. In her memoirs Alma wrote, "I feel a desperate longing for Manon."[63]

Another replay of an earlier life ensued as Alma and Werfel traveled to New York, where a biblical pageant that Werfel had written with Kurt Weill was being prepared. Denying the deteriorating political conditions in Europe and Werfel's vulnerability as a Jew, neither Alma nor Werfel had any desire to emigrate. The chief rationalization was that each was too famous on their side of the Atlantic, however much it was crumbling. It was 1936, and if there was any perception that they might be in danger, their lives were too gratifying at the time to entertain any change. But after *Kristallnacht*, 9 November 1938, they went to the village of Sanary in the south of France where they enjoyed some respite among other refugees. After other avenues of escape proved unfeasible, the couple came to America in 1940, barely escaping with their lives as their reputations won them friendly assistance in crossing the French border and eventually obtaining passage on a Greek ship.[64]

Franz Werfel died at their Beverly Hills home in 1945. He and Alma had joined a community of émigrés, many of whom they knew from Europe—the writers Thomas and Heinrich Mann, Bertolt Brecht, and Lion Feuchtwanger; the composers Arnold Schoenberg and Erich Wolfgang Korngold; Bruno Walter and the theatrical director Max Reinhardt. America embraced Werfel in part for his late-life novel, *The Song of Bernadette*, which sold four hundred thousand copies and was made into a successful motion picture. Alma might have thought herself back in Vienna as, isolated from the war, and once again on good financial footing, she continued to entertain the German-speaking members of the transplanted circle.[65]

She mourned Werfel deeply—this most enduring of her lovers and husbands. He had gone as far as to renounce Judaism in order to marry her. Yet even this was not enough. Ever collecting attractive men, Alma befriended the Jesuit Georg Moenius, who had advised Werfel in his work on St. Bernadette. She invited him to give the eulogy at Werfel's funeral. It was heavily edited by Alma even as the large assemblage awaited Father Moenius's arrival. When Moenius spoke, rather inappropriately, of the various forms of baptism, it became apparent to all present (although denied by Alma) that she had had Werfel baptized after death—a form of the rite called, ironically in this case, "baptism by desire." Clearly, it was Alma's desire to see Werfel a Catholic at last.

As she entered her seventies Alma moved to an apartment on East Seventy-third Street in New York. Her appearance, it was said, changed little. She had long since habitually worn a loose-fitting, shape-concealing black dress set off with pearls; her hair, now frequently beauty-saloned, was piled on top of her head.[66] Expectably, she did not take kindly to aging. She occupied herself with writing her memoirs.

Alma Mahler Gropius Werfel died in 1964, at the age of eighty-six.

18

EPILOGUE

Gustav Mahler, at age fifty-one in 1911, was the first to die of all the major figures in his biography. Alma survived him by more than half a century; and Anna (Gucki) was nearly seven when her father died. Carl and Anna Moll lived through World War II, although Anna not quite to its end. Walter Gropius matured into a major figure in architecture; a teacher and a pioneer in design. The New York doctors Emanuel Libman and George Baehr both went on to brilliant careers in clinical and academic medicine. Joseph Fraenkel continued an honorable practice in a shortened career. Sigmund Freud, who would outlive Mahler by nearly three decades, of course created psychoanalysis as we know it today, changing the way we think of the mind.

Gustav Mahler is survived by his music.

Anna (Gucki) Mahler (1904–1988)

If Alma was born, as she said, into an artistic tradition, what can we say of her daughter Anna? Like her mother, who spent hours in the studio of her father, Emil Schindler, the ten-year-old Anna spent much of her time in the new Haus Mahler on the Semmering watching Oscar Kokoschka paint. The young critic asked, "Can't you paint anything but Mummy?"[1] She was heiress to a manifold artistic tradition: music through her parents; art through Kokoschka and step-grandfather Carl Moll; design through Gropius; and literature through Werfel. Early on she showed some gift for music but later focused her talents on sculpture.

After her father's death, young Anna's life was peopled with household help of various kinds—housekeepers, cooks, governesses—and an idiosyncratic family consisting of her mother, the grandparents Moll, and Alma's lovers and husbands. Some of the affairs and marriages went on concurrently and Anna had affectionate relationships with several of the men, especially Kokoschka and Franz Werfel, who overlapped as figures in the household. Kammerer early on amused the child with his experimental snakes and lizards always escaping down the stairs in Villa Mahler. The handsome Walter Gropius was a more distant figure, away for most of World War I and later in Berlin and Weimar, where occasional visits were made. But at thirteen years of age Anna had a crush on him.

Besides the instability of family life, there was considerable trauma in Anna's childhood. She was present in Maiernigg when, a few days after her third birthday, her sister Putzi died the lingering and strangulating death of diphtheria. When her parents left for the first American season soon after, Anna was left behind in Vienna in the care of a governess.

Three and a half years later, in the suite at the Savoy Hotel, she was witness to the comings and goings of doctors and the talk of prognosis and treatment. She would probably have known that her father was dying. There was no doubt at all about the death-bed scene in which she was called to Mahler's bedside: "Stay good, my child."[2] When she was fourteen, there was not only her mother's hemorrhage and the premature birth of her infant brother, Martin, but a year of watching the poor hydrocephalic and unresponsive child deteriorate.

Such childhood events, experienced before the mental capacity to master trauma has developed, may be revived, along with the earlier anxiety and dread, when comparable events occur later in life. In gifted individuals like Anna, such events tend to become externalized, symbolized, and even frankly depicted in art.

Alma herself stated that during these family "calamities" she was "neglected."[3] But chronic neglect of a different kind characterized Anna's growing up. Dependent on one person—her mother—she became a caretaker herself when Alma took to bed weeping over one of her love affairs. At such times, Anna would be "beside herself."[4] She felt it was her role to cheer her mother up. Of her daughter, Alma wrote, "Her feelings, at that age, always reflected mine."[5] There is no indication that Anna had childhood friends or playtime and consequently she grew up too fast. When she was about twelve, she shed the name Gucki and insisted on Anna or Annie. She became the big sister as someone else was born into her life: her half sister, Manon Gropius.

Naively, Alma prided herself on their closeness and claimed, "Anna and I never knew the kind of jealousy that often sours mother-and-daughter relationships."[6] Whether emulating or competing with her mother (or both), Anna had a disastrous love life. It tracked that of her mother, just as her mother's had tracked that of grandmother Anna Moll—but without the gratifications Alma had enjoyed. An affair at age sixteen resulted in Anna's first brief marriage, then divorce, when "Anna came back to me."[7] Alma alleged that neither the bride nor the groom knew what to do in bed. Had the veteran mother failed to educate the young woman in matters of sex?

Anna's divorce occurred about a year after Alma's divorce from Gropius in 1920. Around that time, Alma wrote in her diary, "We worry a lot about Anna, who is starving herself. One might say she has gone on a kind of hunger strike."[8] Anna may have gone through a period of anorexia. By the age of eighteen, she was living with the composer Ernst Krenek; she married him a year later. Anna would later say that she wed to get out of the house.

Alma had exacted a promise from Krenek to wait until he could support Anna before marrying. Both young people traveled to Switzerland, where Anna undertook serious study of painting with Kuno Amiet. Krenek met a musical benefactor there who awarded him 10,000 Swiss francs. This proved to be a not entirely happy outcome, for Anna was less and less eager to marry the difficult Krenek. On her return Anna had begged Alma, "Mummy invent something else so I don't have to get married."[9] But Alma had no recommendations for her at the time, except to remind her the alternative would be living with her and Franz Werfel. The marriage with Krenek lasted scarcely three years when something else sparked. Neighbors and friends, the Zsolnays were a wealthy publishing family and had a son, Paul, who was becoming involved with the business. A marriage was arranged between Paul and Anna; it would last seven years and produced a child, named after Anna's mother, Alma. Although the relationship ultimately failed for Anna, who was proving to be unlucky in love, it was a felicitous match for Werfel, since young Paul published one of his books as his first offering.

Meanwhile Anna Mahler (who kept her maiden name professionally) pursued training and considerable work in art. After her first experiences in Switzerland, she went to Rome to study with Giorgio De Chirico and worked for a period in Paris during her marriage to Zsolnay. She evolved a style of working with naturalistic figures and created busts of many well-known figures of the time.

After Alma purchased a villa in Florence, there were many family reunions. One summer, however, authorities suppressed news of a polio outbreak, and when eighteen-year-old Manon Gropius remained at the villa, she contracted it. During her year-long illness Anna proved to be affectionate, solicitous, and caring toward her half sister. Despite the deaths she had witnessed during her childhood, this was Anna's first adult death. She was involved in a double commemoration. When Alban Berg dedicated his Violin Concerto to Manon—"To the Memory of an Angel"—Anna created a bust of Berg.

Anna divorced Zsolnay in 1937 and the child Alma remained with him. That year saw Anna's greatest triumph at the Paris World Exposition, where she was awarded the Grand Prix for Sculpture.[10] Thereafter she settled in London, where she met Anatol Fistulari, the conductor, who became her fourth husband in 1942. At thirty-eight, she gave birth to a second child, Marina. For most of her adult life, Anna seemed to require some optimal distance from her mother Alma, with whom she had been stiflingly close in the past. She remained in London, where she was able to work regularly with some artistic and fiscal success.

When Franz Werfel died in 1945, Anna stayed with her mother for four weeks in Beverly Hills. Alma felt that the visit "had intensified our new harmony—a gift from heaven that I hoped never to lose." Accordingly, Anna relocated to California in 1950 to be close to her aging mother and to teach at UCLA. She brought Marina with her and remained there except for a brief period when Alma wished to return to New York, and Anna helped get her settled in an apartment.[11]

When Alma Mahler died in 1964 Anna had just turned fifty. With the inheritance from her mother's estate, she was financially secure and purchased a villa in Italy, later in Spoleto. For nearly two productive decades she continued to work there. At some point, having become infirm, she returned to New York just as her mother had. Meanwhile, daughter Marina, now past fifty herself, had married and remained in London. When it appeared to Anna that her life was ending, she returned to London to be with her daughter.

Only once did Anna Mahler create a likeness of her father, a bust that she promptly destroyed. A photograph of the sculpture remains and its similarity to a favorite picture of smiling, benevolent, almost effeminate Mahler is striking. It was said requests to tell journalists, friends, and casual acquaintances about her father were so frequent that Anna had become quite impatient and irritable about it. The multiple traumas of her early life may be seen sublimated in several of her sculptures in which a female figure holds her hands over her eyes in order not to see, and in comparable pieces in which the fields of vision are similarly obscured.

Anna Mahler had the creative means to master these early traumas, separate from a formidable mother—although uncannily tracking her life—and lead a productive life herself, although scarred by her inability to maintain a lasting, caring marriage. In not one of the many photographs and snapshots taken during her life is she seen smiling.

Anna Mahler died on 3 June 1988 and was buried not in the family plot at Grinzing with Gustav, Alma, and Putzi but at Highgate Cemetery in London.

Carl Moll (1861–1945) and
Anna Schindler Moll (1857–1938)

At Gustav Mahler's funeral in 1911, Carl Moll was the first to cast a handful of earth into the grave. At that time, Moll had moved on from his influential role in the Vienna Secession and was the guiding spirit—and financial wizard—of the Neukunstgruppe, the New Art Group, which had its inaugural exhibition that same year. Long involved in the commerce of art, he gave up his ownership of the gallery Miethke in Vienna the following year but continued to advise and trade. Oskar

Kokoschka was one of the New Art Group and Moll mounted exhibitions of his work that were pivotal in Kokoschka's career. Meanwhile, after years of involvement in the marketplace and politics of art, Moll returned to his own painting, which took a new direction in color and balance. Perhaps his most characteristic works are interiors that reveal the lives of their owners and the space they occupied.[12] Late in World War I, Moll auctioned his extensive collection of old masters but enjoyed his wealth only briefly, as postwar inflation encroached. In 1921, on his sixtieth birthday, he was honored by an exhibition of his life's work at the Kuenstlerhaus in Vienna. More than fifty of his paintings were assembled.

Moll was sympathetic to the cause of national socialism, and his friendships with Jewish figures in the art world became strained with its rise. He was a staunch adherent to the Nazi doctrine of the necessity and legitimacy of power.[13] His daughter Maria, from a first marriage, wed a man who had been a longtime supporter of Hitler, the lawyer Dr. Richard Eberstaller; the Molls remained close with them. In fact, Alma resented this attachment and was piqued when Moll made alterations in her girlhood home in the Hohe Warte by adding two stories for their use. When Alma and Werfel finally fled Vienna, Moll and Eberstaller took possession of the Haus Mahler in Semmering. (It was the locale of a farewell garden party for 160 guests.) Renamed Haus Eberstaller, it was decorated with flags of the Third Reich and swastikas.[14]

Moll and the Eberstallers believed to the end in the certainty of Hitler's final victory. In April 1945, as the Red Army closed in on Berlin and Vienna, Carl Moll, his daughter, and his son-in-law committed suicide.[15]

Anna Moll did not live to witness the fall of the Third Reich and the politics of power that she and Carl Moll had embraced. The intimacy she and Alma shared in the days of the Gropius affair had eroded. Although Alma Mahler herself was never free from anti-Semitism, her destiny was "inescapably tied to the fate of the Jews" as she became more committed to Werfel. In this she finally shared the sense of the Wandering Jew that was so much a part of Gustav Mahler: "Now I must wander to the ends of the earth with this strange people—there is no road back."[16] This was a path that Anna Moll, her personal anti-Semitism now buttressed by

Nazi doctrine, finally could not tolerate. It shattered both Alma's attachment to her mother and Anna Moll's secret gratification in the reliving of her own earlier affairs.

In the spring of 1938, when Alma left Vienna for the last time, Anna Moll was already ill. "I said good-bye to my mother, whom I knew I was not going to see again. I let her think that I would return in a week." By then it was dangerous to drive without a swastika on the car, which Alma, in token protest, refused to do. Richard Eberstaller, stepbrother-in-law, drove her to the station, where Carl Moll appeared "gazing dolefully at us with his sad hound's eyes."[17] As a final tribute to her mother, Alma denied that Anna Moll was ever a Nazi and attributed her "worship of this monster, Hitler" to Carl's persistent influence.[18] By the time the Werfels had fled to Paris, Anna was dying and already beyond being reached by Alma's phone call. Alma wrote, "I had lost my mother a long time before this, to Hitler, who had robbed me of everything except Werfel and Anna (Gucki)."[19]

Anna Bergen Schindler Moll died in November 1938. Alma: "I felt for the first time that I was flesh of her flesh—that the heart that was congealing in Vienna made *me* freeze in Paris."[20]

Walter Gropius (1883–1969)

Gropius met Alma Mahler at a critical turn in his creative life. As the affair became more passionate in 1910 and early 1911, the twenty-eight-year-old architect was engaged in a project that was destined to become a defining achievement. An industrial building called the Faguswerke already featured the simplicity, light, and lightness that would characterize his life's work. More than this, the associated philosophy that Gropius articulated early on anticipated that of the Bauhaus school that he founded after the war in Weimar in 1918–1919: "Work must be established in places that give the workman, now a slave to industrial labor, not only light, air, and hygiene, but also an indication of the great common idea that drives everything." The spirit of the Bauhaus in its subsequent incarnations in Dessau, Berlin, and, later, Chicago, was already inherent in "the joy of working together for that greater common good previously unobtainable by a single individual."[21]

Throughout Gropius's career the idea of communal endeavor in crafts-manship was a part of his teaching and he would remain a teacher until nearly the end of a long life. "The school is the servant of the workshop," he declared.[22]

At thirty-five, devastated by the war and still married, he picked up the pieces of his life in the Bauhaus endeavor and started new relationships since Alma would rarely leave Vienna. Their child, Manon Gropius, called Mutzi, remained with her mother, to Gropius's dismay. A rela-tionship with the vivacious artist Lily Hildebrandt, again a married woman, soon developed as unrestrainably as that with Alma had, and predictably with due respect to her husband, an art historian. When after much turmoil Alma, now living with Werfel, granted Gropius a divorce, he, ironically, was declared the guilty party.

In 1923 he met the beautiful Ilse Frank, fourteen years younger and the woman with whom he would spend the rest of his life despite intermit-tent affairs by both. She was already on the verge of marriage to another when the brilliant and attractive architect won her over. With her con-sent, they celebrated the occasion by renaming her Ise. Painfully sepa-rated from Manon, hence wary of procreation, Gropius did not wish to have children. But both were devoted to a niece, Ati, whom they adopted after the death of one of Ise's sisters. Rare reunions with Mutzi in Vienna, chiefly on the occasion of his lectures, were marred by the hov-ering presence of Alma, embittered at the success of his marriage. When Mutzi died in 1935, Gropius had not seen his daughter since the onset of her illness nearly a year earlier.[23]

Gropius and Ise sojourned in England as World War II threatened. At the same time there were overtures from Harvard University, which eventually resulted in Gropius's receiving an appointment and settling in the United States in 1937. Gropius never denied his German identity. He did not denounce the Nazis or renounce his citizenship until late in the war.[24] Strongly anti-Semitic during his early years, he softened consider-ably as the war progressed and he was besieged in Cambridge with requests for jobs and other aid. Gropius helped former Bauhauslers and both Jewish and Gentile friends trapped in Europe. Branded as an "enemy alien" during the war, he did not become a U.S. citizen until 1944, at the age of sixty-one.

Gropius had a remarkable career that lasted long past his resignation from Harvard after a dozen years. Monuments to his late-life creativity remain in locales throughout the world, including New York's Pan Am building and its stunning view from Park Avenue; and the John F. Kennedy Federal Building in Boston. When eighty of his students gathered at Harvard's Harkness Commons, a building Gropius had designed some fifteen years earlier, to celebrate his eightieth birthday, his place in the history of art and architecture was secure but his career not yet over. Projects continued in the United States and Canada before the celebration of his eighty-fifth, at which time he was offered a commission from the German Foreign Office for the design of the embassy in Argentina, which he accepted. Nor was this his final project.

Walter Gropius died at eighty-six, in July 1969, in Boston's Pratt Diagnostic Hospital, his window overlooking the site of the Tufts Medical Center, which he had a hand in designing.

When Alma Mahler Werfel published her memoir, *And the Bridge Is Love*, in 1958, revealing the details of their affair nearly a half century earlier, Gropius was stunned. He wrote to her:

> The love story which you connect with my name in the book was not ours. The memory of Mutzi should have prevented you from taking away the essential content of our *Erlebnis* and its literary exposure is bound to kill also in me the blossom of memory.
>
> The rest is silence.[25]

Doctors

In July 1920 Alma Mahler noted in her diary the passing of Dr. Joseph Fraenkel, devoted physician in Mahler's final illness and her would-be lover: "Joseph Fraenkel is dead. I forgot to note it." That autumn Fraenkel's brother came to visit with a dying man's message. "Joe asked me to come," he said. "He told me on his deathbed that he had loved only you, that the separation from you was the tragedy of his life."[26] Returning to New York after having been turned down by Alma, Fraenkel was deeply troubled when he learned of her marriage to

Walter Gropius. An avid lover of music, Fraenkel met Polish opera singer Ganna Walska, a friend of Alma's, and married her. It was said that he was drawn to her because of the a's in her name, an echo of Alma.

At the time Dr. Fraenkel attended Mahler, he was in private practice in New York and held the post of lecturer and clinical instructor in Medicine at the Cornell University Medical College. He was one of the founders of the Neurological Institute in New York. In addition, he had been the medical director of Montefiore Hospital in the Bronx, then a facility for chronic diseases. He himself suffered from a chronic intestinal illness that caused his death.

Emanuel Libman (1872–1946), already a famous doctor when he consulted on the Mahler case, became a legendary figure on the New York scene. Although he readily responded to difficult diagnostic problems throughout the city, one had to know someone to see him in his office and his fees set the high-water mark in the community. However, because of his teaching and philanthropic work, he was said to have earned about a quarter of what he might have. Noted for his generativity, he mentored numerous young physicians and paved the way for their further studies in Europe through his reputation and many friendships, often offering financial support. Gifts from grateful patients funded this as well as Libman's numerous philanthropic causes. He was benefactor to such widespread institutions as the Royal College of Physicians in London, the Hebrew University in Palestine, the Tuskegee Institute in Alabama—and of course the Mount Sinai Hospital, his clinical base of operations. Mount Sinai did not have a medical school at that time and his academic appointment was at the Columbia-Presbyterian School of Medicine.

In 1939, the sixty-seven-year-old Libman was profiled in the *New Yorker* by S. N. Behrman, who depicted a mercurial and alert man with interests beyond medicine, in music, food, and people.[27] A prodigious letter writer, Libman corresponded with Sarah Bernhardt, Fanny Brice, Albert Einstein, and Thomas Mann, among others. At the time of his death at seventy-four, Dr. Libman he was still active as practitioner and teacher. In an ironic turn, the master diagnostician missed his own terminal diagnosis, insisting it was an acute abdomen requiring immediate surgery. The reluctant surgeon found nothing significant. Nevertheless, Libman correctly predicted the time of his death, which was from "arteriosclerotic complications."[28]

When Dr. George Baehr (1887–1978) drew Mahler's blood for testing at the Hotel Savoy, he was only beginning a seventy-year career as romantic, exciting, and productive as ever there was in the field of medicine. After graduate studies in Europe, he did research at Mount Sinai Hospital in typhus, which led to an appointment to a commission to the Balkans. Caught in the Serbian-Bulgar War, he ran a hospital and was decorated by both sides.

Learning of his work on typhus, the Austrian War Department recruited Baehr for work in epidemics in the Ukraine and Poland. To reach his destinations he drove a model-T Ford through Bulgaria, Hungary, and Austria. With America's entry into World War I, Dr. Baehr headed the Mount Sinai Hospital unit in France.

During World War II Dr. Baehr served as chief medical officer for the U.S. Office of Civil Defense. Blessed with productive longevity, he served for thirty-five years on the New York Public Health Council under four successive governors. Dr. Baehr was an advocate of national universal health insurance and traveled frequently to Washington to promote the cause during the Truman administration.[29] When in 1973 he ventured the prediction that "many of us would no longer be around by the time the ultimate program became a reality," a voice from the back of the room cried out, "We won't, but you will."

In 1974 the author interviewed Dr. Baehr at his home on the East Side of Manhattan. Well groomed, alert, and in full possession of memory, Baehr recounted his meeting with Gustav Mahler in February 1911.

Sigmund Freud (1856–1939)

As Freud's biographer Peter Gay points out, "Most of Freud's writings bear traces of his life."[30] And a good part of his life was his involvement with his analysands—not excluding colleagues or himself. "One must learn something from everything," said Freud in seeking psy-

chological enlightenment from patients, associates, acolytes, and the arti-
facts of civilization.[31] Just as the analyst remains a part of the patient's life
in spirito, the opposite is true too, although almost never does one hear
of the impact knowing a patient intimately might have on the life of the
therapist. Can some mental residue of Freud's encounter with Mahler be
found in his life? There is no indication that any subsequent interest in
listening to Mahler's music developed, but Freud was distinctly unmusical. Nor was there any reference to the meeting outside of Freud's two
accounts and his brief remarks to the Vienna Psychoanalytic Society.
Where then might one seek repercussions of Freud's meeting with Mahler?

There are two possibilities. First is the aggregate effect of working with
many patients in the formulation of new theory. Just as the diagnosis and
treatment of Mahler's heart disease was absorbed, along with the data
from similarly afflicted patients, into Dr. Emanuel Libman's ground-
breaking monograph *Subacute Bacterial Endocarditis,* so did Mahler's
emotional problems join anonymously in the mass of data that inspired
Freud's later contributions to psychoanalysis. In his late-life treatise
Inhibitions, Symptoms, and Anxiety, for example, Freud catalogued the
changing faces of anxiety through the life cycle; issues such as the fear of
annihilation (the basic anxiety of birth); separation anxiety; fear of loss
and the loss of love; the anxiety of corporeal harm; guilt and the fear of
death.[32] Although these are believed to be universal phenomena, one can
readily see the tracings of each in the life of Gustav Mahler.

Beyond this, and more specifically, the fifty-nine-year-old Freud was
invited in 1915 by the Berlin Goethe Society to write an article for a com-
memorative volume.[33] The list of authors, which included the playwright
Gerhard Hauptmann, placed Freud among the distinguished intellectu-
als of the time. His article, *On Transience*, is about "a summer walk
through a smiling countryside in the company of a taciturn friend and
of a young but already famous poet." The pessimistic poet experienced no joy, rather was "disturbed by the thought that all this beauty
was fated to extinction." The depressed young man felt that "all that
he would otherwise have loved and admired seemed to him to be shorn
of its worth by the transience which was its doom."[34] Sensibly, Freud,
while interpreting the universal wish for immortality, did not "dispute" the ephemerality of all things beautiful. But he did not agree that

impermanence involves a loss of worth. "On the contrary," he argued, "transience value is scarcity value in time."[35]

Freud wrote that the walk occurred before the war and we now know that the poet in question was Rainer Maria Rilke. But could this "walk" have been informed by the walk in Leiden? Freud's conclusion to the brief *On Transience* was that the poet's attitude comprised a "revolt against mourning." In its inevitable passing, the transience of beauty involved a "foretaste of mourning."[36] Freud was much occupied with the "great riddle of mourning" during this period, which eventually produced his classic *Mourning and Melancholia.*"[37] Mahler's life was a study in the vicissitudes of mourning and, conflated with the then anonymous poet Rilke, may have found its way into the writings of Freud.

Both *On Transience* and *Mourning and Melancholia* were conceived during 1915–1917. In Austria at the time, Alma Mahler and her husband, Franz Werfel, assuming safety in their Austrian proto-Nazi connections, were arrogantly denying Werfel's vulnerability. Not so Freud, who wrote to Arnold Zweig in 1925, "An anxious premonition tells us that we, the poor Austrian Jews, will have to pay part of the bill. It is sad that we even judge world events from the Jewish point of view, but how else could we do it any other way?" The following year, at age seventy, he told an interviewer, "My language is German. My culture, my attainments are German. I considered myself German intellectually, until I noticed the growth of anti-Semitic prejudice in Germany and German Austria. Since that time, I prefer to call myself a Jew."[38] But despite his premonition, Freud, like Alma and Franz Werfel, remained in Vienna, which remained the heart of the psychoanalytic movement until national socialism seemed unstoppable with Hitler's arrival in 1938. At that point a cohort of colleagues such as Ernest Jones, with connections to Parliament; Marie Bonaparte, with her wealth and international influence; and William Bulitt, the American ambassador who had once coauthored a book with Freud, arranged safe passage for the psychoanalyst and his family to England.

There, although frail as he turned eighty, he "was still capable of work, love and hate."[39] Celebrating his birthday, 191 artists and writers signed a congratulatory message written by Stefan Zweig and Thomas Mann.[40] Freud was suffering from cancer that required successive operations but he had come to London, he said, "to die in freedom."[41]

Gustav Mahler (1860–1911)

"... and my time will yet come ..."[42]
—Gustav Mahler

Mahler in Holland, 1906.

ACKNOWLEDGMENTS

First thanks are to Henry-Louis de La Grange, whose magisterial multivolume, multilingual biography of Mahler made much material available through the years it was being created. Professor de La Grange was also generous in sharing documents at the Bibliothèque Mahler in Paris. I am grateful to Stephen E. Hefling, who read a late draft of the present book and offered many helpful suggestions. At the Internationale Gustav Mahler Gesellschaft in Vienna, Reinhold Kubic provided useful primary materials from the collection. Other scholars who were helpful in Mahler research are Steven D. Coburn, Susan M. Filler, Jonathan Kramer, Stephen McClatchie, Eveline Nikkels, and Morten Solvik.

At what is now the Médiathèque Musicale Mahler, librarians Marie-Gabrielle Soret, Marie-Joe Blavette, and Alena Parthonnaud patiently retrieved documents from the Mahler archive. Barbara Niss, archive librarian at the Library of Mount Sinai School of Medicine, New York, provided information related to Mahler's final illness. The library at Montefiore Hospital, Bronx, New York, was also consulted. Other research was conducted at the New York Public Library for the Performing Arts and the Juilliard Library, also in New York. Matthew von Unwerth at the Brill Library of the New York Psychoanalytic Library helped trace Freud sources and other psychoanalytic references.

Jeffrey Langford provided me with the opportunity to teach a graduate seminar on Mahler at the Manhattan School of Music, during which I learned much from the students. Likewise, Katherine Gertson of the

Juilliard Evening Division invited me to offer a course on Mahler. Thanks, too, to Reinhold Brinkmann for an invitation to participate in his "Mahler and Ives" graduate seminar at Harvard. The collegiality of the New York University Biographical Seminar chaired by Kenneth Silverman and Brenda Wineapple was encouraging.

Jiři Rychetský and Willem Smith hosted informative and orienting visits to locations in the Czech Republic relating to Mahler's ancestry and early life. Phillip Bohlman supplied information and references relevant to this period, as did Petr Vasicek. Others who answered queries include Jerry Bruck, Gerald Fox, Henry Mahler, Mortimer Ostow, and Leonard Shengold.

Thanks to "first reader" Charlotte R. Kaufman, and to friends and colleagues who read complete early drafts or chapters-in-progress: Phyllis Ackman, Donald Gerard, Stan Ruttenberg, Herbert D. Saltzstein, Alexander Stein, Arnold Winston, Beverly G. Winston, Howard Zucker, and Marjorie Zucker.

At Yale University Press Larisa Heimert, Keith Condon, Kim Hastings, and Nancy Moore skillfully turned a manuscript into an actual book. Harry Haskell, formerly of YUP, initially saw its possibilities.

If I have missed any of those who have helped me over the inevitable long gestation period of a biography, I am thinking of you in spirit if not by name.

ILLUSTRATION CREDITS

Frontispiece.
Mahler-Rosé Collection, Music Library, University of Western Ontario, London.
Figs. on pp. 10, 32, 37, 95, 249.
Médiathèque Musicale Gustav Mahler, Paris.
Figs. on pp. 13, 46, 55, 63, 127, 168, 174, 200.
Bild-Archiv der Österreichischen Nationalbibliothek, Vienna.
Fig. on p. 49.
Courtesy of the Herbert F. Johnson Museum, Cornell University.
Figs. on pp. 67, 76, 84, 112, 123, 128, 255.
Van Pelt Library, Alma Mahler and Franz Werfel Collection of Photographs, Rare
Book and Manuscript Library, University of Pennsylvania.
Fig. on p. 107.
Netherlands Music Institute, The Hague/The Willem Mengelberg Archive
Foundation.
Figs. on pp. 140, 278.
Reproduced from *The Mahler Album*, ed. Gilbert Kaplan (The Kaplan Foundation,
New York).
Fig. on p. 143.
By kind permission of Marina Mahler.
Fig. on p. 157.
New-York Historical Society.
Figs. on pp. 161, 196.
Stuart Feder, private collection.
Fig. on p. 180.
Courtesy of the Society for the Preservation of New England Antiquities.
Figs. on pp. 209, 231.
By permission of A. W. Freud et al./Paterson Marsh, Ltd., London.

Fig. on p. 264.
New York Public Library for the Performing Arts, Lincoln Center.
Fig. on p. 268.
Mount Sinai Archives, New York.
Fig. on p. 282.
Courtesy Galerie St. Etienne, New York.
Fig. on p. 315.
Gemeentearchief Amsterdam.

ABBREVIATIONS

AMB   Alma Mahler. *And the Bridge Is Love*. Translated by E. B. Ashton. New York: Harcourt Brace, 1958.

AMD   Alma Mahler-Werfel. *Diaries, 1898–1902*. Selected and translated by Antony Beaumont. From the German edition transcribed and edited by Antony Beaumont and Susanne Rode-Breymann. London: Faber and Faber, 1998.

AMM   Alma Mahler. *Gustav Mahler: Memories and Letters*. 4th ed. Translated by Basil Creighton. Edited by Donald Mitchell and Knud Martner. London: Cardinal Books, 1990.

COM   *The Mahler Companion*. Edited by Donald Mitchell and Andrew Nicholson. Oxford: Oxford University Press, 1999.

DOC   *Mahler: A Documentary Study*. Compiled and edited by Kurt Blaukopf with contributions by Zoltan Roman. New York: Oxford University Press, 1976.

GRO1   Reginald R. Isaacs. *Walter Gropius: Der Mensch und sein Werk*. Volume 1. Berlin: Mann Verlag, 1983.

GRO2   Reginald R. Isaacs. *Gropius: An Illustrated Biography of the Creator of the Bauhaus*. Boston: Little, Brown, 1991.

HLG1   Henry-Louis de La Grange. *Mahler*. Volume 1. Garden City: Doubleday, 1973.

HLG2   Henry-Louis de La Grange. *Mahler*. Volume 2, *Vienna: The Years of Challenge, 1897–1904*. Oxford: Oxford University Press, 1995.

HLG3   Henry-Louis de La Grange. *Mahler*. Volume 3, *Vienna: Triumph and Disillusion, 1904–1907*. Oxford: Oxford University Press, 1999.

HLGFR2   Henry-Louis de La Grange. *Gustav Mahler—Chronique d'une Vie: L'Age d'Or de Vienne, 1900–1907*. Fayard, 1983.

HLGFR3   Henry-Louis de La Grange. *Gustav Mahler—Chronique d'une Vie: Le Génie Foudroyé, 1907–1911*. Fayard, 1984.

NBL   Natalie Bauer-Lechner. *Recollections of Gustav Mahler.* Translated by Dika Newlin. Edited and annotated by Peter Franklin. London: Faber and Faber, 1980.

RUH   *Ein Glück ohne Ruh': Die Briefe Gustav Mahlers an Alma.* Published and illustrated by Henry-Louis de La Grange and Günther Weiss. Edited by Knud Martner. Berlin: Siedler Verlag, 1995.

SEL   *Selected Letters of Gustav Mahler.* Original edition selected by Alma Mahler. Enlarged and edited by Knud Martner. Translated by Eithne Wilkins, Ernst Kaiser, and Bill Hopkins. New York: Farrar Straus Giroux, 1979.

SFR   *The Standard Edition of the Complete Psychological Works of Sigmund Freud.* Translated from the German under the general editorship of James Strachey. In collaboration with Anna Freud. Assisted by Alix Strachey and Alan Tyson. London: Hogarth Press, 1974.

UNK   *Mahler's Unknown Letters.* Edited by Herta Blaukopf. Translated by Richard Stokes. Boston: Northeastern University Press, 1987.

NOTES

Chapter 1. The Summer of 1910

1. Marie Bonaparte, unpublished diary manuscript, courtesy of Celia Bertin.
2. Josef Bohuslav Förster, *Der Pilger: Erinnerungen eines Musikers* (Prague, 1955). Translation from HLG1, 313–314.
3. Karen Monson, *Alma Mahler: Muse to Genius* (Boston: Houghton Mifflin, 1983), 22.
4. AMM, 172.
5. Ibid.
6. GM to AM, 26 June 1910, RUH, no. 314, 434.
7. GM to AM, 5 July 1910, RUH, no. 317, 436.
8. HLG1, 272.

Chapter 2. The Family Mahler

1. HLG1, 11 and 12. Genealogy and dates are from this major biography of Mahler.
2. *Encyclopaedia Judaica*, vol. 12 (Jerusalem: Keter Publishing, 1972), s.v. "Moravia."
3. AMM, 224.
4. *Journey's Beginning: Gustav Mahler and Jihlava in Written Sources* (Jihlava: Statni Okresni Archiv, 2000), 17, 18. [Author unknown]
5. Petr Vasicek, "The Hilsner Case," in *Encyclopedia of Anti-Semitism, Anti-Jewish Prejudice, and Persecution*, ed. Richard S. Levy (Chicago: University of Chicago Press, forthcoming 2005).
6. *Journey's Beginning*, 17.
7. HLG1, 8.
8. NBL, 164.
9. HLG1, 8.

10. Ibid., 7.

11. Ibid., 8.

12. Ibid., 17.

13. *Journey's Beginning*, 17.

14. HLG1, 14.

15. Stuart Feder, "The Childhood of the Composer: The Auditory Environment," in *Neue Mahleriana: Essays in Honour of Henry-Louis de La Grange on His Seventieth Birthday*, ed. Günther Weiss (Bern: Peter Lang, 1997), 27–38.

16. HLG1, 16.

17. Eva Krekovicova, *Zwischen Toleranz und Barrieren: Das Bild de Zigeuna und Juden in der Slowakischen Folklore*, Studien zur Tsiganologie und Folkloristik, vol. 21 (Frankfurt am Main: Peter Lang, 1998).

18. HLG1, 22.

19. Norman Lebrecht, *Mahler Remembered* (New York: Norton, 1987), 11–12.

20. Jiři Rychetsky, "Eits a Binkel Kasi (Hrasi)," *News about Mahler Research* (International Gustav Mahler Society 17), 7.

21. Jiři Rychetsky, "Eits a Binkel Kasi (Hrasi)," *Musical Times* (London), December 1989, 729.

22. HLG1, 18.

23. *Das himmliche Leben* [Heavenly Life], trans. Deryck Cooke, liner notes to Mahler Symphony no. 4, BBC MM2044, 2001.

24. NBL, 152–153.

25. Fredda M. Herz and Elliott J. Rosen, "Jewish Families," in *Ethnicity and Family Therapy*, ed. Monica McGoldrick, John Pearce, and Joseph Giordano (New York: Guilford Press, 1982), 364–392.

26. Susan M. Filler, "The Missing Mahler: Alois (Hans) in Chicago," in *Neue Mahlerian*, ed. Weiss, 39–46.

27. GM to Friedrich Löhr, undated [spring 1894], SEL, no. 119, 153.

28. *Journey's Beginning*, 18.

29. HLG1, 24–25.

30. Ibid., 5.

31. Ibid., 26.

32. NBL, 164.

33. HLG1, 26.

34. GM to Josef Steiner, 17 June 1879, SEL, no. 2a, 54–55. Trans. from HLG1, 56–57.

35. HLG1, 28.

36. Stefan Zweig, *The World of Yesterday* (New York: Viking Press, 1943), 11.

37. HLG1, 30.

38. Ibid., 29.

39. *Die drei Pintos*, Mahler's reconstruction of an opera after the sketches of Carl Maria von Weber (1786–1826).

40. Mahler's First and Second symphonies.

41. GM to Annie Mincieux, 2 March 1896, UNK, 119.

Chapter 3. Family Crisis, 1889

1. HLGi, 185.
2. Ibid., 188.
3. Ibid.
4. Ibid., 198.
5. GM to Friedrich Löhr, undated [July 1889], SEL, no. 72, 119.
6. Ibid., 121.
7. HLGi, 201.
8. GM to Friedrich Löhr, undated [October 1889], SEL, no. 77, 121–122.
9. NBL, 160–161.
10. HLGi, 212.
11. Ibid., 222.
12. Ibid., 218.
13. *Mahleriana* comprises the notes of Natalie Bauer-Lechner in MSS. A selection appeared as *Erinnerungen an Gustav Mahler*, ed. Johann Killian (Leipzig: Tal, 1923). NBL is the English translation.
14. GM to Friedrich Löhr, undated [January 1891], SEL, no. 95, 130.
15. GM to Friedrich Löhr, undated [28 November 1891], SEL, no. 99, 138.
16. HLGi, 226.
17. Ibid., 171.
18. GM to Justine Mahler, 27 January 1893, UNK, 108.
19. GM to Emil Freund, undated [late autumn 1891], SEL, no. 100, 140.
20. HLGi, 241.
21. GM to Emil Freund (as above n. 19).
22. HLGi, 240.
23. Ibid., 258.
24. Stephen McClatchie, "'Liebe Justi!' Mahler Family Letters," in *Mahler Studies*, ed. Stephen E. Hefling (Cambridge: Cambridge University Press, 1997), 68.
25. HLGi, 266.
26. McClatchie, "'Liebe Justi!'" 69.
27. Ibid.
28. Ibid.
29. Susan M. Filler, "The Missing Mahler: Alois (Hans) in Chicago," in *Neue Mahleriana: Essays in Honour of Henry-Louis de La Grange on His Seventieth Birthday*, ed. Günther Weiss (Bern: Peter Lang, 1997), 39–46.

Chapter 4. The Music of Fratricide

1. HLGi, 249.
2. Ibid., 198.
3. Ibid., 287.
4. DOC, 198.
5. NBL, 33.

6. Genesis 32:26.

7. HLG1, 276.

8. GM to Arthur Seidl, 17 February 1897, SEL, no. 205, 212.

9. Edward R. Reilly, "*Das Klagende Lied* Reconsidered," in *Mahler Studies*, ed. Stephen E. Hefling (Cambridge: Cambridge University Press, 1997), 42.

10. Ibid., 25.

11. HLG1, 241.

12. Ibid., 300.

13. Ibid.

14. GM to Arthur Seidl, 17 February 1897, SEL, no. 205, 212.

15. Ibid.

16. Theodore Reik, *The Haunting Melody: Psychoanalytic Experiences in Life and Music* (New York: Grove Press, 1953), 253–254.

17. GM to Friedrich Löhr, 29 June 1894, SEL, no. 121, 154–155.

18. GM to Friedrich Löhr, undated postcard [postmark: Berlin, 16 June 1893], SEL, no. 114, 150 and 415 n.

19. HLG1, 319.

Chapter 5. Mahler at Midnight

1. HLG1, 749.

2. Sigmund Freud, *The Interpretation of Dreams* (1900), SFR, vol. 5, 357.

3. HLG1, 609.

4. NBL, 74.

5. HLG1, 390.

6. Ibid., 412.

7. AMM, 14.

8. HLG1, 614.

9. Ibid.

10. Herta Blaukopf, "Villa Mahler on the Wörthersee," in *Gustav Mahler on Wörthersee: Documents, Reports, Photographs Relating to the Composer's Life and Work*, ed. International Gustav Mahler Society (Klagenfurt: Kulturamt der Landeshauptstadt Klagenfürt, n.d.), 5–7.

11. HLG1, 579.

12. Ibid., 617, 938 n. 26.

13. Ibid., 236.

14. Natalie Bauer-Lechner, *Erinnerungen an Gustav Mahler*, ed. Johann Killian (Leipzig: Tal, 1923). Translation courtesy Stephen E. Hefling.

15. NBL, 167.

16. Ibid., 70.

17. Gustav Mahler, *Um Mitternacht*, in *Twenty-four Songs for Voice and Piano* (New York: International Universities Press, n.d.), 15–20.

18. Stuart Feder, "Gustav Mahler: Um Mitternacht," *International Review of Psychoanalysis* 7 (1980): 11–26.

19. Edward F. Kravitt, "Mahler's Dirges for His Death," *Musical Quarterly* 64 (1978): 329–353.

Chapter 6. Family Romances

1. Karen Monson, *Alma Mahler: Muse to Genius* (Boston: Houghton Mifflin, 1983), 22.

2. Stuart Feder, "Before Alma: Gustav Mahler and *Das Ewig-Weibliche*," in *Mahler Studies*, ed. Stephen E. Hefling (Cambridge: Cambridge University Press, 1997), 78–109.

3. HLG1, 313–314.

4. NBL, 23.

5. Ibid., 24.

6. Feder, "Before Alma," 101.

7. HLG1, 218.

8. Jonathan Carr, *Mahler: A Biography* (Woodstock: Overlook Press, 1998), 63.

9. Feder, "Before Alma," 102.

10. HLG1, 374.

11. Ibid., 355.

12. Ibid., 636.

13. HLG2, 361.

14. Natalie Bauer-Lechner, *Erinnerungen an Gustav Mahler*, ed. Johann Killian (Leipzig: Tal, 1923), 195.

15. Peter Franklin, foreword to NBL, 11.

16. HLG1, 699.

17. AMM, 13.

18. AMB, 13.

19. Ibid., 9.

20. Ibid., 5.

21. Ibid., 4.

22. Sigmund Freud, *Family Romances* (1909), SFR, vol. 9, 240.

23. AMD, 141.

24. Ibid., 307.

25. Freud, *Family Romances*, 239.

26. AMB, 6.

27. Susanne Keegan, *The Bride of the Wind: The Life and Times of Alma Mahler-Werfel* (New York: Viking, 1992), 9.

28. AMB, 6.

29. Ibid., 9.

30. AMD, 131.

31. AMB, 10.

32. AMD, 300.
33. Ibid., 12.
34. Ibid., 123.
35. AMB, 14.
36. AMD, 124.
37. Ibid., 297.
38. AMB, 129.
39. AMD, 142–143.
40. Ibid., 157.
41. Ibid., 119.
42. Ibid., p. 121.
43. Ibid., 351.

Chapter 7. Mahler in Love

1. AMD, 76.
2. Ibid., 84.
3. Ibid., 163.
4. Ibid.
5. AMM, 3.
6. AMB, 14.
7. Ibid., 15.
8. HLG1, 681.
9. AMD, 443.
10. Ibid., 441.
11. HLG1, 669.
12. AMM, 17.
13. Ibid., 16.
14. HLG1, 671.
15. HLG2, 435.
16. HLG1, 692.
17. AMM, 17.
18. Ibid.
19. AMB, 52.
20. Ibid., 18.
21. HLG1, 673.
22. AMD, 451.
23. AMM, 207.
24. Stuart Feder, "Before Alma: Gustav Mahler and *Das Ewig-Weibliche*," in *Mahler Studies*, ed. Stephen E. Hefling (Cambridge: Cambridge University Press, 1997), 86.
25. Ibid., 96.
26. AMB, 18.

27. HLG1, 677.

28. Ibid., 618.

29. Ibid., 675.

30. AMD, 457.

31. Ibid.

32. Ibid.

33. AMM, 211.

34. AMB, 19.

35. HLG1, 684–690.

36. AMB, 19.

37. AMM, 218.

38. Ibid., 219.

39. Gilbert Kaplan, preface to *Gustav Mahler, Adagietto: Facsimile, Documentation, Recording* (New York: Kaplan Foundation, 1992), 21.

40. AMB, 19.

Chapter 8. The "Splendid" Years

1. AMD, 466.

2. Ibid., 467.

3. Ibid., 468.

4 AMB, 22.

5. HLG1, 697.

6. Ibid.

7. AMM, 31–32.

8. Ibid., 26.

9. Ibid., 53.

10. GM to Anna Moll, undated [9 December 1901], SEL, no. 282, 257.

11. AMM, 29.

12. AMB, 20.

13. HLG2, 759.

14. Ibid., 815.

15. AMM, 41.

16. Michael Kennedy, *Richard Strauss* (New York: Schirmer Books, 1996), 16.

17. Ibid., 32.

18. AMM, 27.

19. GM to AM, 31 January 1902, RUH, no. 18, 129.

20. Richard Newman with Karen Kirtley, *Alma Rosé: Vienna to Auschwitz* (Portland: Amadeus Press, 2000), 24.

21. Ibid., 16.

22. AMM, 26–28.

23. AMB, 30.

24. Ibid., 19.

25. Kennedy, *Richard Strauss*, 41.

26. Ibid., 31.

27. Ibid., 26.

28. AMM, 282–286.

29. Ibid., 287.

30. Ibid., 282.

31. Kennedy, *Richard Strauss*, 41.

32. Ibid., 76.

33. Stephen E. Hefling, "The Rückert Lieder," COM, 361.

34. Ibid., 364.

35. AMB, 27.

36. Ibid., 28.

37. AMM, 76.

38. AMB, 28.

39. AMM, 68.

40. Ibid., 70.

41. HLG3, 401.

42. Ibid.

43. AMM, 100.

44. HLGFR2, 453.

45. AMM, 70.

46. AMB, 31.

47. AMM, 235.

48. GM to Franz Bartolomey, undated [March 1903], SEL, no. 296, 268.

49. AMB, 29.

50. AMM, 69.

51. Ibid., 237.

52. Ibid., 250.

53. Ibid., 252.

54. Ibid., 236.

55. AMB, 28.

56. AMM, 105.

57. Joseph Albrecht, "Epilogue: Mahler's Smile," COM, 593.

58. Ibid., 590.

59. Ibid., 593.

60. AMM, 89.

61. AMB, 31.

62. Jonathan Carr, *Mahler: A Biography* (Woodstock: Overlook Press, 1998), 151.

63. AMM, 116.

64. Ibid., 81.

65. Antony Beaumont, *Zemlinsky* (Ithaca: Cornell University Press, 2000), 137.

66. Ibid.

67. HLG3, 198.

68. AMM, 102.

69. GM to Friedrich Löhr, 21 June 1906, SEL, no. 333, 292.

70. AMM, 328.

71. Johann Wolfgang von Goethe, *Faust I and II*, ed. and trans. Stuart Atkins (Cambridge: Harvard University Press, 1985), 79.

72. AMM, 106.

73. GM to AM, 21 October 1906, RUH, no. 185, 296.

74. HLG3, 545.

75. Ibid., 550.

76. Ibid., 463.

77. Ibid., 647.

78. GM to AM, 5 June 1907, SEL, no. 206, 320.

Chapter 9. A Child's Death

1. AMM, 121.

2. Ibid., 122.

3. 2 Samuel 18.

4. GM to Bruno Walter, undated [summer 1908], SEL, no. 372, 321.

5. AMM, 121.

6. HLG3, 697.

7. Ibid.

8. Alma Mahler, diary manuscript, University of Pennsylvania, Rare Book and Manuscript Library. This excerpt is provided courtesy of Henry-Louis de La Grange, to be published in volume 4 of the English edition of his *Mahler*. Translation by Mac Stock.

9. HLG3, 743.

10. Ibid., 744.

11. Anna Mahler, interview for Austrian TV, circa 1984.

12. AMB, 35.

13. Anna Mahler, interview.

14. *Die Bildhauerin Anna Mahler*, ed. Franz Willnauer and Marina Mahler-Fistoulari (Salzburg: Verlag Galerie Welz, 1988), 38, 84, 87.

15. AMB, 35.

16. HLG3, 851.

17. Ibid.

18. Ibid., 698.

19. AMM, 123.

20. Ibid., 129.

21. Donald Mitchell, *Gustav Mahler: Songs and Symphonies of Life and Death* (Berkeley: University of California Press, 1985), 173.

22. HLG3, 851.

23. Mitchell, *Gustav Mahler*, 241.

24. GM to Carl Moll, undated [10 March 1909]; SEL, no. 387, 333 no. 1.

25. Sigmund Freud, *Mourning and Melancholia* (1917), SFR, vol. 14, 237–258.

26. David Aberbach, "Grief and Mysticism," *International Review of Psychoanalysis* 13 (1987): 509–526.

27. Gustav Theodor Fechner, *The Little Book of Life after Death*, trans. Mary C. Wadsworth (Boston: Little, Brown, 1905).

28. HLG3, 851.

29. William James, introduction to Fechner, *The Little Book of Life after Death*, vii–xix.

30. Jonathan Kramer, personal communication, March 2002.

Chapter 10. Old World, New World

1. Flysheet, December 1907, DOC, 251.

2. HLG3, 792.

3. Carl E.Schorske, *Fin-de-Siecle Vienna: Politics and Culture* (New York: Knopf, 1980), 246.

4. Alfred Roller, "A Portrait of Mahler," in *The Mahler Album*, ed. Gilbert Kaplan (New York: Kaplan Foundation, 1995), 21–22.

5. AMM, 126.

6. Ibid., 129–130.

7. Marvin L. Von Deck, "Gustav Mahler in New York: His Conducting Activities in New York City, 1908–1911" (Ph.D. dissertation, New York University, 1973), 100–101.

8. Ibid., 116.

9. Joseph Horowitz, *Understanding Toscanini* (London: Faber and Faber, 1994), 68.

10. AMM, 136.

11. Ibid., 135.

12. Roller, "A Portrait of Mahler," 22.

13. GM to Willem Mengelberg, undated [February 1908], SEL, no. 362, 314.

14. Howard Shanet, "New York's Musical Culture: The Transformation of an Orchestra," in *Mahler in New York: The Mahler Broadcasts, 1948–1982* (n.d.), 56 ff.

15. Marion Casey, "Mary Sheldon: A Woman of Substance," in *Mahler in New York*, 108–117.

16. Von Deck, "Gustav Mahler in New York," 120.

17. AMM, 128.

18. Ibid., 137.

19. Roller, "A Portrait of Mahler," 22.

20. AMM, 139.

21. Ibid., 142.

22. Ibid., 140.

23. Ibid., 148.

24. Zoltan Roman, *Gustav Mahler's American Years, 1907–1911: A Documentary History* (New York: Pendragon Press, 1989), 143.

25. Ibid., 63.

26. *The Letters of Arturo Toscanini*, comp., ed., and trans. Harvey Sachs (New York: Knopf, 2002), 69.

27. Ibid., 70.

28. Ibid., 447.

29. Horowitz, *Understanding Toscanini*, 55.

30. Ibid.

31. Von Deck, "Gustav Mahler in New York," 180.

32. GM to Bruno Walter, undated [December 1909], SEL, no. 407, 346.

33. Horowitz, *Understanding Toscanini*, 70.

34. Howard Shanet, *Philharmonic: A History of New York's Orchestra* (Garden City: Doubleday, 1975), 214.

35. Roman, *Gustav Mahler's American Years*, 234.

36. AMM, 162.

37. Ibid., 159.

38. GM to Carl Moll, undated [10 March 1909], SEL, no. 387, 333.

39. AMM, 150.

40. Stephen E. Hefling, "The Ninth Symphony," COM, 468.

41. Ibid., 467.

42. Ibid., 476.

43. AMM, 322–323.

44. Ibid., 151.

45. DOC, 258.

46. Roman, *Gustav Mahler's American Years*, 305 n. 81.

47. Ibid., 242.

48. AMM, 166.

49. Roman, *Gustav Mahler's American Years*, 252.

50. Ibid., 314.

51. Horowitz, *Understanding Toscanini*, 75.

52. Roman, *Gustav Mahler's American Years*, 486.

53. Shanet, *Philharmonic*, 216.

54. Roman, *Gustav Mahler's American Years*, 320.

55. Ibid., 406.

56. Horowitz, *Understanding Toscanini*, 72.

57. AMM, 184.

58. DOC, 265.

Chapter 11. Alma at Tobelbad

1. AM in DOC, 231.

2. Ibid., 258.

3. Edward R. Reilly, *Gustav Mahler and Guido Adler: Records of a Friendship* (London: Cambridge University Press, 1982), 108.

4. Ibid., 108–109.

5. Ibid., 110–111.

6. AMM, 170.

7. Ibid., 140–141.

8. AMB, 50.

9. HLGFR3, 715 n. 35.

10. Sigmund Freud, *Studies on Hysteria* (1893–1895), SFR, vol. 2.

11. AMB, 53.

12. GM to AM, 28 June 1910, RUH, no. 315, 435.

13. Susanne Keegan, *The Bride of the Wind: The Life and Times of Alma Mahler-Werfel* (New York: Viking, 1992), 7.

14. HLGFR3, 732.

15. AMB, 50.

16. GRO1, 98–105.

17. HLGFR3, 715.

18. Ibid.

19. Françoise Giroud, *Alma Mahler, or The Art of Being Loved*, trans. R. M. Stock (Oxford: Oxford University Press, 1991), 82.

20. HLGFR3, 715.

21. GM to AM, 6 June 1910, RUH, no. 302, 422.

22. GM to AM, 21 June 1910, RUH, no. 311, 432.

23. GM to Anna Moll, undated [June 1910], SEL, no. 422, 359.

24. GM to AM, 18 June 1910, RUH, no. 309, 429.

25. GM to Anna Moll, undated [June 1910], SEL, no. 422, 359.

26. Ibid., 363.

27. GRO1, 276.

28. GM to Anna Moll, undated [July 1910], SEL, no. 428, 362–363.

29. Marianne Trenker, handwritten account of Mahler's sojourn in Altschluderbach, summer 1910, Médiathèque Musicale Mahler.

30. Colin Matthews, "The Tenth Symphony," COM, 495.

Chapter 12. Marital Crisis

1. GRO1, 102.

2. Françoise Giroud, *Alma Mahler, or The Art of Being Loved*, trans. R. M. Stock (Oxford: Oxford University Press, 1991), 13.

3. AMD, 4 n. 3.

4. Ibid., 136.

5. AMB, 51.

6. Sigmund Freud, *The Psychopathology of Everyday Life* (1901), SFR, vol. 6.

7. AMB, 51.

8. GRO2, 33–34.

9. Ibid., 34.

10. GRO1, 99.

11. GRO2, 83–83.

12. AMM, 172.

13. Ibid.

14. Ibid.

15. Ibid., 173.

16. Ibid., 333.

17. Ibid., 173.

18. AMB, 52.

19. AMM, 333.

20. Ibid., 333–334.

21. AMB, 53.

22. HLGFR3, 764.

23. GRO1, 100.

24. AMB, 53.

25. Jörg Rothkamm, "Wann entstand Mahlers Zehnte Symphonie?: Ein Beitrag zur Biographie und Werdeutung," *Musik-Konzepte* 106 (October 1999): 103.

26. Colin Matthews, "The Tenth Symphony," COM, 508.

27. Rothkamm, "Wann entstand Mahlers Zehnte Symphonie?," 6–7.

28. Steven D. Coburn, *Mahler's Tenth Symphony: Form and Genesis* (Ph.D. dissertation, New York University, May 2002).

29. Ibid., 300.

30. David Matthews, "Wagner, Lipiner, and the 'Purgatorio,'" COM, 514.

31. Ibid.

32. Ibid., 515.

33. Matthew 27:46; the Lord's Prayer or Matthew 26:39.

34. HLG1, 1.

35. D. Matthews, "Wagner," 512.

36. Maynard Solomon, *Beethoven* (New York: Schirmer, 1977), 121.

37. GRO2, 34.

38. AMB, 176.

39. Susan M. Filler, "A Composer's Wife as Composer: The Songs of Alma Mahler," *Journal of Musicological Research* 4 (1983): 427–442.

40. AMB, 54.

41. AMM, 177.

42. GRO2, 34.

43. AMM, 332.

44. Ibid., 333.

Chapter 13. The Walking Cure

1. Peter Gay, *Freud: A Life for Our Time* (New York: Norton, 1988), 207.

2. Ibid., 213.

3. Ibid., 218.

4. *The Correspondence of Sigmund Freud and Sándor Ferenczi*, vol. 1, *1908–1914*, ed. Eva Brabant et al. (Cambridge: Harvard University Press, 1992), 195.

5. Ibid., 169.

6. Sigmund Freud, *On Beginning the Treatment: Further Recommendations on the Technique of Psychoanalysis* (1913), SFR, vol. 12, 126.

7. Marie Bonaparte, unpublished diary manuscript, courtesy of Celia Bertin.

8. Ernest Jones, *The Life and Work of Sigmund Freud*, vol. 2 (New York: Basic Books, 1955), 79.

9. Gay, *Freud*, 59.

10. Ibid., 60.

11. Paul Roazan, *Freud and His Followers* (New York: Knopf, 1975), 48.

12. Ibid., 56.

13. Gay, *Freud*, 76.

14. *The Correspondence of Freud and Ferenczi*, 204.

15. Ibid., 157.

16. Alfred Roller, "A Portrait of Mahler," in *The Mahler Album*, ed. Gilbert Kaplan (New York: Kaplan Foundation, 1995), 20.

17. AMM, 294.

18. Ibid., 274.

19. Ibid., 304.

20. Sigmund Freud, *Jokes and Their Relation to the Unconscious* (1905), SFR, vol. 8, 174.

21. Peter Gay, *A Godless Jew: Freud, Atheism, and the Making of Psychoanalysis* (New Haven: Yale University Press, 1987).

22. Sigmund Freud, *Address to the Society of B'nai B'rith* (1926), SFR, vol. 20, 274.

23. Josef Hayim Yurushalmi, *Freud's Moses: Judaism Terminable and Interminable* (New Haven: Yale University Press, 1991), quoted in Edward W. Said, *Freud and the Non-European* (London: Verso, 2003), 31.

24. Roller, "A Portrait of Mahler," 27.

25. Bruno Walter, *Gustav Mahler* (New York: Knopf, 1966), 139.

26. Morten Solvik, personal communication, August 2002.

27. Marsha L. Rozenblit, *The Jews of Vienna, 1867–1914: Assimilation and Identity* (Albany: State University of New York Press, 1983), 17.

28. AMM, 226.

29. Gay, *Freud*, 19.

30. Sigmund Freud, *An Autobiographical Study* (1925), SFR, vol. 20, 7.

31. Freud, *Address to the Society of B'nai B'rith*, 241.

32. HLG1, 57.

33. Phyllis Grosskurth, *The Secret Ring: Freud's Inner Circle and the Politics of Psychoanalysis* (Reading, Mass.: Addison-Wesley, 1991), 57.

34. Ibid., 17.

35. Ibid., 46.

36. NBL, 76.

37. Freud, *An Autobiographical Study*, 8.

38. Leonard Shengold, *This Boy Will Come to Nothing* (New Haven: Yale University Press, 1993), 28–46.

39. Sigmund Freud, *A Childhood Recollection from Dichtung und Wahrheit* (1917), SFR, vol. 17, 156.

40. Gay, *Freud*, 11.

41. Ibid., 89.

42. Sigmund Freud, *The Interpretation of Dreams* (1900), SFR, vols. 4 and 5.

43. Ibid., vol. 4, xxiii.

44. HLG1, 272.

45. Freud, *An Autobiographical Study*, 8.

46. Gay, *Freud*, 168.

47. Walter, *Gustav Mahler*, 153.

48. William McGrath, *Dionysian Art and Popular Politics in Austria* (New Haven, Yale University Press, 1974), 247.

49. AMM, 20.

50. HLG1, 465.

51. AMM, 124.

52. Ibid., 9.

53. Sigmund Freud, *Dostoyevsky and Parricide* (1928), SFR, vol. 21, 177.

54. Sigmund Freud, *On Psychoanalysis* (1913), SFR, vol. 12, 210.

55. Jones, *The Life and Work of Sigmund Freud*, 220.

56. Gay, *Freud*, 58.

57. Freud, *The Interpretation of Dreams*, vol. 4, 265.

58. HLG3, 468.

59. Ibid., 698.

60. Gay, *Freud*, 130.

61. HLG3, 59.

62. Ibid., 376.

63. Max Graf, *Composer and Critic: Two Hundred Years of Music Criticism* (New York: Norton, 1946), 25.

64. David M. Abrams, "Freud and Max Graf: On the Psychoanalysis of Music," in *Psychoanalytic Explorations in Music*, 2nd series, ed. Stuart Feder, Richard L. Karmel, George H. Pollock (Madison, Conn.: International Universities Press, 1993), 279–308.

65. Sigmund Freud, *Analysis of a Phobia in a Five-Year-Old Boy* (1909), SFR, vol. 10, 1–50.

66. Bruno Walter, *Theme and Variations: An Autobiography* (London: Hamish Hamilton, 1947), 181.

67. Ibid.

68. Ibid.

69. Ibid.

Chapter 14. The Precious Word

1. Marie Bonaparte, unpublished diary manuscript, courtesy of Celia Bertin.

2. Celia Bertin, *Marie Bonaparte: A Life* (San Diego: Harcourt Brace, 1982), 7.

3. Ibid., 154.

4. Bonaparte, diary.

5. Sigmund Freud, *Recommendations to Physicians Practising Psychoanalysis* (1912), SFR, vol. 10, 111.

6. Sigmund Freud, *Family Romances* (1909), SFR, vol. 9, 237–241.

7. Sigmund Freud, *The Question of Lay Analysis* (1926), SFR, vol. 20, 179–250.

8. Theodore Reik, *Listening with the Third Ear* (New York: Farrar, Straus, 1948).

9. Theodore Reik, *The Haunting Melody: Psychoanalytic Experiences in Life and Music* (New York: Grove Press, 1953), 343.

10. Ibid.

11. Sigmund Freud, *A Short Account of Psychoanalysis* (1924), SFR, vol. 19, 203.

12. AMM, 175.

13. Bonaparte, diary.

14. Sigmund Freud, *Inhibitions, Symptoms, and Anxiety* (1926), SFR, vol. 20, 75–176.

15. Ibid., 137.

16. Ibid., 140.

17. Arnold Winston and Beverly Winston, *Handbook of Integrated Short-Term Psychotherapy* (Washington, D.C.: American Psychiatric Press, 2001), 60.

18. AMM, 175.

19. Ibid., 334.

20. Ibid.

21. Ibid., 335.

22. *Minutes of the Vienna Psychoanalytic Society*, ed. Herman Nunberg and Ernst Federn, vol. 3 (New York: International Universities Press, 1971), 263–264.

23. Ibid., 275.

24. Ibid.

25. Emanuel E. Garcia, "Gustav Mahler's Choice: A Note on Adolescence, Genius, and Psychosomatics," in *The Psychoanalytic Study of the Child*, vol. 55 (New Haven: Yale University Press, 2000), 100.

26. Ibid., 101.

27. Aaron Esman, personal communication, August 2003.

28. Sigmund Freud, *The Ego and the Id* (1923), SFR, vol. 19, 1–66.

29. Garcia, "Gustav Mahler's Choice," 102.

30. Sigmund Freud, *Dostoyevsky and Parricide* (1928), SFR, vol. 21, 173.

Chapter 15. Triumph and Despair

1. AMM, 181.

2. Ibid.

3. GRO2, 34.

4. Ibid., 35.

5. HLGFR3, 787.

6. Ibid.

7. AMM, 178.

8. GRO1, 103.

9. Alma Mahler, diary manuscript, University of Pennsylvania, Rare Book and Manuscript Library. Courtesy of Henry-Louis de La Grange. See chap. 9 n. 8.)

10. GRO2, 35.

11. GRO1, 103.

12. GRO2, 35.

13. HLGFR3, 792.

14. Ibid., 796.

15. Ibid., 793.

16. HLGFR3, 828.

17. Thomas Mann, *Death in Venice*, trans. and ed. Clayton Koelb (New York: Norton, 1994), 12.

18. HLGFR3, 804.

19. Ibid., 804.

20. Zoltan Roman, *Gustav Mahler's American Years, 1907–1911: A Documentary History* (New York: Pendragon Press, 1989), 391.

21. Ibid.

22. Ibid., 377.

23. Ibid., 397.

24. Ibid.

25. Ibid., 405.

26. Ibid., 369.

27. GRO2, 35.

28. Roman, *Gustav Mahler's American Years*, 397.

29. GRO1, 104.

30. Ibid.

31. Roman, *Gustav Mahler's American Years*, 418.

32. AMM, 136.

33. GRO1, 105.

34. Roman, *Gustav Mahler's American Years*, 410.

35. GRO1, 105.

36. GRO2, 36.

37. Roman, *Gustav Mahler's American Years*, 409.

38. AMM, 186.

39. Ibid., 187.

40. Ibid.

41. GRO1, 110.

42. Roman, *Gustav Mahler's American Years*, 448.

43. Ibid., 404.

44. Ibid., 427.

45. Ibid., 429.

46. Ibid., 434.

47. Ibid., 446.

48. Henry-Louis de La Grange, "Mahler and the New York Philharmonic," in Philip Reed, ed., *On Mahler and Britten: Essays in Honor of Donald Mitchell on His Seventieth Birthday* (Aldeburgh: Boydell Press, 1995), 71.

49. Roman, *Gustav Mahler's American Years*, 441.

50. Minutes of the Guarantors' Advisory Committee, New York Philharmonic, Archives of the New York Philharmonic, New York.

51. AMM, 185.

52. Norman Lebrecht, *Mahler Remembered* (New York: Norton, 1987), 295.

53. AMM, 189.

54. Ibid.

55. Philharmonic Society of New York, Program Notes (1910–1911), Program of 21 and 24 February 1911.

Chapter 16. Mahler Dying

1. GM to Anna Moll, undated [February 1911], SEL, no. 442, 370–371.

2. AMB, 57.

3. AMM, 190.

4. AMB, 58.

5. Dr. Joseph Brettauer, file, Mount Sinai Hospital Center Archives.

6. Ibid.

7. Alma Mahler, diary manuscript, University of Pennsylvania, Rare Book and Manuscript Library. Courtesy of Henry-Louis de La Grange. See chap. 9 n. 8.

8. Dr. Emanuel Libman, file, Mount Sinai Hospital Center Archives.

9. Dr. George Engel, oral history of Emanuel Libman, Mount Sinai Hospital Center Archives.

10. Ibid.

11. Ibid.

12. Emanuel Libman and H. L. Celler, "The Etiology of Subacute Infective Endocarditis," *American Journal of Medical Science* (1910): 140. Also Emanuel Libman and Charles K. Friedberg, *Subacute Bacterial Endocarditis*, ed. Henry A. Christian (New York: Oxford University Press, 1947).

13. Nicholas P. Christy and Beverly M. Christy, "Mahler's Final Illness," *Chord and Discord* 3, 2 (1998): 69–76.

14. AMM, 197.

15. Stuart Feder, "Mahler Dying," *Chord and Discord* 3, 2 (1998): 84.

16. Stuart Feder, interview with Dr. George Baehr, April 1974.

17. Christy and Christy, "Mahler's Final Illness."

18. Stuart Feder, *The Diagnosis: Terminal but Not Final, Chord and Discord* 3, 2 (1998): 78.

19. AMM, 185.

20. Ibid., 199.

21. Ibid.

22. GRO1, 110.

23. AMM, 194.

24. Ibid.

25. Kurt Blaukopf and Herta Blaukopf, *Mahler: His Life, Work, and World* (London: Thames and Hudson, 1976), 248.

26. AMM, 196.

27. Blaukopf and Blaukopf, *Mahler*, 247.

28. GRO1, 111.

29. AMM, 199.

30. Blaukopf and Blaukopf, *Mahler*, 248.

31. Ibid.

Chapter 17. Forever Alma

1. AMB, 66.

2. Alma Mahler, *Mein Leben* (Frankfurt am Main: Fischer, 1949).

3. Alma Mahler, *And the Bridge Is Love*, trans. E. B. Ashton (New York: Harcourt Brace, 1958).

4. Ibid., 68.

5. Ibid.

6. Ibid.

7. Ibid.

8. Ibid., 39.

9. Susanne Keegan, *The Bride of the Wind: The Life and Times of Alma Mahler-Werfel* (New York: Viking, 1992), 170–171.

10. AMB, 72.

11. Frank Whitford, *Oskar Kokoschka: A Life* (New York: Atheneum, 1986), 90.

12. Keegan, *The Bride of the Wind*, 171.

13. AMB, 72.

14. Ibid., 75.

15. Keegan, *The Bride of the Wind*, 174.

16. Ibid., 176.

17. GRO1, 111.

18. Ibid.

19. Ibid., 112.

20. Ibid.

21. GRO2, 37.

22. GRO1, 113.

23. Alfred Weidinger, *Kokoschka and Alma Mahler* (Munich: Prestel, 1996), 7.

24. Ibid.

25. AMB, 72.

26. *Letters of Oskar Kokoschka*, selected by Olga Kokoschka and Alfred Marnau (New York: Thames and Hudson, 1992), 20.

27. Ibid., 22.

28. Whitford, *Oskar Kokoschka*, 90.

29. Weidinger, *Kokoschka and Alma Mahler*, 11–12.

30. AMB, 76.

31. Weidinger, *Kokoschka and Alma Mahler*, 15.

32. AMB, 77.

33. *Letters of Kokoschka*, 20.

34. Weidinger, *Kokoschka and Alma Mahler*, 20.

35. GRO1, 115.

36. GRO2, 38.

37. Whitford, *Oskar Kokoschka*, 91.

38. AMB, 74.

39. Weidinger, *Kokoschka and Alma Mahler*, 34.

40. Ibid., 82–83.

41. AMB, 84.

42. GRO1, 142.

43. Ibid., 48.

44. Ibid.

45. Ibid., 53.

46. Ibid., 52.

47. Ibid., 55.

48. Ibid., 54.

49. Ibid.

50. Ibid., 58.

51. AMB, 62.

52. GRO2, 82.

53. Peter Stefan Jungt, *Franz Werfel: A Life in Vienna, Prague, and Hollywood* (New York: Grove Press, 1990), 59.

54. Ibid.

55. AMB, 93.

56. Jungt, *Franz Werfel*, 89.

57. Ibid., 122.

58. Ibid., 131.

59. Friedrich Buchmayr and Jörg Rothkamm, "Unknown Sketches to Mahler's Second Symphony from the Estate of the Theologian Johannes Hollnsteiner," *News about Mahler Research* 47 (autumn 2002): 3.

60. Keegan, *The Bride of the Wind*, 255.

61. Ibid., 254.

62. Jungt, *Franz Werfel*, 130.

63. AMB, 277.

64. Ibid., 170.

65. Keegan, *The Bride of the Wind*, 287.

66. Ibid., 306.

Chapter 18. Epilogue

1. AMB, 79.

2. Ibid., 65.

3. Ibid.

4. Ibid., 87.

5. Ibid., 91.

6. Ibid., 90–91.

7. Ibid., 156.

8. Ibid., 153.

9. Ibid., 164.

10. *Die Bildhauerin Anna Mahler*, ed. Franz Willnauer and Marina Mahler-Fistoulari (Salzburg: Verlag Galerie Welz, 1988). Biographical material on Anna Mahler's career has been drawn from this monograph.

11. AMB, 305.

12. G. Tobias Natter and Gerbert Frodl, *Carl Moll* (Salzburg: Verlag Galerie Welz, 1998).

13. Ibid., 37.

14. Peter Stefan Jungt, *Franz Werfel: A Life in Vienna, Prague, and Hollywood* (New York: Grove Press, 1990), 173.

15. Ibid., 225.

16. AMB, 247.

17. Ibid., 240.

18. Ibid., 247.

19. Ibid.

20. Ibid.

21. GRO2, 26.

22. Ibid., 68.

23. Ibid., 196.

24. Ibid., 231.

25. Ibid., 283.

26. AMB, 155.

27. S. N. Behrman, "Emanuel Libman." *New Yorker*, 8 April 1939.

28. Dr. George Engel, oral history of Emanuel Libman, Mount Sinai Hospital Center Archives.

29. Ibid.

30. Peter Gay, *Freud: A Life for Our Time* (New York: Norton, 1988), 267.

31. Ibid., 277.

32. Sigmund Freud, *Inhibitions, Symptoms, and Anxiety* (1926), SFR, vol. 20, 75–176.

33. Sigmund Freud, *On Transience* (1916), SFR, vol. 14, 303–307.

34. Ibid., 305.

35. Ibid.

36. Ibid., 306.

37. Sigmund Freud, *Mourning and Melancholia* (1917), SFR, vol. 14, 237–258.

38. Gay, *Freud*, 448.

39. Ibid., 614.

40. Ibid., 612.

41. Ibid., 629.

42. GM to AM, 31 January 1902, RUH, no. 18, 129.

INDEX

Adler, Alfred, 204
Adler, Guido, 24, 163, 173–76, 248, 251
Adler, Victor, 98, 223
Amiet, Kuno, 304
anti-Semitism, 11, 38, 63–64, 135; of
    Alma Mahler, 91, 297; of Alma
    Mahler's family, 91, 97, 98, 109, 113,
    189, 297–98, 307–8; ; of Gustav
    Mahler, 91; of Richard Strauss, 115; of
    Walter Gropius, 295
Arnim, Achim von, 40
Arnold, Richard, 169

B'nai B'rith, 214, 215, 216
Baehr, George, 271–73, 302, 312
Bahr, Hermann, 248
Bauer–Lechner, Natalie, 12, 19, 28, 34,
    38, 51–52, 66, 68–69, 70, 77–83, 101,
    102, 212
Bauhaus school, 308, 309
Bechstein, Ludwig, 61
Beethoven, Ludwig von, 14–15; *Fidelio*,
    153; *Heiligenstadt Testament*, 201–2;
    Klimt's interpretation of, 153;
    Symphony no. *3* (Eroica), 201;
    Symphony no. *5*, 164; Symphony
    no. *9*, 57, 58, 71, 132, 164
Behn, Hermann, 144
Behrman, S. N., 311
Bekker, Paul, 113

Berg, Alban, 167, 305
Berliner, Arnold, 243
Bernays, Emmeline, 208
Bernays, Minna, 210–11
Bethge, Hans: *The Chinese Flute*, 144,
    145, 151
Blumenthal, Carl, 137
Bonaparte, Lucien, 227
Bonaparte, Marie, 211, 227–32, 314
Bonaparte, Napoleon, 227
Boston Symphony Orchestra, 158, 160
Brahms, Johannes, 38
Brecht, Bertolt, 300
Brentano, Clemens, 40
Brettauer, Joseph, 266–67
Breuer, Josef, 178
Bulitt, William, 315
Bülow, Hans von, 47–48, 56–57
Burckhard, Max, 88, 91, 93, 97, 98, 99,
    104, 116, 177
Busoni, Ferruccio, 125, 171, 278; *Berceuse
    Elégiaque*, 263–64

Caruso, Enrico, 156
Casella, Alfredo, 247
Catholicism: Alma Mahler's return to,
    299; Gustav Mahler's conversion to,
    64, 91
Chadwick, George, 261
Chaliapin, Fyodor, 156

Chantemesse, Andre, 277, 279–80
Charlton, Loudon, 251, 260
Chinese Flute, The (Bethge), 144, 145, 151
Christy, Beverly M., 273
Christy, Nicholas P., 273
Chvostek, Franz, 277, 281–82, 283
Clark University, 207
Clemenceau, Georges, 116
Clemenceau, Paul, 116, 132, 133, 166, 177, 247
Clemenceau, Sophie, 93, 94, 116, 132, 166, 177
Conried, Heinrich, 135, 136, 154, 160
Coolidge, Calvin, 269–70

Damrosch, Leopold, 158
Damrosch, Walter, 158, 159, 162
Debussy, Claude, 176
De Chirico, Giorgio, 305
de La Grange, Henry–Louis, 23, 141–42, 144, 178, 182
Des knaben Wunderhorn, 16, 20, 40, 46, 47, 48, 50–52, 54, 56, 70, 113
Diepenbrock, Alphonse, 247
Dostoyevsky, Fyodor, 59, 221, 242
Dreyfus, Alfred, 116
Dreyfus affair, 132–33
Dürer, Albrecht: *Melancholia,* 48–50, 59
Dvorák, Antonín, 158

Eberstaller, Maria Moll, 307
Eberstaller, Richard, 307, 308
"Eits a binkel Kasi," 17–18
Engel, George, 269
Epstein, Julius, 26–27, 90

"family romance": Alma Mahler's, 85–86; Freud's concept of, 85–86, 231–32; Gustav Mahler's, 90–91
Farwell, Arthur, 260, 261
Fechner, Gustav Theodor, 150
Federn, Paul, 239, 240
Ferenczi, Sándor, 209, 211, 217, 234
Ferrier, Kathleen, 163
Feuchtwanger, Lion, 300
Filler, Susan, 203

Fistulari, Anatol, 305
Fistulari, Marina, 305, 306
Fliess, Wilhem, 211
Förster, Josef, 4, 48, 76
Förster-Lauterer, Bertha, 76
Fraenkel, Joseph, 156, 165, 254–56, 257, 263, 302; death of, 310; and Mahler's final illness, 266, 268, 270, 277–78; romantic interest in Alma, 284–85, 310–11
Francis Joseph I, 15
Frank, Ilse, 309
Franklin, Peter, 83
Freud, Ernst, 209
Freud, Jacob, 215
Freud, Julius, 218
Freud, Martha Bernays, 208, 210, 211
Freud, Oliver, 209
Freud, Sigmund, 62, 149, 302; and Marie Bonaparte, 227–32; commonalities with Mahler, 212–19, 220–26; and "family romance" concept, 85–86, 231–32; and Sándor Ferenczi, 211; *Inhibitions, Symptoms, and Anxiety,* 236; *The Interpretation of Dreams,* 217, 218, 219–20; Jewishness of, 213–18; later years of, 313–16; "libido" as understood by, 233–34; losses suffered by, 232; Mahler's consultation with, 1, 3, 7, 8, 12, 204–5, 206, 208, 209, 211–12, 226, 227, 229–30, 232–34, 313; *Psychopathology of Everyday Life,* 190; as scientist, 219–20; and sister-in-law Minna Bernays, 210–11; *Studies on Hysteria,* 178; and Bruno Walter, 224–26, 235–36; on vacation, 208–10; and wife Martha, 210
Freund, Emil, 24, 41, 242
Fried, Oskar, 203–4, 253

Gabrilowitsch, Ossip, 142, 171
Garcia, Emanuel E., 241–42
Gardner, Isabella Stewart, 156
Gatti-Casazza, Frances-Alda, 265
Gatti-Casazza, Giulio, 155–56, 160
Gay, Peter, 210, 213, 313

Geiringer, Gustav, 92
George of Greece, Prince, 227
Goethe, Johann Wolfgang von, 133, 220
Gorky, Maksim, 132
Graf, Max, 223–24, 239
Grimm brothers' fairy tales, 61
Gropius, Ise, 309
Gropius, Manon (Alma and Walter's daughter), 228, 294, 296, 298, 299–300, 304, 305, 309
Gropius, Manon (Alma's mother–in–law), 294, 295
Gropius, Martin, 296, 297, 299
Gropius, Walter, 248, 303; Alma Mahler's relationship with, 6–7, 142, 179–84, 188, 189–90, 243–44, 245, 252–53, 256, 259, 265, 291–92; architecture of, 310; divorce from Alma Mahler, 297; encounter with Gustav Mahler, 194–95, 198; interest of in Mahler's work, 257–58; later years of, 302, 308–10; marriage to Alma Mahler, 293–96; relationships with women, 191; during World War I, 292, 293
Gutmann, Emil, 172, 244–45, 259

Harding, Warren G., 269–70
Hartmann, Eduard von, 281
haskalah movement, 14
Hauptmann, Gerhart, 131, 247, 313
Hefling, Stephen, 120
Heller, Hugo, 240
Hellmesberger, Joseph, 77
Henderson, William, 260
Hermann, Abraham, 11, 12
Hermann, Marie. See Mahler, Marie Hermann
Higginson, Henry Lee, 160
Hildebrandt, Lily, 297, 309
Hoffmann, Josef, 59, 135
Hoffmann, Nina, 44, 59
Hofmannsthal, Hugo von, 135
Hollnsteiner, Johannes, 299
"Huntsman's Funeral, The," 61

Isaacs, Reginald R., 191

Jacob (biblical), 52, 217
James, William, 150
Jews: Freud and Mahler as, 213–18; Freud's concerns for, 314–15; humor of, 213; in Moravia, 9–11, 15; music of as influence on Mahler, 17; in Vienna, 215. See also anti-Semitism
Johner, Thomas, 261–62, 263
Jones, Ernest, 217, 222, 314
Joseph (biblical), 217–18, 237
Joseph II, 9, 11
Judenzoll, 9
Jung, Carl, 207, 217

Kahn, Otto, 156, 165, 254
Kammerer, Paul, 286–87
Karpath, Ludwig, 64
Keegan, Susanne, 299
Kestenbaum, Richard, 273
Klimt, Gustav, 88–90, 93, 116, 135, 189; Beethoven Frieze, 153; and the Mahlers' departure for America, 152–53
Klopstock, Friedrich Gottlieb, 56, 58, 75
Kokoschka, Oskar, 228, 289–92, 293, 302, 303, 306–7
Korngold, Erich Wolfgang, 300
Kovacs, Friedrich, 138
Krasny, Arnold, 90
Kraus, Karl, 279
Krefeld Festival, 114, 120
Krehbiel, Henry E., 155, 164–65, 170–71, 260, 261
Krenek, Ernst, 304
Krisper, Anton, 71
Kurtz, Selma, 248

Lehár, Franz, 167
Lehman, Lotte, 118
Lehmann, Lilli, 248
Libman, Emanuel, 267–73, 276–77, 302, 311–12
Liechtenstein, Prince Karl, 87
Lipiner, Siegfried, 77, 90–91, 98, 109–10, 166, 168, 173, 177
Livy, 169

Loew, Anton, 282
Löhr, Fritz, 21, 32, 33, 34–36, 37, 38, 43–44, 59, 77, 133
Löhr, Uda, 33, 34, 36, 37

MacDowell, Edward, 261
Mahler, Abraham, 9
Mahler, Alma Schindler, 2, 172; abortion undergone by, 291; ambivalence of toward children, 141, 154; anti–Semitism of, 91; compositions of, 202–4, 265–66; death of, 301; death wishes of, 245–46, 267, 291; disapproval of by Gustav's friends, 109–10, 173–76; in New York City, 154–55, 156–57, 255–57; pregnancies of, 109, 123–24, 165–66, 290–91, 294–95; relationship with father, 83–85, 87–88, 89, 99; relationship with stepfather, 88; at Tobelbad, 178–84
—psychoanalytic considerations: depression, 5, 123, 141–42, 166, 167–69, 176, 178; "family romance," 85–86; medical/psychiatric problems of, 3–5; mourning process after Putzi's death, 139–40, 141–42; narcissism, 178, 192; sexual origins of depression, 178–79; superstition as factor in, 158
—relationships: with Guido Adler, 174, 175; with Anna Mahler (daughter), 304–6; with Justine Mahler (sister–in–law), 100–103, 109; with Pauline Strauss, 117–18
—relationship with Walter Gropius, 6–7, 142, 179–84, 188, 238, 243–44, 245, 252–53, 265, 291–92; and Alma's desire for child with Gropius, 246; divorce from, 297; fears associated with, 189–90; and Mahler's changed feelings about Alma's music, 202–4; after Mahler's death, 287–89; during Mahler's illness, 277, 280–81; Mahler's learning of, 190–92; Mahler's response to, 192–94; marriage to, 293–96

—relationship with Gustav Mahler: concerns about age difference, 100, 103; courtship, 94–100, 104–7; dissatisfaction with, 122–23, 154, 167–68, 183; Freud's oedipal interpretation of, 237–38; initial meetings, 74, 75, 92–94; during Mahler's final illness, 266, 267, 279; married life, 4–5, 113–14, 134; musical ambitions discouraged by, 105–7, 122–23; resentments involving, 130–31; sexual passion, 108; wedding, 111
—romantic involvements, 83, 88–90, 228: with Joseph Fraenkel, 284–85; with Ossip Gabrilowitsch, 142; with Paul Kammerer, 286–87; with Gustav Klimt, 88–90, 189; with Oskar Kokoschka, 228, 289–92, 293; with Franz Schreker, 285–86; with Franz Werfel, 228, 284, 294, 295–96, 297, 298–301; with Alexander von Zemlinsky, 83, 89, 93, 94, 98, 99–100, 105, 132
Mahler, Alois (brother), 19, 20, 33, 34, 36, 37, 42, 44, 45, 71, 111
Mahler, Anna Justine (Gucki) (daughter), 124, 129, 130, 142, 153–54, 167, 178; artistic pursuits of, 305, 306; childhood traumas of, 303–4; death of, 306; marriages of, 304–5
Mahler, Bernhard (father), 9, 10, 16, 17, 30, 32–33, 36, 215; as businessman, 21–22, 90; children of, 14–15, 18–19; death of, 32, 62; health problems of, 31–32; as influence on Gustav, 20–21; marriage of, 12–13
Mahler, Emma (sister), 19, 33, 34, 36, 37, 38, 71, 78, 101, 248
Mahler, Ernst (brother), 18, 111; death of, 23, 25, 61, 218
Mahler, Gustav: artwork in study of, 48–51; birth of, 14–15; birthplace of, 11; as book lover, 21; composing routine of, 121–22; crises in life of, 7–8; criteria for a wife articulated by, 4, 76–77; and daughter Putzi's death, 2; death of, 283; departure for

America, 152; describing himself,
28–29; early education of, 22; early
musical interest of, 16–17; encounter
with Walter Gropius, 194–95, 198;
family of origin, 9–11; as father,
128–30; financial worries of, 34–35, 39,
43–44, 131; and Icarus myth, 125; in
New York City, 154–55, 156–57, 250–51;
as outsider, 30–31, 35, 41–42, 78,
216–17; on his parents, 12; religious
conversion of, 63–64, 91, 216;
Toscanini's view of, 162–63; at
the Vienna Conservatory, 26–27,
215; as "Wandering Jew," 35, 68,
216
—family relationships: with brother
Alois, 44–45; with brother Otto, 36,
37–38, 39–40, 42, 43, 44–46, 51, 54,
55, 203, 221; Ernst's death, 25–26, 61,
111; with his father, 24, 215; father's
influence, 20–21; Gustav as focal
point of, 19; with his mother, 19–20,
24, 222–23, 229, 236; with sister
Justine, 100–103, 116; as strain,
38–39, 42
—and Sigmund Freud: bill for
consultation, 242; Marie Bonaparte's
recollections of, 229–31, 234;
commonalities with, 212–19, 220–26;
consultation with, 1, 3, 7, 8, 12, 204–5,
206, 208, 209, 211–12, 226, 227,
229–30, 232–34; Freud's discussion of
with other psychoanalysts, 239–42;
Alma Mahler's recollections of,
234–35; "Mahler's choice" as
articulated by, 241–42; Mahler's
improvement following consultation,
238–39
—health problems of, 33, 60, 65–66, 68,
80, 160–61, 251–52; as affected by
emotional state, 273–76; final illness,
266–83; heart disease, 6, 64, 138–39;
psychological component of,
64, 221; restrictions imposed because of, 138–39, 153, 157–58; throat
inflammations, 244–45, 257,
263–64

—as music director/conductor, 39, 44,
120, 129, 132; of the Budapest Opera,
30–32, 38; of the Hamburg Opera,
40; Krehbiel's criticism of, 164–65,
170–71, 261; of the Metropolitan
Opera, 135, 136, 155–56, 170; of the
New York Philharmonic, 160, 162,
163–65, 169–72, 250–51, 254–64,
275; of the Vienna Court Opera,
62–64, 70, 134–35, 156; of the
Vienna Philharmonic Orchestra,
65, 153
—music of: as autobiography, 8, 57,
61–62, 70, 72–73, 119–21, 124, 125–26,
128, 158, 197–202; death as recurring
theme in, 8, 15, 18–19, 28, 34, 42, 61,
62, 73–74, 126, 222, 274; Eastern
philosophy as influence on, 149–51;
folk music as influence on, 17;
fratricide as theme in, 40, 53–54, 57,
61; French composers' response to,
176–77; importance of text in, 56;
irony in, 212–13; Jewish music as
influence on, 17; loss and separation
in, 147, 149; mourning as theme in,
142–51; nature sounds in, 146, 151;
progressive tonality in, 212–13;
resurrection as theme in, 57–59, 274;
sleep symbolism in, 73, 146; suicidal
ideas in, 200–201; superstition
associated with, 124, 125–26, 158, 165,
203, 222, 241; *Wunderhorn* as source
for, 16, 20, 40, 46, 47, 48, 50–52, 54,
56, 70, 113, 125, 264. *See also* Mahler,
Gustav: works
—psychoanalytic considerations: death
instinct, 240–41; depression, 41–42,
43, 48, 146; dreams, 68–69; "family
romance," 90–91; and final illness,
272–76; fratricidal fantasies, 43, 57, 61;
guilt, 20, 69, 71; mastery of crises,
7–8, 59, 74, 135–36, 144, 151; mourning
through music after Putzi's death, 5,
8, 139–40, 143–51, 274; narcissism,
76–77, 105–6; separation anxiety,
236–37; sibling deaths, 60–61, 111,
218; survivor's guilt, 218–19, 222.

Mahler, Gustav (*continued*)
See also Mahler, Gustav: and Sigmund Freud
—relationships: as affected by marriage to Alma, 109–10; with Natalie Bauer–Lechner, 38, 51–52, 66, 68–69, 70, 77–83, 102, 212; with Hans von Bülow, 47–48, 57; with Max Graf, 223–24; with Fritz Löhr, 34–35, 43–44; with Arnold Rosé, 111, 116, 258; with Richard Strauss, 114–15, 118–19; with Bruno Walter, 55; with women, 75–76, 82, 133–34; with Alexander von Zemlinsky, 132
—relationship with Alma Schindler Mahler: anxieties associated with, 182–83, 192–94, 199–200, 275; attitude regarding Alma's musical talent, 105–7, 122–23, 202–4, 265; courtship, 94–100, 104–7; defensiveness regarding, 175–76, 258; impact of Alma's infidelity on, 6, 8, 190–94, 202–4, 274–75; initial meetings, 74, 75, 92–94; married life, 4–5, 113–14, 134; Hans Sachs story (*Die Meistersinger*) as applicable to, 100, 103, 108, 191, 195, 223; sexual passion, 108; wedding, 111
—works: *Der Abschied,* 145, 149, 150; *Der Einsame im Herbst,* 146–47; *Ernst von Schwaben,* 25, 26, 27, 143; *Fünf Humoresken,* 47, 51; *Das himmlische Leben,* 113; *Ich bin der Welt abhanden gekommen,* 274; *Das irdische Leben,* 53, 199, 200, 274; *Kindertotenlieder,* 15, 72, 126–28, 148, 149, 272; *Liebst du um Schoenheit,* 119, 120; *Das klagende Lied,* 15, 40, 53–54, 56, 57, 61, 73, 99–100, 143; *Lieder eines fahrenden Gesellen,* 18, 62, 143; *Das Lied von der Erde,* 2, 3, 8, 144–51, 158, 162, 169, 264, 274; *Purgatorio* movement (Tenth Symphony), 196–99; Symphony no. 1 ("Titan"), 35, 38, 54, 61–62, 81, 143, 170; Symphony no. 2 ("Resurrection"), 7, 28, 35–36, 46, 47, 51, 52–53, 55–59, 73, 75, 90, 125, 136, 143, 149, 172, 176, 214, 221, 274; Symphony no. *3,* 56, 80, 98, 120, 221; Symphony no. *4,* 20, 56, 67, 113, 149, 261; Symphony no. *5,* 8, 106–7, 114, 120–21, 122, 125, 132, 224; Symphony no. *6,* 124, 125–26, 133, 158, 165; Symphony no. *7,* 130, 257; Symphony no. *8* ("Symphony of a Thousand"), 3, 8, 56, 133–34, 172, 177, 186, 195, 201, 223, 239, 241, 245, 246–50; Symphony no. *9,* 2–3, 165, 166–67, 176, 290; Symphony no. *10,* 3, 6, 8, 157, 172, 187, 188, 192, 196, 199–200, 235, 238, 241, 257, 274, 275; *Der Tamboursg'sell,* 70, 71–72; *Todtenfeier,* 35, 46, 51, 52, 143; *Das Trinklied von Jammer der Erde,* 145, 146; *Der Trunkene im Frühling,* 146; *Um Mitternacht,* 72–74, 96, 125, 146; *Urlicht,* 52, 57; *Von der Jugend,* 147, 148; *Von der Schönheit,* 147, 148; *Wenn dein Mütterlein tritt zur Tür herein,* 127. See also Mahler, Gustav: music of
Mahler, Isador (brother), 14, 15, 61, 218
Mahler, Justine (sister), 19, 20, 38, 42–43, 51, 65, 71, 79, 248, 282–83; as caregiver for parents, 31, 32, 34; daughter born to, 116; health problems of, 33–34; and Alma Mahler, 100–103; and Arnold Rosé, 101–2, 109, 111
Mahler, Karl (brother), 19
Mahler, Leopoldine (Poldi) (sister), 18, 20, 30, 32, 33, 34, 37
Mahler, Maria (Putzi) (daughter), 123, 128, 129–30, 250; burial of, 166, 272; death of, 2, 5, 8, 137–38, 139, 303
Mahler, Marie Hermann (mother): children of, 14–15, 18–19; death of, 34, 42; Gustav's attachment to, 19–20; health problems of, 31, 32, 33–34; marriage of, 11–13; St. Ursula associated with, 20, 48

Mahler, Otto (brother), 19, 20, 33, 34, 35, 54, 55; as composer, 40–41; emotional instability of, 36–38; Gustav's concerns about, 39–40, 42, 43, 44–46; suicide of, 59, 62, 111

Mahler, Rudolf (brother), 19

Mahler, Simon (grandfather), 9, 10, 11, 14

Mankiewicz, Henriette, 82

Mann, Heinrich, 300

Mann, Thomas, 247, 248–50, 251, 300, 316

Maria Theresa, 9

Matthews, David, 198–99

McCormack, John, 253

Mendelssohn, Felix: *Wedding March*, 120

Mengelberg, Willem, 39, 106–7, 120, 158, 163, 247, 295

Metropolitan Opera, 135, 136, 155–56, 170, 255

Mildenburg, Anna von, 75, 100–101, 108, 109, 120, 223, 248

Mitchell, Donald, 144, 147

Moenius, Georg, 300

Moll, Anna, 2, 84, 86, 87, 88, 89, 97, 99, 109, 142, 152, 153, 162, 248, 252, 253, 302; and Alma's relationship with Gropius, 181, 184, 188, 189, 244; later years of, 306–8; relationship with Mahler, 111–13, 183, 184–85, 189, 258, 276

Moll, Carl, 87, 88, 92, 97, 108, 109, 142, 152, 153, 166, 188, 248, 252, 289, 302; later years of, 306–8; relationship with Mahler, 111, 258, 279, 283

Moll, Ernst, 90

Moll, Hanna, 90

Moll, Maria, 307

Moravia: Jewish families in, 9–11, 15

Morgan, J. P., 160

Moser, Kolomon, 109

Mozart, Wolfgang Amadeus: *The Magic Flute*, 65

Nazis, 307–8

Nepallek, Richard von, 204

New York Philharmonic, 158, 160, 162, 163–65, 169–72, 250–51, 254–64

New York Symphony, 158, 162

Nietzsche, Friedrich Wilhelm, 98–99, 103, 104, 177, 220–21

Olbrich, Joseph, 90

Painleve, Paul, 132–33

Palladino, Eusapia, 165, 255

Pfitzner, Hans, 131

Picquart, Georges, 116, 132, 133, 166

Pierné, Gabriel, 176

Pollock, Theobald, 92

psychoanalysis: acceptance of in America versus Europe, 207; Nürnberg congress, 207–8. *See also* Freud, Sigmund

Puchstein, Hans, 134

Pulitzer, Joseph, 160

Quittner, Ludwig, 33

Rank, Otto, 217

Reik, Theodore, 57, 232–33, 234

Reinhardt, Max, 248, 300

Richter, Joanna, 62, 75

Rilke, Rainer Maria, 314

Rockefeller, John D., 160

Rodin, Auguste, 166

Roller, Alfred, 153, 158, 161, 162, 212, 214, 248

Roman, Zoltan, 170

Roosevelt, Theodore, 159

Rosé, Alma, 124

Rosé, Arnold, 66, 101–2, 248; as friend and brother to Mahler, 111, 258; as husband to Justine Mahler, 115–16

Rosé, Eduard, 248

Rosé, Justine Mahler. *See* Mahler, Justine

Rott, Hans, 71

Rückert, Friedrich, 8, 72, 119, 126–27, 128, 146, 274

"St. Anthony's Sermon to the Fish," 7, 50–52, 106

Sax, Hans Emanuel, 40–41

Schindler, Alma. *See* Mahler, Alma Schindler

Schindler, Anna Bergen. *See* Moll, Anna

Schindler, Emil Jacob, 83–85, 87–88, 179, 188, 229

Schindler, Gretl, 86, 188

Schlesinger, Bruno. *See* Walter, Bruno

Schnitzler, Arthur, 135, 144, 223

Schoenberg, Arnold, 126, 131, 135, 300

Schreker, Franz, 285–86

Schubert, Franz: *Erlkönig*, 53, 69, 199

Schuschnigg, Kurt, 299

Schwartz, Gustav, 25, 26, 27, 37

Secession movement, 88–89, 153

Seidl, Anton, 158

Seidl, Arthur, 53, 56

Shanet, Howard, 164

Sheldon, George R., 159

Sheldon, Mary Seney, 159–60, 259, 260, 261, 262

Shengold, Leonard, 217–18

Soldat-Röger String Quartet, 78, 83

Solomon, Maynard, 201–2

Somerfeld-Mincieux, Annie, 28

Spiegler, Nanna, 109

Spiering, Theodore, 251

Stefan, Paul, 247

Steiner, Josef, 25–26, 27

Steiner, Maximillian, 240

Strauss, Johann, Jr.: *Freut euch des Lebens*, 167

Strauss, Pauline, 115, 116–18

Strauss, Richard, 39, 175, 248; *Feuersnot*, 115, 117; *Intermezzo*, 119; Mahler's relationship with, 114–15, 118–19; married life of, 115, 116–17; *Sinfonia Domestica*, 118, 119, 132; *Tod und Verklärung*, 197

Taft, William Howard, 159

Tiffany, Louis, 165

Titian: *Concert*, 48

Toleranzpatent, 9–10, 11, 14

Toscanini, Arturo, 160, 162–63, 170

Trenker family, 6, 186–87

Turner, Miss, 179, 180

Untermeyer, Minnie, 171, 262, 278

Untermeyer, Samuel, 251, 262

Ursula, Saint, 20, 48

Verdi, Giuseppe: *Requiem*, 162

Vereinigung Schaffender Tonkünstler, 126, 224

Vienna Conservatory, 26–27, 77, 215

Vienna Court Opera, 3, 62–64, 70, 134–35

Vienna Philharmonic Orchestra, 65, 153

Vienna Psychoanalytic Society, 224, 239, 240, 313

Wagner, Cosima, 117

Wagner, Richard: *Die Meistersinger* (Hans Sachs story), 100, 103, 108, 191, 195, 223; *Parsifal*, 198; *Ring* cycle, 31, 32; *Tristan und Isolde*, 155, 163, 246; *Die Walküre*, 197

Walska, Ganna, 311

Walter, Bruno, 97, 138, 140, 144, 163, 166, 169, 173, 214, 220, 250, 283, 300; as Freud's patient, 224–26, 235–36; as Mahler's assistant, 55, 134

Weber, Carl Maria von: *Pinto* sketches, 29

Webern, Anton von, 152

Weill, Kurt, 300

Weingartner, Felix, 140–41

Weisman, Avery, 273

Werfel, Franz: Alma's affair with, 294, 297; death of, 300–301; as father of Alma's child, 295–96; Alma's marriage to, 228, 284, 298–301; and Anna Mahler, 303

Wolf, Hugo, 71

World War I, 292

Wunderhorn. See *Des knaben Wunderhorn*

Yeats, William Butler: *Lapis Lazuli,* 147
Yiddish language, 10–11
Yurushalmi, Josef, 214

Zemlinsky, Alexander von, 83, 89, 93,
    94, 98, 105, 126, 131, 132
Zola, Emile, 133

Zsolnay, Alma, 305
Zsolnay, Paul, 304–5
Zuckerkandl, Bertha, 93, 94, 116, 177,
    292–93, 297
Zuckerkandl, Emil, 93, 177, 267
Zweig, Arnold, 314
Zweig, Stefan, 26–27, 135, 247, 316